Accountability in Global Governance

Accountability in Global Governance

GISELA HIRSCHMANN

OXFORD
UNIVERSITY PRESS

OXFORD
UNIVERSITY PRESS

Great Clarendon Street, Oxford, OX2 6DP,
United Kingdom

Oxford University Press is a department of the University of Oxford.
It furthers the University's objective of excellence in research, scholarship, and education by publishing worldwide. Oxford is a registered trade mark of Oxford University Press in the UK and in certain other countries

First Edition published in 2020

Published in the United States of America by Oxford University Press
198 Madison Avenue, New York, NY 10016, United States of America

British Library Cataloguing in Publication Data
Data available

Library of Congress Control Number: 2019954850

ISBN 978–0–19–886124–9

Preface

The purpose of United Nations (UN) peace operations is to protect people in conflict-ridden environments from further harm.[1] Thousands of military, civilian, and other associated personnel around the globe work dedicatedly to fulfil these laudable intentions. Usually, the population of a country where a peace mission is deployed has suffered already for a long time before the start of an operation. When the state is not able or willing to protect the rights and lives of its citizens, the hopes of the population lie on the "blue helmets" that are sent by the UN to bring peace and stability. But what if the presence and actions of peacekeepers and their cooperating partners even actively cause harm when implementing a UN-mandated peace operation?

This is not an academic figment but has indeed happened in various forms in different peace operations around the globe. In operations in West Africa and the Democratic Republic of Congo, for example, "blue helmets" raped local women and girls or had sex with them for the exchange of a dollar or a piece of bread, abuses that have been termed "survival sex." In Cambodia and Sierra Leone, numerous peacekeeping soldiers and civilian staff took local women as their wives, had children with them, and then disappeared at the end of their appointment, leaving behind stigmatized women and hundreds of "peacekeeper babies." On the Balkans, international police officers protected human-trafficking networks in the areas where they were deployed to take advantage of trafficked women working as prostitutes. In Haiti, a peacekeeping contingent polluted the water around the base so that more than 8,000 local people died of cholera, a plague that had been extinct in Haiti before the arrival of peacekeepers. These are just a few examples, where the behavior of actors implementing a peace operation caused further harm for the local population.

This puzzle that international organizations (IOs), while set up to do good, can have detrimental effects on individuals' human rights, is not unique to UN peacekeeping but characterizes many issue areas of global governance. The complexities of these governance structures have blurred responsibilities and

[1] See the UN Security Council Resolutions on the protection of civilians, the Council's Presidential Statements, and the reports of the Secretary-General to the Council on this topic at http://www.securitycouncilreport.org/un-documents/protection-of-civilians/ (last access November 4, 2014).

have thus rendered traditional and legal accountability rather difficult. At the same time, however, these complexities have enabled new mechanisms of accountability as IOs are embedded in an international society of actors who provide novel checks and balances.

This book is a contribution to a more encompassing analysis of IO accountability, taking into consideration the standard-setting, monitoring, and sanctioning activities exercised by third parties that populate the environment of IOs. By identifying the push and pull factors that enable these third parties to enact accountability, this book sheds light on the conditions for pluralist accountability. While pointing out these alternative avenues for accountability, the book also does not shy away from highlighting the difficulties and downsides of pluralist accountability. With the UN celebrating its seventy-fifth anniversary in 2020 and an increasing number of states openly rejecting cooperation in multilateral institutions, I believe it is of utmost importance to enhance pluralist as well as traditional and legal accountability mechanisms in order to improve the credibility and legitimacy of IOs.

Throughout writing this book, I have been supported by an amazing network of friends, family, and colleagues to whom I would like to express my gratitude.

First of all, I am immensely grateful for all my interview partners, who dedicated their time and shared their insights with me, either confidentially or open for disclosure. Their accounts, documents, and ideas have been invaluable for the success of this project, even if the final product might not do fully justice to the level of details they provided. This field research was further enabled by the German Academic Exchange Foundation, to which I am thankful for financing my research stays in New York City, Michael Doyle and the Center on Global Thought, who hosted me at Columbia University, and Jonathan Bach, who hosted me at the New School earlier.

Cornelia Ulbert, Marianne Beisheim, Thomas Risse, and the ATASP crew of 2006–2010 at the Free University Berlin have set my foot on the path of academic research and have remained great mentors. When writing my PhD dissertation on accountability in UN peace operations, I could rely on critical but encouraging feedback from Monika Heupel, Christian Kreuder-Sonnen, Sophie Eisentraut, Benjamin Faude, Tanja Abendschein-Angerstein, and my cohort of the Berlin School of Transnational Studies. In particular, my work in the project "International Organizations and the protection of fundamental human rights," funded by the German Science Association and conducted between 2010 and 2014 at the Berlin Social Science Research Center under the leadership of Michael Zürn and Monika Heupel, became a constant source of inspiration. Thank you, Monika, for your patience, respect, and friendship! Similarly, the feedback from both of my supervisors, Michael Zürn and Thomas Risse, as well as from the other members of my defense committee Ingo Peters and Anna Holzscheiter, stimulated my thinking—thank you. My other colleagues at the Berlin Social Science Research Center took my project apart in numerous colloquia and helped me put it together afterwards. Thank you, Matthias Ecker-Ehrhardt, Martin Binder, Christian Rauh, Autumn Lockwood-Payton, Pieter de Wilde, Lora Viola, and Thomas Rixen. Finally, I am grateful to Jonas Tallberg and his colleagues at Stockholm University, who hosted me for a productive and motivating research stay and who gave important critical feedback in the final stages of my PhD dissertation.

The Max Weber post-doctoral fellowship at the European University Institute (EUI) in Florence then allowed me to start exploring pluralist accountability in other issue areas and develop the book proposal. Dominic Byatt at Oxford University Press was an enthusiastic and patient supporter of the project from the start and the critical comments from the three reviewers helped greatly to improve the manuscript. At the EUI, I further received crucial feedback and encouragement from Jennifer Welsh and Peter Dietsch as well as great support through their friendship from Anna Beckers, Cynthia Salloum, Jordi Teixido-Figueras, Miriam Gonzàlez Avià, and Stefano Verde.

Throughout the writing process I could rely on the editorial support of Roisin Cronin, the staff from the EUI language center, and Amanda Pierson for a great final round of language editing, my student assistants Hannah Bliersbach and Marius Stemmer for helping with editing the references. I also thank the Institute of Political Science of Leiden University for carrying the costs for some of this assistance.

I would further like to thank Fundación Gego in Caracas, Venezuela, for the permission to use the picture of Getrud Goldschmidt's artwork "Esfera No. 5, 1977" (photographed by Anne and Thierry Benedetti") for the cover of this book. Gego was a German artist who was forced into emigration in 1939 and built a successful career in Venezuela. Her work "Esfera No. 5" is an expression of both transparency and complexity and thus resonates well with the topic of this book, accountability in global governance.

Finally, there are my close friends and family on whose support I could always rely. Sonja, Marcel, Anne, Katia, Mira, Helen, and Angelika, thank you for your friendship, emotional support, and for reminding me of the importance of a life outside of the PhD. Thank you, AnnSo, for helping me select the artwork for the cover with your expertise as an art historian. My sister Judith rescued the manuscript when Word was inserting random black spots; thank you for always being there. Thank you, Mama and Papa, for introducing me to debates about politics and encouraging me to never stop asking questions. Rainer Wolters, Sebastian, Sergej, Ilona, Christina, and Sophia never stopped believing in me, have helped me to keep the music in my life and to realize my parallel career as a professional violinist. Thank you, Claire, for teaching me how to grow plants and for being this wonderful inspiring office-mate and friend. Thank you, Niels, for being you, for your love, trust, support, and patience—we have survived *the book* together.

Contents

List of Figures

List of Tables

List of Abbreviations

AEFI	adverse events following immunization
AIHRC	Afghan Independent Human Rights Commission
AMIS	African Union Mission in Sudan
AMISOM	African Union Mission to Somalia
ANP	Afghan National Police
COMKFOR	Commander KFOR
DoD	Department of Defense
ECB	European Central Bank
ECCHR	European Center for Constitutional and Human Rights
ECON	Economic and Monetary Affairs Committee (EU)
EMPL	Committee on Employment and Social Affairs (EU)
EP	European Parliament
ESM	European Stability Mechanism
EU	European Union
GAVI	Global Alliance for Vaccines and Immunisation
GPPHP	global public–private health partnerships
HPV	human papilloma virus
ICC	International Criminal Court
ICRC	International Committee of the Red Cross
ICTY	International Criminal Tribunal for the former Yugoslavia
IFOR	NATO-led Implementation Force in Bosnia and Herzegovina
IL	International Law (studies)
IMF	International Monetary Fund
IO	international organization
IOM	International Organization for Migration
IPTF	International Police Task Force
IR	International Relations (studies)
ISAF	International Security Assistance Force in Afghanistan
KFOR	NATO-led Kosovo Force
LIBE	Committee on Civil Liberties, Justice and Home Affairs (EU)
LSMS	Legal Systems Monitoring Section
MDG	Millennium Development Goal
MoU	Memorandum of Understanding
NATO	North Atlantic Treaty Organization
NDS	National Directorate of Security (Afghan)
NGO	nongovernmental organization

NTAG	National Technical Advisory Group for Immunization
OEF	Operation Enduring Freedom
OHCHR	Office of the High Commissioner for Human Rights (UN)
OIK	Ombudsperson Institution of Kosovo
OSCE	Organization for Security and Co-operation in Europe
PATH	Program for Appropriate Technology in Health
SDG	Sustainable Development Goal
SFOR	NATO-led Stabilization Force in Bosnia and Herzegovina
SRSG	Special Representative of the Secretary-General (UN)
TCC	troop-contributing countries
TNA	transnational actor
UK	United Kingdom
UN	United Nations
UNAMA	United Nations Assistance Mission in Afghanistan
UNAMID	United Nations/African Union Mission in Darfur
UNHRC	United Nations Human Rights Council
UNICEF	United Nations Children's Fund
UNMIBH	United Nations Mission in Bosnia and Herzegovina
UNMIK	United Nations Mission in Kosovo
UNPROFOR	United Nations Protection Force
US	United States
WHO	World Health Organization
WTO	World Trade Organization

1

Introduction

Human Rights Accountability in Complex Global Governance

Many international organizations (IOs) not only facilitate interstate cooperation but also promote and foster respect for human rights. At the same time, however, the actions and policies of IOs and their implementing partners can—unintentionally or purposefully—harm human rights (Aoi et al. 2007; Heupel and Zürn 2017; Verdirame 2011). Over the last twenty-five years, there have been numerous cases in which IO staff, partners of IOs, or national actors under the mandate of IOs have violated human rights, most prominently in the area of peace operations. United Nations (UN) peacekeepers and their cooperating partners, such as regional organizations, national actors, and private military and security companies, have caused severe harm when implementing an operation through the sexual exploitation and abuse of women and children, for example, and the organization of human-trafficking networks, torture, or systematic killings of civilians (Amnesty International 2007b; Aoi et al. 2007; Bolkovac and Lynn 2011; Hirschmann 2017a, 2017b; Human Rights Watch 2009; Mégret and Hoffmann 2003; Mendelson 2005; Smith and Smith 2011). The effects of IOs' actions and policies on human rights have raised great concern in other areas, such as economic governance or global health policies. In programs funded by the World Bank and the International Monetary Fund (IMF), the implementing states and companies have harassed and detained critics and people negatively affected by these programs (Human Rights Watch 2015). The austerity measures implemented by governments in Southern Europe, as required by the European Union (EU) and the IMF in response to the economic and financial crisis, negatively affected social and economic rights (Dowell-Jones 2015; Salomon 2015). Researchers on global health governance see the growth of public–private partnerships with growing concern as they can severely affect individuals' rights to healthcare (Clarke 2012; Hesselmann 2011).

Accountability in Global Governance. Gisela Hirschmann, Oxford University Press (2020). © Gisela Hirschmann.
DOI: 10.1093/oso/9780198861249.001.0001

Legal scholars still debate to what extent human rights are applicable to IOs and whether they are, thus, legally able to violate human rights (Mégret and Hoffmann 2003; Zagel 2018). In the wider public, the malfeasance of IOs and their implementing partners in the context of global governance arrangements has evoked strong criticism and threatens to undermine the legitimacy of IOs (Daugirdas 2015; Heupel and Zürn 2017).[1] But how can organizations like the UN, the EU, or the World Bank regain legitimacy both in the eyes of the affected populations and within the international community? As a strategy of relegitimation, legal scholars as well as political scientists argue that IOs and their member states should hold the implementing actors accountable for their deeds (Buchanan and Keohane 2006; Verdirame 2011; Wouters et al. 2010). However, the complexity of contemporary global governance renders the exercise of accountability rather difficult. Virtually all IOs, in particular the most prominent global ones such as the UN, the World Bank, the IMF, or the World Trade Organization (WTO), have been accused of being "unaccountable" to their members and even more so to those citizens affected by their policies (Chesterman 2009; Nye 2001; Woods 2001). Moreover, IOs increasingly delegate tasks mandated by their member states to private actors, national actors, or other IOs. The World Bank, for example, encourages recipient states to hire private agencies to implement economic programs. Peace operations mandated by the UN Security Council are increasingly delegated to regional organizations, national actors, or even private military and security companies (Pingeot 2012; Yamashita 2012). For the implementation of millennium development goals put forward by the UN, such as the reduction of child mortality, public–private partnerships have become the new mode of governance in the global community (Liese and Beisheim 2011). IOs might also form their own networks to adopt rules, norms, and regulations, which may result in "informal law-making" (Pauwelyn et al. 2012).

These new forms of global governance imply that a variety of actors—who often are not part of the first delegation step—exercise important governance functions. By delegating tasks, IOs exercise "sovereign powers" and, thus, make delegation chains in global governance even more complex (Alvarez 2005; Sarooshi 1999; Weaver 2008). This prolonged delegation is more than just simple cooperation or influence in general; the implementing actors are formally entrusted with certain tasks and they enjoy a certain degree of

[1] See Daily Yomiuir 2007: UN Legitimacy Eroding like Festering Sore, article by Ramesh Thakur, May 21, available at: http://www.cigionline.org/articles/2007/05/un-legitimacy-eroding-festering-sore (last access March 30, 2016).

discretion, which implies having the authority to make autonomous decisions and actions (Hawkins et al. 2006a, 7; Tierney 2006). As a consequence of this complex delegation, traditional conceptions of accountability, for example, accountability whereby implementing actors are held accountable for their actions directly by their mandating authorities (Schedler et al. 1999), have become difficult to achieve (Wilde 2006). Instead, alternative forms of accountability have evolved, in which third parties act as "accountability holders" vis-à-vis the implementing actors.

This book sets out to explore these forms of "pluralist accountability," as I call it, which is a recent trend in global governance that deserves further analysis. Some of the most prominent examples of accountability exercised by third parties have been studied in the areas of trade and development, in particular with regard to the World Bank, the IMF, and the WTO (Brown and Fox 1998). The "new intrusiveness" of these three institutions has led to the evolution of accountability regimes which include a broader audience than just the institution's member states as accountability holders (Woods and Narlikar 2001). Similarly, new forms of accountability exist in global health governance, for example, in the development of an International Code for the Marketing of Breast Milk Substitutes in the context of the World Health Organization's (WHO) policies (Kickbusch 2000).[2] Also, the study of private regulatory agencies, which increasingly set standards for financial and economic actions, has revealed how third parties act as accountability holders for public actors (Büthe and Mattli 2011; Mattli and Woods 2009). These examples demonstrate that various international and domestic actors act as "accountability holders," independent from the mandating authority.

So far, however, we know little about the reasons for and the effects of pluralist accountability. This book provides a conceptual framework for analyzing the various forms of third-party accountability and asks *under which conditions we can expect pluralist accountability to evolve*. In order to answer this question, the analysis focuses on accountability for actions that affect individuals' *human rights*. Despite the fact that there are many actions (as well as omissions) of IOs and their partners for which the question of accountability has become highly relevant, the focus on human rights provides an analytical framework that is operationalizable and coherent enough to reduce the conceptual ambiguity of the concept of accountability. Moreover, the fact that IOs and their implementing partners have repeatedly been accused

[2] Gavin Yarney 2002: Why Does the World Still Need the WHO? Available at: http://www.bmj.com/content/325/7375/1294?goto=reply (last access September 19, 2014).

of negatively affecting human rights stands in direct contrast to the IOs' objectives, at least to those that are mandated to promote and protect human rights. In the legal debate about IOs' human rights obligations (see also Reinisch 2001; Schrijver 2013), I follow the argument by Mégret and Hoffmann (2003), who argue with regard to the UN that human rights standards can be applicable to an IO in three ways: first, to the extent that these standards have become customary international law (*external conception*); second, to the extent IOs are mandated to promote human rights according to the internal legal order (*internal conception*); and third, to the extent that their member states are bound to respect human rights (*hybrid conception*). The demands for greater accountability that I analyze in this book refer to actions and policies that have affected four human rights: the right to physical integrity, the right to a fair trial (due process), social and economic rights as provided by the International Covenant on Economic, Social and Cultural Rights, and the right to informed consent. In all of the cases that I analyze, the policies and actions of IOs in the context of global governance have negative effects on these rights, both directly and indirectly. While the distinction between the explicit and implicit attribution of human rights violations is crucial for legal accountability (Reinisch 2010; Sari 2008), this book compares those political accountability mechanisms that evolve in response to violations of different types of human rights. In all of the analyzed cases, accountability has become increasingly linked to the issue of legitimacy in the public and scholarly debates about global governance. The rationale for this book follows up on this debate; I focus on human rights accountability to present a novel argument about the conditions for pluralist accountability in complex global governance.

Pluralist Accountability: The Empirical Phenomenon and the Concept

In 2013, two nongovernmental organizations (NGOs) filed a complaint in the Southern District of New York federal court claiming that the UN Stabilization Mission in Haiti had caused serious harm to the Haitian population by spreading a cholera epidemic that killed at least 8,000 people.[3] The European Court of Justice in its *Kadi* case of 2008 ruled that by implementing the UN

[3] See http://www.ijdh.org/wp-content/uploads/2013/10/Georges-v.-United-Nations-Complaint.pdf (last access January 31, 2016).

Security Council's sanctions policy, EU member states would violate their human rights obligations as outlined in EU treaties.[4] In 2002, a British court decided that the dismissal of a police officer who worked for the International Police Task Force of the UN mission in Bosnia and exposed the involvement of her colleagues in human trafficking was unlawful.[5] These examples demonstrate that human rights violations that occurred in the context of global governance activities do not go unnoticed but are investigated and sanctioned by independent third parties. This book puts forward the concept of pluralist accountability to analyze these new empirical phenomena.

The growing interest of academic scholarship in accountability across several disciplines has led to a proliferation of definitions and concepts (Bovens et al. 2014b). Instead of putting forward yet another new concept, I propose a concept of accountability that sets it apart from democracy and responsiveness and that encompasses the core elements shared by most common terminators in the existing literature. I thereby hope to bridge the fragmented scholarship and enable more coherent and commensurable research in the future. I do so with one caveat: I embark on a sociopolitical understanding of accountability, which relies on a much broader conceptualization than pure legal accountability. While legal accountability focuses on accountability through jurisprudence and legal sanctioning that is limited to rights that can be subjected to judicial review, the broader notion of political accountability includes both procedural and substantive aspects of accountability.

In line with existing research, I define accountability as the relationship between two actors by which one actor (the accountability holder) sets the standards for the other actor's (the accountor's) behavior and monitors and sanctions the other if his actions deviate from the standards (Bovens 2007; Buchanan and Keohane 2006; de Wet 2010; Grant and Keohane 2005; Grigorescu 2008; Koenig-Archibugi 2004; Macdonald and Macdonald 2006). In contrast to other studies that have focused on accountability components (Koppell 2010; Scholte 2011a), in my analysis of the process of accountability, I focus on accountability functions (i.e., the actions that are undertaken). Depending on which actor exercises these core accountability functions, and is thus the main accountability holder, I distinguish two ideal types of accountability.

[4] Case C–402/05 P and C–415/05, *P. Kadi and Al Barakaat International Foundation* v. *Council and Commission* [2008] ECR I-6351.

[5] UK Employment Tribunal 2002, *Bolkovac* v. *Dyncorp*, Case no. 3102729/01, Reserved Decision, July 1, 2002, para. 38.

In the classical, vertical form of accountability, the accountability relationship takes the inverse direction of the delegation relationship. The mandating authority as the accountability holder defines the standards for implementation, monitors the agent through self-reporting mechanisms or "police patrol" investigations, and sanctions misbehavior by normative shaming, revising the mandate, or, ultimately, by withdrawing the authorization. Others have used the term internal accountability if the accountability holder is institutionally linked to the organization, while differing on the extent to which accountability exercised by IO member states would fall under this category (Keohane 2003; Krisch 2010; Risse 2008).

In contrast to vertical accountability, I define pluralist accountability as an accountability form whereby third parties outside of the original delegation relationship act as accountability holders. External third parties—parallel operating institutions, regional organizations, NGOs, or courts—initiate accountability functions. Pluralist accountability holders thus may be transnational, national, judicial, or nonstate actors who, individually or together, engage in standard setting, monitoring, and sanctioning. The accountability relationship, therefore, is independent of the delegation relationship. I borrow the term "pluralist" from legal scholarship that uses the concept of pluralism to describe different coexisting, nonhierarchical, or fragmented systems of law in contrast to the more hierarchical understanding of constitutionalism (Krisch 2010). Scholars in the tradition of the "New Haven School" in particular use this concept of legal pluralism to highlight the increasingly plural character of actors involved in lawmaking, in contrast to the classical view that emphasized the role of sovereign states in the creation of law (Berman 2007; Burke-White 2004; Stone Sweet 2009; Teubner 1996). Other authors use the term "horizontal" accountability to describe this phenomenon, which would be semantically the logical opposite (Deshman 2011; Grigorescu 2008; Schillemans 2011; Woods and Narlikar 2001), "diagonal or new forms of accountability" (Bovens 2007), or "non-institutionalized accountability mechanisms that operate outside of a given regime" (Krisch 2010). However, both horizontal and diagonal accountability imply connotations about the position of the accountability holder in relation to the implementing actor. They require the accountability holder to be situated on either the same or a different level, which imposes important limitations on the analysis of accountability relationships. Schedler (1999, 22) very strongly rejected the use of the term horizontal accountability as a "euphemism" that would lead to the negation of asymmetric power structures. The term pluralist accountability, to the contrary, does not limit the analytical focus to a specific actor type nor does it disregard status asymmetries. This concept thus allows us to analyze the accountability mechanisms enacted by a variety of actors, which would otherwise be overlooked when focusing on traditional conceptions of accountability. Compared to vertical accountability, pluralist accountability is especially intriguing for current research on IOs because external actors independently set—and even enforce—the rules for the "accountability game."

The Argument

The core research question of this book asks under what conditions pluralist accountability evolves in response to human rights violations. The argument of this study builds upon a dynamic theoretical understanding of IOs that regards IOs as social institutions interacting independently with a wide array of national and transnational actors (Martin and Simmons 2002). Conceiving IOs as actors, and not only as agents of their member states, is a necessary theoretical assumption for the study of accountability. Only when granting IOs the status of an actor can we logically assume that they care about their agents' behavior (da Conceição-Heldt et al. 2015). Moreover, I open up the "black box" IO and distinguish its internal components, such as, the authorizing member state body, the bureaucratic structure, and the implementing sub-components. With this diversified understanding, I am able to identify the different accountability holders and targets of accountability.

I argue in this book that a combination of two factors influences the evolution of pluralist accountability. First, I argue that a specific opportunity structure characterized by a competitive environment is a condition for third parties to become active as accountability holders. This argument is based on the research on norm entrepreneurship and regime fragmentation, which has demonstrated that competition among third parties can take place among NGOs, between NGOs and intergovernmental organizations (Cooley and Ron 2002), and also between courts (Schimmelfennig 2006). If the institutional context is populated by actors who conceive themselves as norm entrepreneurs and compete for resources and the reputation as guardians of human rights, these third parties are more inclined to act as accountability holders in order to enhance their profiles. I assume that this competition leads to the evolution of pluralist accountability via a distinct causal mechanism, which I call the mechanism of "profiling": the desire to distinguish itself from other concurring parties in the area of human rights motivates an actor to develop certain niche capacities, thus a distinct profile. The exercise of accountability functions serves this purpose of distinction: acting as an accountability holder can enable a third party to demonstrate its particular contributions to the promotion of human rights in a competitive environment.

As a second condition, I argue that the degree of vulnerability of the implementing actor or of the mandating authority with regard to human rights demands influences the evolution of pluralist accountability. This argument is based on research about states' compliance with human rights norms (Risse et al. 2013). If implementing actors are able to justify their actions by a strong normative frame other than human rights, their vulnerability is less dependent on their human rights record (Risse and Ropp 2013: 21). As a consequence, they refuse to accept third parties as accountability holders. On the other hand, if the identity or the mandate of the implementing actor or the mandating authority renders them highly vulnerable to human rights demands, they are more inclined to recognize third parties as accountability holders. This condition takes into consideration that accountability requires the mutual recognition between the accountability holder and the implementing actor (Grant and Keohane 2005: 29). I hereby assume that vulnerability influences the evolution of pluralist accountability through the causal mechanism of recognition. The implementing actors and their mandating authorities do not operate in a social vacuum. Instead, they are embedded in communities that share certain social norms, such as the protection of human rights. If actors violate these norms, their reputation within this community is damaged. The recognition of third parties as accountability holders demonstrates that the implementing actor or the mandating authority—despite the violations—is still committed to these norms and aims to rehabilitate their social status within their respective communities.

These two conditions cover both the institutional context and particular actor characteristics. While regarding them as two independent factors, I further advance the argument that the combination of both is necessary for pluralist accountability. Each of the conditions individually explains only specific aspects of the evolution of pluralist accountability. While competition explains the motivation of third parties to act as accountability holders, it cannot explain why their exercise of accountability functions is recognized by either the implementing actor or the mandating authority. In turn, while vulnerability explains the acceptance of third parties as accountability holders, it cannot explain why third parties are available and willing to exercise core accountability functions in the first place. Therefore, in line with the research on the participation of civil society organizations in IOs, I argue that only the combination of "push factors" and "pull factors" provides a comprehensive explanation for such a complex phenomenon (Steffek 2013). Due to the explanatory limitations of each individual condition, I thus advocate for a combined theoretical approach that takes into consideration both the institutional environment as the "supply side" and the specific actor characteristics as the "demand side" (Steffek 2013).

Research Strategy: A Qualitative Comparative Approach

I introduce pluralist accountability as an alternative analytical concept to grasp the standard-setting, monitoring, and sanctioning activities of third parties outside of a given delegation relationship. Given that most of the existing research has neglected these forms of pluralist accountability so far, the empirical-analytical framework I develop in this book aims to foster our understanding about the conditions for pluralist accountability and its underlying causal mechanisms. As there is no available systematic data on accountability in global governance, I conduct a qualitative comparative case study in order to, first, identify a variety of cases of pluralist accountability in complex global governance (as well as cases of failed pluralist accountability), and second, conduct an in-depth analysis that evaluates the underlying causal processes conducive to the evolution of pluralist accountability. Empirically, I illustrate the argument of this book with a set of different case studies, ranging across the domains of UN peace operations, EU economic austerity policies, and global health governance, in order to provide a comprehensive account of the conditions for pluralist accountability that can be generalized across different areas of complex global governance.

I followed two steps in the process of selecting the cases: in the first selection step I identified allegations of human rights violations committed in the implementation of IO policies. I acquired relevant data from publicly available NGOs and media reports, which I examined both manually as well as through an evaluation of newspaper articles published between 1992 and 2012. With regard to the allegations of human rights violations, I focused on the rights that are regarded as universally accepted and are not legally disputed any more, such as the right to physical integrity, the right to fair trial and due process, as well as basic socioeconomic rights. In the second selection step I identified instances of pluralist accountability while at the same time assuring for variation in the outcome of the dependent variable by juxtaposing pairs of cases. Thus, even if we expect pluralist accountability to be a rising trend in global governance, it is by no means an automatism in reaction to legitimacy problems in complex delegation but depends on specific conditions.

The empirical analysis starts with a set of case studies on UN peace operations, where human rights violations by UN staff and associated personnel and partner organizations—such as the sexual abuse and exploitation of civilians and the violation of the rights of detainees—have become a serious threat for the organization's legitimacy. My comparative analysis of UN-mandated operations in Afghanistan, Bosnia, and Kosovo demonstrates how a competitive environment and the increasing vulnerability of the implementing actors to human rights demands foster pluralist accountability. I selected six cases from all UN-mandated peacekeeping operations after 1992 with a duration of more than one year, in which implementing actors have allegedly committed human rights violations. Most importantly, I selected these three countries because they allow me to juxtapose three pairs of cases that display a clear variance with regard to whether or not pluralist accountability evolved within the same country. In Afghanistan, pluralist accountability evolved in response to human rights violations in Afghan detention centers, to which the North Atlantic Treaty Organization (NATO)-led International Security Assistance Force (ISAF) transferred captured terrorist suspects. In contrast, attempts of pluralist accountability failed in the case of the violation of the rights of detainees transferred by ISAF to the United States (US)-led Operation Enduring Freedom (OEF) in the same country. In Bosnia, pluralist accountability evolved in response to the involvement of private security actors and the UN-mandated International Police Task Force in human trafficking. In the same country, however, no pluralist accountability evolved in response to the violation of the rights of detainees by the NATO-led Stabilization Force (SFOR). Pluralist accountability occurred in the case of detentions by the UN mission in Kosovo (UNMIK) but not in the case of detentions by the NATO-led Kosovo Force (KFOR).

While peacekeeping might be an issue area in which the evolution of pluralist accountability has been most noted, I also analyze the conditions for pluralist accountability in response to human rights violations in other contexts of complex global governance. Regional economic governance in response to the financial crisis after 2008 is a field in which human rights violations have become an issue of great concern and governance has become most complex. Similarly, the "private turn" in global governance, most pointedly exemplified by the rise of public–private partnerships and governance networks, has raised concerns about the implications for traditional accountability and legitimacy (Bäckstrand 2008; Papadopoulos 2007). Therefore,

I examine two additional cases from these issue areas that illustrate the argument of this book.

In the case of economic governance, I examine the conditions for pluralist accountability with regard to the EU Troika's austerity policies in Greece and Portugal. The economic hardship that followed from the Troika's intervention in these two countries significantly affected fundamental rights, especially in terms of citizens' living conditions and the right to health. My analysis reveals that pluralist accountability differed with regard to the three institutions that formed the Troika: the European Commission, the European Central Bank, and the IMF. While competition stimulated various international and domestic actors to enhance pluralist accountability, the varying degree of vulnerability of the different Troika institutions explains the differences in pluralist accountability across these institutions.

Regarding public–private governance networks, my analysis focuses on how pluralist accountability emerged in response to human rights violations resulting from global health partnerships. For the WHO, the cooperation with public–private partnerships has become crucial to implement the Millennium Development Goals. My study looks at the contested issue of vaccination and vaccine development in India, where the implementing actors have reportedly violated the right to consent in clinical trials and the right to physical integrity in vaccination. This case in particular reveals the difficulties for pluralist accountability in complex governance: the lack of a formal delegation relationship, and the strong ideological cleavage in the context of a moral dilemma, hindered the development of pluralist accountability and enabled the implementing actors to refuse to recognize any accountability mechanisms.

With this comparative research strategy, this book seeks to demonstrate the general applicability of the argument by covering various types of complex governance arrangements with a variety of implementing agents, be it regional organizations, state actors, or nonstate actors, and different types of human rights violations in different issue areas.

The Implications for International Relations and International Law Research

This book speaks to three different strands of existing scholarship, namely, the International Relations (IR) literature on delegation, IR research on IOs, and international law (IL) research on accountability and the human rights obligations of IOs. Most of the existing IR research on delegation has thus far focused on the first delegation step, whereby IOs implement the rules for cooperation agreed upon by their member states, equipped with a certain degree of autonomy (Hawkins et al. 2006b; Heldt 2017; Martin and Simmons 1998). Only recently have researchers started to analyze further delegation steps, in which IOs turn from agents into principals themselves, for example, in the area of development aid (Dann 2006). Thus, the authority of IOs has not only increased in terms of the range and intrusiveness of their activities, but it has also changed in character as IOs now increasingly design and delegate policies autonomously. This prolonged delegation as a feature of contemporary complex global governance has not yet been sufficiently captured by either IR scholarship or principal-agent approaches (Lenz et al. 2015). One major contribution of this book is to address this lacuna and to highlight some of the consequences for accountability.

My argument in this book furthermore addresses contemporary IR research on IOs in global governance. One important implication is the contextualization of IOs beyond their relationships with their member states. My findings thus speak to the results of recent research on the interaction of IOs with nonstate actors (e.g., Nanz and Dingwerth 2016; Tallberg et al. 2013) and regional organizations (e.g., Brosig 2010; Jetschke and Lenz 2013), which demonstrate that the institutional environment in which IOs operate is too important and too varied to be reduced to state–IO relations only.

My analysis also has implications for the normative debate among IR scholars about the legitimacy of IOs (Dingwerth 2007; Scholte 2011b; Verdirame 2011; Zürn 2012). Previous studies focused on the prospects of the democratization of IOs or advocated for a greater accountability as a means to enhance the legitimacy of IOs (Scholte 2011a). While existing research often subsumed accountability under the criteria of democratization, the findings of this book provide a nuanced picture by evaluating the effect of pluralist accountability on IO legitimacy with regard to core legitimacy demands, both in the absence of and in comparison to vertical accountability. This responds to the recently growing literature on the legitimation practices of international institutions (e.g., Zaum 2013). Moreover, this study also points to some limitations of accountability as a legitimation strategy in terms of the degree of legalization and potential pitfalls, such as multiple accountability disorder.

The findings of this book also have implications for IL scholarship, although most legal scholars will not be satisfied with the broad, political conception of accountability in this study. Scholars of IL have so far focused on the difficulties of holding IOs legally accountable, and they have discussed problems of command and control that amplify with an expansion of delegation (Abass 2004; Curtin et al. 2010; Lake 2007; Sarooshi 1999). Inspired by the concept of legal pluralism (Krisch 2010), this book supports legal scholars who broaden the state-centered perspective and argue for a greater responsibility of IOs, in particular with regard to human rights obligations (e.g., Besson 2015; Schrijver 2013). Moreover, my findings are a response to those who remain skeptical about the prospects of legal accountability with regard to human rights violations by IOs (von Bogdandy and Steinbrück Platise 2012). Instead, the findings support recent contributions to IL scholarship that explore a "new terrain of international law" by, for example, highlighting the importance of "new-style" international courts, which issue compulsory jurisdiction and grant nonstate actors access to the courts' procedures (Alter 2014). By analyzing the conditions for the evolution of pluralist accountability, I emphasize how important legal *and* political institutions are for the overall dynamics of pluralist accountability.

In addition to these theoretical contributions, this book further provides an empirical study on the evolution of accountability in complex global governance. So far, there is no systematic empirical overview that compares the dynamics of accountability after allegations of human rights violations by IOs and their implementing partners have become public. With the help of primary documents and interviews, I depict the processes of accountability in peace operations, in response to global economic policies and in global public–private health partnerships, and I explain how competition and vulnerability influence the evolution of pluralist accountability in these different cases. This will help to understand the development of pluralist accountability in complex global governance against the background of a broader comparative framework while at the same time do justice to the empirical realities of each individual case.

Structure of the Book

This book contains eight chapters, including the introduction and the conclusion. Following this introduction, Chapter 2 outlines the theoretical framework of this book. This comprises a review of the concept of accountability in the existing literature, which summarizes the perspectives of principal-agent research, legal scholarship, and the research on transnational actors in global governance. It also contains a section on the challenges for accountability and legitimacy in complex global governance structures, illustrated by the phenomenon of prolonged delegation relationships. The theoretical framework further comprises the conceptualization of pluralist accountability as the dependent variable, the conceptualization of the model specifying the conditions for pluralist accountability, and the research design with a section on case selection, methods, and data acquisition. This is followed by five empirical chapters, containing case studies on peace operations in Afghanistan, Bosnia, and Kosovo, the EU Troika's austerity policies in Greece and Portugal, and the vaccination and vaccine development in the context of global public–private health partnerships in India specifically.

Chapter 3 analyzes the conditions for pluralist accountability in response to the violation of the rights of detainees in Afghanistan and comprises two case studies. Under the leadership of NATO, ISAF captured numerous individuals who were suspected of terrorist activities and were handed over to detention facilities run by US-led coalition forces of OEF and, after 2006, also to the Afghan government. My analysis demonstrates that the lack of competition among third parties to rise as advocates for the rights of suspected terrorists in Afghanistan, as well as the low vulnerability of the US government with regard to human rights demands in the immediate aftermath of the attacks of September 11, 2001, hindered the emergence of pluralist accountability in the case of detentions by the US-led coalition forces. In contrast, the case on the rights of detainees transferred by ISAF to the Afghan government shows how competition within the UN-led political operation Assistance Mission in Afghanistan, and the increasing vulnerability of the transferring ISAF states with regard to human rights demands, fostered pluralist accountability.

Chapter 4 contains two case studies on the accountability of peace operations in Bosnia. The first case study analyzes how pluralist accountability evolved in response to allegations that a significant number of international personnel, partly under contract with private security companies, were involved in sex trafficking. The competitive environment in which third parties operated stimulated the Bosnian Office of the High Commissioner on Human Rights to become an accountability holder vis-à-vis the international personnel involved in human trafficking. The second case study on Bosnia demonstrates how pluralist accountability failed to evolve in response to the violation of detainees' rights by the NATO-led SFOR operation. In this case, competition was rather weak as there were no concurring transnational NGOs or intergovernmental human rights organizations that competed for promoting the rights of detainees. Moreover, SFOR's low vulnerability with regard to human rights demands hindered the evolution of pluralist accountability.

Chapter 5 contains two case studies analyzing the evolution of pluralist accountability in response to the violation of the rights of detainees held in Kosovo by the Special Representative of the UN Secretary-General and the NATO-led military operation KFOR. My analysis reveals that while pluralist accountability evolved in the case of detentions by UNMIK, it failed with regard to KFOR detentions. The competitive environment stimulated regional organizations to sharpen their profiles as external accountability holders, in both cases by establishing an Ombudsperson Institution and a Human Rights Advisory Panel. However, the difference in UNMIK's and KFOR's vulnerability with regard to human rights demands explains why pluralist accountability evolved only in the case of UNMIK.

Chapter 6 analyzes the conditions for pluralist accountability in response to alleged human rights violations that were attributed to the EU Troika's austerity policies that were implemented in Greece and Portugal between 2010 and 2015 in response to the global financial crisis, especially in terms of citizens' living conditions and the right to health. I demonstrate how a competition between national and EU institutions, as well as between different EU institutions, led the Portuguese Constitutional Court and the European Parliament, in particular, to develop distinguished profiles as accountability holders. Major differences, however, existed with regard to the degree of vulnerability of the different Troika institutions to human rights demands: while the IMF, and to a certain extent the European Central Bank, managed to render themselves immune against human rights demands, the European Commission was more vulnerable due to its broader mandate and the declining trust of the public in EU institutions' capacity to address the crisis. This explains why a pluralist accountability framework was most active with regard to the European Commission.

Chapter 7 analyzes the conditions for pluralist accountability regarding public–private health partnerships in the areas of vaccination and vaccine development in India. While in many other fields complex global governance is still characterized by formal delegation relationships with IOs as the mandating authorities, global health governance has become very fragmented and consists of primarily informal governance structures. This case study reveals in particular the limitations of pluralist accountability in complex global governance: it demonstrates how the evolution of pluralist accountability was inhibited by both a politicized environment that does not incentivize the exercise of accountability and a moral dilemma situation in which actors adopted a strong counter-norm to render themselves invulnerable against human rights demands. In this context, the core question concerning what implementing actors should be held accountable for remains disputed, which thus makes a pluralist accountability relationship impossible. The chapter also highlights the danger of a lack of pluralist accountability for the legitimacy of vaccination and public–private health partnerships as a whole.

In the conclusion, Chapter 8, I summarize the main arguments, discuss the theoretical and practical implications of the findings, and outline avenues for future research. Moreover, I reflect upon the normative-theoretical implications of pluralist accountability for IO legitimacy and demonstrate why pluralist accountability is not a panacea for the (re)legitimation of IOs. This normative assessment proceeds in two steps. I first argue that, in the absence of vertical accountability in light of human rights violations in global governance, pluralist accountability is an important means of procedural control that restrains the exercise of authority. In a second step, I demonstrate the legitimacy-enhancing potential of pluralist accountability in comparison with vertical accountability. I evaluate pluralist accountability in terms of two criteria, namely, participation and transparency (Dingwerth 2007, 27–31). The book concludes by pointing out the potential limitations of pluralist accountability in terms of the danger of "multiple accountability disorder" (Bovens and Schillemans 2011; Koppell 2005) and the degree of legalization.

2

Pluralist Accountability

A Theoretical Framework

The Concept of Accountability in Global Governance

Accountability has become a new buzzword in contemporary research as well as in the realm of practical governance.[1] The recent publication of an *Oxford Handbook on Public Accountability* certainly pays tribute to this fact (Bovens et al. 2014b). Within the domestic-level research, Schedler's (1999) definition of accountability as a three-dimensional concept of enforcement, monitoring, and justification to prevent and redress the abuse of power has become the point of reference for an increasing number of studies that strive to adapt the concept of accountability to the international or global level. Taking the research on accountability in domestic politics further, several strands of literature deal with the concept of accountability in the context of global governance. In the following sections I examine the most prominent contributions from principal-agent research, legal perspectives, and the research on transnational actors (TNAs).

Within the political science literature, the arguments about IO accountability are, to a great extent, rooted in principal-agent theory. These rely on the concept of delegation, which—although originally developed in the area of domestic politics—has increasingly been applied to the international level in order to explain the nature and work of international institutions (e.g., Koremenos et al. 2001). States agree to delegate a task to an IO and try to prevent potential delegation costs, such as agency losses, by establishing mechanisms of control, such as rules for behavior, monitoring mechanisms and institutional checks, as well as means of sanctioning (Hawkins et al. 2006b; Lake 2007). These control mechanisms presume a hierarchical relationship between principals and agents, and they are not necessarily mechanisms of democratic accountability. Most of the principal-agent literature on IO

[1] Parts of this chapter have been published in Hirschmann 2019. I thank Cambridge University Press for the permission to reprint sections of this article.

Accountability in Global Governance. Gisela Hirschmann, Oxford University Press (2020). © Gisela Hirschmann.
DOI: 10.1093/oso/9780198861249.001.0001

accountability focuses on the interactions between the IO and its member states. The central argument of this literature posits that it is the member states that hold IOs accountable according to the delegation "contract." This is the classical conception of vertical accountability between an agent and its principals. Hereby, accountability is regarded as a constitutive element in the delegation relationship between an IO, as the agent, and its member states, as the principals. Accountability works in the opposite direction of the delegation chain, as a means for the principal to cope with agency misbehavior. Accountability is both to prevent and to sanction cases of "agency slack," in which parts of the agent's actions betray the principal's interests. In an extreme form of agency slack, the agent deliberately uses its authority against the principal's interests (Kiewiet and McCubbins 1991, 26). However, principal-agent researchers argue that principals will refrain from oversight procedures that are too costly (Lake 2007, 222). Moreover, too much control by member states would also threaten the independence and neutrality of IOs (Abbott and Snidal 1998). Accountability, therefore, remains a rational balancing act for the principal between respecting the independence of the agent while retaining the possibility to act in case of misbehavior. Principals do not aim to fully control their agents, but instead weigh carefully the political and material costs of control mechanisms at the outset of the delegation relationship (Hawkins et al. 2006a, 31). According to these rationalist-institutionalist perspectives, accountability mechanisms such as self-reporting are expected to be much more common and favorable to the principals' interests than independent (let alone external) oversight mechanisms.

In an ideal-type conceptualization rooted in domestic principal-agent research, each agent is accountable to a single principal (Strøm 2003, 65). However, as some authors recognize, the role of third parties as potential accountability mechanisms has been neglected by a majority of the existing research so far. Lake and McCubbins (2006) suggest that principals might revert to third parties, for example NGOs, as alternative sources of information when they are dissatisfied with the effectiveness of the classical accountability relationship or when vertical accountability is very costly. This is expected to happen in those cases in which principals lack the power to exercise accountability or if institutional features hinder vertical accountability, such as unclear formal accountability rules for principals or an institutional culture in which a highly autonomous bureaucratic structure, constituted mainly of independent international bureaucrats, constrains the principals' influence (Hawkins et al. 2006a, 26). Thus, from a principal-agent perspective there can be another type of accountability beyond the classical vertical accountability relationship. However, this conception of a broadened accountability, in which member states deliberately employ third parties as a means to enhance their monitoring capacities, has not yet played a prominent role in principal-agent research. This might be attributed to the state-centered focus of most principal-agent studies of IOs. Instead, it has become the subject of legal theories on transnational accountability as well as in the research on the role of TNAs.

Scholars of IL have become particularly concerned about the accountability of IOs. One of the most prominent IL scholars, José Alvarez, argued in a speech in 2006:

> The increased levels of legally significant activity by our Frankenstein monsters, our IOs, are making people notice them and more people do not like what they see. Recent events suggest that states (like a gang of drunken teenagers) can do more harm sometimes when they act as a group. Our beloved "representatives of the international community" do not always respect the law. Our international financial institutions are charged with malfeasance. UN peacekeepers engage in trafficking and forced prostitution. Multilateral sanctions programs—such as the Oil for Food Program for Iraq can be just as corrupt as comparable efforts by government agencies and still do a very effective job of undermining the economic and social rights of women and children—almost as much as less effectual, unilateral efforts. Even the alternative to those—"smart" UN sanctions that focus on individual perpetrators, such as the SC's [Security Council] 1267 list of alleged terrorists—have a dark side: these can be nearly as contemptuous of due process and the need for independent review over "executive" action as the actions of P-1 with respect to unlawful combatants.[2]

As a consequence, and quite similar to the arguments of principal-agent research, classical IL scholarship emphasizes the role of states for holding IOs accountable. But not all scholars of IL share this state-centered perspective. Pluralist legal theorists, for instance, are increasingly concerned about the challenges for accountability on the global level when a variety of different actors are involved. Krisch (2010), for example, highlights that multiple principals or shared responsibilities, as in complex delegation contexts, render

[2] Alvarez 2006, available at: http://www.temple.edu/law/ils/CCILspeech.pdf (last access September 15, 2014). This terminology was also used by other legal scholars, e.g., Guzman 2013: Doctor Frankenstein's International Organizations, available at: http://escholarship.org/uc/item/8r8416mf (last access September 15, 2014).

effective vertical accountability or domestic control mechanisms as advocated by constitutionalist theories rather difficult. Hence, he argues for a pluralist conception of law as an effective accountability mechanism by combining overlapping layers of law. In this conceptualization, courts are important for sanctioning and revising decisions. Others go even further: according to the International Law Association, accountability does not necessarily imply a legal relationship between the parties. Instead, accountability can be exercised by "all component entities of the international community at large provided their interests or rights have been or may be affected by acts, actions or activities of IOs" (International Law Association 2004, 5). The committee distinguishes between legal, political, administrative, and financial accountability, and it explicitly addresses peacekeeping in several paragraphs. However, this perspective, which also takes into consideration the role of NGOs as potential accountability holders, remains the exception.

Most legal scholars still focus on states as the relevant actors for IO accountability. In order to ensure liability, they argue, this presupposes a legal personality of the different actors involved (Zaum 2006; Zwanenburg 2005). Much of the debate discusses questions of immunity and the applicability of international law to IOs as well as private actors. While some authors argue that principles of responsibility can be applied to IOs as well (Mégret and Hoffmann 2003; Zwanenburg 2005), others are more skeptical about the question of to whom actions can be attributed (Häußler 2010; Reinisch 2001). A recent milestone is the report of the International Law Commission on the Responsibilities of International Organizations, a body established by the UN General Assembly.[3] The members of the commission took into account several recent court rulings and identified effective control as the criterion for attribution. However, with regard to the sanctioning capacity, legal theorists remain skeptical since immunity regulations continue to prevent the legal enforcement of remedies against IOs (Wellens 2002). Thus, very few scholars have proposed measures of "naming and shaming" as alternative horizontal sanctioning mechanisms (de Wet 2010, 856). These measures, however, remain outside of the core legal research on IO accountability.

The notion that there might be alternative avenues of accountability that involve a broader audience to which IOs are (to be) held accountable has gained traction with the growing prominence of research on the normative and legal power of TNAs. Research on accountability in a globalized world

[3] See the Articles on the Responsibilities of International Organizations adopted by the UN General Assembly in 2011 (UN doc. A/RES/66/100).

points out that the delegation of tasks to external and especially nonstate actors weakens the direct influence of citizens as accountability holders (Kersbergen and Waarden 2004; Papadopoulos 2003; Scholte 2004). The central argument points to the difficulties of achieving accountability of (mostly nonstate) TNAs in global governance (Risse 2002, 269). This argument is especially prevalent in the literature and the public policy discourse on NGOs and has since been extended to private actors particularly in the security sector (Pingeot 2012; Singer 2003; Steffek and Nanz 2008). The role of third parties as accountability holders can potentially compensate the lack of traditional accountability at the transnational level (Sperling 2009).

In particular, the research on the democratization of global governance emphasizes the underestimated potential of TNAs for achieving (democratic) accountability beyond the state-level context (Bexell et al. 2010; Held 2006; Koenig-Archibugi 2010; Scholte 2011a; Uhlin 2011).[4] These scholars criticize principal-agent and mainstream legal scholarship for its focus on the role of nation-states as the sole accountability holders. TNA researchers propose to take the transnational realm as an additional point of reference and highlight the (positive) influence of nonstate actors on IO accountability through advocacy and policy evaluation. They argue, often informed by a cosmopolitan understanding of how to make international institutions more democratic, that greater participation of nonstate actors in IO policymaking increases transparency. Accountability in the transnational realm, therefore, relies on the naming and shaming activities of human rights groups (Macdonald and Macdonald 2006; Woods and Narlikar 2001). TNAs, thus, can influence both norm-setting and enforcement processes. Additionally, TNAs are recognized as an important element in a pluralistic process of international lawmaking with regard to their normative power, particularly in the area of human rights; a role that even lawyers have begun to acknowledge (Fischer-Lescano and Liste 2005, 233).[5]

To summarize, the concept of accountability as used in the various strands of IR and IL literature differ strongly, from a rather restricted concept of legal

[4] See also the recent Global Accountability Reports since 2006, available at: http://oneworldtrust.org/index.php?option=com_content&view=article&id=73&Itemid=60 (last access January 31, 2015) and the research project on the "Democratization of Global Governance" at the universities of Stockholm and Lund, available at: http://www.transdemos.se/publications/transdemosStvTidskr.pdf (last access January 31, 2015).

[5] The authors introduce the concept of a "law-making civil society" ("rechtsetzende Zivilgesellschaft") and give an example of a Belgian ad hoc judge, who argued that "advocacy organizations, such as, Amnesty International, Avocats sans Frontières, Human Rights Watch, The International Federation of Human Rights Leagues (FIDH) and the International Commission of Jurists, have taken clear positions on the subject of international accountability. This may be seen as the opinion of civil society, an opinion that cannot be completely discounted in the formation of customary international law today" (Fischer-Lescano and Liste 2005, 233).

accountability to the very broad notion of democratic accountability by a greater involvement of TNAs. As others have highlighted, there are probably as many concepts of accountability as there are researchers (Bovens et al. 2014a, 2). However, an important insight to be taken away from this review is the notion of two basic types of accountability, one that is restricted to the relationship between two actors (the agent and its principal) and one that allows for the inclusion of other actors as a broader "audience" of accountability. This distinction is the basis for my development of a more systematic conceptualization of different types of accountability in this book.

Complex Global Governance: The Challenge for Accountability

Although IR scholars continue to debate the role of nation-states in a globalized world, "new modes of governance" involving a number of different public and private actors have emerged that pose new conceptual and empirical challenges (Koenig-Archibugi and Zürn 2006). The very distinct characteristics of complex global governance, namely, the prolonged delegation relationships and informal governance arrangements, are particularly challenging when it comes to the question of how to hold the various implementing actors accountable. IOs hereby play an important role as the solution to globally relevant problems in areas such as peace and security, economics, or the environment (Hooghe et al. 2017; Zürn 2018). The delegation of authority to IOs has intrigued IR researchers for a long time (e.g., Hawkins et al. 2006b; Lake 2007; Sarooshi 1999). Researchers have investigated states' motivations behind the delegation of powers to IOs (Abbott and Snidal 1998; Pollack 1997) as well as the reasons for choosing specific types of institutional designs (e.g., Koremenos et al. 2001). Some scholars conceive of IOs as implementing (with a certain degree of autonomy) the rules for cooperation agreed upon by their member states (e.g., Martin and Simmons 1998). But what happens after an IO has been entrusted with these powers? This important question is the point of departure for this book, which looks at complex governance arrangements in which IOs do not merely function as arenas for cooperation between interdependent states (Keohane 1984) or as agents of their member states for the implementation of certain tasks, but instead further delegate these tasks to other actors. One major contribution of this book is to highlight the implications of complex governance arrangements for accountability.

By further delegating tasks, IOs can increase their autonomy (Barnett and Finnemore 2004; Weaver 2008), which in turn makes member states lose control over them (Heldt 2017; Johnson 2014). IOs can gain higher independence from their original mandate by designing new mandates themselves and assigning them autonomously to other actors. Thus, the authority of IOs has not only increased in terms of the range and intrusiveness of their activities (Heupel and Zürn 2017), but it has also changed in character, as they increasingly design and delegate policies themselves. These new forms of IO authority imply that a variety of unforeseen actors participate in the exercise of governance functions. IOs hereby extend the delegation chain by mandating nonstate actors, regional organizations, or individual states to implement certain tasks. This can include all kinds of actors, independent of the IO or a body within the IO itself, that enjoy a certain degree of autonomy in a particular policy field. If there is no implementing actor available, the IO might also create one that is then mandated to implement specific tasks. One common example for this is the position of the Special Representative of the UN Secretary-General (SRSG) established to lead transitional administrations mandated by the UN Security Council. The core feature of complex governance arrangements implies that the implementing actor enjoys a certain degree of discretion and has the authority to take autonomous decisions and actions (Hawkins et al. 2006a, 7; Tierney 2006).

In order to disentangle the complex governance arrangements between an IO, the IO bureaucracy, the sub-organs, and external implementing parties, I embody the terminology of principal and agent as put forward in delegation theory.[6] Principal-agent theorists define delegation as "a conditional grant of authority from a principal to an agent that empowers the latter to act on behalf of the former, that is limited in time and scope and is revocable by the principal" (Hawkins et al. 2006a, 7; Lake 2007, 228). For the purpose of this study, I define delegation as the act by which an actor (the principal) entrusts another actor (the agent) to implement a decision or a certain task. This can happen through a formal authorization that concludes a delegation contract with an existing party or by establishing a new institution that is mandated to implement particular tasks. Moreover, delegation can also take place

[6] Using this terminology, however, is not supposed to conceal the autonomy of the implementing actors. From a legal perspective, the use of the term "agent" might raise the connotation of a lack of autonomy and independence. Principal-agent research, in contrast, has always focused on issues of agency discretion and autonomy. Moreover, it is important to note that I do not rely on the theory's further assumptions that all actors have fixed preferences and act purely rationally. I use this terminology only for descriptive purposes without further theoretical implications.

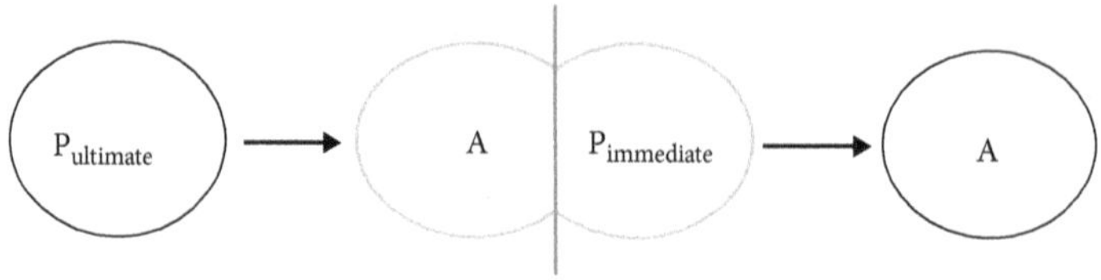

Figure 2.1 Illustration of prolonged delegation, whereby the ultimate principal delegates a task to an agent who, as an immediate principal, further delegates this task to another agent.
Note: P = principal, A = agent

informally or implicitly (Hawkins et al. 2006, 7). Crucial for identifying an act of delegation is that the principal grants and is able to withdraw such authorization.

In order to conceptualize prolonged delegation chains, my analysis distinguishes between *ultimate principals* and *immediate principals* (see Figure 2.1). The immediate principal has a double role: it is an agent to the ultimate principal but a principal to another agent. The ultimate principal is the original authorizing body that stands at the beginning of the delegation chain after states have conferred power to an IO. Therefore, it is a collective decision-making body that consists of several actors that adopt one single delegation agreement that cannot be revised by an individual member state (Lyne et al. 2006; Tierney 2006). This distinction is different from another concept of complex delegation, namely that involving "multiple principals." Multiple principals characterize situations "when a single agent has more than one contract with organizationally distinct principals" (Lyne et al. 2006, 44). In contrast, prolonged delegation chains contain several principals that individually contract with a single agent by further delegating the task. In this case, the delegation chain is based on one single authorization and contains agents that simultaneously act as principals toward another agent.

The phenomenon of prolonged delegation in global governance can be best illustrated with the example of peacekeeping. In the context of peace operations, prolonged delegation chains are nothing new; the implementation of peacekeeping missions has always been delegated. With the founding of the UN, states entrusted the UN Security Council with providing international security. However, UN member states never officially authorized the body to conduct peacekeeping operations. Peacekeeping is not mentioned in the UN Charter; instead, the authorization of peace operations has grown incrementally through an expansion of the Security Council's own tasks. The Security

Council bases the authorization of peace operations on Article 39 of Chapter VII of the UN Charter, which determines that the body "shall determine the existence of any threat to the peace, breach of the peace, or act of aggression and shall make recommendations, or decide what measures shall be taken in accordance with Articles 41 and 42, to maintain or restore international peace and security."

Prolonged delegation chains are a particularly useful conceptual framework for researching the changing patterns of actors involved in peacekeeping after 1990. When authorizing a peace operation, UN Security Council member states collectively delegate the implementation of peace operations on the basis of Chapter VII or Chapter VIII powers to other actors (Lake 2007, 232; Lipson 2008). This usually implies the relocation of core mission tasks such as security sector reform, disarmament, demobilization, reintegration of former combatants, and police reform as well as military tasks. The actors that are entrusted with the implementation of these tasks can be the UN bureaucracy, regional organizations, or individual member states. The UN bureaucracy is mandated to assemble troop-contributing countries (TCCs), which are since 1999, for the most part, not the same Security Council members that authorized a mission. Moreover, certain aspects of the mission are increasingly delegated to the host state in which the operation takes place. Finally, with the growing influence and capacities of regional organizations, the Security Council, under Chapter VIII of the UN Charter, also increasingly delegates the implementation of a complete operation or parts of an operation to regional organizations (Yamashita 2012).

All these implementing actors enjoy a comparably high degree of autonomy, either legally or de facto. In legal terms, the UN bureaucracy and a peacekeeping operation are conceived as subsidiary organs that are entrusted with Chapter VII powers (Häußler 2010, 238). The implementing TCCs are legally sovereign and retain the command and control over their troops (Buchan et al. 2011). The degree of transferred authority, as well as questions of operational control, depends on individual mandates and additional agreements, such as the Status of Forces Agreements between the host state and the troop-contributing state.[7] A similarly high degree of autonomy can be identified in delegation contexts in which agents are entrusted with the implementation of a complete mission. Transitional administrations, such as in Kosovo and East Timor, are examples of such delegated authority. In these cases, the

[7] See United Nations Department for Peacekeeping Operations and Department of Field Service 2008.

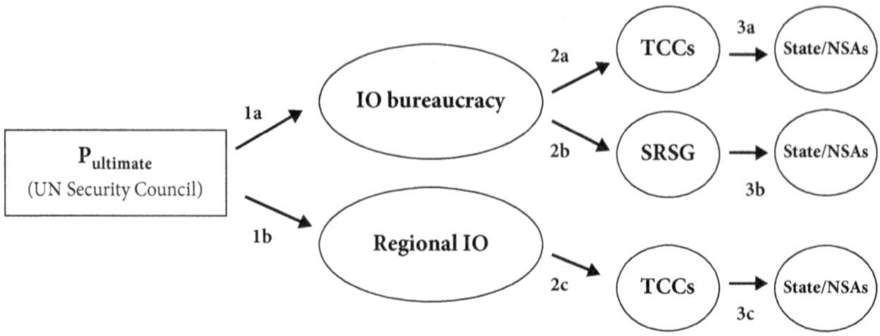

Figure 2.2 Peacekeeping delegation chain from ultimate principal (the UN Security Council) to the IO's bureaucracy or a regional organization, to troop-contributing countries or the Special Representative of the Secretary-General, to state and/or nonstate actors.

Note: TCCs = troop-contributing countries, SRSG = Special Representative of the Secretary-General, NSAs = nonstate actors

SRSG was empowered to establish governmental authorities and undertake binding decisions (Chopra 2002; Zaum 2006). Regional organizations, by the nature of their own mandate, also enjoy a high degree of autonomy. The UN itself has identified three types of delegation to regional organizations: operational support, co-deployment, and joint operations.[8] NATO, for example, was entrusted with the implementation of the military aspects of the operations in Kosovo and Bosnia. Figure 2.2 illustrates the possible empirical delegation relationships in peace operations.

The UN Security Council, as the ultimate principal, authorizes peace operations to be implemented by the UN bureaucracy (1a) or by a regional IO (1b). The UN bureaucracy, in general the Department for Peacekeeping Operations, then asks TCCs to implement the military aspects of the operation (2a). TCCs may further delegate individual tasks to state or nonstate actors (3a). The UN bureaucracy may also entrust an SRSG with certain powers to implement an operation, with the highest powers conferred during transitional administrations (2b). The SRSG may in turn delegate certain aspects of the implementation to state or nonstate actors (3b). The regional IO usually also delegates the implementation to its TCCs (2c), which in turn may employ state or nonstate actors to implement parts of the operation (3c). The issue area of peace operations thus very nicely illustrates the complex governance arrangements of today's world and the role that IOs play in prolonged delegation relationships.

[8] United Nations Department for Peacekeeping Operations 1999.

Complex governance arrangements are not restricted to the realm of peace operations, though. Much attention has been given to prolonged delegation in the context of the EU, for example, which has shown an "unlimited appetite" for creating new agencies to develop policies and implement a wide range of tasks in the fields of health, finance, economics, environment, and energy (Busuioc 2012; Busuioc et al. 2011; Curtin and Wessel 2005). Even more complex are the fields of global environmental governance and global health governance, in which a combination of different actors coordinates themselves under the leadership of an IO (Holzscheiter et al. 2016; Kickbusch 2000; Kramarz and Park 2016). These areas involve more indirect and informal governance arrangements that have also been characterized as "orchestration" (Abbott et al. 2015) or "meta-governance" (Holzscheiter et al. 2016), in which IOs play a coordinating role. Whether IOs formally delegate the implementation of tasks to other actors or coordinate and oversee the implementation of such tasks, the question of how the implementing actors can be held accountable if they violate human rights has become crucial for the legitimacy of IOs.

These complex governance arrangements pose significant conceptual and empirical challenges to accountability. Existing research on accountability mostly focuses on the first delegation step—the transfer of power from states to IOs—and highlights the importance of accountability in particular for an IO's legitimacy (e.g., Heldt 2017; Henderson 2014; Heupel and Zürn 2017; Lake and McCubbins 2006). From an international law perspective, accountability is expected to be much more difficult in prolonged delegation chains due to further problems of command and control that amplify with a delegation expansion (Abass 2004: 83; Ferstman 2017; Sarooshi 1999: 31). Human rights violations might be committed under the name of an operation mandated by the UN, while the complex delegation relationships would make it hard for the UN Security Council, as the mandating authority, to actually control the behavior of the different implementing actors.

Not all scholars are so pessimistic, however. Lake (2007, 231) posits that while in simple delegation the principal retains residual rights to control and sanctions its implementing agent, this might or might not be the case in prolonged delegation. This, however, requires the willingness of the principal to hold the agent accountable, which in many situations of global governance is not the case, as pointed out by recent literature on "drifting principals" (Schillemans and Busuioc 2014). Due to the difficulty with finding the balance between discretion and control, which some scholars have characterized as the "discretion dilemma" (Hawkins et al. 2006a; Tallberg 2002), principals in complex governance arrangements seem to be increasingly reluctant to invest in accountability mechanisms (Schillemans and Busuioc 2014). Moreover, the blurred lines of responsibility in more informal governance settings make accountability rather difficult as it remains increasingly unclear who should hold whom accountable when responsibilities are "diffused" (Nollkaemper 2018). Thus, while the empirical research on the "new intrusiveness of IOs" (Woods and Narlikar 2001) and the research on the increasing complexity of global governance arrangements have revealed the importance of accountability, there has been less theoretical and conceptual work that would allow us to formulate clear expectations for how accountability features in these contexts (Macdonald 2014). In the words of one legal scholar, new institutional forms such as complex delegation and new accountability demands are "two 'moving targets' that are still in search of accommodation" (Rached 2014). Against this background, I now turn to the question of how to analyze accountability in these complex governance structures.

Conceptualizing the Dependent Variable: Pluralist Accountability

The concept of accountability as it is used today is fairly recent and has its origins in the Anglo-American management realm (Bovens 2007, 449). Researchers with other linguistic backgrounds have found it difficult to come up with corresponding semantic translations that adequately capture the meaning of the concept. Therefore, the public and scientific discourses about accountability often remain vague. So far, conceptualizations of accountability originate mainly in the national democratic realm (Schedler et al. 1999). Schedler (1999) defines accountability as a mechanism to constrain power by ensuring that the powerful act transparently, justify their actions, and are subject to sanctions. However, the strong reliance on domestic conceptualizations of accountability has produced conceptual ambiguities, in which the boundaries between accountability and other concepts such as democracy and responsiveness have become blurred. In this section, I first show why this conceptual ambiguity is problematic before outlining the conceptual framework for accountability that I use in this study.

The first clarification is about the relationship between accountability and democracy. Accountability is often understood as democratic accountability, a conceptualization that encompasses a priori provisions for participation and ex-post electoral responsibility toward those affected by policy decisions (Benz 2007; Curtin et al. 2010). This conceptualization is predominantly put forward by cosmopolitan theorists who argue that there are no substantial conceptual differences between governance on the domestic and transnational levels that would restrict accountability to the domestic context only (Held 2006; Koenig-Archibugi 2010). Therefore, cosmopolitan theorists advocate for the democratization of international institutions by transporting the concept of accountability from the domestic context to the global level. Their argument is often linked to normative prescriptions of how IOs should be reformed in order to include accountability mechanisms familiar to the domestic level. This is also supported by research on the influence of TNAs, which argues that nonstate actors play a crucial role in enhancing accountability beyond the nation-state (e.g., Scholte 2011a; Steffek 2010). In contrast, according to the pessimists' view, accountability cannot be applied to the transnational context due to fundamental differences in structure and character, that is, the absence of an international demos as well as the size, heterogeneity, and inaccessibility of the international system for the ordinary citizen (Goodhart 2011; Krisch 2010). In this understanding, accountability is a concept genuine to the nation-state, and it is, therefore, impossible to attribute it to IOs because of the rather undemocratic setting of global governance.

This divide between cosmopolitans and skeptics is due to the problematic conceptual intertwinement of accountability and democracy that always implies democratic means of participation and popular control of the governing authority when referring to accountability. Thus, disentangling the concepts of accountability and democracy is essential if we are to gain a richer picture of the empirical realities of accountability. In order to avoid conceptual overstretch when applying accountability to the transnational level, scholars suggest looking more closely at how various forms of accountability differ across specific governance characteristics (e.g., Benner et al. 2004; Grant and Keohane 2005; Krisch 2010, ch. 8). The fact that multinational corporations are internally accountable to their shareholders or private investors, for example, highlights that there are forms of accountability beyond electoral mechanisms and outside of the democratic context (Koenig-Archibugi 2010; Warren 2014).

One conceptualization of accountability that is independent from the democratic context is inherent to the concept of responsiveness, which highlights the role of shareholders as accountability holders (Kingsbury et al. 2005). Responsiveness implies that an organization adheres closely to the demands and the expectations of its constituents (Koppell 2010, 39). Confounding accountability with responsiveness, however, stands in stark contrast to the two central features of IOs that render them valuable for states: their independence and neutrality (Abbott and Snidal 1998). Responsiveness thus does not adequately capture the fact that IO member states need to continuously find the right balance between respecting an organization's independence while retaining the possibility to act in case of transgression. Moreover, we could also imagine situations in which an organization responds to the demands of actors other than its shareholders. This could be in situations in which organizations respect general normative standards that have been established by its surrounding community, for example.[9] The concept of accountability to responsiveness furthermore ignores the responsibilities that IOs might have toward affected people. The World Bank, for example, might be very responsive to the US government as its most influential shareholder, but it often remains unaccountable to those affected by its policies (Woods and Narlikar 2001). Hence, defining accountability by responsiveness limits the possibility to grasp the empirical varieties of account holders.

The definition that I put forward in this book thus distinguishes the concept of accountability from democracy and responsiveness. I define accountability as the relationship between two actors by which one actor (the *accountability holder*) sets the standards for the other actor's behavior and monitors and sanctions the other (the *accountor*) if its actions deviate from the standards. This definition is in line with recent research that, for the most part, agrees on these three functions: standard setting, monitoring, and sanctioning (Bovens 2007; Buchanan and Keohane 2006; de Wet 2010; Grant and Keohane 2005; Grigorescu 2008; Heldt 2017; Koenig-Archibugi 2004; Macdonald and Macdonald 2006). On this basis, Grant and Keohane (2005) have developed a detailed typology of seven accountability forms that includes hierarchical, supervisory, fiscal, legal, market, peer, and reputational mechanisms. Other conceptualizations have defined accountability on the basis of components, namely the four components of transparency, consultation, evaluation, and correction (Scholte 2011a), or the five components of transparency, liability, controllability, responsibility, and responsiveness (Koppell 2005, 2010).[10] However, for the purpose of this analysis, I find that the distinction of accountability *functions* is more useful than accountability components to identify different types of accountability.

Standard setting is the first necessary accountability function. This implies that the accountability holder prescribes the norms that the accountor should

[9] In the economic realm, recent standards include corporate social responsibility, environmental protection, or sustainability standards.

[10] See also the dimensions used for the Global Accountability Reports (http://www.oneworldtrust.org/globalaccountability/gar, last access October 10, 2013).

be respecting in the course of the implementation. These standards are derived from norms that are regarded as generally legitimate by both the accountability holder and the accountor (Grant and Keohane 2005, 29). Standard *setting* does not necessarily imply that accountability holders themselves *develop* these standards, although this might happen in specific circumstances.[11] Rather, standard setting means that accountability holders identify existing rules and norms and establish them as a frame of reference for the accountor's actions in the context of implementing a specific task. By arguing that the IO and its implementing actors should adhere to these standards, they engage in standard setting, but not in developing standard. The accountability holders hereby specify to which (often pre-existing) rules the accountor should be held accountable. Not every delegation contract or implementation mandate contains references to norms. Usually mandates include tasks to be fulfilled without necessarily referring to applicable standards for behavior. An accountability holder then specifies which norms must be respected in the course of the implementation; these norms can be binding or nonbinding.[12] They are expressed in the external international discourse and the legal framework, describing the nexus between the implementing actions and generally accepted norms, such as human rights (Reinisch 2005). Holding someone accountable for human rights violations, for example, means to provide a framework that embeds actions into national and international human rights obligations.

Of course, different actors have different opinions about how human rights apply to IOs and their agents, whereas only a quite homogenous discourse can have norm-generating effects that contribute to standards of appropriate behavior. Depending on the homogeneity in standard setting, this might imply that actors are asked to be accountable to potentially conflicting principles (Schedler 1999, 22). Generally speaking, there may be two frames in the discourse, one establishing a weak, implicit, or even contradictory link between actions and human rights, and another establishing a strong, explicit, and univocal link that generates a sense of obligation. Cases in which no link is drawn between human rights and actions indicate that a generally accepted standard does not yet exist.

[11] In the field of human rights, the roles of standard developing and standard setting might often overlap, for example NGOs who develop and monitor human rights standards for peace operations. I am grateful to one of the reviewers for highlighting this point.

[12] To give an example, the "responsibility to protect" has evolved as a global norm, though not yet legally binding, that became the standard for judging UN interventions (Peters 2011).

Monitoring is the second necessary accountability function. Monitoring defines mechanisms of oversight that are established to accompany the implementing process in order to ensure that the mandate is effectively implemented. To make transparent whether the accountor respects the standards set by the accountability holder, the latter establishes mechanisms for reporting and surveillance. The principal-agency literature identifies several modes of control that actors employ to minimize agency slack (Hawkins et al. 2006a, 28; McCubbins and Schwartz 1984). These oversight mechanisms include self-reporting or unannounced on-site visits ("police patrol"), for example. This accountability component is most closely linked to the concept of transparency and constitutes the basis for sanctioning, as it provides the accountability holder with the relevant information needed to determine whether the agent's behavior is in line with the standards set (Schedler 1999).

Sanctioning is the third necessary accountability function, although it is contested in its effects and applicability to the global level (Grant and Keohane 2005, 41). Nevertheless, the possibility to sanction misconduct and the misuse of power remains essential for the concept of accountability (Bovens 2007; Schedler 1999). The accountability holder must be able to sanction misbehavior and the lack of respect for the established standards. The central questions for assessing this dimension are: are there costs attached to misbehavior and, if yes, what types of costs? One possible sanction category entails normative-political sanctions, through measures of "naming and shaming," for example. This leads to a loss in the accountor's authority and reputation (de Wet 2010, 856). Here, the transnational human rights groups play an important role to signal "public disempowerment" (Macdonald and Macdonald 2006). Material sanctioning includes budget cutbacks, revisions to the agent's mandate, or any form of monetary penalties (Pollack 1997, 118). The accountability holder can also completely withdraw the mandate or the delegated tasks, which constitutes the most powerful and encompassing form of sanctioning.

In order to distinguish different types of accountability, the crucial question to ask is who are the accountability holders? Surprisingly enough, there is no agreed-upon definition for a verb that describes what an accountability holder actually does when it engages in standard setting, monitoring, and sanctioning. However, it is not its mere presence that characterizes an accountability holder but only its actions. Therefore, I employ the term "to exercise accountability" that Schedler (1999) uses to describe the actions of an accountability holder. The analytical framework I use in this study distinguishes two modes of accountability—vertical and pluralist—depending on what actor performs these three accountability functions (standard setting, monitoring, and sanctioning) (see Figure 2.3).

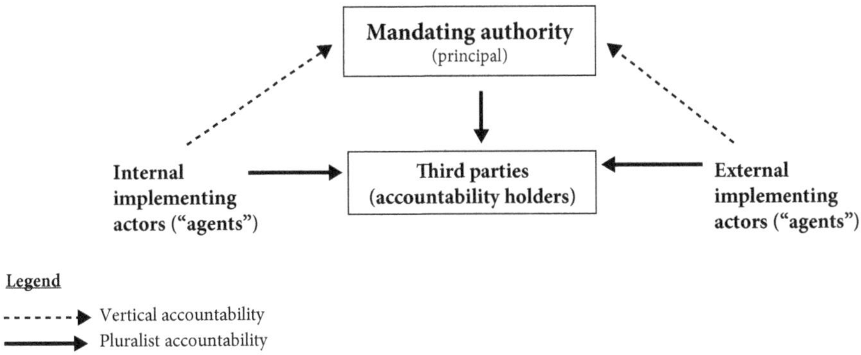

Figure 2.3 Vertical and pluralist accountability. The analytical framework I use in this study distinguishes two modes of accountability—vertical and pluralist—depending on what actor performs the three accountability functions (standard setting, monitoring, and sanctioning). In vertical accountability, the internal (bottom left) and external (bottom right) implementing agents are held accountable by the mandating authority, i.e., the principal (top). In pluralist accountability, the internal (bottom left) and external (bottom right) implementing agents as well as the mandating authority (top) are held accountable by third parties who act as accountability holders (bottom center).

Previous researchers have also labelled vertical accountability internal accountability, which characterizes all forms in which the accountability holder is institutionally linked to the organization (Grigorescu 2008; Keohane 2003; Krisch 2010; Risse 2008). In this accountability type, the agent is held accountable directly by its immediate and ultimate principals. This means that accountability takes the inverse direction of the delegation chain: the delegation goes from a principal to the agent whereas accountability chains go back from the agent to the principal. In vertical accountability, the principal defines the standards for implementation, monitors the agent, and sanctions misbehavior by normative shaming, revising the mandate, or ultimately by withdrawing the authorization. In vertical accountability, the mandating authority thus acts as the accountability holder.

In contrast to the concept of vertical accountability, I put forward the concept of *pluralist accountability*. This concept takes into consideration that third parties, which operate externally to the delegation relationship between the mandating authority and the accountor, also act as accountability holders. In pluralist accountability, the accountability relationship is thus independent of the delegation relationship as third parties initiate their own accountability functions. Previous researchers have used the terms external, diagonal, or horizontal for this form of accountability (Bovens 2007). There are, however, several reasons for choosing the term pluralist to describe this accountability type. Initially, external accountability was defined as "stakeholder" accountability, in which actors are held accountable to the people who are affected by its actions and policies (Keohane 2003; Sperling 2009). Indeed, some scholars have examined how affected individuals can file complaints if their rights are violated by an IO (Grigorescu 2010; Heupel and Zürn 2017; Hirschmann 2017a, 2017b, 2017c, 2017d). Grant and Keohane (2005) have used a broader notion of external accountability which also includes peer or reputational accountability to all kinds of external actors (Grant and Keohane 2005). Other authors have termed this "horizontal accountability" (Deshman 2011; Woods and Narlikar 2001), "diagonal or new forms of accountability" (Bovens 2007), or "non-institutionalized accountability mechanisms that operate outside of a given regime" (Krisch 2010). They point to other actors such as a transnational civil society, peer international institutions, or other stakeholders that can act as accountability holders. According to the International Law Association, accountability holders can comprise "all component entities of the international community at large provided their interests or rights have been or may be affected by acts, actions or activities of IOs" (International Law Association 2004, 5). Rubenstein (2007) has used the term "surrogate accountability" if third parties act on behalf of the "real" accountability holder, that is, the affected people.

One of the main reasons why I use the term pluralist accountability to refer to accountability relationships in which third parties act as accountability holders is the fact that the existing terms mentioned above all bear connotations that have important implications for the understanding of the concept. External accountability has been used in different ways and therefore it risks being misunderstood. Given the fact that it has often been used to refer to stakeholder accountability, external accountability (as well as surrogate accountability) does not rightly capture the phenomenon this study intends to describe. Horizontal or diagonal accountability in turn both imply connotations about the position of the accountability holder in relation to the implementing actor. As previous research on accountability in the domestic context points out, the concept of horizontal accountability is limited to very specific contexts and euphemizes the structural asymmetries that might exist between the accountability holder and the accountor (O'Donell 1994; Schedler 1999).

The second reason for choosing the term pluralist accountability is linked to how the concept of pluralism has been used in international law. Describing different layers of law, this term reflects best the fragmented and nonhierarchical character of accountability relationships (Krisch 2010). Pluralist accountability holders may be transnational, national, nonstate, or judicial actors who—individually or together—engage in standard setting, monitoring, or sanctioning. They can be parallel operating institutions, regional organizations, NGOs, or courts, for instance. Examples of third parties who perform accountability functions are the International Committee of the Red Cross (ICRC), which has repeatedly developed standards for specific circumstances such as international and noninternational armed conflicts, NGOs like Amnesty International or Human Rights Watch, which often undertake monitoring activities, or the International Criminal Court (ICC), which has a singular sanctioning authority in the international arena.

The distinction between vertical and pluralist accountability does not exclude the use of existing concepts that describe the individual accountability forms as identified, for example, by Grant and Keohane (2005). Hierarchical, supervisory, and fiscal accountability forms can most often be found in vertical accountability. In contrast, legal, market, peer, and reputational accountability forms are more likely to be characterized as pluralist accountability. Therefore, while the dichotomous concept of vertical and pluralist accountability focuses on actor relations, the classification of accountability forms emphasizes the type of action that is undertaken by the accountability holder. The conceptualization of this study thus provides an additional analytical layer to existing concepts of accountability for the purpose of clarification.

Note that pluralist accountability is not specific to the international context but exists in the domestic realm as well. Often, the activities of accountability holders target not only the implementing actors but also the delegating principal and its responsibilities as a vertical accountability holder. This might result in a contest about who is the legitimate accountability holder and might constrain the principal's authority as the primary accountability holder. Pluralist accountability may be seen as a sign of a transnational community growing together, with a common understanding about the rules for global governance and a new sense of responsibility. Using the concept of "cosmopolitan accountability" (Beck 2006, 143), however, would be misleading since it does not lead to the evolution of a world state. Nevertheless, pluralist accountability implies that there is a wider community outside of the delegation relationship in which both the principal and the agent are embedded (Buzan 1993, 336).

How can the concept of pluralist accountability be applied to the context of governance failures at the global level? The crucial aspect here is that third

Table 2.1 Vertical and pluralist accountability

	Vertical accountability	Pluralist accountability
Standard setting	Standards set by the mandating authority, the organization/headquarters	Standard development by third parties (norm-entrepreneurs, experts, etc.)
Monitoring	Internal reporting mechanisms: self-reporting or "police patrol"	Information collection and oversight of agents' behavior by third parties: "police patrol" or "fire alarms"
Sanctioning	Imposition of material and normative costs by the principal	Imposition of material and normative costs by third parties, e.g., national, regional, or international courts; shaming by NGOs

parties decide to exercise accountability functions on their own and independently of actors involved in the delegation relationship. Table 2.1 summarizes how pluralist accountability operates in contrast to vertical accountability. If the delegating authority develops standards at the outset of the delegation process or in reaction to lessons learned from previous delegation acts, I characterize this as vertical standard setting. Pluralist accountability, on the contrary, is characterized by standard setting by external third parties, for example norm entrepreneurs (Finnemore and Sikkink 1998) or other standard-setting actors, such as NGOs, courts, or expert commissions that develop new guidelines for the implementing actor. In the area of peacekeeping, the ICRC is a very important standard setter with regard to applying human rights principles to the use of force in military operations.

Vertical monitoring implies oversight that takes place within the delegation relationship. This includes the mechanism of self-reporting, which requires the agent to report regularly to its principals on certain aspects of its actions. In self-reporting, there is no independent evaluation and the agent itself can decide what to report. Vertical monitoring can also imply the mechanism of "police patrols," the regular and direct monitoring by principals that guarantees more detailed insights into the agent's actions through spontaneous onsite visits (Lake and McCubbins 2006, 348). In pluralist monitoring, independent third parties collect information and monitor compliance of the implementing actor's behavior through initiating "police patrols." Through the "fire alarm" mechanism, third parties can alert the general public, other external actors, or the original delegating authority about misbehavior of the implementing actor. This can also include briefings to the IO itself on wrongdoings that happened in other parts of the organization or within the implementing partner's group.

Vertical sanctioning implies the imposition of material or normative costs directly by the mandating authority. Only the principal can exert the most harmful material sanction—the termination of the delegation relationship. Nevertheless, third parties, which independently assess the penalty for the implementing actor's misbehavior, can impose significant sanctions. Third parties can for example "exit" the institutional context, thereby terminating the cooperation in order to materially sanction another actor within this specific context (Kuyper et al. 2017). Moreover, pluralist legal theorists highlight the increasingly important role of courts for sanctioning and revising decisions (Alter 2014; Krisch 2010). This presupposes a legal personality of the implementing actor in order to ensure liability (Zaum 2006; Zwanenburg 2005). Usually, however, immunity regulations prevent the legal enforcement of remedies in the context of IOs (Wellens 2002). Thus, in pluralist accountability, normative sanctioning in the form of "naming and shaming" remains more likely (de Wet 2010). This form of sanctioning increases the reputational costs of the implementing actor and the mandating authority.

The overview of these indicators reveals that both vertical and pluralist accountability comprise formal and informal elements of accountability functions. In vertical accountability, standards may be set formally in the delegation contract or informally through mutual agreement. Self-reporting and "police patrol" monitoring can take place through formal reporting lines or on an informal ad hoc basis. Sanctioning might involve material and thus more formal costs, or immaterial, normative costs in terms of social shaming. In pluralist accountability, aspects of formal standard setting may include legal norms whereas informal standards may be established by independent expert commissions, for example. Formal monitoring might include agreements on onsite visits or invitations to hearings, while informal monitoring includes spontaneous and unregulated acts of information collection. Formal sanctioning in pluralist accountability can be undertaken through legal proceedings, for example, whereas informal sanctioning refers to actions that imply immaterial, normative costs. Therefore, the differences in formal and informal elements across the two accountability types need to be assessed empirically on a case-by-case basis.

Of course, in reality, this ideal-type binary distinction of accountability is not always so clear-cut. In some cases, third parties that act outside the delegation relationship may be institutionally part of the principal. One example of this "grey zone" is the World Bank Inspection Panel that reviews human rights complaints from third parties regarding the bank's projects. Consequently, other studies refer to this type of institutional accountability as internal (Grigorescu 2008; Heldt 2017). If we consider its status regarding the delegation relationship between the World Bank and the implementing partner country, however, the World Bank Inspection Panel's monitoring activities can be characterized as external as it stands outside of this delegation relationship. What makes it even more complicated is the fact that the panel has no sanctioning power independent from the World Bank. Thus, while being an independent monitoring mechanism, it is not a pluralist accountability mechanism with regard to the sanctioning function. The same ambiguity characterizes the UN Office of Internal Oversight Services, which is institutionally part of the UN Secretariat. It can undertake independent monitoring but, again, has few sanctioning powers independent from the secretariat. In this mixed form, the principal delegates some accountability functions to either external preexisting third parties or ones that the principal creates. Delegated accountability thus displays features of vertical accountability as well as pluralist accountability. Sometimes, institutions that principals created for the purpose of delegated accountability may become more independent over time (Alter 2014). The ICC, for example, usually can act only if the court is invited to do so, for instance by the UN Security Council. Recently, however, the chief prosecutor has become active as a more independent accountability holder, or has threatened to do so, which indicates a development toward pluralist accountability.[13] Recent studies on when IOs open up to nonstate actors (Tallberg et al. 2013) outline the conditions for when and why principals delegate accountability functions, as does the literature on judicalization (Zangl et al. 2011). However, it is important to note that I focus on cases of "pure" pluralist accountability, in which third parties act as accountability holders independent of the principals.

The ideal-type complete pluralist accountability that I define in this study encompasses all three functions of standard setting, monitoring, and sanctioning exercised by third parties. If the accountability holder performs only one or two of the three functions, I describe such cases as attempts of pluralist accountability when the evolution of a complete pluralist accountability failed. I assign equal value to all three functions because I consider each of them equally important for accountability. However, standard setting, monitoring, and sanctioning do not have to be undertaken by one single third party; instead, several third parties who all act as accountability holders with regard

[13] See the recent statement by the ICC's President Bensouda to the UN Security Council with regard to allegations that the UN mission in Sudan had covered up important information about war crimes, http://www.unmultimedia.org/tv/unifeed/2014/06/un-darfur-bensouda/ (last access September 12, 2014).

to the same implementing actor can exercise these three functions. For an NGO to monitor and shame the UN regarding its treatment of detainees, it needs to establish the rights of detainees as a standard to be respected in peacekeeping operations. This standard setting can be done by the NGO itself, whereby it would enact all three accountability functions. Alternatively, the NGO can rely on other actors who identify the rights of detainees as a standard applicable for peacekeeping operations, whereby accountability would be exercised in conjunction with another standard setter.

This plurality of actors is a core characteristic of pluralist accountability. I developed the indicators for the individual dimensions according to the family structure concept formation to account for differences across organizations and implementing actions (Goertz 2006, 63). This means that even one indicator can signal the presence of the respective dimension, even if the others are not present. While this provides a more nuanced picture of more or less successful attempts of pluralist accountability, it is important to note that the evaluation of the strength or quality of pluralist accountability is not the main objective of this book. I only use the distinction between strong and weak accountability to evaluate the existing accountability framework at the outset of the delegation in order to control for potential effects of path dependency; otherwise, it is not relevant for my subsequent analysis of the evolution of pluralist accountability. Conceptualizations of accountability based on accountability components such as Scholte's will thus provide better frameworks to capture the variation in the degree of accountability (Scholte, 2011a: 17). While assessing the quality of accountability in terms of its effectiveness remains outside the scope of this study, I focus on the question of when pluralist accountability emerges, conceptualized as the exercise of three core accountability functions by external third parties.

By operating with a concept of accountability that does not rely on democratic (i.e., electoral or participatory) components, this research project cannot (and does not intend to) derive significant implications for the prospects of democracy at the global level. Other researchers argue that the conceptual and empirical differences between the domestic and the transnational level are quite low (Koenig-Archibugi 2010). Instead of entering the debate of whether and how democratic accountability can be achieved beyond the domestic context, my research takes a closer look at the conditions and causes for accountability at the transnational level. Conceptualizing accountability through a democratic lens would unnecessarily blur the analytical clarity that the concept originally provides for the purpose of this study.

At the same time, I take into consideration the norms under which the implementing actors are held accountable in my empirical analysis. In contrast to principal-agent and delegation research, which care mostly about whether the agent is actually doing what it is supposed to do according to its mandate, this analysis focuses on accountability with regard to core human rights principles. This focus is in line with recent research that emphasizes norms, such as the respect for human rights, instead of actors as the baseline for a conceptualization of accountability. I thus agree with Goodhart (2011), who argues that the questions of to what principles actors are held accountable ("accountability for what") matters for more legitimate—and in his understanding also more democratic—global governance. This conceptualization allows more variation about how IOs and their implementing partners are held accountable to human rights standards, which can in some instances conflict with other standards. With this understanding, I present my theoretical framework and analyze the conditions for pluralist accountability in the following section.

Conditions for Pluralist Accountability: Competition and Vulnerability

Despite frequent calls for greater accountability, the theoretical expectations about the implications of accountability as a strategy to regain legitimacy remain unclear and ambiguous. There are at least two concurring views about which type of accountability is enhanced in response to legitimacy problems and how accountability can contribute to greater legitimacy. These can be found in principal-agent and legalization theories. Principal-agent theories consider human rights violations committed by the implementing actor as "agency slack" through which parts of the agent's actions betray the principal's interests (Hawkins et al. 2006a, 24). Human rights violations, in this case, are unintended consequences of the implementation process. If the behavior of the implementing actor impugns the legitimacy of the mandating authority, principal-agent theories expect principals to demonstrate greater commitment to the implementation of their decisions by enhancing vertical accountability. The principal, consequently, needs to demonstrate that the agent's behavior violated the original standards outlined in the mandate. Reinforced monitoring such as "police patrols" allows the principal to clearly implicate the implementing actor for not complying with the principal's standards (Dai 2002, 242). Vertical accountability can thus also be a blame-shifting strategy by which the principal distances itself from the implementing agent (Hood 2002). If the behavior of an implementing actor fundamentally contradicts the mandate and threatens to thwart the overall objective, vertical accountability can help depict the implementing actor as "the bad" and the delegating authority as "the good," at least with regard to their intentions. By demonstrating full control over potential agency slack by vertical standard setting, monitoring, and sanctioning, an IO can thus regain legitimacy among member states as well as within its respective constituencies.

Legalization theories, however, have a different view on how to regain legitimacy (e.g., Finnemore and Toope 2001). The implicit assumption is that the greater the degree of legalization (conceptualized as precision, obligation, and delegation), the greater the legitimacy (Abbott et al. 2000; Bernstein 2004, 11). This is rooted in the Weberian notion that legalization increases compliance, which generally leads to a higher legitimacy of the rules. Although legalization theories do not deal explicitly with the concept of accountability, from this assumption I deduce that if accountability increases compliance, it also enhances the legitimacy of the mandating authority. Moreover, regarding the study of pluralist accountability, the delegation component of the legalization concept is of particular interest. The delegation of dispute-settlement functions to independent international institutions arguably promotes compliance because noncompliance would potentially lead to a greater loss of reputation and credibility domestically and internationally.[14] Compliance is enhanced by not only judicial mechanisms but also external nonlegal institutions (Raustiala 2004). Thus, monitoring and sanctioning by external judicial and political institutions, as it is done in pluralist accountability, is valuable because it is expected to increase compliance.

Legalization theories also regard the delegation of disputes to adjudication bodies as being more legitimate because of the third parties' independence and objectivity. "Different actors have access to the process, and they are constrained to make arguments different from those they would make in a nonlegal context. Legal decisions, too, must be based on reasons applicable to all similarly situated litigants" (Abbott et al. 2000, 419). The delegation of claims assessment and jurisdiction to independent third parties, such as dispute-settlement bodies, is to guarantee a more independent jurisprudence, which

[14] See the arguments presented by Simmons 2002; Zangl et al. 2011. For the "compliance benefit" of delegation see Guzman 2005, 600.

Keohane et al. (2000, 458) say is "more autonomous of national interests."[15] In the optimal form, the judicalization of disputes increases the rule of law (and therefore also its legitimacy), because similar violations face similar sanctions before an independent body (Zangl 2006, 42). Legalization theories would thus expect accountability types that involve third parties as accountability holders to enhance legitimacy, such as in pluralist accountability. While legalization research does not provide concrete implications for the question of which conditions we can expect in the evolution of pluralist accountability, I use these insights to evaluate the effect of pluralist accountability on IO legitimacy in the concluding chapter.

These theoretical views thus do not offer an unambiguous causal link for the relationship between legitimacy and the accountability type. The empirics also provide a diverging picture. There are cases in which the endangered legitimacy of peacekeeping led to enhanced vertical accountability (Heupel et al. 2018), and there are others in which it led to pluralist accountability (Hirschmann 2019). This empirical variety of accountability regimes suggests that we need to know more about the scope conditions for pluralist accountability before we evaluate the relationship between IO legitimacy and accountability. Thus, in the following paragraphs, I outline the theoretical framework of this book that explores the conditions and the underlying causal mechanisms that lead to the exercise of accountability by third parties in response to human rights violations.

The theoretical argument of this study builds upon a dynamic theoretical understanding of IOs that regards IOs as social institutions interacting independently with a wide array of national and transnational actors (Simmons and Martin 2002). Conceiving IOs as actors and not only as agents of their member states is a necessary theoretical assumption for the study of accountability. Only when granting IOs the status of an actor can we logically assume that they care about their agents' behavior (Heldt 2017). Moreover, it is essential for this study to open the "black box" of IOs and distinguish their internal components, such as the authorizing member state body, the bureaucratic structure, and the implementing sub-components. With this diversified understanding, I can identify the different accountability holders and targets of accountability.

In order to find out when third parties act as independent accountability holders, we need to look at both the "supply side" and the "demand side," as

[15] However, critics warn that the delegation of accountability is a hegemonic move by states to support special interests (e.g., Koskenniemi 2004, 205).

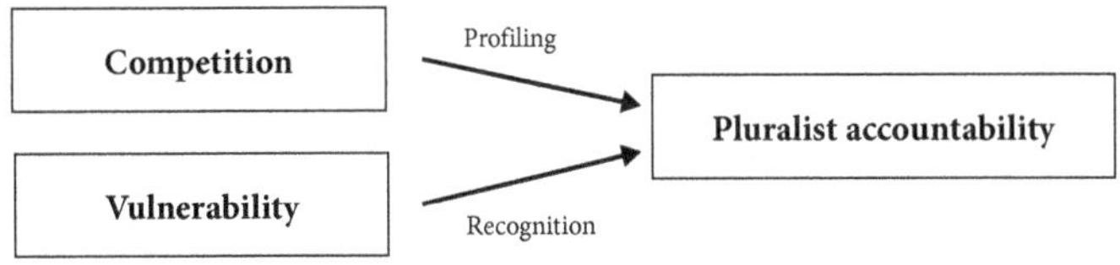

Figure 2.4 Two conditions contribute to the emergence of pluralist accountability. Competition stimulates third parties to act as accountability holders through the mechanism of profiling; vulnerability stimulates the implementing actor to accept third parties as accountability holders through the mechanism of recognition.

research on the participation of civil society organizations in global governance institutions suggests (Steffek 2013). What are the "push factors" that motivate external actors—not only civil society organizations but also courts or regional intergovernmental organizations—to exercise accountability functions? What are the "pull factors" that make them act as accountability holders? I argue that the combination of a specific opportunity structure characterized by a competitive environment and certain characteristics of the implementing actor, in particular its vulnerability within a specific community, are all conditions to the evolution of pluralist accountability (see Figure 2.4).

One important push factor can be described as the "independent global civil society effects" of human rights regimes (Hafner-Burton and Tsutsui 2005; Martens 2011). External third parties, such as civil society, courts, or intergovernmental organizations, consider themselves as accountability holders of "last resort" to compensate for nonexistent or ineffective vertical accountability.[16] This effect is especially strong if there are multiple principals who shift the blame and the responsibility for the exercise of vertical accountability to each other or in delegation relationships that involve collective principals with institutional overlap, that is, in which some parts of the principal also function as implementing agents. However, there is no automaticity in which pluralist accountability is exercised every time classical accountability mechanisms are absent or ineffective. Instead, existing research on norm entrepreneurship or

[16] Tarrow quoted an American lawyer's perspective on the role of accountability holders in times of a lack of government accountability, saying that "the rule of law is not coming back on its own. It will come back only when you go out and grab hold of it by the ears and drag it back. In the ballot box and the courtroom and the newspaper and the public street" (Tarrow 2013, 56). According to Tarrow's argument, only the contention of human rights by legal and societal advocacy coalition can effectively protect human rights in times of war (Tarrow 2013, 38). This points to the competitive dynamics that are implicit in the social movement literature.

regime fragmentation suggests that competition, which characterizes the institutional context of third parties, is a further condition for their participation in pluralist accountability (Brosig 2011; Gehring and Faude 2014). This competition among third parties can take place between not only NGOs but also NGOs and intergovernmental organizations (Cooley and Ron 2002), or between courts. In all cases these third parties consider themselves as guardians of human rights (Schimmelfennig 2006). Competition is especially strong (but does not necessarily have to occur solely) between third parties concurring about the reputation as guardians of human rights. A third party thus develops a "niche capacity" and a distinct profile by exercising core accountability functions, which allows it to distinguish itself from other concurring parties in the same field. The causal mechanism of "profiling" that links competition to pluralist accountability, therefore, can comprise both a rational cost-benefit analysis of how the exercise of accountability could possibly lead to greater material resources as well as normative considerations that aim to promote human rights in new areas.

Thus, when effective vertical accountability does not exist, pluralist accountability is enacted if there is an institutional competition that motivates third parties to act as accountability holders (*context-related hypothesis: third party competition*). This hypothesis is falsifiable if pluralist accountability systematically appears complementary to principal-led accountability or is exercised by third parties who do not face any competition. If there are one or two cases with instances of overlapping accountability modes, however, I will consider them as crucial cases for refining the hypothesis, for example with regard to possible reverse effects. We can, for instance, assume that pluralist accountability puts the principal under normative pressure to increase vertical accountability.

Given that this is a context-related hypothesis, I propose the following observable implications that need to be identified in the environment of third parties. A competitive environment exists if the institutional context is populated by actors who all consider themselves as norm entrepreneurs in the transnational system and compete with others in the same area for resources and reputation. This pushes third parties to act as accountability holders. Another indicator for competition is a third party's perception of another actor as having equal standing, or if a new actor enters the issue area and has to develop its reputation. I identify these indicators by examining the mandates of the potential accountability holders and other material revealing their discourse directed towards perceived competitors or towards those providing them with resources.

Besides the institutional context, however, I argue that it is also important to take into consideration how the implementing agent and its characteristics can affect the accountability type. The theoretical framework thus also includes the "demand side" for pluralist accountability. The research on accountability emphasizes that a precondition for accountability is that the accountability holder and the accountor mutually recognize each other (Grant and Keohane 2005, 29). This mutual recognition is different from the concept of compliance. Compliance means that an actor follows the rules imposed by another actor. Recognizing an actor as an accountability holder, however, implies that the accountor regards the standards set by this actor as legitimate, that it allows monitoring activities to accompany the implementation process and that the accountor subjects itself to the other's sanctioning authority. Some actors that engage in accountability relationships might be without standard-setting authority in the formal or legal sense, however, through the accountor's recognition they become accountability holders whose standards become the point of reference for the implementation of a specific task. This process of recognition should not be taken for granted, since the implementing actors might not be interested in entering an accountability relationship in the first place. If we follow this line of reasoning it is only logical to assume that the characteristics of the implementing agent have an influence on the accountability type. The crucial question therefore is: when do actors recognize third parties as relevant accountability holders and allow them to undertake standard-setting, monitoring, and sanctioning activities?

As the research on accountability has not yet examined the subject of recognition, I recur to a recent argument in the literature on compliance. Even if the underlying logic of action might be different, the conditions for compliance might also be applicable for understanding when actors are more likely to recognize accountability holders. According to the authors of the "spiral model," material and social vulnerability are two important scope conditions for actors to comply with human rights norms (Risse and Ropp 2013, 20). A less powerful actor can be materially vulnerable if its resources depend on respecting certain norms within a specific community. In addition, even powerful states like the US, though materially less vulnerable than others, can be sensitive to domestic and international pressures. Being socially vulnerable implies that the reputation and the social status of an actor within a specific community depend on its respect for certain norms. In contrast, an actor reduces its social vulnerability by referring to a powerful counter-norm to justify its behavior (Risse and Ropp 2013, 21). Previous research uses this argument to explain how the US government engaged in the strategy of "discursive legitimation" in order to undermine the prescriptive status of the antitorture norms regarding detainees during the Bush era after 2001 (Hurd 2013, 180; Ohlin 2010; Sikkink 2013). In this case, the US was able to appeal to a powerful counter-norm, namely the fight against terrorism, to justify torturing detainees in the denial phase of the spiral model (Sikkink 2013, 146). With a "stream of rule-following justifications around apparently rule-breaking behavior," the government was able to legitimate torture and thus render itself invulnerable to human rights demands, at least to some degree (Hurd 2013, 180).

Building upon this, I argue that the willingness of an actor to recognize third parties as accountability holders depends on its degree of vulnerability. Implementing actors are able to reduce their social vulnerability if they can justify their actions by a different normative frame, as the US did with its "war on terror" or NATO does when the UN asks it to implement "security-related aspects." This requires a competing, widely accepted normative frame that allows the implementing actor to play conflicting principles, inherent to accountability relationships, against each other (Schedler 1999, 22). On the other hand, implementing actors are much more likely to recognize other community members as their accountability holders if they conceive their actions as being part of the tasks of a community that has enshrined certain norms as part of its identity and its portfolio. Thus, in order for pluralist accountability to emerge, the accountor and the accountability holder need to agree on the substance of accountability, that is, the question of *for what* the implementing actor should be held accountable. Hence, as a second hypothesis, I assume that the implementing actor is more inclined to accept external accountability holders if it is highly vulnerable in terms of its social status and human rights reputation within a specific normative community (*accountor-related hypothesis: vulnerability*).

The underlying causal mechanism for this condition is the mechanism of recognition by which third parties are accepted as accountability holders due to the implementing actor's sensitivity to domestic or international pressure. On the basis of this logic, I expect the degree of vulnerability of the principal in the delegation relationship to affect the emergence of pluralist accountability in a similar way. If the principal, in particular the immediate principal, is vulnerable to human rights demands, it is more inclined to recognize third parties as external accountability holders for the implementing agents. This recognition can in turn influence the implementing actor's inclination to recognize external accountability holders.

A common strategy in peacekeeping to decrease vulnerability is to invoke a dilemma between security and human rights. In this context, human rights are often conceptualized as private or individual interests that might be in opposition to the general public's interest in security and stability as promoted by the peace operation. Often, the argument points to exceptional circumstances under which peacekeeping takes place: "It is clear that there are fundamental [human rights] standards that are irreducible but in many cases there must be a recognition that the circumstances of most of these deployments equates to a state of emergency that would permit certain derogations under the various human rights conventions" (Kelly 2005, 119). Such dilemmas are not exclusive to peacekeeping but exist also in other issue areas, such as with regard to individual versus group rights, and economic development versus human rights. The main observable implications for this dilemma construction are indicators that reflect arguments of operational necessity, which limit the power of human rights within peacekeeping (e.g., references to Chapter VII of the UN Charter), or arguments referring to a greater public good being served through the implementation of the specific action (Häußler 2010, 261; McGoey 2017; Moran 2011; Pacquée and Dewulf 2006; Wouters and Schmitt 2010, 106).

Both conditions have independent effects as they contribute differently to the evolution of pluralist accountability. The competition among third parties influences the motivation of third parties to act as accountability holders. The vulnerability of the implementing actors instead contributes to the recognition of pluralist accountability by both the implementing actors and the mandating authority. Given that each of the two conditions explains only certain aspects, I argue further that the combination of both conditions is necessary for explaining the evolution of pluralist accountability. If there is strong competition among third parties but the implementing actors are less vulnerable to human rights demands, we might see attempts of pluralist accountability, in which a few accountability functions are exercised by third parties but remain without recognition. With low competition but strong vulnerability we might also see some attempts of pluralist accountability without placing much effort and resources, however, into the exercise of accountability functions. Thus, if only one of the conditions is present, attempts of pluralist accountability will remain limited and will not amount to complete pluralist accountability as with the cases in which both conditions are present. My argument in this study therefore contains a combined theoretical approach, similar to the argument that Steffek (2013) puts forward on the participation of civil society actors in international institutions. Given that pluralist accountability is a complex phenomenon, its theoretical explanation needs to consider both the "demand side" in terms of the institutional opportunity structure and the "supply side" in terms of specific actor characteristics.

Two potentially relevant alternative explanations, from other important research strands, need to be taken into consideration when examining the conditions for pluralist accountability. First, why doesn't path dependence explain the turn to pluralist accountability (Pierson 2000; Rixen and Viola 2015)? To control for possible path-dependent effects, I focus on cases with different accountability regimes in which the same institution acts as the principal in the delegation relationship. Path dependence would imply that the principal's past decisions, for example when mandating an actor to implement a task, influence the nature of the accountability regime. As this is a very valuable argument, I evaluate each case through process-tracing whether the prior accountability regime, at the outset of the delegation contract, has had an effect on the nature of the enacted accountability after human rights violations have become apparent (Bennett and Elman 2006).

Second, researchers have identified the rise of a general norm in terms of more democratic and, therefore, more participatory global governance (Steffek and Nanz 2008). On the basis of this assessment, we should also expect a possible trend toward pluralist accountability mechanisms (Tallberg and Uhlin 2011). In line with advocates of the world society theory, one could argue that the respect of TNAs as accountability holders is a consequence of the emergence of a "transnational political space," in which IO legitimacy depends on not only stakeholders' consent but also the approval by transnational societal actors (Albert et al. 2009; Buzan 2004). A political community of actors that share a common concern about compliance with human rights is expected to shape the environment for the implementation of the IO's policy. Other researchers, however, have also identified a normative trend toward the respect for the rule of law by IOs, which might explain a reinforcement of vertical accountability mechanisms (Chesterman 2008; Heupel and Zürn 2017; Kingsbury et al. 2005). Thus, due to these two trends, we are not able to draw unambiguous conclusions about the type of accountability enacted in response to human rights violations in complex delegation relationships. The empirical variance between cases with vertical and pluralist accountability seems to reflect these various normative demands. For this reason, I propose a systematic comparison of cases across different policy fields to find out more about the underlying conditions for the individual accountability types.

Research Design

Case Selection

Since there is no available systematic data on accountability in global governance, I designed this study as a qualitative comparative case study in order to first identify cases of both active pluralist accountability and failed pluralist accountability, and second, to analyze in depth the underlying causal processes conducive to the evolution of pluralist accountability. The case studies cover several empirical areas, ranging from peace operations, to economic adjustment policies, to global health policies. The problem of accountability is most clearly illustrated by UN peace operations, in which human rights violations—such as the sexual abuse and exploitation of civilians and the violation of the rights of detainees—by UN staff, associated personnel, and partner organizations have become a serious threat to the organization's legitimacy. I conduct a comparative analysis of UN-mandated operations in Afghanistan, Bosnia, and Kosovo to demonstrate how a competitive environment and the vulnerability of the implementing actors to human rights influence the emergence of pluralist accountability. In order to probe whether my theoretical framework is applicable to other issue areas, I include two case studies on the emergence of pluralist accountability in other governance contexts, focusing on the EU Troika's austerity policy and public–private health partnerships' immunization campaigns. By adding these probing case studies, this book provides a comprehensive account of the conditions for pluralist accountability that can be generalized across different areas of complex global governance.

I based my selection of cases for the analysis on three steps. First, I identified cases of complex governance arrangements in which implementing actors were accused of alleged human rights violations. All cases are cases of complex governance par excellence; they involve several delegation steps or modes of informal governance. Second, the selection ensures systematic variation with regard to the dependent variable, that is, the evolution of pluralist accountability. With this setup, the case selection on the one hand covers instances in which pluralist accountability is most likely, but on the other hand shows that pluralist accountability is no automatism in complex global governance but depends on specific conditions. Third, the selection criteria control for variation in terms of types of human rights violations and path dependence with regard to institutional characteristics of the mandating authority.

To select the peacekeeping operations, I first identified all UN peace operations mandated after 1992 with a duration of more than one year that were accused of human rights violations.[17] Between 1992 and 2011, the UN Security Council authorized forty-eight peace operations under Chapter VII with a duration of more than a year. While the majority of peacekeeping operations throughout the 1990s involved the same implementing agents as in the years before the end of the Cold War, a new variety of implementing agents entered the scene at the end of the 1990s (Coleman 2007; Yamashita 2012). The tasks and components of a peacekeeping mission have become increasingly complex and include a wide range of civilian and military aspects. The new type of integrated missions in 2006 introduced the position of the SRSG to all peacekeeping missions, with the objective of coordinating the various military, civilian, and humanitarian agents, including developmental aspects (Lipson 2008; United Nations Department for Peacekeeping Operations 2009). Moreover, core parts of the peacekeeping mandate (de-mining, disarmament, security, policing, border control, etc.) are further outsourced to different sub-agencies, other IOs, or nonstate actors. This outsourcing has become an increasing trend in the UN bureaucracy (Pingeot 2012) but even more so with regard to the implementing TCC.

With the authorization of NATO operations in Bosnia (1996; SFOR), Kosovo (1999; KFOR), and Afghanistan (2001; ISAF), a first wave of Chapter VIII delegations to regional organizations commenced. Further operations were delegated to the African Union to implement operations in Sudan (2004; AMIS and 2007; UNAMID) and Somalia (2007; AMISOM), as well as to the EU (2009; EUFOR) in Kosovo.[18] The literature acknowledges this increasing cooperation between the UN Security Council and regional organizations under the terms of delegation, subsidiarity, and burden sharing (Abass 2004; Berman 1998; Brosig 2010; O'Brien 2000; Sarooshi 1999). Some of the operations analyzed by these studies, however, were not mandated originally by the UN Security Council. The operation in Liberia, for example, was authorized by the Economic Community of West African States, and had already been on the ground before it was approved by the UN Security Council (Abass 2004). Similarly, the operation by the Cooperation of Independent States in Georgia, although later approved by the UN Security Council, derived its mandate from an agreement by the Cooperation's heads of state (Korkelika 1999). These types of operations are usually legally justified ex-post through reference to Chapter VIII, but they do not constitute acts of prolonged

[17] In 1992, the UN Secretary-General Boutros-Ghali introduced landmark changes to the UN's peacekeeping policy with the new "Agenda for Peace," which had a significant impact on the character and mandates of all subsequent operations (Boutros-Ghali 1992).

[18] Note that UNAMID was a hybrid mission, in which the African Union operated alongside the UN.

delegation as conceptualized in this study, since they were not originally mandated by the UN Security Council.

In addition to the operations that the UN Security Council delegated to regional organizations, I include in this study UN-mandated transitional administrations, namely the one in Cambodia (1992–3), Eastern Slavonia (1996–8), Kosovo (since 1999[19]), and East Timor (1999–2002). For these operations, the Secretary-General appointed Special Representatives who acted as heads of the administrations. To control for general organizational characteristics and mandate types, I excluded all operations that had not been authorized by the UN Security Council, such as interventions in Iraq or Kosovo, as well as all non-Chapter VII missions, such as special political or Chapter VI operations.

When identifying peacekeeping operations that allegedly violated human rights, I focused on two categories of rights: the rights of civilians (e.g., sexual exploitation and abuse and human trafficking); and the rights of detainees (e.g., the right to bodily integrity and due process rights). These two categories pose the greatest challenges to the legitimacy of peace operations. Moreover, these rights are universally accepted and are not legally disputed, in contrast to other "third-generation" rights, such as the right to development for the countries of the Global South. Referring to data from NGO and media reports, I identified twenty-eight operations that allegedly violated these types of human rights (as shown in Table 2.2): twenty-four operations mandated under Chapter VII or Chapter VIII of the UN Charter and four transitional administrations.[20] I relied on reports that were publicly available, which I then examined both manually and with the help of the search function in the database LexisNexis, which includes a systematic evaluation of all available articles published by the *New York Times*, *Guardian*, and *Washington Post*.[21]

As a second step, I evaluated these operations with regard to pluralist accountability, the dependent variable of this study. I thus followed the approach of a backward-looking research design (Scharpf 1997, ch. 2), also named "y-oriented" research (Ganghof 2005) or the "cause-of-effects approach" (Bennett and Elman 2006). Given the unsystematic evidence that

[19] Although UNMIK has not yet been officially terminated, the transition to EUFOR in 2007 marked the end point of the far-ranging involvement as stipulated by UN Security Council Resolution 1244.

[20] This number is a conservative estimate as I included only those operations in which reliable sources revealed clear allegations of human rights violations.

[21] Assuming that these three newspapers display a generally positive attitude towards IOs, I expect reports on their wrongdoings to be scrutinized particularly diligently. I restricted the search through a number of keywords, including a combination of "United Nations" and human rights violations, as well as peacekeeping and sexual exploitation and abuse.

Table 2.2 List of UN-mandated operations since 1992 alleged of human rights violations

	Name of the operation	Duration
UNPROFOR	United Nations Protection Force	Feb 1992–Mar 1995
UNTAC	United Nations Transitional Authority in Cambodia	Mar 1992–Sept 1993
UNOSOM I	United Nations Operation in Somalia I	April 1992–Mar 1993
ONUMOZ	United Nations Operation in Mozambique	Dec 1992–Dec 1994
UNOMIL	United Nations Observer Mission in Liberia	Sept 1993–Sept 1997
UNAVEM III	United Nations Angola Verification Mission III	Feb 1995–June 1997
UNMIBH	United Nations Mission in Bosnia and Herzegovina	Dec 1995–Dec 2002
UNOMSIL	United Nations Observer Mission in Sierra Leone	July 1998–Oct 1999
UNMIK	United Nations Interim Administration Mission in Kosovo	June 1999–present
UNAMSIL	United Nations Mission in Sierra Leone	Oct 1999–Dec 2005
UNTAET	United Nations Transitional Administration in East Timor	Oct 1999–May 2002
MONUC	United Nations Organization Mission in the Democratic Republic of the Congo	Nov 1999–June 2002
UNMEE	United Nations Mission in Ethiopia and Eritrea	July 2000–July 2008
UNMISET	United Nations Mission of Support in East Timor	May 2002–May 2005
UNMIL	United Nations Mission in Liberia	Sept 2003–present
UNOCI	United Nations Operation in Côte d'Ivoire	April 2004–present
MINUSTAH	United Nations Stabilization Mission in Haiti	June 2004–present
ONUB	United Nations Operation in Burundi	June 2004–Dec 2006
UNMIS	United Nations Mission in the Sudan	Mar 2005–July 2011
UNMIT	United Nations Integrated Mission in Timor-Leste	Aug 2006–present
UNAMID	African Union-United Nations Hybrid Operation in Darfur	July 2007–present
MINURCAT	United Nations Mission in the Central African Republic and Chad	Sept 2007–Dec 2010
MONUSCO	United Nations Organization Stabilization Mission in the Democratic Republic of the Congo	July 2010–present
Missions delegated to regional IOs		
KFOR	SC 1244 NATO mission in Kosovo	June 1999–present
ISAF	SCR 1386 NATO mission in Afghanistan	Dec 2001–present
SFOR	SCR 1088 NATO mission in Bosnia and Herzegovina	1996–2004
AMIS	SCR 1564 African Union mission in Sudan	2004–7
AMISOM	SCR 1725 African Union mission in Somalia	2007–present

Table 2.3 Selected cases (peacekeeping)

	Pluralist accountability	No pluralist accountability
Afghanistan	Afghan National Directorate of Security detentions	Operation Enduring Freedom detentions
Bosnia	Human trafficking	SFOR detentions
Kosovo	UNMIK detentions	KFOR detentions

is available about accountability in peace operations, I relied on a collection of preliminary evidence about the accountability type for the case selection. In line with the y-oriented research question, I selected three pairs of cases that cover the operations in Afghanistan, Bosnia, and Kosovo. These cases cover both early and recent operations mandated after the Cold War across Central Asia and Europe. The implementing actors include all types of different actors, namely regional organizations, state actors, or nonstate actors. Moreover, the case selection allows me to control for potential country-specific context factors in terms of a most similar case design, as each pair differs with regard to the two conditions that are expected to influence the outcome variable (Seawright and Gerring 2008). Each analysis of peacekeeping contrasts a "positive" case (i.e., a case with active pluralist accountability) with a "negative" case (in which there was no pluralist accountability). Table 2.3 depicts the selected cases. The case studies on Afghanistan consist of a diachronic comparison whereas the cases in Bosnia and Kosovo contain a synchronic comparison.

In addition to these six peacekeeping cases, I expand the analysis to two further case studies in other issue areas of global governance, namely in the fields of global economic and global health governance. I selected two cases that show similar features of governance complexity in order to probe whether the conditions for pluralist accountability also hold in other issue areas and when different types of human rights are affected. First, in global economic governance, one of the most complex governance arrangements with significant impact on human rights were the reactions to the financial and economic crisis of 2008: the austerity measures that were promoted by the so-called Troika, composed of the European Commission, the European Central Bank, and the IMF. These policies were implemented in several European countries, but I focus on Greece and Portugal. Similar to the structural adjustment programs included in the lending portfolios of the World Bank and the IMF in the 1970s (Heupel 2017), the Troika's austerity measures were strongly criticized because of their negative impact on human rights, in particular fundamental social and economic rights as provided by the International

Covenant on Economic, Social and Cultural Rights. These included the right to work, the right to health, the right to education, and the right to adequate living standards (Kilpatrick and De Witte 2014; Nolan and Dutschke 2010). Following these allegations, several national and international actors enacted a pluralist accountability framework, making the Troika's austerity measures an ideal case to probe the applicability of the theoretical framework on the conditions for pluralist accountability.

I chose the second case from the context of global health governance, a policy field that features extremely complex governance arrangements with a high number of private actors involved in its implementation (Andonova 2017, ch. 5; Holzscheiter 2014; Holzscheiter et al. 2016). After the adoption of the Millennium Development Goals in 2000, global public–private health partnerships have become the most important governance arrangements through which policies are implemented (Clarke 2014; Rushton and Williams 2011). Most of the existing research highlights the difficulties of holding these partnerships accountable given the complexity of the governance arrangements (Bruen et al. 2014, 3). However, the scholarly debate on the accountability of partnerships rarely focuses on human rights aspects but mainly centers on how partnerships are held accountable by their members (Steets 2010). Concerns for human rights have in particular become public in the context of vaccinations and vaccine development, in which implementing actors were accused of violating the right to informed consent (Terwindt 2014). Despite several attempts, however, no significant pluralist accountability framework has evolved. I investigate why this has been the case by focusing on the conditions that are expected to foster pluralist accountability. As an insightful addition to the case studies on more successful developments of pluralist accountability, this case on global health governance reveals the limitations of accountability in current complex global governance areas.

Through this comparative research strategy, the analysis aims at demonstrating the general applicability of the argument by covering various types of complex governance arrangements with a variety of implementing actors, such as regional organizations, state and nonstate actors, as well as different types of human rights violations. The allegations cover rights violations that can be directly attributed to an individual's (criminal) behavior (e.g., human trafficking) or an organization's actions (e.g., violation of due process rights in detentions), as well as rights violations that occur indirectly from the implementation of an organization's policies (e.g., austerity measures; vaccination). While the difference in types of human rights in terms of their attributability might matter for legal accountability, previous research shows that these human rights violations are comparable with regard to how they affect an

IO's legitimacy (Heupel and Zürn 2017). By allowing for a variation in the type of human rights that does not coincide with the evolution of pluralist accountability, I therefore control for the potential effects that the type of human rights might have on accountability.

I examine each case systematically with regard to how the two conditions—competition and vulnerability—influence the evolution of pluralist accountability and how their absence can explain the lack of pluralist accountability. In order to control for the potential influence of path dependence, each case study contains an analysis of the accountability regime at the outset of the operation. In all cases, I apply the method of process tracing to assess the dynamics of accountability and its underlying conditions (Checkel 2005; Mahoney 2012; Mayntz 2004). This method is particularly suitable for the development of middle-range theories (George and Bennett 2005). Process tracing is also essential to cope with complex causality and to control for the effects or interactions of alternative mechanisms that I may have overlooked when designing the theoretical framework (George and Bennett 2005, 207). Starting with the dependent variable, my analysis looks backward to identify the fine-grained causal processes that lead to the observed outcome. In the analysis of the "positive cases" in particular, I examine the causal chain that links the development of pluralist accountability back to the competition among third parties and the vulnerability of the implementing actors.

Methods of Data Acquisition

My empirical analysis relies on a variety of sources. I acquired the relevant data for evaluating the causal processes from primary documents of the different IO bodies, such as the UN Security Council, the UN Secretariat, and individual peace operations, as well as the EU, the IMF, and the WHO. This includes official resolutions, meeting protocols, draft resolutions, reports, commissioned studies, and internal documents. Additionally, the material for the analysis includes data provided by both implementing actors and accountability holders, such as public–private health partnerships, the Council of Europe, and regional courts. I also used data from national institutions, such as the archives of the US Congress and the British High Court. Finally, reports by the media and NGOs on the individual operations, the human rights violations, and the reactions after these violations have been made public are important additional documentary sources for my analysis. I paid particular attention to documents provided by field operations, which have the closest access to local developments on the ground. I also used secondary sources, which mostly include materials by experts of IOs, former or present members of IOs and courts, former members of NGOs, or international legal scholars.

To complement this documentary analysis, I conducted thirty-seven qualitative expert interviews either in person or via Skype with present and former IO staff as well as member states' representatives and members from other organizations, such as regional IOs (e.g., the Council of Europe), public–private partnerships (the Global Alliance for Vaccines and Immunizations), research institutes and NGOs, and private actors (e.g., the ICRC; Gates Foundation).[22] I based my selection of interviewees on the "snowball system": I selected some interviewees in advance on the basis of primary and secondary sources, and I selected others throughout the interview phase.

Although the interview questions were similar for all thirty-seven interviewees, I adapted each questionnaire so that it was relevant to the individual interviewee (Kvale and Brinkmann 2009). For example, I asked some background questions to clarify the role of the individual in the respective case. Thereafter, I asked the interviewee to give an account of the "story" of the case in his/her own terms. On the basis of this account, I then asked probing questions to reveal more insights in the accountability process, and I asked more targeted questions regarding specific dimensions of the dependent variable or the two conditions. These nonstandardized interviews were based on the expertise of the respective interview partners and were used as additional sources of information for the analysis when primary documents could not provide sufficient information. In some cases, the interviewees provided primary documents on certain aspects, for example, documents that revealed accountability dynamics that I had not been aware of. Depending on the interviewee's expertise, I also asked transfer questions with regard to other cases of the study. Most interviews were confidential, whereas a few interviewees agreed to be quoted directly. Therefore, I refer to the sources of information only when possible; otherwise I give a general description of the source (e.g., the interviewee's institutional affiliation) if the interviewee wished to remain anonymous. Moreover, as much as possible I tried to corroborate any information revealed by the interviews with written confirmation from other sources.

[22] Among the interviewees were individuals who were important drivers for initiating accountability, such as the former commissioner for human rights of the Council of Europe, Niels Muižnieks, the former special rapporteur of the European Parliament, Alejandro Cercas Alonso, the former ombudsman of the UN in Kosovo, Marek Nowicki, the former SRSG in Afghanistan, Kai Eide and Tom Koenigs, the former representative of the Office of the UN High Commissioner for Human Rights in Bosnia, Madeleine Rees, a former law clerk of the Portuguese Constitutional Court, and staff members of the Global Alliance for Vaccines and Immunizations.

3

"We cannot rule out that torture is going on"

Accountability Regarding the Rights of Detainees in Afghanistan

Introduction

The operation in Afghanistan has become an important litmus test for the international community in its quest to promote peace, stability, and democracy in this particular region.[1] Mandated by the UN Security Council after the attacks of 9/11, ISAF was motivated by the fight against Al-Qaeda and the Taliban regime and to foster the respect for the human rights of the Afghan people. In reality, these proved to be good intentions with contrary effects. Not only did the operations fail to bring a lasting peace to the country, international forces were also strongly criticized for violating human rights themselves. Two main concerns have become prominent over the last years: the first was raised in relation to the increased number of civilian casualties that the implementing partners could no longer justify by referring to their mandate (Amnesty International 2006b, 2007a; Eide 2012). The second relates to the treatment of detainees. Detaining Al-Qaeda and Taliban suspects was an important component of the military operations in Afghanistan, which gave rise to significant human rights concerns.[2] ISAF was strongly criticized for capturing and transferring detainees without ensuring that the detainees' rights were not violated by the respective detaining authorities. In this chapter, I analyze the accountability regimes that evolved in response to the violation of the rights of detainees.

[1] The quotation in the chapter title is from Liv Monica Stubholt, Norwegian Ministry of Foreign Affairs, interviewed by the Norwegian News Agency NTB, July 27, 2007, quoted in Amnesty International 2007b: 20.

[2] See New York Times 2005: In US Report, Brutal Details of 2 Afghan Inmates' Deaths, article by Tim Golden, May 20, available at: http://www.nytimes.com/2005/05/20/international/asia/20abuse.html?pagewanted=all&_r=0 (last access August 8, 2014).

Accountability in Global Governance. Gisela Hirschmann, Oxford University Press (2020). © Gisela Hirschmann.
DOI: 10.1093/oso/9780198861249.001.0001

Initially, ISAF was mandated to "assist the Afghan Interim Authority in the maintenance of security in Kabul and in surrounding areas" (United Nations Security Council 2001a).[3] Soon it became clear, however, that the international community's presence in the country would require a more long-term engagement. Eventually, NATO took over leadership of ISAF in August 2003 and gradually expanded the mission in accordance with UN Security Council Resolution 1510. By 2006, ISAF was present throughout the whole country and took over some activities of the US-led OEF, which was operating in parallel but without a UN mandate.

ISAF's mandate required it to establish a secure and stable environment by using "all necessary means" under Chapter VII of the UN Charter (United Nations Security Council 2001a). In interpreting this mandate, ISAF not only conducted joint military operations with the Afghan National Security Forces but also captured numerous individuals who were suspected of threatening this stability. ISAF however had neither the capacities nor the mandate to detain these individuals for a longer term. Therefore, ISAF member states cooperated with the US-led OEF coalition forces. Between 2002 and 2005, ISAF handed over detainees to the OEF detention facilities at the Bagram airport base, which was under US command, where investigations and interrogations took place. When operations expanded significantly, ISAF member states arranged agreements with the Afghan government to also transfer detainees within ninety-six hours to facilities run by the Afghan intelligence service, the National Directorate of Security (NDS), and the Afghan National Police (ANP) (NATO 2006a). ISAF thus delegated the acquisition of security-related information from captured suspects to other actors by transferring the detainees to OEF and NDS authorities (see Figure 3.1).

The conditions and treatment of detainees transferred by ISAF to the different detaining authorities soon became cause for concern. From early on, nongovernmental human rights organizations informed the US government and the international public about the mistreatment and torture of detainees in the two main OEF detention facilities, Bagram and Kandahar, which were under US control (Amnesty International 2002, 2004c, 2005). Detainees in OEF facilities such as the Parvan Detention Facility at the Bagram US military base had no access to judicial procedure, which violated the right to due process. Moreover, detainees in Bagram were tortured by their investigators. Two innocent inmates, who had just happened to be at the wrong place at the wrong time, died after they were chained by their wrists to the

[3] See ISAF, available at: http://www.isaf.nato.int/mission.html (last access June 18, 2012).

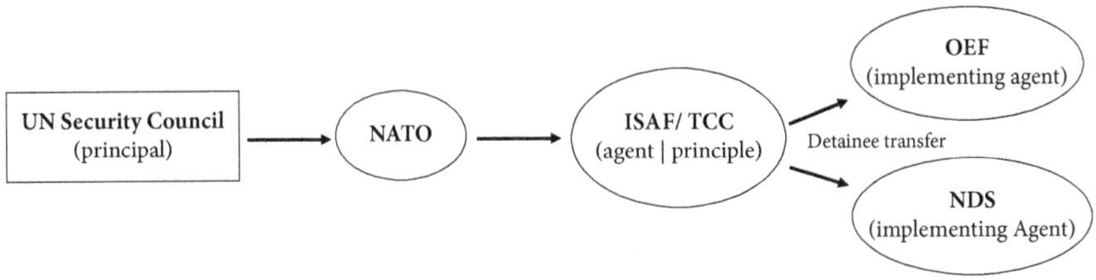

Figure 3.1 ISAF detainee transfers, delegation chain.
Note: The UN Security Council as the ultimate principal mandated ISAF via NATO on the basis of Chapter VIII of the UN Charter. The individual troop-contributing countries of ISAF further delegated the handling of detainees to the OEF or the Afghan NDS. UNSC = UN Security Council, TCC = troop-contributing countries

ceiling of their cells.[4] Although the question of which interrogation techniques could be characterized as torture was debated by the US government for a long time, observers and scholars agree that "at least between 2002 and 2008," detainees were tortured in US detention facilities (Forsythe 2007, 475; Sikkink 2013, 149).

Similar allegations were made in relation to detainees transferred by ISAF member states to the detention centers run by the Afghan NDS and ANP. NDS officials themselves referred to their detention facilities as the "Afghan Guantánamo."[5] "I saw many people who were beaten for five months, six months. They want to put pressure on people and make them say lies. If the beating is one or two days, okay. But six months?"[6] Over the last years, newspapers and human rights organizations reported in great detail how detainees were tortured after being transferred by ISAF member states to Afghan custody:

> They were whipped with electrical cables, usually a bundle of wires about the length of an arm. Some said the whipping was so painful that they fell unconscious. Interrogators also jammed cloth between the teeth of some detainees, who described hearing the sound of a hand-crank generator and feeling the hot flush of electricity coursing through their muscles, seizing them with spasms. Another man said the police hung him by his ankles for eight days of beating. Still another said he panicked as interrogators put a

[4] See New York Times 2005, quoted in fn. 2.

[5] Reporters sans frontiers 2007: Website Editor Freed after Being Held for Nine Hours in Afghan "Guantanamo," August 10, available at: http://archives.rsf.org/article.php3?id_article=22847 (last access August 8, 2014).

[6] A victim quoted in Globe and Mail 2007: Personal Account: A Story of Torture, article by Graeme Smith, April 24.

> plastic bag over his head and squeezed his windpipe. Torturers also used cold as a weapon, according to detainees who complained of being stripped half-naked and forced to stand through winter nights when temperatures in Kandahar drop below freezing.[7]

This treatment of detainees constitutes a violation of fundamental human rights guaranteed to any individual in detention by international human rights law and international humanitarian law, even if the detainees are suspected to have committed serious crimes (Amnesty International 2002, 2). All individuals in detention or in prison enjoy fundamental rights, including the right to access to council and legal assistance, the right to be questioned only in the presence of a lawyer, the right to be presumed innocent until an independent judicial body decides otherwise, the right to apply to an independent court and an impartial trial, the right to be released if the detention was found unlawful, and the right not to be subjected to torture or other cruel, inhuman, or degrading treatment or punishment, among others. These rights were violated after ISAF member states transferred detainees to their operating partners.

How were the two detaining authorities, the OEF and the Afghan National Security forces, held accountable for violating the rights of detainees? In this chapter, I analyze the conditions for pluralist accountability: when do external actors become engaged in standard setting, monitoring, and sanctioning? The analysis reveals that while no significant pluralist accountability evolved in response to the violation of the rights of the detainees who were transferred by ISAF to OEF forces, pluralist accountability did evolve in response to the transfer of detainees from ISAF to the Afghan government. Taking the allegations of rights violations in 2005 as a starting point, I demonstrate how the competition among third parties and the vulnerability of the implementing actors with regard to human rights demands influenced the evolution of pluralist accountability in the two cases.

In each case, I first explore the accountability mechanisms that existed at the outset of the delegation relationship. I then explain why there was no pluralist accountability with regard to OEF detentions and demonstrate how the combination of competition among third parties and vulnerability with regard to human rights demands led to the development of pluralist accountability regarding the transfer of detainees to Afghan authorities. This chapter also

[7] Globe and Mail 2007: From Canadian Custody into Cruel Hands, article by Graeme Smith, April 23. Globe and Mail 2007: Personal Account: A Story of Torture, article by Graeme Smith, April 24, 2007.

demonstrates that these two cases are interlinked: the delegation relationship in the second case evolved as a consequence of the lack of accountability in the first case. And the effective pluralist accountability in the second case, in turn, had feedback effects for attempts to enhance pluralist accountability in the first case. The two conditions, competition and vulnerability, combined can also explain these feedback effects.

The Transfer of Detainees by ISAF to OEF Forces

As the leading authority in the OEF, the US held several hundreds of detainees in Afghanistan, even without being mandated by the UN Security Council (Amnesty International 2002, 16). According to the US Department of Defense, there were twenty-five sites in Afghanistan run by the US where detainees were held and interrogated (United States Department of Defense 2004c). Most of the detainees were captured by OEF forces, but a significant number was captured and transferred by ISAF or captured in joint operations. It is difficult to establish the number of detainees transferred by ISAF to OEF forces, as most of the ISAF member states did not keep record of their transferals.

At the outset of the operation, the accountability framework with regard to detentions was basically nonexistent. Neither the UN Security Council nor NATO provided ISAF with standards for how to deal with and transfer detainees. When NATO took over the leadership of ISAF in 2003, the only requirement set by the Security Council was that "the alliance would operate according to current and future Security Council resolutions" (United Nations Security Council 2003a) and that ISAF would deliver quarterly reports through the Secretary-General (United Nations Security Council 2002b, para. 4). The US entered into an agreement with the ICRC which had allowed the organization to access and monitor the US detention facilities on a regular basis, under the condition that its reports were kept confidential.[8] However, in practice, access to detention facilities remained limited even for the ICRC (Forsythe 2007, 489). Due to the fact that the OEF intervention had been launched without a Security Council mandate, the Council and ISAF had no means to enhance accountability with regard to OEF detentions.

[8] See the document available at: http://www.icrc.org/eng/resources/documents/misc/united-states-detention-2012-01-09.htm (last access August 8, 2014).

When the death of two tortured inmates in Bagram became public, an internal investigation was conducted by the US army's Criminal Investigation Command in 2002. Although this report investigated the OEF's detention procedures in greater detail, it did not result in further accountability. A year later, the Security Council sent a monitoring mission to Afghanistan to "observe the operations of the International Security Assistance Force in Afghanistan," among other activities; however, the question of detainee transfers by ISAF to OEF forces was not addressed in the mission report. Instead, the Council members welcomed the cooperation between ISAF and OEF coalition forces (United Nations Security Council 2003b). There was, thus, no mechanism at the outset of the operation that would have held ISAF accountable for detainee transfers or which would have enabled ISAF to monitor and sanction human rights violations in US-led detention centers.

Attempts to Enhance Pluralist Accountability with Regard to OEF Detentions

The lack of vertical accountability became grounds for a growing international and domestic concern, both within the US as well as among ISAF partnering states (Amnesty International 2002, 33). Human rights organizations such as Amnesty International were the first to try to outline some standards for detainees. The organization argued that "those captured and held by the USA in the armed conflict in Afghanistan must be presumed to be prisoners of war" and thus enjoyed the rights under the Third Geneva Convention to have a fair trial by a "competent tribunal" (Amnesty International 2002, 2).

At the domestic level, the role of courts as accountability holders had been severely limited by the US Congress, which had introduced the Detainee Treatment Act of 2005 and the Military Commissions Act of 2006 as legal protections for US personnel who oversaw detentions (Silverstein and Hanley 2010, 1494).[9] On the basis of these acts, the US conducted internal investigations and held court-martials for over 330 cases of abuse in detention facilities in Iraq, Afghanistan, and Guantánamo in 2006 alone (Sikkink 2013, 159). While other courts were prevented from taking up prosecutions by these acts, the US Supreme Court ruled in 2006 that the Geneva Conventions applied to both Al-Qaeda and Taliban detainees. It further decided that the military commissions set up by the US government to try detainees had to be

[9] United States Congress 2005: Detainee Treatment Act (42 USC. 2000dd-l(b)).

authorized by the US Congress, and that they violated US law as well as the Geneva Conventions in their present form (*Hamdan* v. *Rumsfeld*).[10] Although this decision was not unanimous but adopted by a 5 to 3 majority, the court thus enforced the Geneva Conventions as the appropriate legal standards for detentions (Cole 2013). However, this remained one of the exceptional decisions after 9/11, which imposed legal constraints for the undertaking of detentions. There were no further legal accountability mechanisms introduced for detentions in Afghanistan.

The US Supreme Court rejected the Congress's Detainee Treatment Act and granted detainees in Guantánamo the right to challenge the legality of their detentions before national courts in another decision in 2008 (*Boumediene* v. *Bush*). However, the Court of Appeals of the District of Columbia in 2010 ruled that the detainees at the Bagram detention center in Afghanistan had no constitutional right to habeas corpus.[11] Thus, despite a promising start and further improvements in the accountability regime for detentions in Guantánamo, the attempts of the US Supreme Court to act as an accountability holder for detentions in Afghanistan did not significantly exceed the standard-setting activities of 2006.

Domestic actors in other nations supported the US Supreme Court in becoming a standard setter for detentions. In 2004, for the first time in history, 175 members of the British House of Lords and Commons issued an amici curiae brief addressing the cases of *Rasul* v. *Bush* and *Al Odah* v. *United States*.[12] The authors argued that detainees transferred to Guantánamo should be guaranteed independent judicial review and strongly criticized the US government for not complying with core legal standards. This strong intervention of members of another nation's parliament, a nation that was, moreover, an operating partner within the context of ISAF, was exceptional.

Further attempts to enhance accountability were undertaken by the Parliamentary Assembly of the Council of Europe, which determined that the practice of its member states of "capturing and handing a person over to the United States whilst knowing that such a person would be unlawfully transferred into a US-administered detention facility, constituted a serious human rights violation" (Council of Europe Parliamentary Assembly 2006b, para. 10.2). Although the assembly's debate focused on the role of European states

[10] See http://www.supremecourt.gov/opinions/05pdf/05–184.pdf (last access August 10, 2014).

[11] See http://digitalcommons.wcl.american.edu/cgi/viewcontent.cgi?article=1610&context=aulr (last access August 10, 2014).

[12] See https://ccrjustice.org/sites/default/files/attach/2015/05/2004-01-14SCOTUS_RasulAmicusUK Ireland_0.pdf (last access August 10, 2014).

that allowed the US Central Intelligence Agency to undertake secret detentions on their territory, the transfer of detainees to OEF detention facilities in Afghanistan was also strongly criticized (Council of Europe Parliamentary Assembly 2006a, 2006b). The language used in the resolution indicates normative sanctioning: the parliamentary assembly complained that "across the world, the United States has progressively woven a clandestine 'spiderweb' of disappearances, secret detentions and unlawful inter-state transfers, often encompassing countries notorious for their use of torture" (Council of Europe Parliamentary Assembly 2006b, para. 5). It emphasized that this stood in stark contrast to the fact that the US was an observer state to the Council and "Europe's long-standing ally in resisting tyranny and defending human rights and the rule of law" (Council of Europe Parliamentary Assembly 2006b, para. 5). The assembly further exercised some monitoring activities by mandating an inquiry into "alleged secret detentions and unlawful inter-state transfers of detainees involving Council of Europe member states." In the report, the assigned investigator used even stronger language, stating that the US had instituted a "legal apartheid" for its detentions. This one-time inquiry of the Council of Europe Parliamentary Assembly including the normative sanctioning in the report, however, was not followed by further, more regular, monitoring activities.

Despite these attempts to enhance accountability, there was no general NATO policy for handling and transferring detainees. Nor did ISAF states ask the Security Council to explicitly include detentions in the operation's mandate, as the Council did, for example, for the Multinational Forces in Iraq (Deeks 2008). In addition to that, a proposal by the Dutch government to establish a genuine ISAF detention facility and, thereby, end the prolonged delegation of detentions, was not pursued further by the ISAF partnering countries.[13] The only policy that ISAF states could agree upon was an operational detention policy for Afghanistan, which introduced a ninety-six hour rule after which detainees had to be either released or transferred.[14] This policy, however, did not refer to any human rights standards to guide the transfer of detainees. The OEF under US command, therefore, remained unaccountable for human rights violations that occurred after the transferal of detainees from ISAF to OEF facilities.

[13] Toronto Star 2009: Why Didn't Safe Prison for Detainees Get Built?, article by Tonda MacCharles, December 18, available at: http://www.thestar.com/news/canada/2009/12/18/why_didnt_safe_prison_for_detainees_get_built.html (last access January 21, 2015).

[14] NATO ISAF SOP 362 of August 31, 2006, available at: https://info.publicintelligence.net/ISAF-DetaineeSOP.pdf (last access January 31, 2015).

Explaining the Lack of Pluralist Accountability: Varying Competition, Strong Invulnerability

Neither ISAF/NATO nor the Security Council was motivated to increase accountability regarding OEF detentions. Given the dual role of the US as a leader of the OEF as well as within ISAF, and a veto player in the UN Security Council, it comes as no surprise that all attempts to develop general NATO guidelines for handling detainees failed. As the main detaining authority, the US would be affected by any measure taken. This institutional overlap hindered ISAF and the Security Council to act as vertical accountability holders. But how can we explain the lack of pluralist accountability?

In the immediate aftermath of the attacks of September 11 in 2001, it was extremely difficult to advocate for the rights of terrorist suspects held in Afghanistan and Guantánamo (Davis 2007). A member of the Senate who compared the treatment of detainees in US detention facilities to the German Nazi regime faced a storm of indignation and the debate was quickly silenced (Forsythe 2007, 482). Although there were always individuals who spoke up for the respect of human rights in the "war on terror," competition among human rights organizations was low, as there was no profile to be gained from acting as the detainees' advocate in the state of emergency after 2001, due to overarching security concerns.[15]

After some time, however, there was a "growing unease concerning Bush's detention practices" (Forsythe 2007, 481), which provided an opportunity for several domestic institutions to sharpen their profile by acting as accountability holders towards the US government's detention policies in Afghanistan and Guantánamo. The state of emergency could not be maintained forever, support for the limitation of civil liberties among the population was declining, and dissatisfaction with the executive was growing (Davis 2007). The release of photographs of tortured detainees in the Abu Ghraib facility in Iraq in 2004, particularly, completely changed the discursive environment for domestic and transnational human rights organizations.[16] The public consternation caused by these pictures led to a significant increase in human rights networks both

[15] Zinck et al., 2014; LA Times 2002: Petition Assails US on Prisoners, article by Eric Lichtblau, February 20, available at: http://articles.latimes.com/2002/feb/20/news/mn-28934 (last access January 31, 2015).

[16] Huffington Post 2009: What's Wrong with This Picture?, article by Geoffrey T. Stone, June 14, available at: http://www.huffingtonpost.com/geoffrey-r-stone/whats-wrong-with-this-pic_b_203572.html (last access August 11, 2014).

within and outside the US who took US detentions under scrutiny (Sikkink 2013, 156). The organizations used the Freedom of Information Act to reveal more documents to the public, which then helped others to initiate lawsuits on behalf of detainees against the US government (Forsythe 2007, 482).

Consequently, the potential for third parties to raise their profile as accountability holders in the "war on terror" increased after 2004. The landmark *Hamdan* v. *Rumsfeld* decision of the US Supreme Court fell in this period. The increasing willingness of the court to act as an accountability holder has been linked to the declining support of US citizens for President George W. Bush (Silverstein and Hanley 2010, 1488). The Supreme Court used this momentum to advocate for the Geneva Conventions in order to re-establish its role as a guardian over the executive. This growing competitive environment between judiciary and executive alone, however, cannot explain why pluralist accountability over US detentions did not move beyond the standard-setting activities of the US Supreme Court.

I argue that in this case the US government's high degree of invulnerability with regard to human rights demands hindered a further evolution of pluralist accountability. For a significant period of time after the attacks of September 11, the US government successfully managed to make itself immune to human rights demands (Foot 2006; Sikkink 2013). Although recent studies revealed that Bush lost his popularity, and that the majority of the population rejected the torture of detainees, the public's interpretation of the data came to a different conclusion (Gronke et al. 2010, 437). National and international media and politicians during the Bush administration interpreted public opinion polls in a way that conveyed the impression that most Americans supported torture and other degrading treatment of detainees if it deterred terrorist attacks (Gronke et al. 2010, 437). According to media accounts, the American public was "afraid that terrorists will be released, or that their trial in open court will uncover information that will make Americans less safe" (Silverstein and Hanley 2013, 1494). This concern for safety and security that dominated the public discourse was used by the US government to counter any human rights demands.

Several actors tried to increase the US government's vulnerability by referring to its embeddedness in a Western liberal value system. The signatories of the amici curiae brief of the British Parliament argued that an independent review of detentions would be "inimical to the United States' commitment to the rule of law and its international obligations."[17] The Council of Europe's Parliamentary Assembly emphasized that the OEF detention practices stood in stark contrast to the fact that the US was an observer state to the Council and "Europe's long-standing ally in resisting tyranny and defending human rights and the rule of law" (Council of Europe Parliamentary Assembly 2006b, para. 5). This would severely threaten the "moral authority" of the US as a country "regarded as a model of democracy and respect for individual freedoms" (Council of Europe Parliamentary Assembly 2007, 65). The report warned that "the world's greatest power is becoming a negative role model for other countries, which feel that they may legitimately follow the same path and flout human rights" (Council of Europe Parliamentary Assembly 2007, 65). Amnesty International tried to increase the US government's vulnerability by reminding "the US Government of its stated commitment to international law and standards, and provides detail on the ways in which its actions are failing to match this rhetoric with focus on detentions in Afghanistan and Guantánamo" (Amnesty International 2002).

Nevertheless, these attempts remained without significant effect for one important reason: the US government successfully invoked security as a counter-norm in a very specific antiterrorist discourse (Sikkink 2013, 146, 148). It framed the debate about international law in the context of an antiterrorist discourse to make itself morally invulnerable (Sikkink 2013, 162). In its rhetoric, the government rejected the validity of human rights norms. Even without openly admitting the use of torture in interrogations, officials justified the treatment of detainees by referring to exceptional circumstances. A senior Pentagon official warned of the potential threat that detainees posed for the American people: "These are the worst of the worst, and if let out on the street, they will go back to the proclivity of trying to kill Americans and others. So that is well established" (Amnesty International 2002, 42). In 2002, President Bush refused to grant detainees in the Guantánamo Bay facility the prisoner of war status and used strong rhetoric in doing so: "These are killers. These are terrorists" (White House 2002a). In his State of the Union address, he declared that "terrorists who once occupied Afghanistan now occupy cells at Guantánamo Bay" (White House 2002b). The statements introduced a fundamental distinction between "we" and "them" on the grounds of values. According to President Bush, "the ones in Guantánamo Bay are killers. They don't share the same values we share" (White House

[17] See https://ccrjustice.org/sites/default/files/attach/2015/05/2004-01-14SCOTUS_RasulAmicusUKIreland_0.pdf (last access August 10, 2014).

2002c). The detainees in Guantánamo and Afghanistan were thus defined as security threats that—in contrast to the US—did not care about human rights. This distinction of values was pointedly illustrated by Senator McCain's statement during the debate with regard to an amendment of the Army Field Material in 2006:

> Mr. President, let me just close by noting that I hold no brief for the prisoners. I do hold a brief for the reputation of the United States of America. We are Americans, and we hold ourselves to humane standards of treatment of people no matter how evil or terrible they may be. To do otherwise, as I have noted, undermines our security, but it also undermines our greatness as a nation. We are not simply any other country. We stand for something more in the world—a moral mission, one of freedom and democracy and human rights at home and abroad. We are better than these terrorists, and we will win. The enemy we fight has no respect for human life or human rights. They don't deserve our sympathy. But this isn't about who they are. This is about who we are. These are the values that distinguish us from our enemies.[18]

This rhetorical strategy worked successfully both within the US population as well as among some partner countries (Sikkink 2013, 146). There were several instances, however, in which the US government had to respond to pressure raised with reference to its international legal obligations. As a consequence of the increased normative pressure, the US government eventually accepted that the legal obligations derived from the Geneva Convention on the Treatment of Prisoners of War applied to Taliban suspects captured in Afghanistan (White House 2002c, 2003). With regard to Al-Qaeda suspects, however, the government rejected any responsibility derived from the Geneva Conventions by defining them as "unlawful enemy combatants" instead of prisoners of war.[19] The government could thus deny these detainees the rights guaranteed by the Geneva Conventions and, at the same time, reaffirm its commitment to human rights in general (Amnesty International 2002, 9; Sikkink 2013, 150).

[18] See http://www.mccain.senate.gov/public/index.cfm/2005/7/post-89b54ca0-574d-496b-8e88-d8edca2a92f8 (last access August 11, 2014).

[19] The Department of Defense and its "Enemy Combatant Review Board" accordingly were responsible to determine whether a detainee received the status of an unlawful enemy combatant; see George W. Bush 2002: Fact Sheet: Status of Detainees at Guantanamo, February 7. Online by Gerhard Peters and John T. Woolley, *The American Presidency Project*, available at: http://www.presidency.ucsb.edu/ws/?pid=79402 (last access January 31, 2015).

The vulnerability regarding human rights demands increased significantly only when pictures of torture in the Abu Ghraib facility were leaked. Amnesty International in its annual report of 2005 described a US detention facility in Iraq as a "gulag," which fueled a heated domestic debate inside the US (Forsythe 2007, 484). Together with the images from the Abu Ghraib scandal, these continued attempts to increase vulnerability not only targeted the US government but also the implementing ISAF partners. As a consequence, "America's partners in Afghanistan found themselves politically unable to transfer detainees to US custody" (Deeks 2008; Rogers 2006). By mid-2006, public opinion within the US believed the unwillingness of the US government to develop appropriate standards for detainees was harmful to the relationship with NATO-partnering countries (World Public Opinion 2006a). Instead of enhancing accountability, however, ISAF member states adopted a new detention policy in 2006 that declared they would, from that point on, transfer newly captured detainees to the Afghan national government.

The Transfer of Detainees by ISAF to the Afghan Government

Accountability Framework at the Outset of the Delegation Relationship

When the concern about the OEF's detention practices rendered the transfer of detainees to the OEF forces increasingly unacceptable, several ISAF member states (the United Kingdom (UK), the Netherlands, Canada, Norway, and Denmark) concluded individual memoranda of understanding with the Afghan government. These bilateral agreements stipulated that, after a period of ninety-six hours, detainees had to be either released or transferred from ISAF custody to facilities of the Afghanistan intelligence service, mainly the NDS. The transfer of detainees to the Afghan authorities became a general ISAF policy in 2006.[20] It is difficult to establish reliable numbers of how many detainees were transferred by the ISAF member states to the NDS, but it is safe

[20] See the letter between the governments of Canada, Denmark, the Netherlands, Norway, and the US and the government of Afghanistan on the access to detainees transferred to the Government of Afghanistan exchanged in 2007 (Government of Canada 2007b). The ISAF Standing Operation Procedures for detention were adopted in August 2006, which authorized ISAF to detain "if the detention is necessary for ISAF force protection; for the self-defence of ISAF or its personnel; for accomplishment of the ISAF mission" (NATO 2006a).

to assume that there were at least several hundred including those captured in joint operations with the Afghan army and police (Amnesty International 2007b, 23, 27).

At this point, however, the accountability framework was almost as limited as in the case of the OEF detentions. Neither the UN Security Council nor ISAF had developed standards that they expected the Afghan government to comply with. This is rather surprising given the previous experience with OEF detentions and demonstrates that the organizations did not learn from the lack of accountability in the other case. However, some of the bilateral agreements of individual ISAF member states with the Afghan government set standards for detainees in NDS custody. The agreement between the Canadian and the Afghan governments of 2005, for example, stipulated that detainees under Afghan authority should be treated in accordance with the Third Geneva Convention (Government of Canada 2005, para. 3). The Memorandum of Understanding between the British and the Afghan government of 2006 was more concrete, and it explicitly demanded that the Afghan government act in accordance with its "international human rights obligations, including prohibiting torture and cruel, inhumane and degrading treatment" (Government of the United Kingdom 2006, para. 3.2). The delegating ISAF member states thus outlined some standards to be respected by the detaining authorities.

Some of the agreements also established procedures to monitor the handling of detainees after the transfer. In particular, the agreements between the British and the Afghan governments provided that the transferring state could conduct some monitoring activities and had "full access" to detention facilities (Government of the United Kingdom 2006, para. 4.1). The bilateral Memoranda of Understanding between the Afghan government and individual ISAF member states, such as the UK, also included provisions that ensured that representatives of the ICRC and the Afghan Independent Human Rights Commission (AIHRC) visited the transferred detainees and reported to the respective transferring state (Amnesty International 2007b, 15). These exchanges, however, were to remain confidential. Moreover, the AIHRC, apparently, was granted only limited access to Afghan detention facilities by NDS prison commanders (Amnesty International 2007b, 25). This allowed the ISAF member states to retain control over the information while complying with international law. The Security Council, although it sent a delegation to visit Afghanistan every two years, did not establish monitoring procedures to control the government's compliance with human rights at the outset of the delegation of detainees. The accountability mechanism in place at the outset of the delegation relationship remained, thus, very limited.

The Role of Domestic Courts and UNAMA as External Accountability Holders

In 2007, Amnesty International released a report on mistreatment and torture in Afghan detention facilities (Amnesty International 2007b). Under pressure to prove their readiness to cooperate and provide ISAF partners with information about potential attacks from Taliban and Al-Qaeda suspects, the Afghan authorities frequently relied on torture when interrogating detainees. Because of the transfer of detainees from ISAF to the Afghan NSD, Amnesty International accused ISAF of "complicity in torture" (Amnesty International 2007b). The organization argued that all ISAF states were part of the International Convention on Civil and Political Rights and the UN Convention Against Torture, which provided that "[n]o state shall expel, return or extradite a person to another State where there are substantial grounds for believing that he would be in danger of being subjected to torture" (UNCAT Art. 3, 1). On this basis, Amnesty International filed a lawsuit against the government of Canada in 2007. In 2008, the court dismissed the claim as nonadmissible on the grounds that the Canadian Charter of Rights and Freedoms could not be applied to the case (Federal Court of Canada 2008).

Despite the fact that the court did not legally sanction the Canadian government, the lawsuit caused an intense domestic controversy about how much the Canadian government had known of mistreatment in NDS facilities and thus contributed to strong normative sanctioning. In the aftermath, the Canadian government substantially modified its agreement with the Afghan government. It outlined in detail which standards the Afghan detaining authorities had to respect, in particular, the provisions of the Third Geneva Convention and the prohibition of torture; and it included some mechanisms to monitor the treatment of detainees in Afghan facilities (Amnesty International 2007b, 12–13). The agreement also granted staff of the AIHRC and Canadian government officials unlimited access to Afghan detention facilities and provided that they could interview detainees without Afghan authorities being present (Government of Canada 2007a).

Other ISAF member states, especially the UK and Denmark, also faced claims in courts (Winkler 2010, 491). An individual human rights activist filed a lawsuit against the UK in 2010 (United Kingdom Royal Court of Justice 2010). As a result, the court requested the suspension of transferals of detainees by British ISAF contingents to the Afghan NDS detention facility in Kabul. These legal proceedings, since 2007, increased the member states' motivation to start a process of standard development at the international level. The government of Denmark initiated several high-level conferences on the handling of detainees, which became known as the Copenhagen process (Hirschmann 2016; Winkler 2010). The main outcome of the conference, however, was a set of nonbinding, best-practice guidelines (Amnesty International 2012). This international attempt to set some standards for detentions had no immediate effects on ISAF's practices in Afghanistan.

Meanwhile, another accountability holder arose, which neither ISAF nor the different detaining authorities—the OEF and the Afghan government—had anticipated. In 2001, the UN Security Council had mandated the Assistance Mission in Afghanistan (UNAMA) to assist the newly established Afghan Transitional Authority under President Hamid Karzai (United Nations Security Council 2002). UNAMA's leadership made human rights one of its core activities, especially after Tom Koenigs became head of UNAMA and UN SRSG in March 2006. Koenigs was a member of the German Green Party and a strong human rights advocate, and under his leadership UNAMA's human rights unit increasingly criticized civilian casualties caused by ISAF operations.[21] Moreover, the unit criticized the lack of a legal framework for NDS detentions and eventually requested investigations into the allegations of mistreatment of detainees (Amnesty International 2007b).

In late 2006, UNAMA's human rights unit set up a detention-monitoring program together with the AIHRC that reported to the UN Secretary-General about the mistreatment of detainees in NDS facilities. This involved the monitoring of 2,000 cases. The findings of these monitoring activities prompted the Secretary-General to issue a strong statement in his own report to the UN Security Council: he demanded that "[t]he Government of Afghanistan must investigate allegations of arbitrary detentions, inhumane treatment and torture of detainees by the authorities, and in particular by the National Directorate for Security" and that the monitoring organization's access to detention facilities should be improved (United Nations Secretary-General 2007). In its resolution on Afghanistan in 2007, the Council recognized the lack of accountability that characterized the implementation of the operation in Afghanistan and—for the first time—it highlighted the need for "further progress in the reconstruction and reform of the Afghan prison sector, in order to improve the respect for the rule of law and human rights" (United Nations Security Council 2007). This drew the attention to the issue of human rights violations in detention facilities at the highest level of the international

[21] Author's interview with Tom Koenigs, member of the German Parliament, Berlin, July 31, 2012.

community. As a result, at least one prison director was replaced.[22] Due to internal disagreements between UNAMA's leadership and the human rights unit, however, a systematic approach to detention monitoring was not developed until 2008.

After the arrival of the Norwegian SRSG Kai Eide in 2008, UNAMA's security personnel became increasingly concerned about the validity and efficiency of security-related information they received from ISAF and the NDS, as it was obviously obtained from torture.[23] Within the mission leadership, the interest in obtaining reliable information—that was not obtained through torture—grew: the unrealistic scenarios of supposed attack plans that UNAMA personnel received from Afghan investigation reports were considered highly irrelevant from a security point of view and even hindered the mission's effectiveness. The leadership realized that new procedures for obtaining information were necessary. As a result, a joint taskforce on detainees was proposed that would unite the different elements of UNAMA. This taskforce was supposed to monitor the treatment of Afghan detainees in NDS and ISAF facilities.

Not surprisingly, this accountability mechanism immediately faced strong opposition from several actors. ISAF member states reportedly were "furious" about this self-authorization of UNAMA as an accountability holder.[24] The Afghan government also opposed monitoring and claimed sovereignty concerns. On the other hand, the existing monitoring actors, especially the ICRC (and also the UN High Commissioner for Refugees) opposed any concurrent monitoring actor that would potentially be more effective and thus push them aside. With a change in the leadership in UNAMA's human rights unit, the mission united and established, nevertheless, an efficient human rights monitoring section under Georgette Gagnon. This unit began requesting access to detention facilities. SRSG Eide managed to convince the ISAF leadership and NATO headquarters in various bilateral and group meetings to accept UNAMA as a monitoring actor for detainee transfers. His previous experiences as the former Norwegian ambassador to NATO gave him a high standing in the eyes of his NATO colleagues when negotiating with ISAF about the recognition of UNAMA as an accountability holder.[25]

As an international actor, UNAMA was more successful in getting access to NDS detention facilities than the national AIHRC. It systematized the

[22] Author's interview with a former staff member of UNAMA, New York, May 22, 2012.
[23] Author's interview with a former staff member of UNAMA, New York, May 22, 2012.
[24] Author's interview with a former member of UNAMA, New York, May 22, 2012.
[25] Author's interview with a former member of UNAMA, New York, May 22, 2012.

monitoring of NDS detention facilities in December 2010, when the NDS director ensured the team had regular access to all facilities. This is quite remarkable since UNAMA depended on the consent of the host state to operate in the country. UNAMA's activities were backed by strong support from the UN Security Council, which reiterated its concern about Afghan detention facilities in a resolution on Afghanistan in 2009 and requested access be granted to UN agencies in the country (United Nations Security Council 2008). Despite the fact that the UN Security Council originally had not mandated UNAMA to act as an accountability holder, it officially endorsed UNAMA's activities.

Backed by this recognition, UNAMA's leadership developed a new strategy together with the human rights unit, which allowed them to also use the reporting as an effective sanctioning mechanism. When having observed mistreatment or other human rights violations in detentions, they notified the Afghan authorities. Instead of announcing their findings publicly, they withheld the date for public release of the reports and gave the Afghan authorities time to react. This increased the pressure on the detaining authorities to react and address the deficiencies before the report was released publicly. The objective of this strategy was not to sanction individual authorities but to establish an effective accountability mechanism for the Afghan detention policy as a whole.[26]

UNAMA's sanctioning became more public with a comprehensive detention report published in 2011, which brought about a turning point in ISAF's detention transferal policy (UNAMA and OHCHR 2011). This report was compiled by a small team within the UNAMA human rights unit and was based on insights from the unit's extensive monitoring activities. It contained detailed analyses of the mistreatment of detainees, with interviews of hundreds of detainees in NDS and ANP detention facilities. In anticipation of the publication in October 2011, ISAF member states announced the suspension of its transferal policies to Afghan facilities in September. The reputational costs of continuing the practice of delegating detentions to NDS authorities were considered to be too high.[27] As expected, normative pressure by the international community increased tremendously after the release of the report.

As a consequence, ISAF initiated a rather comprehensive vertical monitoring mechanism. Following the report, ISAF set up a program to train and

[26] Author's interview with a former member of UNAMA, New York, May 22, 2012.
[27] Author's interview with a former member of UNAMA, New York, May 22, 2012.

monitor Afghan detention facilities, which included a certification process (UNAMA and OHCHR 2013, 76). ISAF could thereby rely on much stronger capacities throughout the whole country than UNAMA's human rights unit with its limited resources. ISAF trained a significant number of personnel in Afghan detention facilities in the treatment of detainees and noncoercive interview techniques. Following completion, detention facilities could obtain a certification by the ISAF commander, who provided clearance to resume detainee transfers to these particular facilities (UNAMA and OHCHR 2013, 77). These facilities were then continually monitored by both ISAF personnel and UNAMA. If further allegations of torture and mistreatment were substantiated, they could lose the certification, as happened, for example, with seven facilities in October 2012 (UNAMA and OHCHR 2013, 78). While this program did not hold individual perpetrators to account, it nevertheless was an important accountability mechanism for Afghan detentions and was a prerequisite for the restart of detainee transfers in 2013.[28] It combined elements of pluralist and vertical accountability and, as the ultimate sanction, led to the suspension of detainee transfers to Afghan facilities that were still without certification. As a direct consequence, detention conditions improved and allegations of mistreatment and torture declined (UNAMA and OHCHR 2013, 79). Its effects would however be only temporary, since ISAF troops were withdrawn in 2014, leaving the task of monitoring Afghan detentions entirely to UNAMA.

To sum up, the self-authorization of UNAMA as an independent accountability holder, later backed by the UN Security Council, established effective monitoring and sanctioning mechanisms of Afghan detaining authorities. As a consequence of this pluralist accountability, ISAF's transfer of detainees to Afghan detention facilities was temporarily suspended. Moreover, UNAMA's role as an accountability holder prompted the ISAF member states to engage in vertical monitoring and sanctioning activities towards the Afghan government.

[28] Transfers were taken up again in 2013; see http://www.bbc.com/news/uk-22784851 (last access August 13, 2014).

Feedback Effects: The Consequences of Pluralist Accountability for OEF Detentions

Despite ISAF's new detention policy, which requested the transfer of detainees to Afghan facilities in 2006, a great number of detainees continued to be held in OEF facilities at the Bagram detention center (Human Rights First 2011). While UNAMA's role as an accountability holder focused on Afghan detention facilities, it also had an effect on OEF detentions. In 2009, for example, the head of UNAMA arranged visits to a number of detention facilities throughout Afghanistan and was granted access to Bagram by the US leadership (Eide 2012, 282). His objectives were to examine the conditions of detentions and to make sure that detainees were granted the right to due process.[29] However, these visits did not become a regular monitoring mechanism and did not contribute to any significant pluralist accountability with regard to OEF detentions.

Encouraged by UNAMA's success as an accountability holder, the AIHRC also increased its monitoring of OEF facilities. This had a significant effect on the delegation of detentions, since it eventually led to the complete handover of OEF detention facilities to the Afghan government. After a report by the AIHRC was released publicly, President Karzai demanded the immediate handover of detainees to Afghan authorities.[30] The Afghan government thus emphasized its standing as a "host state" and demanded the end of detentions under the authority of the international forces. Against the background of a tense relationship between the Afghan and the US governments, the two countries eventually agreed that the control over Bagram be handed over from US to Afghan authorities by the end of 2012 (UNAMA and OHCHR 2013).

Explaining the Emergence of Pluralist Accountability: Competition and Vulnerability

ISAF member states initially refused monitoring by external actors as they were afraid that information about potential human rights violations could not

[29] See UNAMA Press Release, available at: http://unama.unmissions.org/Default.aspx?tabid=12330&ctl=Details&mid=15756&ItemID=31797&language=prs-AF (last access August 13, 2014).

[30] BBC News Asia 2012: Afghan Inmates "Abused" at US-Run Bagram Prison, January 8; BBC News Asia 2012: US Deal to Hand over Bagram and Other Prisons to Afghans, March 9.

be controlled as easily if independent third parties were involved.[31] But in this case, they did not have a choice: they were soon confronted with a pluralist accountability regime exercised by domestic courts as well as UNAMA. What factors explain the development of pluralist accountability in the case of the transfer of detainees to Afghan security forces? This section demonstrates, first, that there was a much higher degree of competition among external actors to act as accountability holders than in the case of OEF detentions. Second, the analysis shows that the degree of vulnerability of the Afghan government and the transferring of ISAF states was higher in this case. Finally, the feedback effects for increased pluralist accountability for detentions implemented by the OEF can also be traced back to the presence of the two core conditions: competition and vulnerability.

The rise of domestic courts as accountability holders has been interpreted as a growing struggle about authority between the judicial and the executive branches in the global fight against terrorism (Benvenisti 2008; Benvenisti and Downs 2009). Engaging with the detention issue became an important means for national courts to demonstrate their independent standing and their position as reviewers vis-à-vis their respective governments. It is therefore a struggle among domestic institutions across several countries about who is best at protecting human rights in an era that is characterized by security concerns. After a period of executive dominance in the aftermath of the terrorist attacks on September 11, courts increasingly took up their role as accountability holders:

> National courts have come to realize that, under conditions of increased external pressures, allowing the government carte blanche to act freely in world politics actually impoverishes the domestic democratic and judicial processes and reduces the opportunity of most citizens to use these processes to shape outcomes. These courts, better insulated from external pressures, may have concluded that, by aggressively restricting their government, they can actually revive the domestic democratic processes and secure their own autonomy. (Benvenisti 2008, 11)

The decisions about detainee transfers in Afghanistan demonstrate that courts have been quick in "climbing up the ladder of judicial review" (Benvenisti 2008, 25) and are an indication that they did not hesitate to sanction certain counter-terrorism measures undertaken by the executive abroad. As a result

[31] Author's interview with a former member of UNAMA, New York, May 22, 2012.

of this domestic competition, national courts increasingly held their governments accountable for their policies in the fight against terrorism in Afghanistan. Moreover, as we have seen in the British court's decision to halt the transfer of detainees to Afghan detention facilities, court decisions can also entail sanctioning effects for foreign governments.

Moreover, the increasing harmonization in decisions against counter-terrorist measures has been interpreted as a sign of competition with transnational dimensions: in order to preserve the judiciary's autonomy against dominant executives in the global realm, courts monitor each other's jurisprudence in order to align their decisions and "forge a united judicial front" against the power of the executive (Benvenisti 2008, 3). The quest for autonomy by national courts in response to the global fight against terrorism, therefore, has become a transnational phenomenon. This has fostered the rise of courts as accountability holders with regard to detainee transfers in several democratic countries.

The rise of UNAMA as an accountability holder was triggered by internal competition within the mission. Given the dominance of military actors in Afghanistan, UNAMA had to demonstrate its importance and to emphasize the civilian aspects of the international community's agenda for Afghanistan. Afghanistan is the country with the highest number of UN agencies, which increased the need for UNAMA as a whole to develop a distinct profile (Harsch 2012, 13). The need to increase visibility could be applied, in particular, to UNAMA's human rights unit. In contrast to other UN operations, UNAMA was a political mission under the leadership of the UN Department of Political Affairs. The human rights unit was integrated into the mission (O'Flaherty 2004, 49). The promotion of the respect for human rights was part of UNAMA's core mandate after the end of the Taliban regime in 2001, although it was not adequately reflected by the institutional structure and the personnel deployed. By 2003, security concerns dominated the priorities of the mission and the human rights unit was further downgraded in 2004, when the head of the human rights unit was asked to report to the deputy SRSG instead of directly to the SRSG and was, thus, referred to a lower level in the mission's hierarchy (Hannum 2006, 65).

After a couple of years without a strong profile within UNAMA, the human rights unit decided to start collecting evidence about civilian casualties caused by the international military in 2006. This led to tensions with ISAF, who considered that by counting the civilian casualties of ISAF operations, UNAMA betrayed the international community's efforts to restore stability in Afghanistan.[32] The UN Secretary-General and the High Commissioner for Human Rights, however, strongly supported these efforts. Moreover, in the annual round of negotiations for the renewal of ISAF's mandate, Security Council member states included the concern to further prevent civilian casualties into the new mandate and in other resolutions on Afghanistan (e.g., in resolutions 1833 and 1943). These resolutions strengthened the human rights components within UNAMA.

The mission leadership under SRSG Kai Eide, who was dissatisfied with the security-related information received from the Afghan security forces, had by then recognized the importance of the monitoring undertaken by the human rights unit for the standing of UNAMA as a whole. As a consequence, the unit continued and expanded its detention-monitoring program under the leadership of Georgette Gagnon. It thus regained a strong profile within UNAMA as an external accountability holder that monitored the detentions transferred by ISAF. The other actor monitoring detentions in Afghanistan, AIHRC, was not competing with UNAMA's human rights unit but instead had been an important cooperating partner since the beginning of UNAMA's monitoring activities in 2006.[33]

But why did the Afghan government, the ISAF member states, and, later, to a certain extent, even the OEF accept UNAMA as an external accountability holder? This leads us to the second core condition for pluralist accountability, which is implementing an actor's vulnerability with regard to human rights demands. The Afghan government faced a dilemma about satisfying the demands of its own population. After the interim administration was installed, the Karzai government needed to demonstrate its commitment to effectively fight the Taliban. When conducting detentions, its main priority was to prove that detentions were increasing the security of the Afghan people. The reasoning was that Afghan society could not worry about the conditions in Afghan detention centers as long as they still needed to worry so much about the lack of stability in the country. The concerns about greater security and stability dominated any human rights paradigm about the treatment of Taliban or Al-Qaeda suspects in Afghan detention facilities. This invulnerability, however, changed over the years. Public support for the Karzai government declined, due to the slow reconstruction process and corruption within the government (World Public Opinion 2006b). While much of the population

[32] Author's interview with Tom Koenigs, former SRSG, Berlin, July 31, 2012.

[33] UNAMA was an important donor for building up the AIHRC's capacities in the context of a UN interagency project entitled "Support for the Afghan Independent Human Rights Commission."

still conceived the Taliban to be the main threat to Afghanistan, people increasingly attributed the ongoing violence in the country to the government or international forces instead of the Taliban (Cordesman 2009). The security paradigm thus slowly began to turn against the Afghan government.

In addition to the growing domestic vulnerability, the Afghan government became increasingly vulnerable to human rights demands from the international community. At the outset of detainee transfers, the Afghan security forces were predominantly concerned with providing the Western partners the security-related information they needed. As the Karzai government demanded more and more sovereignty in the area of security, it was increasingly confronted with demands to prove its capability of undertaking security operations and detentions in line with its international obligations. Already in May 2010, the Afghan government emphasized its desire to assume complete leadership over detentions by January 2011.[34] At the London conference, the Afghan government showed itself determined "to assume greater responsibility for detentions, in keeping with the growth of Afghan capacity, in accordance with international standards and applicable national and international law."[35] With Afghanistan being a party of the Additional Protocols of the Geneva Conventions since 2009, it enabled the international community to refer to human rights norms as the Afghan government strived for greater sovereignty with regard to detentions. Moreover, despite its quest for sovereignty and ownership, Afghanistan depended heavily on donor contributions and foreign aid, especially to finance its army and police. This combined material and moral vulnerability gave the international community the means to increase the pressure on the Afghan government to fulfil its human rights commitments and to highlight that detentions are not just about effective interrogation techniques. Members of the international community thus increasingly pressured the Afghan government to recognize independent human rights monitoring of detentions.[36]

The Afghan government was not the only actor confronted with a growing vulnerability. The contributing ISAF states also faced increased vulnerability

[34] See the discussion of the US Secretary of State Hillary Clinton and the Afghan President Karzai, May 13, 2010, available at: http://www.cfr.org/afghanistan/clinton-karzais-us-afghanistan-discussion-usip-may-2010/p22137 (last access January 31, 2015).

[35] See the "communiqué" of the London Conference, available at: http://www.isaf.nato.int/images/stories/File/factsheets/Documents_Communique%20of%20London%20Conference%20on%20Afghanistan.pdf (last access January 31, 2015).

[36] See the opening remarks of the Office of the UN High Commissioner for Human Rights Navi Pillay, September 17, 2014, available at: http://www.ohchr.org/EN/NewsEvents/Pages/DisplayNews.aspx?NewsID=13734&LangID=E (last access January 31, 2015); UN doc. S/Res/1868, para. 28.

with regard to human rights demands. The legitimacy of the whole operation was linked to the fact that operating countries had intervened with the promise of establishing peace and security for the Afghan people. Promoting human rights was the main argument to gain support for this operation among domestic audiences within the ISAF states.[37] The significant rise of civilian casualties and a deteriorating security situation, instead of the expected operational successes, raised the consciousness among ISAF members that the operation had a reputation to lose both within domestic audiences as well as with the Afghan population. Over the years, public opinion support for the operation in Afghanistan decreased significantly. Within Afghanistan, the support decreased to 37 percent in 2009, compared to two thirds of the Afghan people who still supported ISAF in 2006 (Cordesman 2009). Moreover, the number of those who agreed that attacks on international forces could be justified doubled from 13 percent in 2006 to 25 percent in 2009. More than one third of the Afghan people also blamed the international or Afghan forces, not the Taliban, for the continuing violence in the country and 44 percent supported a withdrawal of international forces. With this increased vulnerability "in theater," even high-ranking US military officials recognized that ISAF needed the trust of the Afghan population for the effectiveness of its operations. ISAF commander Petraeus said in August 2010 that "only by providing them [the Afghan people] security and earning their trust and confidence can the Afghan government and ISAF prevail" (Human Rights First 2011, 1). Human rights violations caused by ISAF would harm this trust significantly.

Within Western societies, public opinion polls showed a similar picture. In Great Britain, where a court decision eventually led to the halting of detainee transfers to the Afghan government, more than half of the population opposed the operation in Afghanistan in 2009.[38] The Dutch government, which also faced court decisions about detainee transfers, resigned in the course of a domestic quarrel about whether to extend its contribution to ISAF or not. Even if the Dutch contingent entertained comparably good relations with the Afghan population, much of the Dutch population opposed the operation.[39] In light of the limited military successes, it became increasingly hard for these

[37] In some countries, for example in Germany, the government could only acquire public support and the parliament's agreement to send troops to Afghanistan by emphasizing the human rights-related aspects of the operation (Müller and Wolff 2011).

[38] BBC 2009: Most "Remain against Afghan War," October 7, available at: http://news.bbc.co.uk/2/hi/uk_news/politics/8292771.stm (last access January 31, 2015).

[39] The Economist 2009: The Dutch Model: The Flower-Strewers Partly Vindicated, March 14, available at: http://www.economist.com/node/13279199 (last access November 11, 2019).

governments to push aside human rights demands on the basis of arguments related to security and stability.

The reactions to NGO reports about transferal practices of individual ISAF members demonstrate the increasing vulnerability of important ISAF member states. By using the term "complicity in torture," for example, NGOs explicitly targeted Canada's role as an ISAF member state when delegating detentions to other agents (Amnesty International 2007b). The domestic debate that followed these allegations caused a governmental crisis and eventually led to a replacement of the defense minister and the withdrawal of Canadian troops in 2011.[40] Similar debates about the moral and legal responsibilities of ISAF states for human rights violations committed by the Afghan government evolved in the parliaments and public discourse of the US, the UK, and the Netherlands (Dimitriu 2013). In these debates, the discrepancy between ISAF's objectives and the practice of detainee transfers rendered ISAF member states vulnerable to human rights demands from their respective domestic audiences. A world public opinion survey conducted in 2008 in nineteen countries revealed that most respondents rejected torture, even if it involved terrorist suspects who could potentially reveal information that would save the lives of innocent people (World Public Opinion 2008). Therefore, the vulnerability that had prompted ISAF member states to reduce detainee transfers to the OEF detention facilities again increased and eventually led to the suspension of detainee transfers to Afghan facilities.

Finally, increasing competition and vulnerability can also explain why UNAMA became an accountability holder with regard to detentions undertaken by the OEF. Competition between various actors increased because of the dynamics of the conflict on the ground. When the Taliban regained power and became the (at first unofficial) negotiation partner in a new attempt to find a solution to the conflict in Afghanistan, their position on detentions started to matter. In late 2010, the treatment of Taliban detainees eventually became a deal breaker for the negotiations led by UNAMA under SRSG Kai Eide in Dubai.[41] At the meeting, the Taliban negotiators showed concern

[40] E.g., Toronto Star 2009: Canada Shamed on Afghan Prisoner Torture, November 19, available at: http://www.thestar.com/news/canada/2009/11/19/canada_shamed_on_afghan_prisoner_torture.html (last access January 31, 2015). The Canadian parliament set up a committee to investigate the allegations. When Prime Minister Harper refused to hand out documents to the committee, members of parliament threatened a constitution shut-down to obtain documents, until an agreement was reached that an independent panel should analyze the documents and decide which of them to make public (see Hill Times 2010, available at: http://www.hilltimes.com/news/2010/03/22/opposition-parties-push-for-a-showdown-over-afghan-documents-pms-power-to-prorogue/23526 (last access August 15, 2014)).

[41] Author's interview with a former member of UNAMA, New York, May 22, 2012.

about the treatment of their fellow inmates in US detention facilities. At the same time, the SRSG had to build up trust and demonstrate that he had influence over the US ISAF leadership with regard to some important issues, in particular detentions. Getting the US to grant UNAMA access to Bagram and other detention locations was an important sign in the peace negotiation process (Eide 2012, 278–95). This allowed UNAMA to establish itself as an independent monitoring actor for detentions undertaken not only by the Afghan government but also by international forces without a UN mandate.

Moreover, the US government's vulnerability with regard to human rights demands increased after President Barack Obama took over office, who had promised to close down the detention center in Guantánamo (Sikkink 2013). When negotiating access to OEF detention facilities, the head of UNAMA devalued any arguments invoking security as a counter-norm to strengthen invulnerability. He argued that detentions needed to be conducted in line with international human rights standards in order to prevent a "further radicalization" of the detainees.[42] The SRSG thus dismantled the supposed dichotomy between security and human rights that was previously often invoked to render the detaining authority immune to human rights demands. In August 2009, US General Stanley McChrystal admitted that the lack of transparency and the lack of due process of detentions in Bagram would become a "strategic liability"; he expected detentions in Afghanistan to become the focus of the critique of US detention practices in the near future (Human Rights First 2011, 1). The Afghan society indeed increasingly rejected the presence of international forces, especially after incidents of disrespect and violence as expressed by the burning of the Koran by US soldiers and the continuously high number of civilian casualties. The approval rating of the US in the Afghan public opinion went down from as high as 83 percent in 2005 to 47 percent in 2009. What is even more important, the security paradigm that initially helped to cement the invulnerability of the US-led OEF was seriously challenged. The number of Afghans who considered the invasion and the overthrow of the Taliban regime by the US to be something good dropped significantly from 88 percent in 2006 to 69 percent in 2009. The number of those who supported the presence of the US military decreased from 78 percent in 2006 to 63 percent. When the AIHRC revealed more data on human rights violations in Bagram, the Karzai government used this moment of vulnerability to claim full Afghan

[42] See the press statement of SRSG Eide of August 2, 2009, available at: http://unama.unmissions.org/Default.aspx?tabid=12320&ctl=Details&mid=15872&ItemID=34326&language=en-US (last access January 31, 2015).

sovereignty over the OEF-led detention facility.[43] This was thus only possible because the US could no longer rely on its role as a security provider for the Afghan people, as a powerful counter-norm to render itself immune against human rights demands.

Conclusion

The complex system of "diversified governance activities" (Bothe and Fischer-Lescano 2002) in Afghanistan provides important insights for the study of pluralist accountability in global governance. In the analysis, I focused on the transfer of detainees by ISAF, the international assistance operation under NATO leadership. ISAF delegated the detention of Al-Qaeda and Taliban suspects to the US-led intervention OEF and after 2006 also to the Afghan security forces. Both detaining authorities violated fundamental human rights, in particular, by using torture to extract confessions and information from detainees.

In this chapter I analyzed two different accountability regimes that evolved in response to the human rights violations of detainees. I first analyzed how pluralist accountability failed to evolve in response to the violation of the rights of detainees transferred by ISAF to detention facilities controlled by the US-led OEF intervention (between 2002 and 2006, in particular). Neither of the two conditions for pluralist accountability was present in this case: the post-9/11 atmosphere hindered the evolution of a competitive environment in which different actors could compete by acting as external accountability holders. Furthermore, the US government, which was the main detaining authority, successfully made itself invulnerable against human rights demands by invoking security concerns as a powerful counter-norm.

In the case of detentions delegated to the Afghan government, by contrast, pluralist accountability did evolve: national courts and the UN's political mission UNAMA exercised important accountability functions and, as a consequence, forced ISAF to suspend detainee transfers to Afghan security forces. In this case, competition enabled the rise of accountability holders, while the detaining authority's domestic and international vulnerability led to the recognition of external accountability holders. My analysis demonstrates that these two cases were interlinked: the delegation of detentions by ISAF to

[43] BBC News Asia 2012: Afghan Inmates "Abused" at US-Run Bagram Prison, January 8; BBC News Asia 2012: US Deal to Hand over Bagram and Other Prisons to Afghans, March 9.

the Afghan government in the second case evolved as a consequence to the lack of accountability with regard to detentions delegated to the OEF in the first case. The pluralist accountability that evolved regarding detentions by Afghan authorities in turn had feedback effects and enhanced the dynamics for pluralist accountability with regard to ongoing detentions by the OEF. The competitive environment of UNAMA's human rights unit and a growing vulnerability of the new US government under President Obama contributed to this development.

Beyond the analysis of pluralist accountability, the OEF case also revealed some insights on the conditions for vertical accountability. The US as the implementing actor (OEF) and a dominant actor within ISAF hindered the development of binding standards. Therefore, for vertical accountability to evolve, the different actors of the delegation relationship—accountability holder and accountor—need to be independent from each other. The analysis further revealed potential links between the two types of accountability. Pluralist accountability regarding detentions by Afghan security forces increased the pressure on ISAF member states and eventually prompted ISAF to exercise vertical sanctioning by suspending its detainee transfers. As a consequence, ISAF introduced a monitoring program to evaluate the conditions of detentions in Afghan facilities. This demonstrates that pluralist accountability does not necessarily replace but can even enhance vertical accountability.

Pluralist accountability continued even beyond the time frame of this analysis. After the suspension of detainee transfers, ISAF member states detained the captured suspects themselves. This might have spared detainees from torture by Afghan authorities but, nevertheless, violated the right of due process, which prompted courts to sanction these prolonged detentions by ISAF. A British court, for example, ruled that keeping detainees in British custody beyond ninety-six hours without judicial oversight constituted a serious human rights violation and requested that these detainees be forwarded to the Afghan government.[44] As a consequence, ISAF member states relaunched its detainee transfers to Afghan facilities, with the new monitoring mechanisms in place.

Recently, another potential external accountability holder evolved, even after ISAF member states had started to withdraw their forces from Afghanistan. The ICC opened a preliminary investigation to examine the

[44] *Mohammed* v.*Ministry of Defence* 2014 EWHC 1369 (QB), May 2, available at: https://www.judiciary.uk/wp-content/uploads/2014/05/mohammed-v-mod.pdf (last access September 20, 2014).

mistreatment and torture of detainees in Afghan and US-led facilities. On the basis of almost 700 victim representations, the prosecutor requested the Pre-Trial Chamber to authorize an investigation on alleged war crimes and crimes against humanity.[45] Had the ICC decided to open a full-fledged investigation, this could have been a significant step towards greater pluralist accountability.

[45] https://www.icc-cpi.int/afghanistan (last access February 28, 2019).

4

Human Trafficking and the Violation of the Rights of Detainees

The Accountability of International Peacekeepers in Bosnia

Introduction

"The apparent lack of accountability of international peace-keeping forces in Kosovo and Bosnia-Herzegovina," such was the title of an NGO report in 2004 (Amnesty International 2004a). This report exposed human rights violations that were committed by international peacekeepers in Bosnia and Herzegovina[1] between 1996 and 2004, namely the involvement of international personnel in human trafficking and the violation of the rights of detainees by military forces. This chapter analyzes the evolution of pluralist accountability in response to these two human rights violations. In the case of human trafficking, the Office of the High Commissioner for Human Rights (OHCHR) in Bosnia as well as domestic institutions acted as accountability holders. By contrast, no comparable pluralist accountability evolved in response to the violations of the rights of detainees.

What can explain the difference in the evolution of pluralist accountability in the two cases? In the case of human trafficking, the competitive environment in which third parties operated stimulated the OHCHR to become an accountability holder vis-à-vis the international personnel involved in human trafficking. On the contrary, in the case of detentions, third parties were hesitant to act as accountability holders as no prestige could be gained by advocating the rights of detainees who were suspected of being terrorists. In addition, the implementing actors' vulnerability with regard to human rights demands varied both over time and across the two cases. In both cases, the implementing actors tried to make themselves immune against human rights

[1] For reasons of space, I refer to the operation in Bosnia throughout the chapter when referring to the operation in Bosnia and Herzegovina.

Accountability in Global Governance. Gisela Hirschmann, Oxford University Press (2020). © Gisela Hirschmann.
DOI: 10.1093/oso/9780198861249.001.0001

demands, with different success. In the case of human trafficking, the strategy of the UN mission leadership to decrease vulnerability by covering up the problem, blame shifting, and dismissing whistleblowers had only limited success. In the case of detentions, however, the detaining authorities could make themselves immune against human rights demands by invoking security as a counter-norm and thus successfully refused to recognize any external accountability holders.

This chapter first analyzes the complex delegation schemes that characterized the two cases and the accountability frameworks present at the outset of the operations. This is then followed by an analysis of the causal processes that led to the evolution of the different accountability types, with a particular focus on the conditions for pluralist accountability, namely competition and vulnerability.

Accountability for Human Trafficking by International Personnel in Bosnia

> When we came to the border of Bosnia, we saw many officers in blue uniforms, like you. And we thought now we were safe. But then this man in blue uniform jumped into the van.[2]

Human trafficking had been no serious issue in Bosnia, or this part of the former Yugoslavia, before the Dayton Peace Agreement and the General Framework Agreement for Peace in Bosnia and Herzegovina was concluded in 1995.[3] However, this changed dramatically when the Security Council, as foreseen in the Framework Agreement, mandated the UN Mission in Bosnia and Herzegovina UNMIBH and a NATO military operation (United Nations Security Council 1996). The influx of predominantly male, well-paid military and civilian personnel in the country was the driving factor behind the rising demand for prostitution. This fueled the mushrooming of brothels, with a significant number of women that had been trafficked from Eastern Europe, particularly from Moldavia and Ukraine (Andreas 2009).[4] While the legality of

[2] A victim's testimony as presented in the movie "The Whistleblower," which is based on the story of a former member of the UN presence in Bosnia, Kathryn Bolkovac.

[3] See the Dayton Peace Agreement, available at: http://www.ohr.int/dpa/default.asp?content_id=380 (last access January 31, 2015).

[4] "Many experts point to the locations and names of the bars as evidence that traffickers not only target but also respond to the demand of international peacekeepers. While SFOR [NATO's peacekeeping force] was stationed in Bosnia, activists claimed that one could drive through Bosnia and know

prostitution is controversially debated in different societies, the sexual exploitation of trafficked women, deprived of their passports, kept in debt and sometimes even under drugs, and treated violently, constitutes a serious human rights violation. The nexus between peace operations and the increase in human trafficking stands in stark contrast to the UN's core objectives and the Security Council's mandates for the operations in Bosnia. Of course, not all international personnel deployed in Bosnia engaged in trafficking or frequented brothels with trafficked women, but those who did seriously endangered the trust of the Bosnian population in the international presence in their country. After the failure to protect civilians from the massacre in Srebrenica, this was the second time that the international community was facing serious legitimacy problems in Bosnia.

The operation in Bosnia was particularly complex due to the various implementing actors that were mandated by the UN Security Council in 1995 and 1996 (see Figure 4.1). The NATO-led SFOR with over 60,000 troops under the direct authority of the North Atlantic Council was mandated to implement the military aspects of the General Framework Agreement through the use of "all necessary means."[5] Furthermore, the UN Security Council mandated a UN presence to implement the civilian aspects of Resolution 1035. This presence consisted of a UN mission (UNMIBH) and an International Police Task Force (IPTF), whose leadership was appointed by the UN Secretary-General.[6] By the end of 1996, more than 1,700 IPTF monitors were deployed (UN Secretary-General 1996). Most importantly for this analysis, however, is the fact that for the first time in UN-mandated peace operations, private actors played a prominent role in the implementation process. Already in the context of the preceding operation by the UN Protection Force (UNPROFOR), private military and security companies were sub-contracted

which international contingent had responsibility for the region by the names on the brothels" (Mendelson 2005, 10).

[5] SFOR was authorized by the UN Security Council in 1996 by resolution 1088 as the successor operation of the multinational implementation force IFOR and also incorporated elements of the peace enforcement operation UNPROFOR. In 2004, SFOR was replaced by an EU mission, EUFOR, mandated by UN Security Council Resolution 1757.

[6] A High Representative was appointed by the Security Council as the "final authority in theatre to interpret the agreement on the civilian implementation of the peace settlement" (Dayton Peace Agreement, Annex 10, available at: http://www.ohr.int/dpa/default.asp?content_id=380 (last access January 31, 2015)). Similar to the SRSG in Kosovo, the high degree of authority granted to the High Representative, which entailed legal power as well as the authority to remove officials from office without any institutional checks, was strongly criticized (Caplan 2006; The Economist 2001). However, these allegations go beyond the specific human rights violations studied in this chapter. UNMIBH and IPTF were terminated in December 2002 and replaced by a smaller EU police mission.

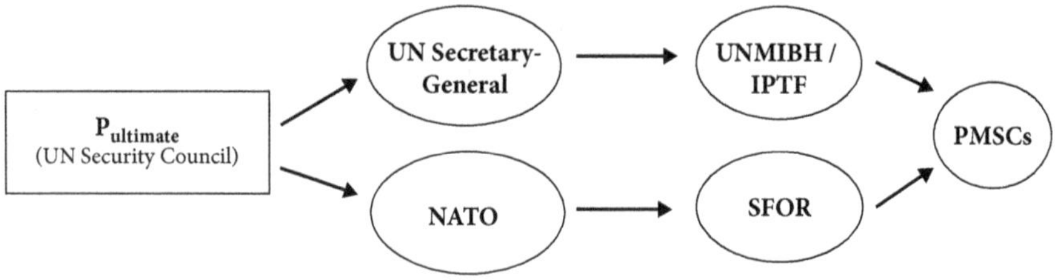

Figure 4.1 Delegation relationships in Bosnia (trafficking case). The UN Security Council mandated the UN Secretary-General and NATO to implement the mission in Bosnia. The Secretary-General delegated the implementation to the UN Mission in Bosnia and its International Police Task Force, of which some police-contributing countries delegated the implementation to private military and security companies. NATO delegated the implementation of the military tasks to the Stabilization Force, of which some troop-contributing countries delegated the implementation to private military and security companies.
Note: UNMIBH = UN Mission in Bosnia, IPTF = International Police Task Force, SFOR = Stabilization Force, PMSCs = private and military security companies

by the participating member states (Pingeot 2012, 22). The US, for example, sub-contracted a private company to implement security-sector reform programs and law enforcement, at that time even against the will of the UNPROFOR leadership (Buchan et al. 2011, 284; Østensen 2013). When the IPTF was mandated by the Security Council after the Dayton Peace Agreement, sub-contracting became officially accepted for the recruitment of police forces by the contributing states (Buchan et al. 2011). Member states, in particular the US, which has no national-level police force from which to recruit for multilateral operations, sub-contracted private companies to provide personnel for SFOR and the civilian police force IPTF (Østensen 2013, 37).[7] This privatization of peacekeeping, which has increased since, poses new challenges for accountability that might be exemplary for other areas of privatization in global governance (Nimkar 2009; Pingeot 2012). Within the complex delegation relationship that evolved from the UN mandate, the analysis of pluralist accountability focuses on these sub-contracted private implementing actors that became involved in human trafficking.

[7] It is not easy to assess the number of private employees in relation to the overall deployed personnel. Around 100–300 private contractors were deployed in Bosnia (*Bolkovac* v. *Dyncorp*, Case no. 3102729/01, para. 14). In total, there were around 1,600–1,800 IPTF officers from over thirty countries deployed in Bosnia in 2002. Around one third of the IPTF personnel were US police officers sub-contracted by Dyncorp (see Colum Lynch 2001: Misconduct, Corruption by US Police Mar Bosnia Mission, available at: http://unclips.blogspot.de/2009/05/us-police-misconduct-mars-bosnia.html, last access January 31, 2015).

How exactly were these implementing actors involved in human trafficking? After the arrival of peacekeeping forces in 1995, Bosnia turned into a flourishing business place for prostitution and trafficking within Europe. Estimated figures amount to 2,000 trafficking victims in Bosnia (Human Rights Watch 2002a, 4). Border control was usually one of the tasks undertaken by UN police forces, some of which were also involved in the smuggling of women or illicit goods.[8] In allegedly 25 percent of the bars and brothels in Bosnia, women were victims of human trafficking. Often, these women, aged between thirteen and thirty-three, had intended to travel to Western Europe to find legal work and ended up in the hands of traffickers, who deprived them of their passports and money and sold them to brothel owners in Bosnia. International clients were providing about 70 percent of the revenue for these brothels: "everyone knew of these places because of all the UN-plated cars outside."[9] A number of IPTF monitors and SFOR private contractors, who were actually mandated to train local police and promote the rule of law, regularly purchased sexual services in brothels, protected the owners from brothel raids, and sometimes even purchased trafficked women themselves, on the pretext of freeing them from their brothel owners (Human Rights Watch 2002a, 49, 62).[10] While civilian employees could freely move around the country, some SFOR contingents also established brothels within their barracks. Although the problem of trafficking did not vanish from the Balkans after the IPTF and SFOR were withdrawn in 2002 and 2004, respectively, the number of brothels significantly decreased with the end of the operations.[11] Thus, the evidence for the involvement of peacekeeping actors was clear and, after 2000, was also reported in international media.[12]

[8] Evidence from the other UN mission on the Balkans provides concrete indicators for the involvement of UN staff in the smuggling of women (see Andreas 2009 on illicit trade facilitated by UN personnel at Bosnia airport; see Mendelson 2005, fn. 69 on trafficking by UNMIK officers in Kosovo).

[9] Author's telephone interview with Madeleine Rees, former head of the Bosnian office of the UN OHCHR, September 14, 2012.

[10] "We had raids in December [2000] against those [brothels], and afterwards several girls came to Doboj IPTF Station and reported to Human Rights Watch that they had been held as sex slaves. Among others, they named several IPTF personnel and language assistants who have visited or frequently visited those places. The reports and girls were taken to Sarajevo for further investigation, but we never heard anything back" (internal UN memorandum quoted in Human Rights Watch 2002a, 52).

[11] "SFOR left the area end last year and there are now no night bars at all... You could plot the closure of the night bars with the removal of troops and the ending of [UN] IPTF" (Mendelson 2005, 12).

[12] E.g. Reuters 2000: UN, SFOR Involved in Bosnian Prostitution, May 1, available at: http://www.balkanpeace.org/index.php?index=article&articleid=11414 (last access January 31, 2015); Washington Post 2000: Six UN Officers in Bosnia Resign after Unauthorized Raid, article by Colum Lynch, November 30.

Accountability Framework at the Outset of the Operation

What were the accountability mechanisms—the standards, monitoring, and sanctioning mechanisms—available at the outset of the deployment of the operations that could have been enacted in response to human trafficking by international personnel? The Framework Agreement included an Agreement on Human Rights, in which the signatory parties committed themselves to "secure to all persons within their jurisdiction the highest level of internationally recognized human rights and freedoms."[13] The agreement referred to several important international human rights treaties, such as the European Convention on Human Rights, the International Covenant on Civil and Political Rights, and the European Convention for the Prevention of Torture and Inhuman or Degrading Treatment or Punishment (Annex 6). The UN, however, was not party to this agreement, with the consequence that it did not have any binding effects for the delegation relationship. In addition, the applicable resolutions by which the UN Security Council mandated the IPTF and SFOR, Resolutions 1035 and 1088, did not mention any human rights standards that should guide the implementing actors' behavior.

This is rather surprising, since standards for international civilian police actors in Bosnia, in particular, had already been introduced by UNPROFOR's Canadian civilian police Commander Mark D. O'Reilly in 1993. He had developed a general and rather broad Code of Conduct, which was integrated in the Standard Operating Procedures and forwarded to the headquarters' unit in New York as a potential role model for future operations in Bosnia, however without response (Chappell and Evans 1999, 243). Despite their existence and O'Reilly's warnings about disciplinary problems, these standards did not play any role for the successor mission UNMIBH and its IPTF under new leadership. Thus, even if the UN leadership was aware of previous issues of conduct within the ranks of international civilian police officers in Bosnia, concrete standards regulating the behavior of IPTF personnel, let alone contractors, were lacking.

A similar lack of accountability can be identified with regard to vertical monitoring mechanisms. The Framework Agreement (Annex 6 Article II) had provided that an independent ombudsman for human rights be appointed by the Organization for Security and Co-operation in Europe (OSCE) and a

[13] Available at: http://www.ohr.int/dpa/default.asp?content_id=380 (last access January 31, 2015).

Human Rights Chamber. However, neither of the two institutions enjoyed jurisdiction over the international presence in Bosnia. Apart from that, the monitoring procedures of the mission in Bosnia relied on the general reporting lines, similar to those in other peacekeeping operations. The Security Council requested the Secretary-General to report every three months about the implementation process by the IPTF (United Nations Security Council 1995b, para. 3), however, there were no on-site visits by the Security Council. Thus, the SRSG in Bosnia remained the most important channel in the UN system through which relevant information about IPTF behavior could be provided to the Security Council.[14] Core monitoring functions were allocated to the IPTF and the UNMIBH human rights office:

> When IPTF personnel learn of credible information concerning violations of internationally recognized human rights or fundamental freedoms or of the role of law enforcement officials or forces in such violations, they shall provide such information to the Human Rights Commission established in Annex 6 to the General Framework Agreement, the International Tribunal for the Former Yugoslavia, or to other appropriate organizations.
>
> (Annex 11, Article 6)

The human rights office was mandated to investigate and monitor human rights violations by law enforcement officers (United Nations Security Council 1996). Both institutions, however, focused on monitoring the human rights compliance of local Bosnian police forces; their activities did not involve any monitoring of international IPTF staff.

The possibilities of sanctioning were greatly shaped by the immunity regulations for the different implementing actors. SFOR military personnel enjoyed functional immunity and the respective contributing states retained exclusive jurisdiction.[15] As a consequence, only the respective contingent commander could sanction the misbehavior of soldiers. For civilian employees, however, this was different. IPTF officers also enjoyed full diplomatic immunity, but their immunity could be waived by the Secretary-General if

[14] "The IPTF Commissioner [appointed by the UN SG] shall periodically report on matters within his or her responsibility to the High Representative, the Secretary General of the United Nations, and shall provide information to the IFOR Commander and, as he or she deems appropriate, other institutions and agencies" (Framework Agreement Annex 11, Article 2, available at: http://www.ohr.int/dpa/default.asp?content_id=380 (last access January 31, 2015)).

[15] As outlined in Annex 1A, Appendix B, Article 7 of the Framework Agreement, available at: http://www.ohr.int/dpa/default.asp?content_id=380 (last access January 31, 2015).

deemed necessary, for example, in the case of illegal or criminal behavior.[16] Thus, the Secretary-General, as the institution overseeing the implementation of peacekeeping operations, could sanction IPTF officers by waiving their immunity to allow domestic prosecution in the host state or dismissing the respective perpetrator from the operation as the strongest disciplinary procedure.[17] The sanctioning procedures for SFOR contractors were even weaker. The Status of Forces Agreement between NATO and Bosnia and Herzegovina provided for claims commissions that should deal with claims for "damages resulting from noncombatant activities" (Amnesty International 2004a, 24). However, this complaint mechanism applied only for claims against SFOR troops and not against contractors employed by the individual contributing states. Even if the NATO agreement between the Republic of Bosnia-Herzegovina and Croatia regarding the status of NATO and its personnel stated that contractors "were not immune from local prosecution if the acts were committed outside the scope of their official duties," there was no mechanism of prosecution outlined that would automatically apply in the case of human rights violations by SFOR contractors.[18]

In sum, the accountability framework which existed at the outset of the delegation relationship for sub-contracted personnel involved in human trafficking was rather limited and did not have any significant path-dependent effects on the accountability regimes after the human rights violations became public.

Attempts to Enhance Vertical Accountability: The "Whistleblower" Bolkovac

Although a widespread phenomenon, human trafficking did not receive much attention within the international community before 1999, until reports by local journalists and NGOs alarmed the OHCHR in Bosnia, which then started to collect information on the issue more systematically. The first attempt to

[16] The Bosnian Criminal Code for example determines human trafficking to be illegal, with up to ten years' imprisonment penalties. This, however, was not known to the implementing actors (Mendelson 2005: 30).

[17] See the press statement of the SRSG in 2001: "The ultimate sanction, at my disposal, against offenders is removal from UN service and repatriation to their home countries," available at: http://www.nato.int/sfor/trans/2001/t010531a.htm (last access September 20, 2014). These immunity regulations basically amounted to impunity, since immunity was never waived in any trafficking-related case.

[18] Kelly Patricia O'Meara 2003: DynCorp Disgrace, Insight on the News, 19 August 2003, available at: www.prisonplanet.com/dyncorp_disgrace.html (last access January 31, 2015).

enhance vertical accountability was undertaken by an American IPTF officer who sent a memorandum entitled "Do not read this if you have a weak stomach or a guilty conscience" to over fifty people within the UN and IPTF including the SRSG on October 9, 2000. In this email, the "whistleblower" Kathryn Bolkovac outlined the problem of trafficking in Bosnia and explained how her colleagues and other international staff contributed to it (Bolkovac and Lynn 2011, 129). Bolkovac herself was on contract with the private military company Dyncorp and had become aware of the problem through her work as a human rights and gender officer within UNMIBH. She found that the UNMIBH leadership was not following up her investigations properly and evidence was being "swept under the rug" (Bolkovac and Lynn 2011, 101). With this email, all actors throughout the delegation chain had information that there was a problem in the mission in Bosnia that needed to be dealt with. The UNMIBH leadership, however, did not take these warnings to enhance vertical accountability. Instead of protecting the "whistleblower," investigations were blocked and senior officials within the IPTF and UNMIBH asked Dyncorp to end her contract (Human Rights Watch 2002a, 56).[19]

The UN Security Council did not enact vertical accountability functions either. In its Resolution 1265 of September 17, 1999, the Security Council requested the Secretary-General to provide "appropriate training in international humanitarian, human rights and refugee law, including child and gender-related provisions" to the UN peacekeeping personnel (United Nations Security Council 1999b, para. 14). However, the resolution did not contain any particular reference to the operation in Bosnia, and the Council did not repeat this request after the allegations in Bosnia became public. Existing monitoring mechanisms, such as briefings of the SRSG to the Security Council and potential means of sanctioning that the Council had at hand when renewing the annual mission mandate, were not used. When the SRSG Jacques Klein came to New York to brief the Security Council about his report on UNMIBH in June 2001, member state representatives did not voice concerns in the official debate regarding the trafficking-related activities by peacekeepers in Bosnia (United Nations Security Council 2001b). NATO denied that there was a problem with SFOR contractors and dismissed early

[19] Washington Post 2001: UN Halted Probe of Officers' Alleged Role in Sex Trafficking; Lack of Support from Above, in Field Impeded Investigators, article by Colum Lynch, December 27, 2001. Bolkovac was first asked to take a leave on the pretext of a burn-out. When she refused, the UNMIBH leadership asked Dyncorp to get her removed. "The irony of it is that the decision to get rid of her was actually made by the SRSG, who told Dyncorp to get rid of her. So the role of the UN was really dubious, to say the least. Hanging out Dyncorp to dry over the Bolkovac fiasco gave them a convenient place to hide behind" (author's telephone interview with Madeleine Rees, September 14, 2012).

allegations in 1998.[20] Until late 2003, human trafficking was a "taboo subject" (Mendelson 2005, 51). Thus, despite the negative effects for UNMIBH's and SFOR's reputation, neither the UN Secretary-General and NATO nor the Security Council enacted vertical accountability to address the problem of international police officers' involvement in human trafficking.

Pluralist Accountability: The OHCHR as an External Accountability Holder

While attempts to enhance vertical accountability failed, the OHCHR became an important accountability holder. The local OHCHR office in Bosnia had been established in 1994 to support the Special Rapporteur of the Commission on Human Rights. The Commission had been mandated by the Dayton Peace Agreement to "monitor the human rights situation in Bosnia and Herzegovina, including through the establishment of local offices and the assignment of observers, rapporteurs, or other relevant persons on a permanent or mission-by-mission basis" and thus decided to send a Special Rapporteur to the area.[21] The mandate of the Bosnian OHCHR office did not explicitly prescribe that it should monitor other international actors with regard to their respect for human rights; nevertheless, the office under the leadership of Madeleine Rees, backed by the headquarters in Geneva, became an important accountability holder for international actors in Bosnia.

The office started to systematically collect information from local NGOs and the police about the relationship between trafficking and the international presence.[22] In 1997, it briefed the outgoing SRSG Kai Eide about its collected evidence on the involvement of international personnel in trafficking.[23] To enhance its monitoring activities, the OHCHR office set up a Joint Trafficking Project together with UNMIBH in 1999. It also established a training program on human rights standards for IPTF and SFOR personnel (United Nations OHCHR 2000, 124).

Being a UN organization itself, the OHCHR first tried to convince the UN leadership to enhance vertical accountability. In 2001, on the basis of the

[20] Reuters 2000: UN, SFOR Involved in Bosnian Prostitution, May 19, available at: https://www.globalpolicy.org/component/content/article/218/46626.html (last access January 31, 2015).

[21] Dayton Peace Agreement Annexe 6, Article 8, available at: http://www.ohr.int/dpa/default.asp?content_id=380 (last access January 31, 2015).

[22] Author's telephone interview with Madeleine Rees, September 14, 2012.

[23] The Norwegian Kai Eide was responsible for introducing NATO's anti-trafficking policy years later, which he determined to be greatly influenced by these experiences from his time in Bosnia (author's telephone interview with Kai Eide, September 4, 2012).

evidence gathered from its own investigations and NGO reports, the High Commissioner for Human Rights, Mary Robinson, together with other UN senior officials, requested an investigation of the Office of Internal Oversight Services into the involvement of UN police in trafficking in Bosnia. A team of two investigators conducted a preliminary inquiry but concluded that there "were insufficient grounds to move ahead with a full-blown criminal investigation."[24] Apparently, UNMIBH officials hindered and blocked internal investigations into IPFT involvement in trafficking (Human Rights Watch 2002a, 56). Thus, the attempt of the OHCHR to enhance vertical accountability through advocating internal investigations failed.

As a consequence, the OHCHR became even more engaged in pluralist accountability. Although in previous years the issue of trafficking had not played a major role for the OHCHR's work, the OHCHR became "one of the key anti-trafficking agencies within the United Nations system" (United Nations Human Rights Commission 2002b, para. 14). On the basis of the experience from its trafficking program launched in 1999 and the input of the Bosnia field office, the organization recognized the "need for practical, rights-based policy guidance on the trafficking issue" and developed the "Recommended Principles and Guidelines on Human Rights and Human Trafficking" (United Nations Office of the High Commissioner for Human Rights 2002). These guidelines also addressed the obligations of international staff:

> The direct or indirect involvement of peacekeeping, peace-building, civilian policing, humanitarian and diplomatic personnel in trafficking raises special concerns. States, intergovernmental and non-governmental organizations are responsible for the actions of those working under their authority and are therefore under an obligation to take effective measures to prevent their nationals and employees from engaging in trafficking and related exploitation. They are also required to investigate thoroughly all allegations of trafficking and related exploitation and to provide for and apply appropriate sanctions to personnel found to have been involved in trafficking.
>
> (United Nations Office of the High Commissioner for Human Rights 2002, guideline 10)

While what "effective measures" and "appropriate sanctions" had to look like remained vague, this was one of the first attempts to set standards applicable to

[24] Washington Post 2001: UN Halted Probe of Officers' Alleged Role in Sex Trafficking; Lack of Support from Above, in Field Impeded Investigators, article by Colum Lynch, December 27, 2001.

international staff in peace operations. This was mainly due to the insights from the monitoring activities of the Bosnia field office (United Nations Human Rights Commission 2002a, 2002b, para. 15).

The OHCHR was able to exercise important monitoring activities also with the help of whistleblower Kathryn Bolkovac. The Bosnian office strongly supported Bolkovac when she faced retaliation from her employers for making the involvement of IPTF police officers in trafficking public. Rees even employed Bolkovac for a new OHCHR project on violence against women when the IPTF regional commander tried to silence her investigations (Bolkovac and Lynn 2011, 61). In April 2000, Rees asked her to become the new gender officer in the UN headquarters in Sarajevo (Bolkovac and Lynn 2011, 86). In this new position, Bolkovac could pursue her investigations throughout the whole country independently with a direct reporting line to the OHCHR. Bolkovac not only monitored the behavior of IPTF officials but also inspected the area around SFOR bases, where a number of bars were located. Despite the OHCHR's position within the UN operation in Bosnia, however, the investigations were continuously blocked by the IPTF and UN-MIBH leadership (Bolkovac and Lynn 2011, 104, 126). The head of UNMIBH, SRSG Klein, even tried to remove Madeleine Rees from her position in 2000 (Bolkovac and Lynn 2011, 141). However, since she was strongly supported by the OHCHR headquarters in Geneva, the SRSG's attempt at that time was without success. Having collected significant evidence on the involvement of IPTF officers in human trafficking, the office then went one step further and engaged in public sanctioning. Rees encouraged Bolkovac to take her case to the British court and gave a testimony in support of Bolkovac, in which she publicly exposed the lack of accountability exercised by the UN leadership and revealed new allegations against a senior official of the UN mission in Bosnia (Bolkovac and Lynn 2011, 211).

The OHCHR's monitoring capacities, however, were significantly reduced when the UN leadership eventually decided not to prolong the appointments of its two most prominent figures, the head of the local office Madeleine Rees and the High Commissioner in Geneva Mary Robinson.[25] With this, the role of the OHCHR as an accountability holder for international actors operating

[25] "I'm sure that Kofi Annan was appalled. I hope that he was appalled by what we showed what happened in Bosnia. But I also noticed that it was his Department of Peace-Keeping Operations that had me removed because I helped to expose it. And it was instrumental in getting rid of Mary Robinson because she had wanted me to expose it. Then you start thinking, well the UN, the UN, it almost doesn't matter who the Secretary-General is, the forces... will protect their own networks" (author's telephone interview with Madeleine Rees, September 14, 2012). Rees filed an administrative appeal against her dismissal (see UN doc. UNDT/2011/156).

in Bosnia came to a halt. As paradoxical as it may sound, the effective exercise of pluralist accountability by the OHCHR with regard to human trafficking eventually prompted the UN Secretary-General to limit the office's independence by removing its two most influential personalities.

The monitoring activities of the OHCHR office in Bosnia, however, were supported by other international actors, such as the UN Commission on Human Rights. Already in 1994, the commission had mandated a special rapporteur who, in his report to the commission, referred to the activities of the OHCHR's local office:

> The Special Rapporteur on violence against women has, along with several OHCHR field offices and other international organizations, identified a link between the presence of international forces and the development of a market for trafficked women and girls. In some situations, international personnel have been implicated as "consumers." However, it has also been suggested that in certain cases, this involvement is more direct and more systematic. (United Nations Human Rights Commission 2002b, para. 17)

This became the basis for the commission to call for a "code of conduct that prohibit all forms of sexual exploitation by United Nations employees and contract workers and humanitarian aid workers, and invites nongovernmental organizations to do the same in their sphere of competence" (United Nations Office of the High Commissioner for Human Rights 2003). Apparently, the UN Commission on Human Rights did not take notice that a UN Code of Conduct for Peacekeeping Personnel ("We Are UN Peacekeepers") had already existed since 1999, which could have been taken as a basis for further detailed regulations.[26] While no further pluralist accountability evolved from this initiative, this demonstrates how the OHCHR's role as an accountability holder was supported also by other UN human rights organizations within the Geneva-based human rights community.

Pluralist Accountability through Domestic Accountability Holders

After Bolkovac was fired from the mission in Bosnia, she filed a lawsuit against Dyncorp in a British court. Bolkovac won the lawsuit, and Dyncorp had to pay

[26] See http://www.un.org/en/peacekeeping/documents/un_in.pdf (last access September 20, 2014).

compensation for her dismissal. The court decision in favor of Bolkovac received widespread attention in the international media, which had sanctioning effects not only for Dyncorp but also for the UN for failing to exercise vertical accountability.[27] Often the UN was mentioned in the title of media reports and received a significant share of the shame and blame in the news, although the court case was against the private sub-contractor and not the UN itself.[28]

When the OHCHR's monitoring capacities were constrained after Bolkovac's dismissal, two NGO reports were important in stimulating further domestic actors to act as accountability holders. The Human Rights Watch "Hopes Betrayed" report of 2002 revealed in great detail how IPTF officers were involved in human trafficking (Human Rights Watch 2002a). In addition to that, another report of 2002 to the UN Committee on the Rights of the Child gave insights into the role of private civilian contractors to SFOR and the US employees' involvement in trafficking (Human Rights Watch 2002b). These reports and further reports by the media about misbehavior by US soldiers in South Korea alarmed the US Congress, the only legislative body that can withhold national funding to international institutions and, therefore, an important potential accountability holder (Allred 2006). Further information was provided to the US domestic institutions by another whistleblower, Ben Johnston, a police officer also employed by Dyncorp. He reported to the US Army Criminal Investigation Division that eight of his colleagues had purchased trafficked women for sexual and domestic servant purposes.[29]

In response to these allegations, the US Congress initiated some monitoring activities. On April 24, 2002, Congress held a hearing entitled "The UN and the Sex Slave Trade in Bosnia; Isolated Case or Larger Problem in the UN System?" to which Martina Vandenberg, the author of the Human Rights Watch report, the whistleblower Johnston, and David Lamb, the leader of the Office of Internal Oversight Services' preliminary investigation in 2001, were

[27] In its decision, the court stated that the failure of the UN administration and the IPTF to "take an adequate grip on the situation and do something about it" was of an "exceptionally serious nature" (UK Employment Tribunal 2002, *Bolkovac* v. *Dyncorp*, Case no. 3102729/01, Reserved Decision, July 1, para. 38).

[28] E.g. International Herald Tribune 2001: Whistleblower Wins Ruling in UN Bosnia Case, article by Barry James, August 9, available at: http://iwpr.net/report-news/un-prostitution-scandal (last access September 20, 2014).

[29] In June 2000, the Investigation Division followed up on a case where a US contractor employed by DynCorp had "purchased" a trafficked woman to "liberate" her from a brothel (Vandenberg 2007, fn. 20). However, the investigation did not lead to any prosecution; the case was closed without any consequences for the Dyncorp employee. Dyncorp introduced a zero-tolerance policy on trafficking in 2000, which however did not prevent further allegations coming up in the following years (available at: http://www.dyn-intl.com/media/Code-of-Ethics-English-12-4-14.pdf, last access January 31, 2015).

invited to give testimonies. During the discussion, members of Congress expressed their dissatisfaction with the UN's vertical monitoring and sanctioning:

> [T] he U.N. needs to do more in this regard, and we have encouraged the U.N., both in New York and directly with the SRSG, the special representative of the secretary general, in Bosnia to ensure that once investigations are initiated that they are completed... There has been a practice at the U.N. where individuals who are being investigated have the opportunity to suddenly leave the country, and then the U.N. tends to drop its investigation. We have encouraged them not to do that and have been assured that they are going to proceed on that basis.[30]

In this hearing, Congress members strongly emphasized the importance of additional US-led investigations and requested "thorough, global, and extensive" investigations. In response to the pressure exerted by members of Congress, the US Department of Defense (DoD) launched in June 2002 a two-phase investigation, the "Human Trafficking Assessment Project," examining the behavior of US troops in South Korea and the Balkans (United States Department of Defense 2003). This attempt of monitoring through domestic procedures, however, did not result in any sanctioning activities, neither by the DoD nor by the US Congress. The Inspector General reported to have "found negligible evidence that U.S. Armed Forces in the Balkans patronized prostitutes or engaged in other activities on a wide-spread basis that supported human trafficking" but identified some "weaknesses," especially regarding contractors (United States Department of Defense 2003, 1–3). It carefully stated that "DoD contractor employees may have more than a limited role in human trafficking. We were unable to gather more evidence of it precisely because there are no requirements and no procedures in place compelling contractors to gather such information regarding their employees or to report it to U.S. military authorities" (United States Department of Defense 2003, 25). Thus, what started out as a promising attempt of pluralist accountability by the US Congress faded away into a weak vertical monitoring.[31] Given the

[30] Robert Gifford in the hearing before the Subcommittee on International Operations and Human Rights of the Committee on International Relations of the House of Representatives, 107th Congress, April 24, 2002, Serial no. 107 85; http://commdocs.house.gov/committees/intlrel/hfa78948.000/hfa78948_0f.htm.

[31] Investigations in Bosnia were systematically hampered or blocked if allegations involved US citizens: "One local NGO activist from Bosnia and Herzegovina told participants at a NATO side meeting that victims who wish to bring charges against their traffickers are advised to remain silent

preparation and investigating methodology, the monitoring activities were designed to fail:

> No DOD/IG investigators had received formal training in how to research trafficking or, more specifically, how to research trafficking in Bosnia and Kosovo in 2003. As numerous reports have made clear, trafficking in the Balkans had moved underground. The DOD investigation's methodology in this environment moreover guaranteed that they would uncover little. For example, in contrast with other reports on trafficking, such as Human Rights Watch's report "Hopes Betrayed," they had no interviews with local non-governmental organizations (NGOs) in Bosnia or Kosovo. They did not speak to any victims, nor drive on the roads where brothels were said to be located. . . . (Mendelson 2005, 42)

Therefore, the monitoring activities initiated by the US Congress did not result in greater accountability.

Already earlier, the Congress had introduced an instrument for sanctioning private contractors with delegation contracts in extraterritorial operations. In 2000, it adopted the US Military Extraterritorial Jurisdiction Act for contractors of the DoD. This was the first legislative act that enabled the government to hold military contractors operating abroad accountable.[32] However, the Dyncorp employees for the police force in Bosnia were under contract with the Department of State and, therefore, did not fall under this act. Thus, although an important sanctioning instrument for other cases of complex delegation in global governance, this law failed to serve as an accountability mechanism in this case.[33]

about any involvement of U.S. personnel. Allegations of U.S. involvement are the fastest way to scuttle a prosecution, even of a local trafficker, the activist said" (see the statement of Martina Vandenberg to the Helsinki Commission, available at: https://chrissmith.house.gov/uploadedfiles/2004.09.21_enforcing_u.s._policies_against_trafficking_in_persons_-_how_is_the_u.s._military_doing.pdf, last access January 31, 2015).

[32] Available at: https://www.justice.gov/sites/default/files/jmd/legacy/2013/10/15/act-pl106-523.pdf (last access January 31, 2015).

[33] In 2009, the US House of Representatives introduced a bill "To require accountability for personnel performing private security functions under Federal contracts, and for other purposes," which prohibits the employment of personnel with a criminal record or who has been dishonorably discharged from the armed or security forces (available at: http://www.gpo.gov/fdsys/pkg/BILLS-111hr2177ih/content-detail.html, last access September 20, 2014). In 2011, another bill was introduced in the US Congress to extend the jurisdiction to contractors employed by the Department of State, but was not enacted: the Civilian Extraterritorial Jurisdiction Act; http://www.govtrack.us/congress/bills/112/hr2136 (last access March 15, 2013).

To complete the role of US domestic institutions as accountability holders, the US government engaged in standard-setting activities. In late 2002, a zero-tolerance policy was adopted by President Bush (White House 2002d). Several subsequent memoranda by the deputy secretary of defense Paul Wolfowitz (United States Department of Defense 2004a) and secretary Donald Rumsfeld (United States Department of Defense 2004b) emphasized this zero-tolerance doctrine especially with regard to the role of sub-contractors of the DoD. In addition to the monitoring activities launched by the US Congress, there were clear standard-setting activities undertaken at the member-state level.

However, despite this promising start with monitoring mechanisms initiated by the US Congress, and clear standards of behavior outlined by the President's zero-tolerance policy, investigations were carried out superficially and were not followed by more regular police patrol-type monitoring activities. Most importantly, despite several hearings, investigations, and a new legal basis for holding military contractors accountable, no significant sanctioning mechanism was enacted in response to human trafficking in Bosnia at the level of US domestic institutions. Thus, the analysis of domestic accountability mechanisms regarding the role of sub-contracted police officers in Bosnia reveals major weaknesses of this accountability regime. The strongest domestic sanctioning effect resulted from the decision of the British court in the Bolkovac case, which was amplified by normative sanctioning through intense media reporting. Comparing the actions of these different external accountability holders, the OHCHR remained the most important third party to exercise core accountability functions.

Conditions for Pluralist Accountability: Competitive Environment and Vulnerability

Why did the OHCHR become such an important accountability holder? The analysis reveals an important condition for the OHCHR's involvement, namely, the competitive environment in which the OHCHR was situated. The OHCHR in Geneva was founded not long before the operation in Bosnia was launched: it resulted from the Vienna Conference on Human Rights in 1993, during which human rights NGOs lobbied for a new, more effective supranational institution monitoring the respect of states for human rights. Under the leadership of Mary Robinson, the OHCHR became an "effective bully pulpit in defense of human rights" with numerous field offices (Weiss 2016, 36). Her outspoken advocacy against human rights violations faced strong opposition from various member states, including the US, but gave the OHCHR an influential voice despite a limited budget. Within the Geneva-based UN human rights institutions, however, the OHCHR had to find its niche as a new institution, especially in the light of notorious budget and personnel shortages that had accompanied the office from the beginning.[34] Two concurring institutions are relevant for this analysis: the human rights offices that are deployed within individual peace operations and the International Organization for Migration's (IOM) work in the domain of human trafficking.

As in other peace operations, there was also a human rights office within UNMIBH that was mandated to investigate misconduct of local police, among other tasks.[35] Nevertheless, the OHCHR maintained a separate office in Bosnia. This parallel maintenance of OHCHR field offices and human rights offices in field presences has often raised concerns about efficiency. Later initiatives sought to mainstream and integrate the human rights offices in the different UN field presences.[36] From the perspective of pluralist accountability, however, the separate mandate enabled the OHCHR field offices to act as an accountability holder. The office in Bosnia could thus monitor the UN peacekeeping presence and report directly to the human rights headquarters in Geneva without having to subordinate itself to the UNMIBH leadership. Acting as an independent monitoring body, the OHCHR field offices could demonstrate their relevance and even provide the Geneva "human rights branch" more leverage vis-à-vis its New York headquarters. Exercising accountability functions through local offices that monitored the peacekeeping policies adopted by the Security Council, therefore, became an important means for the OHCHR to sharpen its profile.

The issue of human trafficking was already in the portfolio of the IOM, which was also active in Bosnia. Nevertheless, soon after Robinson became high commissioner, she decided to make the issue of human trafficking a

[34] See Alston 1997; Ignatieff 2014; see also Mary Robinson 1997: Realizing Human Rights: "Take hold of it, boldly and duly..." Romanes Lecture, Oxford University, November 11, available at: http://www.un.org/rights/50/dpi1938.htm (last access January 31, 2015).

[35] See UNMIBH, available at: http://www.un.org/en/peacekeeping/missions/past/unmibh/background.html (last access May 14, 2013).

[36] See the Memorandum of Understanding signed on November 22, 2002 by the high commissioner for human rights, Sergio Vieira de Mello, and the head of the Department of Peace-Keeping Operations, Jean-Marie Guéhenno: "There are commitments with regard to planning, design and establishment of human rights components of peace-keeping operations, institutional arrangements for these components, procedures for reporting and public statements, arrangements for administration and funding, human rights training for military and civilian staff of peace-keeping operations, provisions on information alert and exchange and an agreement to arrange appropriate exchanges of staff to establish an inter-departmental team" (Clapham 2003).

priority in OHCHR's work.[37] She recognized, however, that they needed to be careful not to duplicate existing activities and indeed cooperated with the IOM in a joint project in Kosovo, for example. Apart from conceiving the OHCHR as a consultative institution that reconciled all international anti-trafficking policies, Robinson was eager to formulate the distinctiveness of the office, especially with regard to the IOM. She outlined a human rights-based approach as the OHCHR's fundamental principle, which distinguished the organization from all other institutions working on this topic. According to Robinson, human rights "must be at the core of any credible anti-trafficking strategy."[38] Mainstreaming human rights in all UN organizations dealing with trafficking would "ensure that trafficking is not simply reduced to a problem of migration, a problem of public order; or a problem of organized crime." This argument was clearly directed against the one-dimensional approach of the IOM's trafficking policy, which dealt with the problem from a migration perspective and focused on the repatriation of trafficking victims, even if many of the women were resmuggled into the country as soon as they left the airport.

The operation in Bosnia thus became the opportunity to demonstrate that the OHCHR was not only able to compete with the IOM in this area but also inhabited—at least around this topic—a unique position within the UN human rights system. The High Commissioner supported the local Bosnian office with a trust fund, to "provide emergency support to trafficked women as well as to provide grants to local NGOs working in this area," which characterized exactly what the IOM was also doing in Bosnia. Robinson further strongly encouraged the office in Bosnia to expose the involvement of IPTF and UNMIBH members in human trafficking.[39] In light of this institutional competition, the office in Bosnia was eager to demonstrate that its role in the fight against human trafficking was more important and more successful than what was done by the IOM.[40] By setting standards for the international personnel with regard to human trafficking and monitoring their compliance, the OHCHR thus gave itself a distinct profile as an accountability holder with

[37] Address by Mary Robinson, UN High Commissioner for Human Rights, Consultation on Trafficking and the Sex Industry, June 21, 1999, available at: http://imadr.org/wordpress/wp-content/uploads/2013/01/T2-1.-NGO-consultation-1999.06.pdf (last access January 31, 2015).

[38] Address by Mary Robinson, UN High Commissioner for Human Rights, Consultation on Trafficking and the Sex Industry, June 21, 1999, available at: http://imadr.org/wordpress/wp-content/uploads/2013/01/T2-1.-NGO-consultation-1999.06.pdf (last access January 31, 2015).

[39] Author's telephone interview with Madeleine Rees, September 14, 2012.

[40] See Madeleine Rees 2012: The Gendered Dimensions of Sex Trafficking, CDDRL Working Papers No. 7, Freeman Spogli Institute for International Studies, available at: http://iis-db.stanford.edu/pubs/23758/Rees_06_19_12.pdf (last access January 31, 2015).

a core focus on human rights that distinguished itself from the IOM as a more executive organization with a more pragmatic approach to trafficking.

While the competitive environment motivated the OHCHR to act as an accountability holder, the vulnerability of the implementing actor and the mandating authority with regard to human rights demands was relevant in this case for the recognition of pluralist accountability. The implementing agent, the private security company Dyncorp, was not morally vulnerable. Its identity was not based on the respect and promotion of human rights. If anything, it was vulnerable materially before the US government, which could decide to suspend the employment of Dyncorp for the recruitment of police officers. This is however no indicator for increased vulnerability but characterizes the general dependence of the implementing agent on the authorization by the principal. Moreover, the rising demand for private military and security companies in the context of peace operations, despite allegations of human rights violations, indicates that human rights did not play a role for choosing the implementing agent, as long the company performed efficiently (Pingeot 2012).

Moral vulnerability, however, was significantly higher for the IPTF and for the UN as a whole, whose reputation in Bosnia had already suffered because of UNPROFOR's failure to protect civilians from the massacre in Srebrenica. NGO reports emphasized that the Security Council Resolution 1088 had mandated the IPTF to investigate human rights abuses by law enforcement personnel and to promote the rule of law (Human Rights Watch 2002a, 2, 9). Vis-à-vis the Bosnian police forces, IPTF officers were expected to act as role models in terms of their respect for human rights. The reputation of the IPTF, and thus also of UNMIBH, was highly endangered if the human rights violations by IPTF officers became public.[41] This vulnerability was also recognized by the UN itself, "Peacekeepers' use of trafficking victims for sexual and other services has been a source of major embarrassment and political damage to U.N. PKOs. Despite the fact that PKO involvement is usually not widespread, the political and moral stigma attached to this behavior can taint entire missions" (United Nations Department of Peacekeeping Operations 2004, 23).

As a consequence, the IPTF and UNMIBH tried to decrease their vulnerability regarding human rights demands through two strategies. The first strategy was to cover up any investigation and to remove those exposing the violations, such as whistleblower Bolkovac. UNMIBH's head, SRSG Klein, also

[41] The verbal attack of SRSG Klein demonstrates the blank nerves: he emphasized that "this was his mission and that nobody interfered with his mission" (Bolkovac and Lynn 2011, 141).

tried to reduce OHCHR's monitoring capacities by demanding that the head of the Bosnian office, Madeleine Rees, be removed. This attempt failed, however, since Rees was backed by the OHCHR headquarters in Geneva, where the fight against human trafficking had become a key priority. The office of the OHCHR in Bosnia thus continued to act as an external accountability holder until the UN Secretary-General Kofi Annan removed Rees in 2004. Apparently, the mission leadership in Bosnia, as well as the UN headquarters in New York, regarded the accountability exercised by the OHCHR as a threat that would only increase the mission's vulnerability. The second strategy to reduce vulnerability was to enact blame shifting: UNMIBH's leadership emphasized that the responsibility to hold their agents accountable lied within the contributing member states, if they decided to sub-contract the recruitment of police officers to private actors. The SRSG argued that repatriation was the only means of sanctioning, that the UN had its hands tied, and that further disciplinary or legal action needed to be undertaken by the respective contributing states.[42]

Despite these strategies, the UN's vulnerability only increased due to the growing attention of the international media. During his visit in New York in June 2001, international news agencies "peppered" the SRSG with questions about the UN's involvement in human trafficking in Bosnia.[43] In June 2001, Klein realized that the reputation of UNMIBH was about to be seriously damaged (Vandenberg 2007, 91).[44] Having learned that Bolkovac had filed a lawsuit against her dismissal by Dyncorp, the SRSG launched the Special Trafficking Operations Programme as a specialized unit within the IPTF in July 2001 (Bolkovac and Lynn 2011, 182). In the context of the program, the IPTF conducted brothel raids together with the Bosnian local police after 2000 (Vandenberg 2007, 91). It dismissed several IPTF officers who were found to be involved in trafficking-related activities, among them eight Americans, including the former deputy commissioner of the IPTF David McBride. The SRSG took care the press would stay informed about the success of his efforts (Human Rights Watch 2002a, 60). The program can thus be taken as an indicator for the high vulnerability of the UN mission in Bosnia that could

[42] Washington Post 2002: Misconduct and the UN System, article by Jacques Paul Klein, January 24.

[43] Tanya L. Domi 2001: UN Prostitution Scandal: The UN Mission in Bosnia Comes Under Fire for Allegedly Trying to Cover Up a Prostitution Scandal, Institute for War and Peace Reporting, available at: http://iwpr.net/report-news/un-prostitution-scandal (last access December 15, 2013).

[44] A number of international newspapers were reporting on the issue, which generated significant negative publicity for UNMIBH, e.g. Washington Post 2001: Ex-UN Officer Sues US Firm over Dismissal; Lawsuit Alleges Retaliation for Reporting Co-Workers' Sexual Misconduct in Bosnia, article by Colum Lynch, June 23.

not leave human rights violations by IPTF officers unanswered any longer. Instead of restoring UNMIBH's reputation, however, the program was strongly criticized for driving trafficking underground by pursuing an aggressive law enforcement policy. Even the UN Department of Peace-Keeping Operations warned that it should not be taken as a role model for other missions when combating trafficking (United Nations Department of Peacekeeping Operations 2004). The Special Trafficking Operations Programme also was declared as a farce: often, the very same officers who raided the brothels were identified by the victims as their clients (Vandenberg 2007). The unit repeatedly raided the same brothels with great fuss while always interviewing the same women (Vandenberg 2007). Hence, the program not only lost legitimacy in the eyes of the Bosnian population, but also exposed the vulnerability of the UN mission in Bosnia to domestic accountability holders, such as the US Congress, who decided to enact monitoring functions themselves after the accountability capacities of the OHCHR had been limited by the UN Secretary-General.

Summary

While human trafficking was not an issue in Bosnia before 1995, the deployment of two operations by the UN (UNMIBH) and NATO (SFOR) led to a dramatic increase in prostitution with a high degree of women trafficked from Eastern Europe to Bosnia. Reports revealed that international staff made up for a significant part of the clientele of these brothels or were involved in trafficking themselves directly. How the international staff was held accountable is a particularly intriguing question, in particular for those who were not directly employed by the UN or by NATO, but by a private sub-contractor of the contributing member states. Thus, in this case study, I analyzed under which conditions pluralist accountability mechanisms evolved with regard to a complex delegation context that included private actors as the implementing agents of a UN-mandated multinational peace operation.

The authorization of the operation did not provide for any substantial vertical accountability mechanisms in the first place. Instead, my analysis shows how pluralist accountability evolved in response to the allegations. Despite knowledge revealed by the "whistleblower" Bolkovac about the misbehavior of sub-contracted international police personnel, no vertical accountability was exercised by the ultimate principal, the UN Security Council, the immediate principals, the UN Secretary-General, or NATO. Instead, denial prevailed, and investigations were blocked by the mission leadership. In light of this lack of vertical accountability, the OHCHR and its local office, under Madeleine Rees' leadership in Bosnia, became important external accountability holders. The OHCHR first requested the UN Office of Internal Oversight to launch an independent investigation as "fire alarm" monitoring to increase vertical accountability. When this effort failed, the office enhanced its own monitoring and sanctioning activities. The office also encouraged the "whistleblower" Bolkovac to take her case to a British court. When the court ruled that Bolkovac was unlawfully dismissed by her employer Dyncorp, this was prominently covered by international media, which also shamed the UN for not having lived up to its responsibilities as a vertical accountability holder. This exposed role as an accountability holder vis-à-vis the other international staff gave the OHCHR a unique position.

Additionally, domestic actors started to exercise pluralist accountability. Concerned by reports of NGOs about peacekeepers' involvement in human trafficking and the UN's lack of vertical accountability, the US Congress initiated "fire alarm" monitoring activities to be undertaken by the US DoD and introduced the Military Extraterritorial Jurisdiction Act in 2000 as a legal grounds for sanctioning US military contractors for misbehavior outside of US territory. The police forces in Bosnia, however, were sub-contracted by the Department of State and, thus, did not fall under this new law. Another attempt of standard setting was undertaken by the US government, which adopted a zero-tolerance policy that also applied to contractors working abroad. These domestic standard-setting and monitoring activities, however, stranded and did not lead to any sanctioning.

To sum up, pluralist accountability was exercised in parallel by the OHCHR and by domestic actors who acted as accountability holders, such as domestic courts and the US Congress. Both conditions for pluralist accountability, the competitive environment of third parties and the vulnerability of the implementing actors regarding human rights demands, explain this development. While competition stimulated the OHCHR to act as an accountability holder, the increasing vulnerability of the UN mission in Bosnia and its IPTF officers contributed to the evolution of pluralist accountability at the domestic level, in which US Congress members were worried by media reports about the behavior of US troops and expressed general skepticism regarding the UN's respect for human rights in Bosnia.

Accountability for SFOR Detentions in Bosnia

NATO's operation in Bosnia was the organization's first peacekeeping operation and the starting point for its new portfolio of activities after the end of the Cold War. It was also the first operation in which potential trade-offs between security and human rights became clearly apparent, in particular, in the context of detentions. The General Framework Agreement determined the UN Security Council should mandate NATO to send a military Implementation Force (IFOR) to Bosnia to take over from the previous UN military operation UNPROFOR (United Nations Security Council 1995a). Through Resolution 1088 of 1996, the Security Council then mandated SFOR as a successor operation under NATO leadership to implement the military aspects of the Agreement "by all necessary means" (United Nations Security Council 1996) (see Figure 4.2).

Although not explicitly mentioned by the Agreement, the arrest and detention of persons who were perceived to be a threat to security became one of the core measures undertaken by SFOR after mid-1997. Before that, detentions were considered a civilian task to be undertaken by Bosnian authorities in terms of its cooperation with the International Criminal Tribunal for the former Yugoslavia (ICTY). More importantly, members of SFOR hesitated to become involved in detentions as they feared retaliation and attacks from the different warring parties, due to the US's experience with detentions in the operation in Somalia (Ryngaert 2012, 681). They even modified their patrolling routes in order to avoid their obligation to arrest indicted war criminals. After 1997, however, cooperation with the ICTY increased and detentions became part of SFOR's activities in Bosnia (Lyck 2009, 115). A significant number of individuals were held in a detention camp at the Eagle Base under US control near Tuzla.

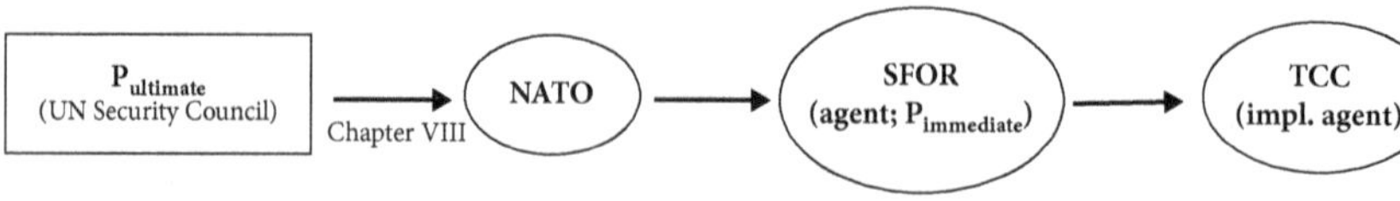

Figure 4.2 Delegation relationships in Bosnia (detentions case). The UN Security Council mandated NATO to implement a military operation in Bosnia. NATO established the Stabilization Force, in which the implementation of the military tasks was delegated to the individual troop-contributing countries.

Note: SFOR = Stabilization Force, TCC = troop-contributing countries

These arrests and the conditions under which detainees were held raised significant concerns about the violation of fundamental human rights, such as the right to counsel and independent review (Amnesty International 2004a, 23). Detainees were not given a reason for their detentions and were not allowed to communicate with their families or lawyers. In May 2001, four men employed to work at the Eagle Base were arrested, detained, and interrogated for several days, without being given access to lawyers, without having their families informed, and without being able to bring their case before an independent judge. They were released when SFOR's suspicion that they were planning a terrorist attack turned out to be false due to mistranslated information (Amnesty International 2004a, 24). Apart from these violations of fundamental due process rights, SFOR was also accused of alleged ill treatment of detainees (Amnesty International 2004a, 2). Media reports revealed that detainees in the Eagle Base detention facilities were heavily beaten and systematically deprived of sleep (Geyer 2007).[45]

In contrast to the aforementioned case study on human trafficking, no significant pluralist accountability regime evolved in this case. The following sections explore why there was no comparable development in this case. I analyze, first, the accountability framework that was available at the outset of the operation and, second, the process of failed attempts of pluralist accountability. I then demonstrate that, in contrast to the case of human trafficking, there was no comparable competitive environment that could stimulate third parties to act as accountability holders. Moreover, SFOR was successful in making itself invulnerable with regard to human rights demands due to its initial hesitation to cooperate with the ICTY and later by invoking the counter-norm of security. As a consequence, SFOR refused to recognize any external accountability holders.

Accountability Framework at the Outset of the Operation

The accountability regime regarding detentions at the outset of SFOR operations was rather limited. Neither the UN Security Council resolutions mandating IFOR and SFOR nor the Framework Agreement mentioned any human

[45] The abuse of detainees in the Eagle Base detention center was made public in the German media, which also revealed that the German secret service and agents of other countries made use of the information gained in interrogations in Bosnia, see http://tsarchive.wordpress.com/2006/11/23/meldung88878/ (last access November 27, 2014), http://www.dw.de/report-germany-suspected-us-prison-abuse-early-in-balkans/a-2213792 (last access November 30, 2014).

rights standards that the implementing actors had to respect. The individual contributing countries retained complete control over their troops and there was no NATO-wide standard-setting activity that would have outlined human rights obligations for the conduct of arrests and detentions. The UN Blue Book on Criminal Justice Standards that had been developed for UN police officers was not referenced by NATO. It is, therefore, safe to assume that these standards did not play any role for SFOR and that the individual detaining authorities were given free rein.

The only potential monitoring instrument in place, apart from the general reporting lines that ran from the detaining authorities to the SFOR Commander and to the NATO Council, was a claims commission established by the Status of Forces Agreement between NATO and Bosnia and Herzegovina, the legal basis for claims against SFOR or its troop-contributing nations. However, this commission was only allowed to deal with claims against damages arising from nonmilitary activities (Paragraph 9 (a) Article VI Annex I-A (The Military Annex) of the Dayton Agreement).[46] As arrests and detentions were considered combat-related, this commission did not provide any adequate monitoring mechanism. Therefore, there was no vertical accountability for SFOR detentions. Moreover, the Ombudsman for Human Rights established by OSCE as foreseen by the Framework Agreement (Annex 6 Article II), focused on monitoring the Bosnian government and had no jurisdiction over SFOR.

Attempts to Enhance Vertical and Pluralist Accountability

Voicing concern about unlawful and arbitrary arrests and detentions by SFOR, Amnesty International attempted to push NATO to enhance vertical accountability. In October 2003, the organization sent a memorandum to the governments of NATO member states, the NATO Secretary General, the two Commanders in Kosovo and Bosnia, as well as the UN Department of Peace-Keeping Operations. In this memorandum, Amnesty International requested investigations into detention practices along the lines of responsibility within NATO. Some of the governments replied and argued that the responsibility to enact vertical accountability lay within alleged member states or NATO as an organization. Overall, however, the organizations denied that there was any problem. The NATO Secretary-General, Lord Robertson, replied that he remained “satisfied that the relevant procedures are in place

[46] Available at: http://www.ohr.int/dpa/default.asp?content_id=380 (last access January 31, 2015).

to deal expeditiously and correctly with any allegations of human rights violations by NATO forces" (Amnesty International 2004, 3).

Meanwhile, some initial steps to enable pluralist accountability were undertaken. In 2002, Bosnia-Herzegovina became a member of the Council of Europe, ratified the European Convention for Human Rights, and became a party to the European Convention for the Prevention of Torture. The Committee for the Prevention of Torture, however, did not pay any visits to NATO detention centers when visiting Bosnia for the first time in April 2003 (Amnesty International 2004). In February 2003, the Ombudsman for Human Rights in Bosnia undertook another attempt to push NATO to enhance vertical accountability: he argued that "even if the Dayton Agreement offers immunity and impunity to SFOR personnel in certain situations, this personnel should reasonably nevertheless in fact be subject to generally accepted legal principles... The reason for the authors of the Dayton Agreement was surely not to leave IFOR, and now, SFOR, free to act arbitrarily" (Amnesty International 2004, 7). He demanded that "allegations [of] improper behavior should therefore be checked as swiftly and properly and due sanctions should be imposed, if there is proper cause" (Amnesty International 2004, 7). In contrast to the UNMIK Ombudsperson in Kosovo (see Chapter 3), however, he did not go so far as to initiate monitoring procedures on his own, and his appeals remained unheard.

Instead, the most important attempts of pluralist accountability were undertaken by domestic legal institutions in Bosnia and in the US. The Bosnian Human Rights Chamber, the Constitutional Court, and the US Supreme Court issued decisions in which they sanctioned the detention practices of SFOR, even if SFOR was not the appellant of the court file.[47] The Human Rights Chamber decided that the Bosnian authorities were to make sure that the claimant Sabahudin Fijuljanin, who was detained for three months at the Eagle Base detention facilities without clear charges and without legal counsel or the possibility to access a lawyer, be transferred to Bosnian authorities.[48] SFOR refused to accept this judgment, but after significant pressure from Amnesty International, it eventually transferred the detainee (Amnesty International 2004, 26). The Bosnian Constitutional Court even went one step further and engaged in normative sanctioning, even without

[47] The Bosnian Human Rights Chamber became the Human Rights Commission within the Constitutional Court in 2004 and all cases of human rights violations committed after January 1, 2004 have to be dealt with by the court (see http://www.hrc.ba/, last access January 31, 2015).

[48] *Sabahudin Fijuljanin* v. *Federation of Bosnia and Herzegovina*, no. CH/02/12499 of January 11, 2003.

having jurisdiction over SFOR. In its 2005 decision on the appeals against arrests and detentions by SFOR, the court judged that Bosnian authorities were liable for not having guaranteed the respect of human rights of their citizens and that "SFOR members exceeded the framework provided by domestic and international law."[49] However, except for the case of the detainee Fijuljanin, SFOR ignored the decisions by Bosnian courts and refused to transfer other detainees to Bosnian authorities. The detaining authorities also ignored the domestic legal sanctioning exercised by the US Supreme Court, which had ordered in a case of six men accused of having bombed the US embassy in Sarajevo that they had to be released. Instead, the detainees were transferred by the US to Guantanamo Bay and the detaining authorities continued their detention practices without modification (Lyck 2009, 116).[50]

Conditions for Pluralist Accountability: Low Competition about Advocating for Detainees' Rights and Low Vulnerability

Why were third parties in this case hesitant to act as accountability holders? In contrast to the case of human trafficking, there were no concurring transnational nongovernmental or intergovernmental human rights organizations that competed about the best strategy for protecting the rights of detainees. Amnesty International was the most active NGO addressing detentions by SFOR; however, its main strategy was not to establish pluralist accountability but to push NATO and the UN to enhance vertical accountability. One reason for this absence of competition is that it was difficult to advocate for the rights of terror suspects in public, especially in the period after 9/11. The populations of the SFOR contributing states and of a war-torn country such as Bosnia were not receptive to empathizing for detained suspected terrorists. Instead, the attitude prevailed that detainees were not suspected for nothing but that there must have been a reason why they were suspects: where there is smoke, there must be fire. Moreover, Bosnia was too far distant, both geographically and emotionally, to stimulate a significant international community of sympathizers for Bosnian detainees. Thus, campaigning for the rights of detainees in Bosnia, in particular for rather abstract rights such as the right to due process, was no strategy through which human rights organizations could sharpen their profile.

[49] *Bogdan Subodic* v. *BiH* of September 23, 2005 and *Dusko Tesic and others* v. *BiH* of January 16, 2005. With these decisions, the court charged the Bosnian government for liability (Bergmann and Porobic 2008).

[50] See *Boumedine* v. *Bush*, at http://www.internationalcrimesdatabase.org/Case/893 (last access November 30, 2014).

The OHCHR had already made the fight against human trafficking a priority for its work in Bosnia, even if it occasionally criticized the lack of respect for the rule of law when transferring detainees to SFOR.[51] Other organizations such as the OSCE or the Council of Europe, which played a significant role in monitoring detentions in Kosovo, showed no ambition to become accountability holders with regard to SFOR detentions. Although human rights monitoring remained the core of the OSCE's work throughout the country, the organization did not compete for monitoring detentions undertaken by international authorities. Instead, it focused on the Bosnian government, domestic institution building, elections, aspects of property rights, and the return of refugees.[52] Through this work, the OSCE became an indispensable and internationally recognized actor in Bosnia for the domestic promotion of human rights. The office in Bosnia, however, did not have any intentions to interfere with SFOR detentions to increase its relevance as a potential accountability holder like the OSCE did in Kosovo when operating under the umbrella of UNMIK's institutional structure. The Special Rapporteur of the Parliamentary Assembly of the Council of Europe on secret detentions and transfers involving Council of Europe member states pointed to cases of detention in the SFOR military base in Tuzla in his final report (Council of Europe Parliamentary Assembly 2006a). However, there was no further attempt to gain access to SFOR detention facilities in order to regularly monitor the conditions of detainees as the Council of Europe's Committee for the Prevention of Torture did in the case of Kosovo. Therefore, neither the OSCE nor the Council of Europe competed for the position of accountability holder with regard to SFOR detentions.

The only area in which we can identify some degree of competition is the domestic realm within Bosnia. Here, competition took place among Bosnian institutions. The newly established Bosnian courts needed to develop a distinct profile in the fresh institutional landscape after the Dayton Agreement and to prove their independent standing vis-à-vis the Bosnian government in terms of a democratic separation of powers and the protection of constitutional rights. The courts decided to do this by criticizing the excess of authority by the international actors and the lack of protection provided by the Bosnian state.[53] Even if SFOR did not fall under the jurisdiction of Bosnian

[51] Washington Post 2002: UN Prosecutors Giving Terrorism Evidence to US, article by Colum Lynch, May 29.

[52] 10 Years OSCE in Bosnia: http://www.oscebih.org/documents/osce_bih_doc_2011030815040118eng.pdf.

[53] http://www.venice.coe.int/wccj/Rio/Papers/BiH_Galic_e.pdf (last access November 30, 2014).

courts and the usual immunity regulations applied, the domestic competition incited the courts to enact normative sanctioning to sharpen their profile as the effective protectors of Bosnian citizens.[54] They thus hoped to generate trust in the Bosnian legal bodies within the population, who did not trust SFOR or any other international presence anyway because of their previous failures in the Srebrenica massacre (Lyck 2009, 187). Thus, while at the international level there was no significant movement to advocate for the rights of detainees in Bosnia, domestic actors nevertheless confronted SFOR's detention policy with a human rights approach.

In addition to the lacking competition, the second condition for pluralist accountability, the implementing actor's vulnerability with regard to human rights demands, remained rather low in this case. SFOR was very successful in keeping its detention practices immune against human rights demands for two reasons. The duty to cooperate with the ICTY had been enshrined as an international norm in the Security Council's Resolution 1031 and, thus, was obligatory for all SFOR contributing states irrespective of any NATO policy (Figà-Talamanca 1996). Although NATO had concluded a memorandum of understanding with the ICTY in 1996, it was heavily accused of not sufficiently cooperating with the ICTY regarding the arrest of war criminals (Ryngaert 2012, 681).[55] Through its increased detention practices after 1997, NATO could demonstrate its willingness to cooperate with the court and thus built an appropriate argumentative basis for refusing to recognize accountability holders that would monitor and sanction SFOR detentions:

> SFOR will continue to contribute to a secure environment in Bosnia and Herzegovina, ensuring the conditions for progress towards full military and civil implementation of the Dayton Peace Agreement. We commend SFOR for . . . its strong support and close cooperation with . . . the ICTY (evidenced by the further successful detention of persons indicted for war crimes).[56]

[54] Constitutional Court of BiH, Decision No. AP 953/05 of July 8, 2006; see also the decision on the limits to the exercise of authority by the High Representative in the case of the Appeal of Milorad Bilbija and others, No. AP 953/05 of March 23, 2007 (http://www.ccbh.ba/eng/odluke/povuci_html.php?pid=59843, last access November 30, 2014).

[55] See http://www.nato.int/cps/en/SID-49C0A60C-5CF4F0F6/natolive/news_24933.htm (last access November 30, 2014). Human Rights Watch even published a map in 1997 to illustrate the close geographical distance between SFOR bases and the whereabouts of indicted war criminals, available at: http://www.hrw.org/sites/default/files/related_material/Bosnia%20and%20Herzegovina%20Map%20%20Location%20of%20SFOR%20Bases%20and%20Indicted%20Ward%20Crimes%20Suspects_0.pdf (last access November 30, 2014).

[56] Meeting of NATO defense ministers at North Atlantic Council on June 8, 2000: http://www.nato.int/cps/en/natohq/official_texts_18203.htm?selectedLocale=en (last access November 30, 2014).

Since the international community had pressured SFOR to cooperate with the ICTY by arresting war criminals, nobody dared to question detentions with regard to their compliance with human rights. SFOR was considered having "not only the right but also the *duty* to execute the Tribunal's arrest warrants" (Jones 1996, 239, emphasis in original). With the failure of the international community to hinder the massacre of Srebrenica still in everybody's mind, SFOR detentions were recognized as an increased commitment of NATO to implement its mandate and thus made it impossible to monitor and sanction detentions with regard to human rights.

After the attacks of 9/11, SFOR moreover confronted any human rights demands by invoking security as a counter-norm. This strategy of establishing a powerful norm to counter human rights demands worked similarly to how the US—the main detaining authority within SFOR—also protected domestic detentions (Sikkink 2013), detentions in Afghanistan (see Chapter 1), and how KFOR protected detentions in Kosovo (see Chapter 3). The statements by the SFOR commander reveal that similar to the US domestic context, the norm of security dominated SFOR's actions and liberated the organization from any obligations that human rights norms entailed. According to his argument, SFOR's authority to detain was provided by Annex 1 of the Framework Agreement, and the length of detentions remained within his own judgment.[57] The commander emphasized that he had been given the final authority to interpret the mandate given to him by the Framework Agreement and thus empowered himself to enact the need for security as a counter-norm. While detentions were not explicitly foreseen by the agreement or the Security Council resolutions, the commander nevertheless defined them as necessary for a successful implementation of the mandate (Amnesty International 2004, 16). Detentions were thus regarded as part of military tasks, in contrast to an understanding that prevailed prior to 1997 where detentions were considered to be part of a civilian mandate, fulfilled by the Bosnian authorities (Lyck 2009, 115). The critique of human rights organizations also indicates that such a counter-norm prevailed at that time: "Amnesty International understands that some of these illegal arrests and detentions were apparently carried out as part of the global campaign: the so-called 'war against terror' led by the USA after the attacks of 11 September 2001" (Amnesty International 2004, 18). Thus, by focusing on security-related aspects in the implementation of the mandate,

[57] "The General Framework Agreement for Peace gives us the authority to detain him as long as we deem necessary to continue our investigations, and his detention will continue for as long as we deem it appropriate" (SFOR commander in reaction to complaints against the prolonged detention of Fijuljanin as quoted by Amnesty International 2004, 16).

SFOR made itself immune against human rights demands. With this immunization, SFOR could refuse to recognize accountability holders that attempted to monitor and sanction its detentions practices on the basis of human rights standards.

Summary

NATO's first peace operation, the operation SFOR in Bosnia, became a case in point for the question of accountability for the violation of the rights of detainees. SFOR established a detention center at the US-led Eagle Base near Tuzla where captured suspected terrorists or other persons alleged of threatening the stability of the country were transferred. They were detained in this facility for a significant amount of time without trial or access to legal counsel, and a number of them were mistreated or tortured during detention. While this constitutes a significant violation of fundamental rights of detainees, there was no accountability framework provided at the outset of the operation that would provide the UN Security Council or NATO the basis for monitoring and sanctioning SFOR's detention practices with regards to human rights standards. In addition to that, pluralist accountability did not evolve in this case. After several failed attempts by human rights organizations to push NATO to enhance vertical accountability, the only significant efforts of pluralist accountability were undertaken by Bosnian courts, which decided in several instances directly and indirectly in favor of the rights of detainees held in SFOR custody.

Why was pluralist accountability limited in this case? First, there was no competition in advocating for detainees' rights among the main international actors that dealt with human rights monitoring in Bosnia. The OSCE focused on domestic human rights promotion and the issues of refugees and property rights, and the OHCHR was already acting as an accountability holder with regard to the issue of human trafficking. The domestic institutional environment, however, was characterized by a higher degree of competition as most of the institutions were newly created after the Dayton Peace Agreement and were still in a process of developing their distinct profiles. The domestic courts, thus, issued several decisions in support of the rights of detainees and sanctioned SFOR's detention practices in order to demonstrate their independence. These attempts of pluralist accountability, however, were limited due to SFOR's invulnerability with regard to human rights demands. In SFOR's 1997 policy, detentions were interpreted by the SFOR Commander as one of the operation's overarching goals to provide for security and stability and were framed in the context of NATO's responsibility to cooperate with the ICTY. Moreover, the ability to invoke the counter-norm of security after 2001 cemented SFOR's invulnerability with regard to human rights demands and allowed SFOR to refuse any pluralist accountability.

Conclusion

The operation in Bosnia, which was mandated by the UN Security Council to implement the Dayton Peace Agreement, was one of the first complex governance arrangements in peacekeeping after the Cold War. The implementation of the civilian and military aspects of the mandate was undertaken by a wide range of state actors and private actors, due to the prolonged delegation relationships that evolved from the Security Council resolution. Despite the intention to promote peace in the conflict-ridden country, the operations seriously affected the human rights of individuals. The question of accountability thus became highly relevant for this operation. This chapter analyzed the evolution of pluralist accountability in response to human trafficking, as an immediate result of the arrival of international personnel, and in response to the violation of the rights of detainees held by SFOR.

While in both cases no significant accountability framework was provided at the outset of the delegation relationship, and any attempts to enhance vertical accountability failed, the two cases fundamentally differed with regard to the evolution of pluralist accountability. In the first case, pluralist accountability evolved in response to the involvement in human trafficking of international personnel and private sub-contracted companies. Important standard setting, monitoring, and sanctioning were exercised by the OHCHR and domestic actors. In contrast to that, the second case did not see a comparable development of pluralist accountability in response to allegations of the violation of the rights of detainees in SFOR detentions, although some important attempts were undertaken by Bosnian courts.

Both conditions explain why the emergence of pluralist accountability differed in these cases. The competitive environment of the OHCHR in Geneva and in Bosnia stimulated the office to develop a distinct profile as an accountability holder vis-à-vis the international presence and its involvement in human trafficking. The office supported the "whistleblower" Bolkovac to sue the private security company that provided most police officers from contributing member states, before a British court. This court ruled in her favor and criticized the refusal of the UN to enhance vertical accountability. In addition, the increasing vulnerability of the UN and its police officers stimulated the evolution of pluralist accountability at the domestic level. The reports by international media and nongovernmental human rights organizations alarmed members of US Congress members, who then asked for additional monitoring through national institutions.

In the case of detentions, on the contrary, no competitive environment prevailed that would have stimulated external third parties to act as accountability holders for the rights of detainees. Potential accountability holders, such as the OHCHR and the OSCE, focused on other issues, namely domestic human rights promotion, human trafficking, the rights of refugees, and property issues. However, competition could be identified as a relevant driving factor within the domestic context: Bosnian courts in particular issued decisions on detentions by SFOR to demonstrate their independence and to develop their profile in a newly created legal landscape. Nevertheless, the detaining authorities managed to preserve their invulnerability with regard to human rights demands by framing detentions in the context of an enhanced cooperation with the ICTY and by invoking the counter-norm of security after September 11, 2001. As a consequence, despite the decisions by domestic courts, SFOR detentions in Bosnia were not challenged with regard to their compliance with human rights standards.

It is important to keep in mind, however, that pluralist accountability does not imply a greater protection of the rights of individuals. Neither the court decision nor the investigations by domestic actors led to an improvement of the rights of trafficked women in Bosnia. As numerous allegations against various other peace operations in Cambodia, the Democratic Republic of the Congo, or Sierra Leone have demonstrated, for example, pluralist accountability was not strong enough to prevent further grave human rights violations and a widespread phenomenon of "sexual exploitation and abuse" in peacekeeping (United Nations General Assembly 2005).

5

Bringing Peace, But Violating Human Rights

The Evolution and Limits of Pluralist Accountability in Kosovo

Introduction

When the UN Security Council authorized the transitional administration in Kosovo in its Resolution 1244 of 1999, this was regarded as the "tip of the iceberg" in the history of international territorial administration (Stahn 2008, 17). UNMIK was equipped with a mandate more encompassing than any other mission before, including a wide range of state-building tasks.[1] Moreover, unlike any other peace operation, UNMIK's authority was even compared to the authority of a state (Marshall and Inglis 2003). The SRSG, nominated by the Secretary-General to implement the mission, determined in his first legal act that "all legislative and executive authority with respect to Kosovo, including the administration of the judiciary, is vested in UNMIK" (UNMIK 1999a). This lack of an adequate separation of powers in the institutional structure of the international administration in Kosovo was characterized as "benevolent despotism" that relied on the "quasi-dictatorial powers" that were granted to the SRSG.[2] All regulations and directives issued by the SRSG, therefore, became applicable law in Kosovo, and the SRSG

[1] In Resolution 1244, the UN Security Council "[a]uthorizes the Secretary-General, with the assistance of relevant IOs, to establish an international civil presence in Kosovo in order to provide an interim administration for Kosovo under which the people of Kosovo can enjoy substantial autonomy within the Federal Republic of Yugoslavia, and which will provide transitional administration while establishing and overseeing the development of provisional democratic self-governing institutions to ensure conditions for a peaceful and normal life for all inhabitants of Kosovo" (United Nations Security Council 1999a: para. 10).

[2] Sergio Vieira de Mello 2000: How Not to Run a Country, unpublished manuscript cited in Joel C. Beauvais 2001: Benevolent Despotism: A Critique of the UN State-Building in East Timor, *New York University Journal of International Law and Politics* 33: 1103–78. Sergio Vieira de Mello himself was nominated the acting SRSG to set up UNMIK in June 1999, followed by the first UNMIK SRSG Bernard Kouchner in July 1999.

Accountability in Global Governance. Gisela Hirschmann, Oxford University Press (2020). © Gisela Hirschmann.
DOI: 10.1093/oso/9780198861249.001.0001

remained the final interpretative authority (UNMIK 1999a). This unlimited authority prompted critics to request that the UN introduce accountability mechanisms in order to restrain SRSG's power (Stahn 2008; Visoka 2011, 2012, 191).

In parallel to the international civil administration, the UN Security Council also mandated NATO to establish a military presence in Kosovo (United Nations Security Council 1999a, Annex II). Following Resolution 1244 of 1999, NATO deployed the (KFOR) peace enforcement operation "Joint Guardian," which consisted of four multinational brigades under the unified command and control of a Commander KFOR (COMKFOR).

There were, thus, two main international main actors mandated by the UN Security Council in 1999, who were present in Kosovo until Kosovo's independence referendum in 2008 (see Figure 5.1). The civilian components of the transitional administration were implemented by UNMIK under the leadership of the SRSG, and the implementation of the military component was delegated to NATO/KFOR. The relationship between the civil and military presences in Kosovo was not hierarchical but rather an equal partnership (Marshall and Inglis 2003, 108). Despite the preeminent powers of the SRSG over Kosovo, KFOR acted independently of UNMIK's authority and had a separate mandate (Cerone 2001, 472).

Both operations, UNMIK and KFOR, operated under Chapter VII of the UN Charter and were equipped with a high degree of authority by Resolution

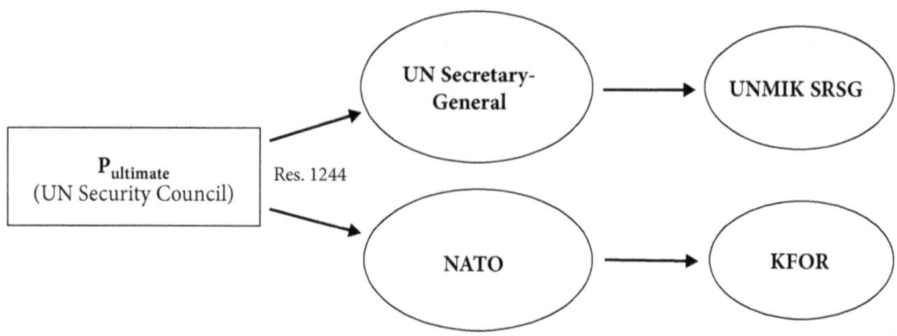

Figure 5.1 Delegation relationships (detentions in Kosovo). The UN Security Council on the basis of Resolution 1244 mandated the UN Secretary-General to implement the transitional administration in Kosovo and NATO to implement a military operation. The UN Secretary-General appointed a Special Representative to be in charge of the UN Mission in Kosovo and NATO established the Kosovo Force to implement the military aspects of the mandate.

Note: SRSG = Special Representative of the Secretary-General, KFOR = NATO Kosovo Force

1244 of the UN Security Council. Their authority had a direct effect on the rights and lives of individuals. Therefore, it is hardly surprising that immediately after their start the two operations were accused of violating fundamental human rights, despite their intention to bring peace and stability to the region. Similar to the operation in Bosnia, the increase in human trafficking as a result of the deployment of international personnel to Kosovo caused great concern (Amnesty International 2004b, 21). Moreover, both UNMIK and KFOR were also accused of the violation of property rights (Visoka 2012, 197). Apart from this, the human rights violation most directly associated to the high degree of authority granted by Resolution 1244 was the violation of the rights of detainees.

Between 1999 and 2005, several types of arrests and detentions were carried out by UNMIK and KFOR. As the civilian authority in Kosovo, the UN SRSG issued executive orders to detain persons for extended periods of time that, according to international law, would otherwise have had to be released. Executive order detentions that caused widespread concern included the extended detention of Afrim Zeqiri and the detention of seventy suspects in relation to an attack on a bus shuttle (Abraham 2003, 1329). The suspects were detained on the basis of executive orders issued by the SRSG, despite the fact that there was no sufficient evidence that would have justified pretrial detentions. Executive order detentions, such as in the case of Zeqiri, often prolonged detentions that had previously been implemented by KFOR as the other international detaining authority in Kosovo. KFOR detentions were, in comparison to UNMIK detentions, much higher in number. The majority of detainees—estimates vary from 140 to over 3,500—were held in Camp Bondsteel between 2001 and 2003, a detention facility run by the US contingent (Council of Europe 2002, para. 95; OSCE 2003).[3] In this facility, KFOR detained individuals that it considered to be a threat to the country's security or suspected to have committed crimes in the previous war.

While in some instances the conditions of detentions and the treatment of detainees became a matter of concern, I focus in this analysis on the effect of UNMIK and KFOR detentions on the right of due process as guaranteed by international human rights law. International human rights standards as outlined by the International Covenant on Civil and Political Rights (Art. 9) and the European Convention on Human Rights (Art. 5) limit the deprivation of liberty and grant detainees fundamental human rights. These include the

[3] After 2005, officially no detainees were held at Camp Bondsteel any longer (Ombudsperson Institution in Kosovo 2005: Quarterly Information Sheet, Pristina, p. 18).

right to information about the reasons for detention, the right to habeas corpus (to challenge the legality of the detention before a judicial body), the right to compensation in the case of illegal detentions, and the right to a timely judicial review in pretrial detentions (Council of Europe 2002: para. 97). In UNMIK and KFOR detentions, especially the lack of the right to habeas corpus—as one of the fundamental, irrevocable principles of international law—prompted major concerns and became the point of reference for criticisms (Amnesty International 2001, 2004a; Marshall and Inglis 2003; Trenkov-Wermuth 2010, 74).

How were the implementing actors held accountable for the violation of detainees' rights? This chapter reveals how pluralist accountability emerged regarding executive order detentions by the SRSG and KFOR. I first analyze the general accountability frameworks that existed at the outset of the delegation relationship. This is followed by an analysis of the accountability regimes that evolved to hold the two detaining authorities accountable. In the case of UNMIK detentions, OSCE and the Council of Europe were the driving forces for pluralist accountability and established the Ombudsperson Institution in Kosovo (OIK). I further analyze the conditions that led to the development of pluralist accountability in the case of UNMIK. While competition can explain why pluralist accountability evolved, the variance in pluralist accountability over time was conditioned by UNMIK's vulnerability to human rights demands.

KFOR's environment was characterized by the same competition as in the case of UNMIK detention and, therefore, remains a constant factor throughout the analysis. By contrast, vulnerability, or rather invulnerability, explains why pluralist accountability in the case of KFOR remained basically nonexistent. The organization successfully invoked security as a counter-norm in order to avoid responding to any human rights demands regarding its detention practices despite the competitive environment in which potential external accountability holders operated.

Accountability at the Outset of the Delegation Context

What standards, monitoring, and sanctioning procedures were present at the outset of the operation that could be used to hold UNMIK and KFOR accountable for their detention practices? The accountability mechanisms provided by UN Security Council Resolution 1244 were limited and differed for the two implementing actors, UNMIK and KFOR (Stahn 2008, 327). The resolution remained rather imprecise and did not establish a strong direct accountability relationship between the UN Security Council, as the mandating authority, and the implementing actors. In the resolution, the UN Security Council broadly stated that protecting and promoting human rights was part of UNMIK's main responsibilities (United Nations Security Council 1999a, para. 11j). This general reference to human rights, however, has become a regular component of multidimensional peacekeeping mandates and does not outline specific standards for the mission's own behavior. Moreover, the paragraphs on the responsibilities of the military operations implemented by NATO do not contain a similar provision (United Nations Security Council 1999a, para. 9). The resolution, furthermore, provided for the usual vertical monitoring by requesting regular reports from the Secretary-General. These also included reports from the various implementing actors, among these, the SRSG and KFOR (United Nations Security Council 1999a, para. 20).

UNMIK's Accountability Framework

In 1999, the Secretary-General adopted the bulletin on the "Observance by United Nations forces of international humanitarian law" (United Nations Secretary-General 1999b). This bulletin laid out the humane and respectful treatment of detainees and guaranteed the ICRC, an internationally renowned expert organization monitoring detentions, access to detention facilities. The ICRC, however, operates on the basis of the principles of neutrality and confidentiality and reports only to the detaining authorities, not to the UN Secretary-General.

The Secretary-General further concretized the general request for UNMIK to protect and promote human rights as outlined in Resolution 1244. In his report of July 1999, he determined that "[in] assuming its responsibilities, UNMIK will be guided by internationally recognized standards of human rights as the basis for the exercise of its authority in Kosovo" (United Nations Secretary-General 1999a, para. 46). The Secretary-General in his initial reports between 1999 and 2002 promoted a "culture of human rights... in all areas of activity" and stipulated that UNMIK "will adopt human rights policies in respect of its administrative functions" (Marshall and Inglis 2003, 142). Most concretely, he determined that international humanitarian law applied to all UN staff (United Nations Secretary-General 1999b). For the first time, a legal framework was outlined in a binding document that set standards for the behavior of the UN's own personnel.

The SRSG subsequently incorporated these standards into UNMIK's legal framework (Pacquée and Dewulf 2006, 4). In his first regulation, the SRSG stated that "in exercising their functions, all persons undertaking public duties or holding public office in Kosovo shall observe internationally recognized human rights standards" (UNMIK 1999a, section 2). This was further specified by UNMIK Regulation 1999/24, which detailed the international human rights instruments referred to in the previous regulation (UNMIK 1999b). The list of international legal obligations relevant for the case of detentions included the Universal Declaration on Human Rights, the European Convention for the Protection of Human Rights and Fundamental Freedoms and its protocols, the International Covenant on Civil and Political Rights and its protocols, and the Convention Against Torture and Other Cruel, Inhumane or Degrading Treatment or Punishment. Despite these comprehensive legal frameworks, however, it remained unclear even to staff members of the mission themselves how international human rights law concretely applied to UNMIK's actions (Marshall and Inglis 2003, 105; United Nations Human Rights Council 2006, para. 8).

This imprecision rendered it difficult for monitoring and sanctioning mechanisms to work. Formally, besides the monthly reports provided to the Secretary-General and the UN Security Council, internal monitoring mechanisms had been integrated into UNMIK's institutional structure from the beginning. A senior human rights advisor within the office of the SRSG was mandated to "ensure the compatibility of regulations issued by UNMIK with international human rights standards" (United Nations Secretary-General 1999a, para. 49). This position however was only filled by mid-2001 (Marshall and Inglis 2003, 139). According to the Secretary-General, human rights monitoring throughout the country was to be undertaken by the OSCE, the parallel implementing actor within UNMIK's institutional pillar structure (United Nations Secretary-General 1999a, Annex). However, neither the report of the Secretary-General nor the OSCE Permanent Council explicitly mandated the OSCE to monitor UNMIK's behavior. The documents remained rather vague and mandated the OSCE to "protect and promote human rights" and to "investigate human rights abuses" (United Nations Secretary-General 1999a, para. 87; OSCE 1999). Whether this implied monitoring UNMIK's own activities was never made explicit (Marshall and Inglis 2003, 105).

The range of possible sanctioning mechanisms was even more restricted. Through UNMIK Regulation 2000/47, UNMIK personnel enjoyed functional immunity from jurisdiction before any national court (UNMIK 2000b). The SRSG and the four deputy SRSGs enjoyed absolute immunity (Pacquée and

Dewulf 2006, 6). This rendered any judicial review of the implementing agents' actions regarding their compliance with human rights impossible. Even in cases in which a national court did accept a claim against UNMIK, the decision could not be enforced (Marshall and Inglis 2003, 96; Stahn 2008, 605). Instead, the immunity regulation provided that "third party claims for property loss or damage and for personal injury, illness or death arising from or directly attributed to KFOR, UNMIK or their respective personnel and which do not arise from 'operational necessity' of either international presence, shall be settled by Claims Commissions established by KFOR and UNMIK, in the manner to be provided for" (UNMIK 2000b). Despite this regulation, no claims procedure for detainees was provided at the outset. Given these limitations, the UN Security Council or the UN Secretary-General could not exercise vertical accountability without restricting the powers that the Council had granted to the SRSG in Resolution 1244. The lack of vertical accountability regarding UNMIK's detentions, therefore, had its origins already in the mandating resolution.

KFOR's Accountability Framework

The accountability framework applicable to KFOR was even less pronounced than the one applicable to UNMIK. In Resolution 1244, the UN Security Council did not set any explicit human rights standards for KFOR. According to the resolution, all activities were justifiable for reasons of law enforcement and the maintenance of a secure environment (Pacquée and Dewulf 2006, 2–3). Nevertheless, international lawyers argued that the fact that KFOR operated under a UN mandate decreed to support the civil presence obliged KFOR to comply with international human rights standards in order not to undermine UNMIK's mandate, which included the promotion and protection of human rights (Cerone 2001, 473; Marshall and Inglis 2003, 109). The acting UN SRSG Sérgio Vieira de Mello, even without having the authority to impose standards on KFOR, stipulated in 1999 in his "Statement on the Rights of KFOR to Apprehend and Detain" that KFOR was bound by international human rights standards when conducting detentions (OSCE 2003, 34). However, this did not lead to any further vertical standard-setting activities by the UN Security Council nor NATO.

Given this lack of explicit human rights standards that could be applied to KFOR, it is not surprising that no substantial vertical monitoring procedure was established at the outset of KFOR's deployment. The ICRC had inspected

NATO detention facilities in Kosovo from 1999; however, the ICRC did not report on its inspections publicly nor to the UN Security Council but directly consulted with KFOR on the monitoring results. In addition to that, the UN Security Council visited Kosovo several times during that period. These visits, however, focused on UNMIK and did not include the monitoring of KFOR activities. KFOR was required to report to the UN Secretary-General and, thus, indirectly to the UN Security Council, but it did not regularly fulfil its reporting duties (García-Orrico 2009). The formal internal reporting chain ran from the KFOR commander (COMKFOR) to the Commander of Joint Force Command Naples in Italy.

Sanctioning was further limited since individual KFOR member states retained exclusive jurisdiction over their respective troops. Moreover, UNMIK Regulation 2000/47 granted KFOR absolute immunity, which could only be waived by the COMKFOR. The COMKFOR directive provided an option for detainees to "submit petitions regarding their detention."[4] As petitions were to be addressed to the detaining authority itself, this can be considered an internal complaint mechanism rather than a mechanism that would enact vertical monitoring or sanctioning by NATO or the UN Security Council.

To sum up, the accountability system that existed at the outset of the mission deployment can be characterized as limited regarding UNMIK, and even more limited regarding KFOR. International human rights standards were integrated into UNMIK's legal framework through an initiative of the Secretary-General, although the consequences of noncompliance remained unclear. The task of human rights monitoring was assigned to the OSCE in a rather broad mandate. The only explicit monitoring obligations were the monthly reports that UNMIK had to provide to the UN Secretary-General and the Security Council as the mandating authority. This limited vertical accountability prompted strong criticisms immediately after mission deployment. The discrepancy between weak accountability and the high degree of authority was one of the major concerns that spurred criticism, especially in the context of detentions. In the following section, I contrast the development of two important pluralist accountability mechanisms, the OIK and the Human Rights Advisory Panel, in the case of UNMIK, with the continuously limited pluralist accountability in the case of KFOR.

[4] Section 5c as quoted by Amnesty International 2004a, 21.

Pluralist Accountability with Regard to UNMIK's Administrative Detentions

The executive detentions by the SRSG were strongly criticized not only by nongovernmental human rights organizations (Amnesty International 2000, 2001), but also by other intergovernmental organizations, such as the OSCE, the Council of Europe, and the UN human rights agencies (Ratner 2005, 715; Stahn 2008, 327). Most of the criticism highlighted that the practice of executive detentions and UNMIK Regulation 1999/26 on pretrial detentions were incompatible with the fundamental rights of detainees as guaranteed by Article 5 of the European Convention for the Protection of Human Rights and Fundamental Freedoms. Especially the case of Afrim Zeqiri, who was held in prolonged detention by an executive order despite the request for release issued by an international court, fueled heated discussions between UNMIK and human rights organizations (Amnesty International 2000, 2001). Substantial critique came also from the OIK, which was established in 2000 to review the actions of UNMIK.

The OIK was a result of the pluralist accountability exercised, in particular, by the OSCE and the Council of Europe. Over the years, the OIK became an important instrument for monitoring the actions of UNMIK and was considered to be a potential role model for future UN peacekeeping accountability systems (Hoffmann and Mégret 2005). I analyze in the following section how the pluralist accountability functions exercised by the OSCE and the Council of Europe led to the establishment of the OIK. I further demonstrate that a competitive environment stimulated the two organizations to act as accountability holders. Despite the fact that competition can explain the role of the OSCE and the Council of Europe as accountability holders, the analysis ultimately demonstrates that UNMIK's vulnerability with regard to human rights demands explains the full dynamic of pluralist accountability, including why third parties failed to establish the Human Rights Advisory Panel as another monitoring instrument after the OIK was turned into a national institution and lost all competences over UNMIK.

Pluralist Accountability by the OSCE and the Council of Europe: The Establishment of the Ombudsperson Institution in Kosovo

At the outset of the operation, the OSCE was not mandated to monitor UNMIK or other parts of the international administration in Kosovo. Instead, it was tasked with the promotion of human rights in more general terms throughout the country. On the basis of this broad mandate from the OSCE Permanent Council, the OSCE nevertheless decided to actively monitor UNMIK's compliance with human rights norms with substantial effects (Marshall and Inglis 2003, 138). In 2000, the OSCE established the OSCE Legal Systems Monitoring Section (LSMS) as an internal reviewing body with a "quasi-independent role to monitor the observance of human rights in Kosovo" (OSCE 2000, 5). Besides its core task of providing advice to UNMIK, the LSMS became an independent monitoring body even though it was institutionally part of UNMIK. From early on, the OSCE suggested amending UNMIK's immunity regulations in order to provide for local judicial review of UNMIK's actions, but to no avail (Pacquée and Dewulf 2006, 7). OSCE staff visited UNMIK detention facilities, reviewed the executive orders issued by the SRSG, and investigated the conditions of detainees.

Moreover, the OSCE developed a forceful mechanism for normatively sanctioning UNMIK's detention practices through the regular publication of reports and reviews. This increased the organization's recognition and reputation within the international community as a human rights organization deeply rooted in Europe's institutional framework, which supported its standing vis-à-vis UNMIK. In surprisingly frank language, the OSCE openly determined UNMIK Regulation 1999/26 on pretrial detentions to be "unlawful" (OSCE 2000). The OSCE further reproached the SRSG, stating that this regulation failed "to strike a proper balance between the imperative duty to safeguard the right to liberty and the need to detain those charged with serious criminal offences" (OSCE 2000). Regarding executive detentions, the OSCE LSMS especially criticized the lack of habeas corpus rights, such as the right to challenge a detention in court. It further argued "the mere existence of [the SRSG's] authority to detain compromises the appearance of judicial independence and the full trust of Kosovo's society in the rule of law" (OSCE 2002, 45). Note that this time it was not an NGO shaming UNMIK for issuing unlawful regulations, but an intergovernmental organization that was part of the international presence in Kosovo. With these reports and reviews, the OSCE established a link between UNMIK's detention practices and the organization's legitimacy both from a human rights law perspective and the viewpoint of the governed people.

In addition to its own monitoring activities, the OSCE, together with the Council of Europe, was the core driving force that led to the establishment of the OIK. The idea of an ombudsperson institution had been developed by the OSCE in the context of the transitional administration in Eastern Slavonia. The intention was to establish a flexible instrument that would be credible for both conflict parties, in order to address human rights violations, and to solve property disputes.[5] The mission in Eastern Slavonia, however, was terminated before any ombudsperson institution was established. When the issue of the responsibility of the international community was raised in Kosovo, the idea of an ombudsperson was reconsidered in the Rambouillet Agreement. Given that the origins of the concept laid with the OSCE, the OSCE Kosovo mission was mandated by the OSCE Permanent Council with the "[m]onitoring, protection and promotion of human rights, including, *inter alia*, the establishment of an Ombudsman institution" (OSCE 1999, para. 4).

The OSCE then asked the Venice Commission of the Council of Europe for legal advice in order to develop the terms of reference for the ombudsperson institution. Moreover, it even offered the Council of Europe to share "the entire responsibility for the running of the ombudsman institution" (Council of Europe 1999). As a consequence, a "Strasbourg man," Marek Nowicki, was proposed as the ombudsman.[6] The two organizations thereby intended to install a human rights monitoring mechanism with a close relationship to the European institutions in Strasbourg that would have the independent standing to oversee UNMIK's activities, despite the high degree of authority of the SRSG.

The initial reaction of the first SRSG, Bernard Kouchner, to the proposal of an ombudsperson institution was generally positive.[7] Also, the UN Secretary-General, who had already outlined some general human rights standards, recognized again in his second report that a "strong system of human rights protection" required mechanisms of independent review (United Nations Secretary-General 2000, para. 89). The OIK was hence mandated to take complaints against the international administration and emerging national institutions and to conduct investigations of human rights abuses, especially underpinned by the European Convention on Human Rights and the

[5] Author's telephone interview with Christos Giacoumopoulos, Council of Europe, October 26, 2012.
[6] Author's telephone interview with Simona Granata-Menghini, Council of Europe, October 22, 2012.
[7] Author's telephone interview with Christos Giacoumopoulos, Council of Europe, October 26, 2012.

International Covenant on Civil and Political Rights (United Nations Secretary-General 1999a, para. 90; UNMIK 2000a). For the first time, UNMIK's exercise of authority was to be independently monitored with respect to a concrete set of human rights standards (Momirov 2012, 8).

Nevertheless, "the UN at that time was not so eager to have this institution established so quickly."[8] In order not to alienate the SRSG by imposing an independent oversight institution that would report to external accountability holders, the ombudsperson was to be appointed by the SRSG and initially mandated for two years only. More importantly, the ombudsperson was to report directly to the SRSG in the form of nonbinding recommendations (United Nations Secretary-General 1999a, para. 90). This emphasized the advisory role of the institution, despite the fact the Secretary-General pointed out that the OIK was to be regarded as an independent body (United Nations Secretary-General 2000, 40).

Given this institutional setting, the OIK's close relationship with its "founding fathers" allowed the Council of Europe and the OSCE to act as accountability holders with regard to UNMIK detentions. Despite its originally intended advisory role, Nowicki's own understanding of his duties and powers as ombudsman, and his personal engagement, tied the OIK to external organizations and rendered the institution effectively independent.[9] Therefore, while on paper being part of UNMIK's institutional framework, the OIK enabled the OSCE and the Council of Europe to act as accountability holders towards UNMIK. The ombudsperson was invited to brief the Council of Europe's member states on a regular basis and used this international backing as a means of leverage in disputes with UNMIK.[10] The ability to express opinions and outspoken criticism to the council's member states meant the ombudsperson could report about UNMIK's human rights account to an external actor and thus engage in normative sanctioning in influential international settings. In addition to the regular interactions with the Council of Europe, the ombudsperson's briefings at the OSCE Permanent Council meeting in November 2001 laid the foundation for continued support by the council members. The delegation of the US, although convinced that executive order detentions were within the SRSG's authority under Resolution 1244, welcomed the ombudsperson's "efforts to provoke useful debate about the

[8] Author's telephone interview with Marek Nowicki, former Ombudsperson in Kosovo, November 28, 2012.

[9] Author's telephone interview with Simona Granata-Menghini, Council of Europe, October 22, 2012.

[10] Author's telephone interview with Marek Nowicki, former Ombudsperson in Kosovo, November 28, 2012.

proper use of such orders" and contributed a significant additional donation to the office's budget.

The OIK was not only created by the two external organizations; great parts of its activities were also funded by voluntary contributions from supportive member states: "With our regular annual budget, we would not have been able to do what we did without these outside donations."[11] This external funding by OSCE member states enhanced the independence of the OIK from UNMIK and provided international backing for the ombudsperson's monitoring activities. Another indicator for how the OSCE exercised accountability over UNMIK through the OIK is that the OSCE mission within UNMIK established an Ombudsperson Support Section, which helped the OIK in all practical aspects of the process of setting up the institution. The OSCE, therefore, was not only the driving force behind the design and conceptualization of the OIK but also key for the implementation and the maintenance of the office.

The office visited detention facilities, conducted its own investigations, and became a focal point for affected individuals to submit complaints. The OIK's reports on detentions were not just delivered to UNMIK itself but were presented to a wider public including the "Strasbourg organizations" and thus exposed UNMIK's detention practice to the greater transnational community. The OIK issued two special reports with an explicit focus on executive detentions, which indicate how the OIK engaged in standard setting and normative sanctioning (OIK 2001a, 2001b). In these reports, the OIK concluded that UNMIK executive detentions violated Article 5 of the European Convention on Human Rights. He demanded that the SRSG should immediately refrain from issuing executive detentions (OIK 2001a). The ombudsperson very outspokenly criticized the SRSG's practice of issuing executive detention orders and pointed to the schizophrenic contradiction between UNMIK's mandate and its practice:

> It is ironic that the United Nations, the self-proclaimed champion of human rights in the world, has by its own actions placed the people of Kosovo under UN control, thereby removing them from the protection of the international human rights regime that formed the justification for UN engagement in Kosovo in the first place. (OIK 2002, 5)

[11] Author's telephone interview with Marek Nowicki, former ombudsperson in Kosovo, November 28, 2012.

The OIK further suggested that a panel of international judges should be established to review UNMIK's detention practices (OIK 2001a, para. 32). Despite being an instrument of pluralist accountability for the OSCE and the Council of Europe, the OIK thereby tried to enhance UNMIK's vertical accountability. As a reaction, the SRSG established a Detention Review Commission for executive order detentions (Council of Europe 2002, para. 78; UNMIK 2001a). The commission's ability to sanction was nevertheless criticized by the OIK for being too limited due to a lack of independence, impartiality, and a legal basis for executive detentions (OIK 2001b). The review commission convened only once in 2001 and expired after three months, with neither the Secretary-General nor the UN Security Council being part of this process (Momirov 2012, 8; Pacquée and Dewulf 2006, 8).

Given that the mandate of the OIK was temporally limited, it was clear from early on that it would be turned into a national institution at some point (Waters 2007). The office would then lose the competency to deal with complaints against the international community. The European Court of Human Rights hence asked the Venice Commission of the Council of Europe to discuss how to establish a more permanent system of accountability for the international administration in Kosovo. With the advisory opinion of a group of international legal experts, the Venice Commission proposed the establishment of the Human Rights Advisory Panel (Council of Europe 2004b). This proposal, which was backed by the Parliamentary Assembly of the Council of Europe, foresaw the establishment of a court-like panel that would complement the work of the OIK until a long-term "Human Rights Court for Kosovo" could be established. Thus, external organizations successfully enhanced pluralist accountability and promoted the establishment of a review mechanism to monitor UNMIK's actions and their compliance with human rights standards.

UNMIK's leadership, however, was not very enthusiastic about establishing the panel.[12] Due to "logistical difficulties," it took UNMIK more than twenty months until the panel was established on March 23, 2006 (Human Rights Watch 2007). At that point, the OIK had already been transformed into a purely Kosovan institution (UNMIK 2006a). As a consequence, the population was left without a substantial complaint mechanism against the international administration for a substantial amount of time. Although the SRSG suggested that an agreement between the national ombudsperson institution and the SRSG could be concluded for dealing with complaints against

[12] Author's telephone interview with Marek Nowicki, former ombudsperson in Kosovo, November 28, 2012.

UNMIK, this was never pursued (Waters 2007, 147). Moreover, the institutional features of the Human Rights Advisory Panel fell short with regard to the criteria for pluralist accountability. First, the panel members were appointed by UNMIK's SRSG on the basis of a list of candidates nominated by the European Court of Human Rights. This granted the SRSG veto power in the selection process. Moreover, in contrast to the OIK, whose independence was guaranteed by its close connection to the Council of Europe and the OSCE, the panel was integrated into UNMIK's structure as an advisory organ. This led to tensions between the panel and UNMIK, as the panel considered itself a court while the SRSG would have preferred a purely advisory body.[13]

Second, while the OIK could ex officio investigate any actions of UNMIK, the panel was mandated to examine complaints about alleged human rights abuses by UNMIK on the basis that "all other avenues for review had been exhausted" (Momirov 2012, 11). In cases of claims that had been approved as admissible and in which UNMIK had been deemed responsible for a human rights violation, the panel had to issue a recommendation to the SRSG (UNMIK 2006b; Visoka 2012, 200).[14] These provisions, as well as its quasi-judicial character, prevented the panel from exercising normative sanctioning in the same way as the OIK. Before publication, any statement had to be handled by UNMIK's department of public information:

> We cannot call to the public and fight for our cases. We must express self-restraint, we must deal with cases like the way the Strasbourg court does. We deliver our opinion whether there was a violation or not and provide recommendations. Then it is up to the SRSG and the UN on how they make use of it. I cannot go to the public and say "this is a scandal, the SRSG does not have any intention to compensate people, etc." As an ombudsman of course I could voluntarily, immediately. This is a big difference.[15]

Further restrictions on the panel were introduced later by the SRSG's Administrative Directive 2009/1 (UNMIK 2009). Limitations regarding the admissibility of claims, shorter mandates of panel members, and a cut-off date for complaints (March 31, 2010) were especially criticized as a "demise" of the panel (Momirov 2012, 11; Visoka 2012, 200). The possibility of submitting

[13] Author's telephone interview with Simona Granata-Menghini, Council of Europe, October 22, 2012.

[14] This critique however does not take into account that UNMIK was in a transition phase, transferring authority to EU operation EULEX.

[15] Author's telephone interview with Marek Nowicki, former ombudsperson in Kosovo, November 28, 2012.

complaints was restricted to human rights violations committed between 2005 and 2008, while the greatest extent of UNMIK authority was before 2005, when the majority of complaints could arise (Visoka 2012, 203).

In sum, contrary to the OIK, the Human Rights Advisory Panel was not recognized by UNMIK as an accountability mechanism as originally intended by the Venice Commission's proposal. Instead, the panel can rather be characterized as a complaint mechanism for affected people.[16] Neither the Secretary-General nor the UN Security Council was involved as vertical accountability holders. The "Human Rights Court for Kosovo" as proposed by the Venice Commission was never established.

Only after 2006, when UNMIK detentions no longer played a major role, did UNMIK recognize another accountability holder, the UN Human Rights Council (UNHRC). In 2006, the UNHRC demanded a human rights report from UNMIK on Kosovo as it did from all of its member states. It hereby acknowledged UNMIK's role as a governing authority over Kosovo and declared that it is "bound to respect and to ensure to all individuals within the territory of Kosovo and subject to their jurisdiction the rights recognized in the Covenant" (UN Human Rights Council 2006, para. 4). In a briefing to the Council, Amnesty International emphasized the unlawfulness of executive order detentions and pretrial detentions by UNMIK as well as the lack of right to habeas corpus (Amnesty International 2006a). UNMIK submitted its report in 2006 and thus accepted its own obligations with regard to an external accountability holder (Pacquée and Dewulf 2006, 14).

The UNHRC noted that

> the Covenant was made part of the applicable law in Kosovo, as defined in UNMIK Regulation 1999/1, and amended in UNMIK Regulation 1999/24, *On the Law Applicable in Kosovo*, binding on all persons undertaking public duties or holding public office in Kosovo, and that it was subsequently included in the Constitutional Framework for the Provisional Institutions of Self-Government, promulgated by UNMIK Regulation 2001/9.
>
> (UN Human Rights Council 2006, para. 5)

It especially criticized the lack of formal independence of the Human Rights Advisory Panel (para. 10):

[16] This form of complaint procedure has become increasingly common among IOs (Heupel and Zürn 2017). The panel became a role model in this regard for the EU mission EULEX when taking over great parts of UNMIK's activities after 2008.

> UNMIK should revoke the Regulation conferring power on the Special Representative of the Secretary-General to detain and expel individuals, seek the cessation of detentions under Commander of KFOR Detention Directive 42, and ensure that all persons arrested under the discretionary powers of UNMIK police or under a court order are informed of the reasons for their arrest and of any charges against them, brought promptly before a judicial authority, granted access to a lawyer and to proceedings before a court to determine the lawfulness of their detention, and are tried without undue delay. (UN Human Rights Council 2006, para. 17)

The UNHRC thus responded to UNMIK's high degree of authority by establishing itself as an accountability holder. As preparations for Kosovo's independence continued, however, this no longer had any substantial effect on UNMIK's executive detentions.

Explaining the Evolution of Pluralist Accountability: Competition

The OSCE, which was the main promoter of the establishment of the OIK, had a special role within the international administration in Kosovo. Mandated to protect and promote human rights, the organization itself was part of UNMIK. UNMIK's structure comprised three pillars, with the civil administration under UN leadership, the reconstruction and economic development tasks under the leadership of the EU, and, finally, the democratization and institution-building activities led by the OSCE (Marshall and Inglis 2003, 100).[17] The institutional division of labor between these three institutions in the years 1999–2008 was the most complex interinstitutional relationship of any other previous or later arrangement between IOs. To use principal-agent terminology, there were three agents—with different degrees of independence[18]—mandated by the Secretary-General to implement the civilian components. Despite their common umbrella, UNMIK, the EU, and the OSCE operated in an environment of institutional competition for resources and

[17] This pillar structure existed between 2000 and 2008. Before 2000, there was another pillar on humanitarian assistance led by the UNHCR, which was transformed into a pillar on police and justice under UN leadership (http://www.un.org/peace/kosovo/pages/unmik12.html, last access November 8, 2012). After 2008, the EU took over several tasks from the UN civil administration.

[18] While the OSCE and the EU pillars understood their own headquarters, UNMIK in legal terms remained a subsidiary organ of the UN (Verdirame, 2011, 110).

recognition. Therefore, the OSCE had to develop competences that rendered its role in Kosovo distinct from the other institutions.

Relying on its mandate from the OSCE Permanent Council, the OSCE mission in Kosovo used its expertise to sharpen its profile by acting as an accountability holder regarding UNMIK's detention practices. The OSCE LSMS's outspoken criticism, however, also implied a danger of becoming marginalized within UNMIK's policymaking process (Baldwin 2006, 491; Marshall and Inglis 2003, 141). Advocating for the establishment of the ombudsperson institution, therefore, was an important means for the OSCE to further demonstrate its distinctiveness without marginalizing itself within the UNMIK pillar system.[19]

At the time when the OIK was turned into a national Kosovar institution, the competition among European institutions to act as accountability holders towards UNMIK remained high. The European Court of Human Rights became increasingly concerned that there was a territory within Europe over which the court had no jurisdiction.[20] Since UNMIK was not a treaty party to the European Convention of Human Rights, the court was concerned that there was a population within Europe that could be denied the possibility of judicial appeal. The suggestion to establish a court for Kosovo was an attempt of the Strasbourg human rights institutions to sharpen their profiles as legitimate accountability holders over the UN mission in Kosovo.

However, despite this ongoing competition among international institutions, the Human Rights Advisory Panel did not enhance pluralist accountability. Also, the "big solution" of establishing a human rights court for Kosovo as proposed by the Venice Commission, which would have significantly increased pluralist accountability, was never implemented. Therefore, the competitive environment, which explained why the OIK was developed, cannot explain the absence of pluralist accountability after the nationalization of the OIK. To explain the variance in the accountability regime for UNMIK detentions, I argue that we need to analyze how UNMIK's changing vulnerability influenced the dynamics of pluralist accountability.

[19] "The OSCE were really fighting for it" (author's telephone interview with the former ombudsperson Marek Nowicki, November 28, 2012).

[20] Author's telephone interview with Simona Granata-Menghini, Council of Europe, October 22, 2012.

Explaining the Variance in Pluralist Accountability: Security and UNMIK's Vulnerability

UNMIK's vulnerability with regard to human rights demands was strongly influenced by its (in)ability to invoke the counter-norm of security in order to justify its detention practices. Executive order detentions were not explicitly requested by the UN Security Council or the Secretary-General. Instead, the UN SRSG used his authority in order to interpret his own mandate provided by Resolution 1244, in a way that defined executive detentions as a necessary measure to cope with an emergency situation (UNMIK 1999a). This self-authorization was only possible due to the institutional powers granted to the office of the SRSG, and it fundamentally affected the rights of individuals in Kosovo. The SRSG argued that it was within his executive authority to order the detention of suspects that threatened public security (OSCE 2001, 33). He defended UNMIK's detention policy by pointing out that there was a trade-off between "ensuring human rights and security" in circumstances of emergency. He thus attempted to invoke the counter-norm of security as a shield to reduce the organization's vulnerability regarding any claims that required UNMIK to protect the rights of detainees. Even two years after the mission's deployment, UNMIK framed its legal environment according to an internationally recognized emergency to argue that, "in such circumstances, international human rights standards accept the need for special measures" (Chesterman 2002, 5).

After the early successes of UNMIK and KFOR in establishing a calm and stable security environment in Kosovo, however, it became harder for UNMIK to argue credibly that it was necessary to prioritize security over human rights, since there was no real emergency any longer.[21] Instead, UNMIK's own priorities of promoting the rule of law and justice throughout Kosovo made it increasingly vulnerable to human rights demands. Eventually, the SRSG became aware of UNMIK's vulnerability. In 2001, he outlined the procedural rights of persons arrested by UNMIK police (UNMIK 2001b). When the OSCE continued to highlight UNMIK's human rights responsibility, UNMIK eventually established a Human Rights Oversight Committee as well as an Inter-Pillar Working Group on Human Rights in 2002 (Visoka 2012, 199). The committee was tasked to "consider and agree on actions and policies to enhance human rights protection in Kosovo and ensure that the

[21] Author's telephone interview with Marek Nowicki, former ombudsperson in Kosovo, November 28, 2012.

actions and policies of all UNMIK Pillars and Offices are in compliance with international human rights standards" (Council of Europe 2004b). After three meetings, however, the work of the committee was suspended. The Inter-Pillar Working Group acted as an advisory body to the Human Rights Oversight Committee and was mandated to "review from a human rights perspective draft Regulations and Administrative Directions prepared under the initiative of the UNMIK components" (OSCE 2003, 51). These two reforms thus indicate that UNMIK's leadership was aware of its vulnerability with regard to human rights claims.

As a consequence, when promoting the OIK, the Council of Europe and the OSCE were careful to frame the discourse in such a way as to suggest it was in UNMIK's interest to have an ombudsperson to avoid losing credibility as an organization that promotes the respect for human rights and the rule of law.[22] It was the first time that a UN operation found itself in a situation of operating like a government: "They were not really accustomed to being accused for human rights violations. We explained to them that they were not just a UN mission, but a government with all consequences of this very fact."[23] Therefore, despite UNMIK's attempts to delay the implementation of the OIK by invoking security as a counter-norm, its own vulnerability eventually led the organization to accept pluralist accountability exercised by the OSCE and the Council of Europe and agreed to establish the OIK.

At a time when the OIK was turned into a purely national institution and lost all competences over UNMIK, however, the situation had dramatically changed. In March 2004, an ethnic cleavage between Serbs and Albanians culminated in a violent unrest in Mitrovica in response to the drowning of two Albanian boys. This was regarded as a serious setback for UNMIK and KFOR in terms of their security mandate (Buerstedde 2005, 145). Both organizations were also targets of the unrest, which was the worst violence seen since 1999, with a UN police officer from Ghana being killed. Moreover, both organizations were accused of being unable to react appropriately to the violence and of having failed to effectively protect minorities in Kosovo. Some media headlines even described the outbreak of violence as a pogrom and suggested that the international community did nothing to hinder it. Since the UN's failure to prevent the massacre in Srebrenica was still in everybody's mind, the provision of security immediately became the overarching norm that determined

[22] Author's telephone interview with Christos Giacoumopoulos, Council of Europe, November 26, 2012.

[23] Author's telephone interview with Marek Nowicki, former ombudsperson in Kosovo, November 28, 2012.

UNMIK's success in Kosovo. The Secretary-General in his report to the Security Council warned that "the situation in Kosovo remains tense, and further violence is possible" (United Nations Secretary-General 2004). As a response to the unrest, UNMIK arrested over 260 individuals who were suspected of having been involved in the violence in Mitrovica. Four hundred more were arrested for having violated the curfew imposed in the aftermath of the killings, and seven individuals were detained (United Nations Secretary-General 2004). At this point, all international and local prosecutors had their hands full with investigating the cases and in this state of emergency, the security paradigm was too strong to let respect for the rights of detainees be of significant concern.

Thus, the proposal of the Council of Europe, which attempted to enhance pluralist accountability after the nationalization of the OIK, came at a time when UNMIK's activities were dominated by security concerns. The adoption of the Human Rights Advisory Panel thus became a compromise, as the prospects for a human rights court were minimal. The European organizations argued that the UN needed to have at least a complaint mechanism for an operation within Europe.[24] Therefore, despite the high number of potential external accountability holders, UNMIK's invulnerability regarding human rights demands after 2004 restricted the ability of third parties to hold UNMIK's detention policies accountable.

KFOR Detentions: The Lack of Pluralist Accountability

Compared to UNMIK detentions, NATO's KFOR detention practices affected far more individuals in Kosovo. More than 3,500 people had been detained by 2003 at Camp Bondsteel under US command for an unlimited time period and without judicial review (OSCE 2003, 34). KFOR's detention policy was outlined in the Directive 42 issued by the COMKFOR, which replaced a previous classified detention directive, FRAGO 997.[25] This directive raised major criticisms: the UN Special Representative of the Commission on Human Rights, Jose Cutileiro, pointed out that the COMKFOR Detention Directive 42 "may be incompatible with basic human rights principles" and demanded that existing legal standards should guide KFOR detentions (United Nations

[24] Author's telephone interview with Marek Nowicki, former ombudsperson in Kosovo, November 28, 2012.

[25] COMKFOR Directive 42 as quoted in Amnesty International 2004a; the document is publicly not available.

Human Rights Commission 2002a, 23–4). The extrajudicial character of KFOR detentions and the lack of legal remedy were especially criticized (Amnesty International 2004a, 22; Council of Europe 2002, para. 97-101; OSCE 2001, 2003, 22). While several actors tried to enact pluralist accountability, KFOR made itself invulnerable to human rights demands by successfully invoking the concern for security as a counter-norm. Thus, in the case of KFOR detentions, no comparable system of pluralist accountability evolved. The following sections describe the attempts of pluralist accountability by the OSCE and the Council of Europe and explain how KFOR's invulnerability hindered the emergence of accountability.

Attempts to Enhance Pluralist Accountability by the OSCE and the Council of Europe

Like UNMIK, KFOR was confronted with attempts by the OSCE and the Council of Europe to enhance accountability. Other IOs such as the OHCHR were present in the area but had no comparably significant effect on the accountability system.[26] When developing the terms of reference for the OIK, the experts sent to the country by the Venice Commission of the Council of Europe also met with the COMKFOR. They considered the possibility of introducing a special formula that would have allowed the OIK to have jurisdiction over at least certain aspects of KFOR operations. Moreover, the COMKFOR in office at that time was generally receptive to the idea of an ombudsperson.[27] However, NATO headquarters strictly refused to accept the OIK as having authority over KFOR (Brand 2001, 483). Consequently, the OIK officially only had jurisdiction over UNMIK. Informally, however, the OIK also exercised some monitoring regarding KFOR detentions. The ombudsman visited Camp Bondsteel in 2000 and 2001 to obtain firsthand information about the conditions of detention. Its offices, moreover, served as focal points where people could come and fill in complaint forms, which were then brought to KFOR.[28] Thus, despite the lack of any formal agreement between KFOR and the OIK, the two actors cooperated informally in so

[26] Author's telephone interview with Marek Nowicki, former ombudsperson in Kosovo, November 28, 2012.

[27] Author's telephone interview with Christos Giacoumopoulos, Council of Europe, November 26, 2012.

[28] Author's telephone interview with Marek Nowicki, former ombudsperson in Kosovo, November 28, 2012.

far as the OIK facilitated people's access to KFOR's internal accountability mechanism. This was a result of the smooth personal relationship between the ombudsman and the COMKFOR at that time: "We were on good operational terms."[29] However, the OIK's monitoring activities were quite restricted and, after 2001, the OIK lost access to Camp Bondsteel (United Nations Human Rights Council 2010).

Besides advocating for the OIK, the OSCE mission in Kosovo also tried to exercise standard-setting, monitoring, and sanctioning functions via its LSMS. Due to the fact that it had no authority over KFOR, however, attempts by the OSCE to hold KFOR accountable remained limited in comparison with its role as an accountability holder regarding UNMIK detentions (Marshall and Inglis 2003, 112). The COMKFOR Directive 42 accepted that the OSCE LSMS would monitor detentions (Council of Europe 2002, para. 89). Hence, the OSCE conducted interviews with detainees in KFOR detention facilities and used its public reviews to report on human rights issues in both UNMIK and KFOR detentions (Marshall and Inglis 2003, 140; OSCE 2002, 2003). Already in its early reports, the OSCE provided an interpretation of KFOR's mandate that set clear human rights standards for KFOR detentions, also under Security Council Resolution 1244. The OSCE argued that the resolution required KFOR to support UNMIK in promoting and protecting human rights and that KFOR should "as a minimum, refrain from undermining this objective" (OSCE 2001, 39). With this understanding, the OSCE limited KFOR's own interpretation of Resolution 1244, as outlined under Directive 42, that said "all necessary means" was the only valid standard for detentions. Instead, it argued that KFOR's mandate could only be fulfilled "through compliance with international human rights standards" (OSCE 2001, 39).

In response, KFOR publicly committed itself to these standards. In a message to KFOR troops, the COMKFOR in 2002 stated that "it is our hallowed responsibility to support the process of justice with professionalism and an unfailing respect for human rights. This is our task and I charge you to remember it in everything you do."[30] These standards however were not issued in any sort of binding regulation that would provide an additional legal accountability framework for KFOR detentions.

The continued lack of legal standards also prompted the Council of Europe to try to enhance pluralist accountability. The Commissioner for Human

[29] Author's telephone interview with Marek Nowicki, former ombudsperson in Kosovo, November 28, 2012.

[30] See KFOR 2002: Message from COMKFOR, available at: http://www.nato.int/kfor/chronicle/2002/chronicle_14/01.htm (last access January 31, 2015).

Rights of the Council of Europe, Alvaro Gil-Robles, expressed his concerns about the questionable legality of KFOR detentions and the lack of remedy against unlawful detentions (Council of Europe 2002, para. 97–101). The commissioner was mandated by the Parliamentary Assembly of the Council of Europe to "visit the Federal Republic of Yugoslavia and Kosovo with a fact-finding mission with the aim of examining the human rights and refugee situation in Kosovo on the whole and elaborating appropriate recommendations" (Council of Europe 2002). In the course of his investigation, the Commissioner also visited the Bondsteel detention facility (Council of Europe 2002, para. 89). In his report to the Parliamentary Assembly, the Commissioner warned that "the continuing practice of extrajudicial arrests and detentions undermines the long-term aim of developing an effective independent judiciary in Kosovo" (Council of Europe 2002, para. 102). He pointed out that the degree of exercised authority of both organizations "substantially deviate[s] from international human rights norms and the accepted principles of the rule of law" and criticized KFOR's practice of detaining "individuals for indefinitely renewable periods of 30 days without judicial supervision" (Council of Europe 2002, para. 3). It further underlined the importance of OSCE's monitoring activities (Council of Europe 2002, para. 103).

KFOR thus was confronted by the attempts from other IOs—such as the OSCE and the Council of Europe—to enhance accountability. The OSCE and the Council of Europe positioned themselves as interpretative authorities that stipulated standards for detentions and undertook monitoring activities. Given that neither of the two organizations had jurisdiction over KFOR, the only way of sanctioning was to engage in public normative shaming that linked KFOR's reputation to the respect for human rights when detaining individuals. In its public reports, the OSCE went so far as to demand that "KFOR cease[d] detentions forthwith and officially renounce[d] its authority in this area" (OSCE 2003, 34). This was a strong claim from an organization that was formally part an implementing partner of KFOR. NGOs such as Amnesty International supported this demand. In a memorandum of October 2003 to NATO, individual KFOR member states and the UN Department of Peacekeeping Operations, Amnesty International criticized the "lack of accountability" of KFOR troops and the lack of a lawful basis for KFOR detentions, thus also engaging in normative sanctioning (Amnesty International 2004a).

KFOR's reactions indicate that the OSCE, the Council of Europe, and even the OIK were recognized as accountability holders by KFOR at least to some degree. In response to their normative sanctioning, KFOR adopted another internal complaint mechanism. Through its Standard Operating Procedure 3023 of March 22, 2003, KFOR established a claims office to which claims against the KFOR headquarters structure could be addressed. If KFOR was able to justify its actions (or omissions) on the basis of "operational necessity," it was relieved of liability.[31] Claims against individual KFOR nations had to be addressed with the respective state, which then bore the sole responsibility for investigating and adjudicating claims. The document was not binding but instead only proposed some procedures that KFOR contributing states and the claims office could adopt for adjudicating claims.[32] Because of the good working relationship with the OIK, the latter was implicitly accepted as a monitoring institution that collected and forwarded claims to KFOR.[33]

In sum, the attempts described above did not amount to pluralist accountability, even if they led to the development of complaint mechanisms. KFOR continued to refuse to officially recognize the OIK and, after 2001, denied the Council of Europe's Committee on the Prevention of Torture access to its detention facilities (Council of Europe 2007). When the Human Rights Advisory Panel was established, it did not obtain jurisdiction over KFOR, although this was strongly advocated for by the Council of Europe's Parliamentary Assembly (Council of Europe Parliamentary Assembly 2006a). Only after 2007 did KFOR accept external monitoring. The Council of Europe's Committee on Torture was permitted to visit detention centers for the first time, after a long-negotiated agreement was concluded with NATO in July 2006 that allowed the monitoring of KFOR detention facilities as well (Council of Europe 2007).[34] At that time, however, KFOR detentions were no longer regarded as a problem. Moreover, the agreement stipulated that the findings from the monitoring were to be published only with UNMIK and NATO's consent, which rendered normative sanctioning through public criticism impossible (Human Rights Watch 2007). Additionally, KFOR established a Kosovo Claims Office in 2007 because the organization felt "obliged to create a procedure of third party claims to be provided for."[35] The Kosovo Claims Office can compensate victims of KFOR wrongdoings after investigating incoming complaints; usually, however, the office forwarded complaints to

[31] The standard operating procedure as quoted in Pacquée and Dewulf 2006, 9.

[32] The standard operating procedure as quoted in Pacquée and Dewulf 2006, 9.

[33] Author's telephone interview with Marek Nowicki, former ombudsperson in Kosovo, November 28, 2012.

[34] With UNMIK, a monitoring agreement had already been concluded in August 2004, but was not implemented due to the ongoing negotiations with KFOR (Council of Europe 2004a).

[35] See http://www.nato.int/kfor/chronicle/2001/nr_010629d.htm (last access November 15, 2011).

the respective national claims offices of troop-contributing countries, often without further consequences. Thus, despite increasing avenues for complaints, accountability remained limited in the case of KFOR detentions. How can this lack of pluralist accountability be explained?

It's NATO, Stupid! Explaining the Lack of Pluralist Accountability

Most of the interviewees, when asked why KFOR was not held accountable by third parties, answered, "well, you know, it's NATO." But what characteristics of NATO hindered the exercise of pluralist accountability in the case of KFOR detentions? This section demonstrates that, although a competitive environment triggered attempts by the OSCE and the Council of Europe to act as accountability holders, KFOR's invulnerability with regard to human rights demands explains why pluralist accountability remained limited.

The competitive institutional environment that characterized the operation in Kosovo, as described in the UNMIK case study above, also triggered attempts to ensure pluralist accountability regarding KFOR detentions. Of course, the relationship of the OSCE to KFOR was different from its relationship to UNMIK, as the military operation was not part of UNMIK's institutional pillar structure. Despite the different mandates, however, the institutional overlap among all the organizations operating under Resolution 1244 required each organization to find its niche in order to gain visibility (Brosig 2011). All three organizations—the OSCE, UNMIK, and KFOR—were tasked with building up a national police force in Kosovo, thus, they had to find ways to make themselves distinct from each other. In this competitive environment, the OSCE enhanced its visibility by becoming the leading monitoring organization over the two main competitors in Kosovo, which had both authorized themselves as detaining authorities on the basis of UN Security Council Resolution 1244. This included attempts to increase civilian control over the military, for example, by trying to enlarge the OIK's mandate to also monitor KFOR. When NATO refused to subject KFOR to the authority of the OIK, the OSCE increased its own monitoring activities via its LSMS. Therefore, due to the institutional setting, the competition that characterized UNMIK's environment also triggered attempts to exercise accountability in the case of KFOR detentions. Competition, however, cannot explain why pluralist accountability was limited in the latter case.

KFOR's invulnerability with regard to human rights demands is the crucial factor that determined the exercise of pluralist accountability regarding KFOR detentions. From the beginning of the operation, KFOR emphasized security as a priority that guided all its actions. It thus invoked security as a counter-norm to make itself immune to human rights demands. This becomes obvious in KFOR's interpretation of Resolution 1244. The COMKFOR determined in Directive 42 of October 9, 2001 that detentions could be ordered if the suspects "constitute a threat to KFOR or a safe and secure environment in Kosovo and civilian authorities are unable or unwilling to take responsibility for the matter" (Section 4a, as quoted in Amnesty International 2004a, 21). Although the COMKFOR emphasized that "no one shall be subjected to arbitrary detention," the directive determined that its "authority to detain is a military decision, not a judicial one" (Section 2e). KFOR, thus, did not try to justify detentions legally. Instead, the organization provided a justification that considered extrajudicial detentions to be a necessary means for the successful implementation of the security-related aspects of its mandate, provided by the Security Council Resolution 1244.[36] KFOR thus referred to security as a priority of its mandate to successfully block any external monitoring mechanism that would not be under KFOR control. The prioritization of security enabled KFOR to make itself immune to any human rights demands. Although a great deal of public attention was directed to KFOR detentions (Marshall and Inglis 2003, 110), the military logic on which the COMKFOR based its argumentation helped KFOR to refuse recognition of the OIK as an instrument of pluralist accountability exercised by the OSCE and the Council of Europe.

In this process of norm contestation, in which security was juxtaposed with detainees' rights, UNMIK supported KFOR's view. UNMIK's SRSG Sérgio Vieira de Mello justified KFOR's authority to detain civilians for an unlimited period of time on the basis of security concerns. In Regulation 2000/47, the SRSG stated that "[a]ll KFOR personnel shall respect the laws applicable in the territory of Kosovo and regulations issued by the Special Representative of the Secretary-General *insofar as they do not conflict with the fulfilment of the mandate* given to KFOR under Security Council resolution 1244 (1999)" (UNMIK 2000b, emphasis added). UNMIK's leadership thus sided with KFOR in prioritizing security over human rights demands in the context of detentions.

[36] See the press releases by KFOR in 2002 (available at: http://www.nato.int/kfor/docu/pr/2002/08/34-08.htm, last access January 31, 2015) and 2004 (available at: http://www.nato.int/kfor/docu/pr/2004/05/28.htm, last access January 31, 2015).

The decision by the European Court of Human Rights in the Behrami and Saramati case of 2007 cemented KFOR's invulnerability in legal jurisdiction. In this decision, the court argued that "KFOR was exercising lawfully delegated Chapter VII powers of the UN Security Council" and that any conditions on the implementation of operations had to be imposed by the Security Council itself, which was outside of the court's jurisdiction (European Court of Human Rights 2007, para. 141, 151).[37] Due to the direct attribution of actions to the UN, KFOR itself could not be held judicially accountable by the court and did not face any legal sanctioning, even if KFOR exercised effective command and operational control (Pejic 2011). By attributing KFOR's actions to the UN Security Council, which under Chapter VII of the UN Charter could provide for the use of "coercive measures" (para. 149), the court acknowledged that any implementation activities needed to be considered in light of the operation's mandate and declared the claims of Behrami and Saramati against KFOR troop-contributing countries inadmissible. The court at that time thus shied away from setting a precedent and did not push for further pluralist accountability.[38] This decision left the human rights community "outraged" but without any means of imposing human rights as a norm for KFOR detentions and holding KFOR externally accountable.[39]

That the court would so strongly support KFOR's invulnerability was not clear before. Legal scholars had argued earlier that KFOR was not operating in a "legal vacuum" (Cerone 2001). Other court decisions, such as by the British High Court in 2004, had attributed the damages caused in the implementation of a peace operation to the respective troop contributing member country (Amnesty International 2004a). With this decision, it had become clear that security would not always continue to trump human rights. Individual contributing countries thus realized that they would become increasingly vulnerable to human rights demands when implementing detentions. Under the leadership of the Danish government, the Copenhagen Process on the Handling of Detainees in multilateral peace operations was launched (Hirschmann 2016; Winkler 2010). In this consultative process, contributing countries,

[37] European Court of Human Rights 2007: Grand Chamber Decision, Strasbourg, May 2, 2007, available at http://hudoc.echr.coe.int/sites/eng/pages/search.aspx?i=001-80830 (last access January 31, 2015).

[38] This stands in stark contrast to the court's active role as an accountability holder in the issue area of UN sanctions (Heupel, 2013). The more recent Al-Jedda jurisdiction to a certain degree revised the previous decision (Messineo, 2009). Here, the court argued that a Security Council resolution had to be interpreted that it did not mandate the implementing agents to act outside or above the law (Pejic 2011; Trenkov-Wermuth, 2010, 74; UK Supreme Court Al-Jedda decision, available at: http://www.bailii.org/uk/cases/UKSC/2013/62.html, last access January 31, 2015).

[39] Author's telephone interview with Jelena Pejic, ICRC, September 18, 2012.

together with UN and NATO representatives as well as experts from the ICRC, developed detention guidelines on the basis of international humanitarian law and international and domestic human rights law. Nevertheless, this process did not create any pluralist accountability mechanism let alone legally binding standards.

Conclusion

The operation in Kosovo, which was launched in 1999 by UN Security Council Resolution 1244, was one of the most complex and authoritative operations in the UN's peacekeeping history. The Security Council established a transitional administration under UN leadership (UNMIK) and asked NATO to deploy a military operation (KFOR). In the course of the implementation, both UNMIK and KFOR detained numerous individuals who they deemed to be security threats. Detainees were held for unlimited periods of time, without having the option to be heard by an independent judiciary or even to notify their families. Through these detention practices, UNMIK and KFOR violated fundamental human rights and the right to due process.

In this chapter I analyzed the accountability regimes that evolved in response to these human rights violations and explored the conditions under which third parties acted as accountability holders. In both cases, there was no significant vertical accountability mechanism provided at the outset of the delegation relationship that could be enacted by the mandating authority. The two case studies, however, fundamentally differed regarding the evolution of pluralist accountability after the human rights violations became public. While in the case of UNMIK, the OSCE and the Council of Europe acted as accountability holders and established the OIK, a lack of pluralist accountability characterized the case of KFOR.

What explains this difference in pluralist accountability? The competitive environment stimulated third parties, in particular the OSCE, to sharpen their profile by engaging in standard-setting, monitoring, and sanctioning activities. Third parties even made some attempts to act as accountability holders in the KFOR case. Only the difference between UNMIK's and KFOR's vulnerability with regard to human rights demands can explain why pluralist accountability evolved in UNMIK's case but not in the case of KFOR. Both organizations tried to render their detention policies invulnerable to human rights demands by invoking the concern for security as a counter-norm. UNMIK, however, was less successful in this endeavor: its mandate to promote the rule of law throughout Kosovo made it particularly vulnerable to human rights demands, especially since the situation in Kosovo became rather stable after 2001. The discrepancy between UNMIK's mandate and its detention practices made it impossible for UNMIK to prioritize security over human rights, at least in the years before the outbreak of violence in Mitrovica in 2004. UNMIK's high degree of authority, which effectively allowed the SRSG to run the whole country on its own, increased its vulnerability. Acting like a government entailed certain human rights responsibilities: this was the argument of third parties, who wanted UNMIK to recognize external accountability holders.

In contrast to UNMIK, KFOR successfully invoked security as a counter-norm to legitimize its detention practices. The COMKFOR argued that extra-judicial detentions were necessary for the successful implementation of the security-related aspects of KFOR's mandate provided by Resolution 1244. KFOR thus made itself invulnerable to human rights demands. "It's NATO, stupid!" characterizes this invulnerability, which allowed KFOR to refuse any pluralist accountability.

6

Pluralist Accountability in Times of Economic Crisis

The Troika Austerity Measures and Their Effect on Human Rights in Greece, Ireland, and Portugal

Introduction

The response of states and IOs to the economic and financial crisis of 2007 raised concerns about the effects of economic policies, in particular the so-called austerity measures, on human rights.[1] These measures were adopted in response to massive public debt that led countries to fall into recession when the financial bubble burst and banks collapsed. Some of the most prominent examples are the measures that were implemented by EU member state governments under the auspices of the "Troika," which is comprised of the European Commission, the IMF, and the European Central Bank (ECB). Greece, Ireland, and Portugal were among the first countries to resort to international borrowing in order to bail out their banking sectors and avoid financial bankruptcy. They each agreed to a Memorandum of Understanding (MoU) with the Troika for financial assistance under the condition that they significantly reduced their public spending and fundamentally restructured their economies.[2]

Setting aside the question about whether these measures constituted appropriate economic responses to the crisis, their effects on human rights has

[1] United Nations 2013: Report of the United Nations High Commissioner for Human Rights on Austerity Measures and Economic and Social Rights, available at: https://www.ohchr.org/Documents/Issues/Development/RightsCrisis/E-2013-82_en.pdf (last access October 9, 2018); United Nations Human Rights Council, Reports of the Independent Expert, UN doc. A/HRC/25/50/Add.1.

[2] See Greece. Memorandum of Understanding on Specific Economic Policy Conditionality, August 6, 2010, available at https://www.imf.org/external/np/loi/2010/grc/080610.pdf (last access October 8, 2018); Portugal. Memorandum of Understanding on Specific Economic Policy Conditionality, May 17, 2011, available at: https://www.imf.org/external/np/loi/2011/prt/051711.pdf (last access October 8, 2018); Portugal. Memorandum of Understanding on Specific Economic Policy Conditionality. First Review Update, September 1, 2011, available at: http://www.imf.org/external/pubs/ft/scr/2011/cr11279.pdf (last access October 8, 2018).

Accountability in Global Governance. Gisela Hirschmann, Oxford University Press (2020). © Gisela Hirschmann.
DOI: 10.1093/oso/9780198861249.001.0001

become a matter of serious concern (Fischer-Lescano 2014; O'Connell 2013; Salomon 2015). These measures implied immense budgetary cuts in governmental social security, education, and healthcare spending as well as structural reforms of the labor markets and pension systems (Correia et al. 2015; Dowell-Jones 2015; Kentikelenis et al. 2014; Nolan 2015). As a consequence, a significant proportion of the population was deprived of access to basic health services, medicine and social security, education, and suffered from welfare and pension cuts. This not only led to a significant rise in unemployment but also to an increase in child mortality, suicides, and poverty in the affected countries. In Greece, for example, the rate of child mortality rose by 40 percent and HIV infections increased by 52 percent in the aftermath of the crisis (Stuckler and Basu 2010), while in Portugal some schools could not start the new academic year as there were not enough funds to hire teachers (Canotilho 2015). This stands in stark contrast to a state's obligations to ensure individuals' fundamental social and economic rights as provided by the International Covenant on Economic, Social and Cultural Rights, in particular Articles 6–8 and 11–13 on the right to work, the right to health, the right to education, and the right to adequate living standards (Kilpatrick and De Witte 2014; Nolan and Dutschke 2010).

While the Troika institutions are not members of the Covenant and can therefore not be held legally responsible for individuals' human rights deprivations, researchers have argued that the Troika should be held accountable for imposing such measures on national governments (Dawson 2015; Fischer-Lescano 2014; Poulou 2014; Salomon 2015). This chapter analyzes how pluralist accountability evolved with regard to the Troika's austerity policies. Between 2011 and 2016, important international and domestic actors, notably the European Parliament (EP), the Council of Europe, and the Portuguese Constitutional Court, established themselves as accountability holders. They determined social and political rights to be relevant standards that had to be respected in the implementation of austerity measures, monitored the actions of the Troika and the implementing member states with regard to these standards, and sanctioned violations.

In line with the theoretical framework proposed in Chapter 2, my analysis reveals that two conditions foster the development of pluralist accountability. First, accountability holders in pluralist accountability are motivated by a competitive environment to engage in standard setting, monitoring, or sanctioning and thereby develop a distinct profile. The second factor that contributes to the development of pluralist accountability is the degree of vulnerability of the mandating authority and/or the implementing actors with regard to human rights demands. I show that while competition stimulated third parties to engage in accountability functions, the varying degree of vulnerability of the different Troika institutions explains the differences in pluralist accountability across these institutions.

I first outline the complex governance scheme that characterized the EU's response to the financial crisis and demonstrate the lack of accountability at the outset of the adoption of the austerity measures. Thereafter, I analyze how pluralist accountability was enacted by European institutions, in particular, and at the domestic level. I then analyze the conditions that triggered the development of pluralist accountability, namely the degree of competition that potential accountability holders were facing and the degree of vulnerability of the mandating and implementing actors. I conclude this chapter by summarizing the findings and the distinct features of this case study in relation to the theoretical framework of the book.

The EU's Response to the Crisis: High Authority with Limited Vertical Accountability

In May 2010, the European Council adopted the first "rescue package" to prevent the bankruptcy of Greece and to provide its government with the financial means to stabilize its banking sector.[3] It also established the "Troika" composed of the European Commission, the ECB, and the IMF as an ad hoc response mechanism to the financial crisis in the Eurozone to provide financial support to and bail out countries that would otherwise go bankrupt (Henning 2017).[4] The Troika assessed the economic and financial situation of the applicant country and concluded an MoU with each government. Usually, the European Commission, representing the Troika, negotiated these MoUs, which were approved thereafter by the IMF and the ECB (Bauer and Becker 2014). Following the MoU, the countries received financial assistance under the condition that they comply with the requirements set in these agreements. In the years after the crisis outbreak, five Eurozone member states received this

[3] See Greece. Memorandum of Understanding on Specific Economic Policy Conditionality, August 6, 2010, available at https://www.imf.org/external/np/loi/2010/grc/080610.pdf (last access October 8, 2018).

[4] See the European Council additional paragraph for Art. 136 of TEU in 2010 decision: "3. The Member States whose currency is the euro may establish a stability mechanism to be activated if indispensable to safeguard the stability of the euro area as a whole. The granting of any required financial assistance under the mechanism will be made subject to strict conditionality" (EUCO 30/1/10 REV 1, ANNEX I).

conditional financial assistance, some of them even several times: Greece and Ireland in 2010, Portugal in 2011, Spain in 2012, and Cyprus in 2013.[5]

To systematize the international assistance in response to the crisis, the primary mechanism of financial assistance since 2013 has become the European Stability Mechanism (ESM) (Rittberger 2014, 1174; Ruffert 2011, 1783). It replaced the European Financial Stabilization Mechanism and the European Financial Stability Facility, which had been established outside the EU's legal framework under the European Council Regulation No. 407/2010 (Curtin 2014, 11). The ESM is based on an intergovernmental treaty, the Treaty on Stability, Coordination and Governance in the Economic and Monetary Union, and is situated with a permanent secretariat in Luxemburg.[6] The eighteen member states can apply to the ESM for financial assistance. The Troika supervised the implementation of the financial assistance by the European Council and later by the ESM, and hereby defined the terms of the last step of the delegation relationship, that is, the conditions attached to the austerity programs (Bauer and Becker 2014) (see Figure 6.1).

In this complex governance arrangement, the high degree of authority of the Troika has become rather contested by the populations of the countries receiving financial assistance. Even if the European Commission and ECB emphasized that the decision-making power rested within the ESM board of governors, the Troika acted at a high level of discretion when negotiating and implementing the MoU (Rittberger 2014, 1178). It decided which financial and economic adjustments should be made, and it monitored how the implementing countries complied with the MoU requirements (Bauer and Becker

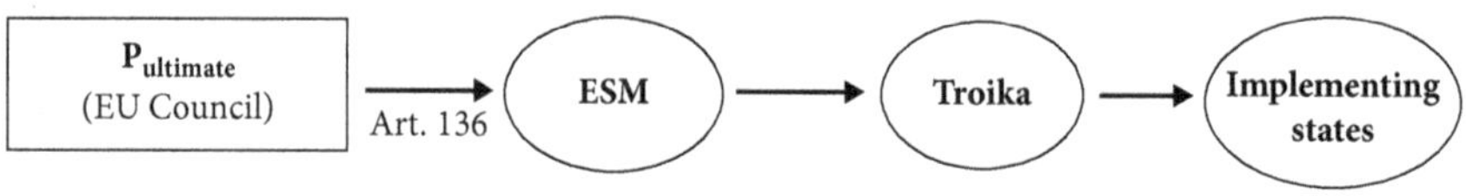

Figure 6.1 Troika delegation relationship (post-2013). The European Council, by amending Article 136 of the Treaty on the Functioning of the European Union, allowed the Eurozone member states to establish the European Stability Mechanism. The implementation of the program adopted by the European Stability Mechanism was monitored by the Troika, which defined the conditions for implementation by the respective member states.

[5] The MoU concluded between the Troika and Spain focused on reforming the banking sector only (http://ec.europa.eu/economy_finance/eu_borrower/mou/2012-07-20-spain-mou_en.pdf). Non-Eurozone members such as Hungary, Latvia, and Romania concluded agreements for financial assistance with a different Troika, i.e., the IMF, the European Commission, and the World Bank.

[6] See https://www.esm.europa.eu (last access October 8, 2018).

2014; de las Casas, 2016). The Troika was permanently present in the countries through a team of experts, and several European Council and Eurogroup member states became concerned about its independence (da Conceição-Heldt 2016). In the domestic public debates of member states, the Troika has been perceived as a powerful institution that has the authority to control a country's budget (Dawson 2015, 982).[7] Thus, the austerity measures are generally considered by the affected populations as being "imposed" or "prescribed" by the Troika as conditions attached to the financial assistance, even if the respective member state actually implemented the austerity measures (Cisotta and Gallo 2014, 2; Sapir et al. 2014). As a consequence, the question of how the Troika was held accountable has become increasingly prominent (Dawson 2015).

Which accountability mechanisms were available within the institutional structure of the delegation relationship to hold the implementing states and the Troika accountable for the effect of austerity measures on human rights? The ESM was established on the basis of an international legal framework that existed outside the EU. Therefore, potential institutional accountability mechanisms within the EU were unavailable (Ginsborg 2017). The European Court of Justice as a legal sanctioning mechanism, for example, was not allowed to deal with the ESM as the latter did not fall under its jurisdiction as provided by Article 273 of the Treaty on the Functioning of the European Union. Moreover, even if the principals of the Troika institutions—the ESM board of governors, the European Council, and the IMF board—retained the authority to approve and monitor the individual Troika member's decisions, the ability of these accountability holders to sanction was severely limited. The IMF board received the decisions too late in order to reject the agreements concluded by the Troika (da Conceição-Heldt 2016; de las Casas 2016). Moreover, the ECB remained outside of the European Council and Parliament's sanctioning capacity (da Conceição-Heldt 2016, 126). Thus, the institutional checks and balances in the aftermath of the crisis were insufficient in light of the complexity and intrusiveness of the responses to the crisis (Dawson 2015).

Besides the lack of institutional monitoring and sanctioning mechanisms, there were also no human rights standards established to guide the implementation

[7] The Independent 2013: Greece Crisis: The Troika's Inflexibility on Austerity Amounts to Nothing Short of an Attempted Coup, available at http://www.independent.co.uk/voices/comment/greece-crisis-the-troika-s-inflexibility-on-austerity-amounts-to-nothing-short-of-an-attempted-coup-10363749.html (last access October 8, 2018); Financial Times 2013: Troika Challenges Greece over 2 Billion Fiscal Gap in Budget, October 17, 2013, available at http://www.ft.com/intl/cms/s/0/06f26484-3707-11e3-9603-00144feab7de.html#axzz32LhERIjo (last access October 8, 2018).

of the austerity policies. In the Treaty on Stability, Coordination and Governance in the Economic and Monetary Union, which provided the basis for the ESM and the Troika's crisis-management activities, the parties were "committed to ensuring the financial stability of the euro area" without any reference to socioeconomic rights.[8] As a consequence, any monitoring activities focused only on the treaty's aspects related to financial stability and how the money was spent and not with regard to human rights-related aspects. The European Commission and the Greek government, for example, agreed to set up a "Taskforce Greece for technical assistance" in 2011 that reported to the Commission and the European Council about the progress in implementing the MoU and macro-economic implications, but not about the effect of the MoU conditions on human rights (Dowell-Jones 2015, 8).[9] Only much later, in 2015, did the Commission conduct an assessment of the social impact of the Troika measures in Greece.[10] Vertical accountability, thus, was mostly limited to the question whether the individual aspects of the delegation contract were implemented in line with the mandate and the desired objectives outlined by the mandating authority.

The Evolution of Pluralist Accountability Regarding the Troika's Impact on Human Rights

In the early years after the crisis, human rights issues mattered mostly in relation to the effect of the crisis itself, not with regard to the institutional measures installed as a response to the crisis (Ivanković Tamamović 2015).[11] However, domestic and international actors became increasingly concerned about the impact of the Troika austerity measures on human rights in the

[8] See ESM Treaty—consolidated version 2012, available at: https://www.esm.europa.eu/legal-documents/esm-treaty (last access October 9, 2018).

[9] See the review reports at: https://ec.europa.eu/info/business-economy-euro/economic-and-fiscal-policy-coordination/eu-financial-assistance_en (last access October 9, 2018).

[10] European Commission 2015: Assessment of the Social Impact of the New Stability Support Programme for Greece, Commission Staff Working Document SWD(2015) 162 final, available at: https://ec.europa.eu/info/sites/info/files/ecfin_assessment_social_impact_en.pdf (last access October 9, 2018).

[11] See the European Parliament Special Committee on the Financial, Economic and Social Crisis 2012: Documentation Relating to the Committee's Work from October 2009 to July 2011, available at: http://www.europarl.europa.eu/document/activities/cont/201109/20110901ATT25750/20110901ATT25750EN.pdf (last access May 28, 2018); European Parliament Committee on Social Affairs, Health and Sustainable Development, The Young Generation Sacrificed: Social, Economic and Political Implications of the Financial Crisis, E.P. Doc. 12951, June 8, 2012; European Commission Director-General for Employment, Social Affairs and Inclusion, Young People in the Crisis, Research Note 5/2012, November 2012.

years between 2011 and 2016 in particular, and a network of pluralist accountability evolved. Three independent institutions started to hold the Troika and the implementing states accountable for human rights: the Council of Europe and the EP at the European level, as well as the Portuguese Constitutional Court at the domestic level. Other IOs, in particular the International Labor Organization, also undertook some monitoring.

None of these institutions had participated in the establishment of the Troika or the implementation of the austerity measures. The EP, although a core EU institution, was not involved in the decision-making process that led to the financial assistance to a number of Eurozone countries. In the EU's institutional response to the crisis, the EP was not mentioned in the ESM treaty at all and was sidelined in the process of the Troika establishment (Dawson 2015, 989). Therefore, in line with the conceptual framework of this study, these institutions are external actors to the complex delegation relationship described above. Crucially, they started to engage in standard setting, monitoring, and sanctioning on their own initiative rather than on behalf of the mandating authority, thereby establishing a network of pluralist accountability regarding the Troika's effect on human rights. This pluralist accountability remained the Troika's only accountability framework, with limited vertical accountability mechanisms.

As I show below, accountability holders targeted individual members of the Troika rather than the Troika as a whole. Thus, the accountability regime differed across the three Troika institutions: the European Commission, the ECB, and the IMF. At the same time, even if the Troika was asked to account as a collective institution, the three Troika members did not recognize external accountability holders to the same degree. While the European Commission became increasingly inclined to recognize the standard-setting, monitoring, and sanctioning activities of pluralist accountability holders, the ECB and the IMF, in particular, mostly refused to be held accountable by these actors. Moreover, pluralist accountability at the domestic level differed across the three countries under a similar austerity program. Pluralist accountability was particularly strong in Portugal whereas it remained comparably limited in the other two countries (Greece and Ireland). The case study of this chapter thus reveals an interesting variation in the dynamics of pluralist accountability.

Pluralist Accountability by the Council of Europe

The Council of Europe had been investigating complaints about the effect of austerity measures on human rights against individual member states since 2011 and was the first international actor to engage in standard setting, monitoring, and sanctioning. The Parliamentary Assembly of the Council of Europe, in its debate in June 2012, adopted Resolution 1884, in which it expressed concern about "the impact of current austerity programmes on democratic and social rights standards." It further argued that the European Social Charter should be taken as the "main reference" when implementing austerity policies and called on its member states to monitor "their short- and long-term impact on democratic decision-making processes and social rights standards."[12] The Parliamentary Assembly thus established human rights as standards to be respected in the implementation of the Troika's austerity measures.

The European Committee of Social Rights also exercised accountability functions. This committee is responsible for monitoring the implementation of the European Social Charter, a treaty of the Council of Europe. It has become the main complaint body for individuals and groups of individuals (for example, workers' unions) claiming that their rights have been violated by austerity measures (Kilpatrick and De Witte 2014, 6). The committee asserted that the member states implementing austerity measures had to respect the European Social Charter regardless of the exceptional nature of the crisis (Nolan 2015, 12). In various decisions on complaints, in particular from Greece and Portugal, the committee ruled that the austerity measures violated important rights guaranteed by the Charter, for example, the right to social assistance and the right to fair remuneration (Canotilho 2015, 67; Poulou 2014, 1164). However, the complaints targeted the implementing member states, not directly the Troika.[13] Moreover, due to weaknesses in its communication strategies, its influence remained limited in comparison with the vocal advocacy of the Commissioner for Human Rights.[14]

The Council of Europe Commissioner for Human Rights, Nils Muižnieks, was "at the forefront of the defense of rights against austerity" (Ivanković Tamamović 2015, 11). The Commissioner undertook important monitoring activities: he visited individual countries and reported on the effect of austerity

[12] Council of Europe Parliamentary Assembly 2012: Resolution 1884 "Austerity measures—a danger for democracy and social rights," Doc. 12948, Strasbourg, available at: http://assembly.coe.int/nw/xml/XRef/Xref-XML2HTML-en.asp?fileid=18916&lang=en (last access October 9, 2018).

[13] See, e.g., *GENOP-DEI/ADEDY* v. *Greece*, Complaint No. 66/2011, May 23, 2012; *IKA-ETAM* v. *Greece*, Complaint No. 76/2012 and the Decisions of the ECSR on Portugal between 2010 and 2014, available at http://hudoc.esc.coe.int/eng?i=2010/def/PRT/4/1/EN.

[14] "This could have been the Social Charter's moment. But the European Social Charter is such an ossified, non-communicative structure, that it missed the boat. This could've been a moment for them to renew themselves and to advertise themselves and to say, We are the standard for social rights here in Europe. But they didn't do that very well" (author's telephone interview with the former Council of Europe Commissioner for Human Rights, Nils Muižnieks, July 2, 2018).

measures on human rights in several reports on Ireland in 2011, Portugal in 2012, and Spain in 2013.[15] In 2013, the commissioner published a policy paper entitled "Safeguarding Human Rights in Times of Economic Crisis."[16] This became the first conceptual framework through which to monitor the effect of austerity measures on human rights: "The EU was pushing some problematic policies without thinking about the consequences. We needed to document those consequences to help defend human rights and give tools to advocates, but also to countries that were trying to resist bad policy being imposed upon them."[17] This issue paper also became very important for member states to counter further austerity demands by the European institutions. In a conversation with the Commissioner, the Minister of Social Welfare of Greece "pulled out the issue paper and said this is my shield against the European Commission, when they are trying to impose more cuts on me in socially sensitive areas."[18] More than any other institution at that time, the Commissioner thus had established human rights as the standard to be respected when implementing austerity measures. This stimulated the accountability functions exercised later by the EP (Ivanković Tamamović 2015, 11).

Pluralist Accountability by the European Parliament

The adoption of the Lisbon Treaty in 2010 initially had raised hopes that EU governance would become more accountable, in particular, by empowering the EP to hold the European Commission accountable (Wille 2010, 1094). The Lisbon Treaty indeed made the EP an important player in the appointment process of the European Commission and prescribed that the European Council and the ECB regularly report to the EP and its committees, such as the Economic and Monetary Affairs Committee (ECON) (Curtin 2014, 26). However, it became clear during the crisis that regarding the EU's economic governance, the role of the EP had been effectively reduced to its characteristics of "pre-Lisbon" times (Dawson 2015, 990). This was partly due to the divide between Eurozone and non-Eurozone countries that became

[15] The reports are available at https://rm.coe.int/16806db80a (last access October 9, 2018).

[16] Council of Europe Commissioner for Human Rights 2013: "Safeguarding Human Rights in Times of Economic Crisis," issue paper published by the Council of Europe Commissioner for Human Rights, Strasbourg: Council of Europe, available at: http://www.enetenglish.gr/resources/article-files/prems162913_gbr_1700_safeguardinghumanrights_web.pdf (last access October 9, 2018).

[17] Author's telephone interview with the former Council of Europe Commissioner for Human Rights, Nils Muižnieks, July 2, 2018.

[18] Author's telephone interview with the former Council of Europe Commissioner for Human Rights, Nils Muižnieks, July 2, 2018.

increasingly apparent during the crisis: the EP is composed of representatives from all EU member states whereas the financial assistance was targeted to Eurozone countries only.

This lack of EP involvement was criticized by members of parliament.[19] However, at the same time, the parliament initially "allowed itself to be sucked into the secretive vortex of closed-door 'negotiations' on legislation" and did not challenge the European Commission or the ECB in hearings (Curtin 2014, 29). The only attempt of accountability by the EP was a resolution in 2012 entitled "Towards a genuine EMU," in which the EP stated that the "social consequences of the crisis have now been exacerbated by the austerity measures" and "called upon the EC to ensure that implementation of troika measures are compatible with employment and poverty reduction targets of Europe 2020."[20] The resolution also proposed that the Eurogroup president and representatives of the European Commission should regularly report to and appear before the EP.[21] Other than that, "parliamentary control and political accountability towards the European Parliament [was] non-existent in the ESM" (Ruffert 2011, 1790).

Over the years, however, the EP became an important accountability holder toward the Troika (Cisotta 2017, 287). An "increasing number of petitions and complaints" about the Troika was forwarded to the EP by the European Ombudsman.[22] In two resolutions in 2013, the EP expressed its concern about the effect of austerity measures on social rights and demanded the European Commission to evaluate the effects of its policies.[23] Several parliamentary committees engaged in standard setting, monitoring, and sanctioning. The Committee on Constitutional Affairs argued that the Troika, as all EU institutions, was obliged to act in accordance with the Charter of Fundamental Rights of the EU (Salomon 2015, 534). This was one of the first standard-setting activities by the EP that referred to human rights as the standards to be respected when implementing austerity measures. This was

[19] European Voice 2011: MEPs Seek Greater Role in Tackling Eurozone Debt Crisis, September 11, 2011, available at: https://www.politico.eu/article/meps-seek-greater-role-in-tackling-eurozone-debt-crisis/ (last access October 9, 2018).

[20] European Parliament 2012: Resolution "Towards a Genuine EMU," EP doc. 2012/2151 (INI).

[21] European Parliament 2012: Resolution "Towards a Genuine EMU," EP doc. 2012/2151 (INI), recommendation 4.4.

[22] The European Ombudsman forwarded these complaints as a petition to the EP in 2012, "in light of the complexity" of the issue, see the European Ombudsman 2012: Decision on Complaint 973/2012/ANA, November 7, 2012, para. 35, available at: https://www.ombudsman.europa.eu/en/decision/en/12113 (last access October 9, 2018).

[23] See the Resolution on the impact of the crisis on access to care for vulnerable groups, July 4, 2013, EP doc. A7/0221-2013, and the Resolution on effects of budgetary constraints for regional and local authorities regarding the EU's Structural Funds expenditure in the Member States, October 8, 2013, EP doc. A7/0269-2013.

followed by increased monitoring and sanctioning by three parliamentary committees, ECON, the Committee on Employment and Social Affairs (EMPL), and the Committee on Civil Liberties, Justice and Home Affairs (LIBE).

ECON had established the "Economic Dialogue" with other EU institutions under the European Semester and held annual hearings reviewing the ECB's economic and monetary policies since 2010 (Rittberger 2014).[24] In 2013, representatives from the Troika institutions were included in this review mechanism (Cisotta 2017, 287; Parra 2017, 109). This allowed ECON to invite the President of the Council, the European Commission, the ECB, the President of the European Council, and the President of the Eurogroup to appear and discuss draft budgetary plans for countries applying for financial assistance. Most importantly, ECON led a parliamentary inquiry about the role of the Troika in 2014. This included a questionnaire sent to Troika institutions and the governments of affected member states, as well as country visits by EP delegates and a public hearing during which representatives of the Troika were questioned by members of the EP.[25] This resulted in a "Report on the enquiry on the role and operations of the Troika (ECB, Commission and IMF) with regard to the euro area programme countries."[26] Interestingly, there was a second report drafted at the same time at the initiative of EMPL, the "Employment and social aspects of the role and operations of the Troika (ECB, Commission and IMF) with regard to euro area programme countries."[27] This was accompanied by hearings, country visits, and a new social media initiative gathering input from EP followers in the affected countries.[28] Both committees also commissioned independent studies from the EP's research service, the Directorate General on Internal Policies, Economic Governance Support Unit (Karantinos 2014; Sapir et al. 2014). Thus, there were two independent monitoring processes taking place in parallel, which resulted in two own-initiative reports: one by ECON, the other by EMPL. With these inquiries, the EP argued that "the Troika monitors if bailout countries carry out the reforms that have been asked for, but it has now been scrutinised in turn."[29]

[24] The schedule of the Economic Dialogues is available at: http://www.europarl.europa.eu/RegData/etudes/BRIE/2015/528782/IPOL_BRI(2015)528782_EN.pdf (last access October 9, 2018).

[25] ECON Public Hearing, "Successes and Failures in Crisis Countries," ECON/7/14301, available at: http://www.europarl.europa.eu/ep-live/de/committees/video?event=20131105-1530-COMMITTEE-ECON (last access October 9, 2018).

[26] EP document A7-0149/2014 (Rapporteurs: Othmar Karas and Liem Hoang Ngoc).

[27] EP document A7-0135/2014 (Rapporteur: Alejandro Cercas).

[28] Author's telephone interview with Alejandro Cercas, March 12, 2018.

[29] European Parliament 2014: Press Statement, January 13, 2014, available at: http://www.europarl.europa.eu/news/en/headlines/eu-affairs/20140110STO32308/inquiry-how-parliament-evaluated-the-impact-of-troika-measures (last access October 9, 2018).

This accountability enacted by the committees of the EP relieved the Council of Europe's Commissioner for Human Rights from its position as the singular accountability holder with regard to the Troika's austerity measures: "the European Parliament subsequently came out with a whole series of country studies on austerity and human rights. Once they started doing that, I was happy about that. I felt that there was less of a need for me to focus in on these issues and actually near the end of my mandate, we began to take a slightly different approach."[30] The monitoring of the effect of the Troika austerity measures on human rights thus was increasingly done by the EP.

On March 12, 2014, the EP held a general debate, during which it adopted the resolution on "Employment and social aspects of the role and operations of the Troika (ECB, Commission and IMF) with regard to euro area programme countries" and the two own-initiative reports by ECON and EMPL. During this debate, members of the EP also asked the European Commission to mandate a study on the economic and social consequences of the austerity policies. While the different parliamentary groups disagreed over the necessity of the Troika in response to the crisis, the members of the EP concluded with the resolution that any further financial assistance should be decided upon by a European institution rooted in EU law and controlled by the EP. This basically called for an end of the Troika, which has been reinforced by public statements by members of the EP and can thus be regarded as an important sanctioning activity.[31] With its 2014 resolution and the adoption of the rather critical reports, the EP not only established human rights as a benchmark for the implementation of austerity measures but also officially claimed its role as an accountability holder vis-à-vis the Troika institutions. This can be considered a milestone in the role of the EP as an accountability holder that shaped the interaction between the EP and the Troika institutions.

Further important monitoring activities were undertaken by LIBE. It organized a public hearing on the "situation of fundamental rights in the EU" in November 2013 (Ivanković Tamamović 2015, 153) and commissioned extensive studies on the effect of the crisis on human rights in 2015, such as the right to education, the right to health, and the right to work (Canotilho 2015). These in-depth country reports became an important source of information for

[30] Author's telephone interview with the former Council of Europe Commissioner for Human Rights, Nils Muižnieks, July 2, 2018.

[31] The public sanctioning was reinforced through four videos on the Troika and how it was held accountable by the EP, available at: https://www.europarltv.europa.eu/de/search?meps=96950&sort=date (last access October 9, 2018).

members of the EP about the effect of the austerity measures on fundamental rights and thus contributed to pluralist accountability.

The recognition of the EP as an accountability holder, however, differed across the implementing and mandating actors. The government of Greece recognized the accountability functions exercised by the EP; in August 2015, President Tsipras wrote the EP president Martin Schulz that he accepted the EP as an accountability holder in the review process of the implementation of Troika measures. He even welcomed this role since he considered the EP to be "the sole European institution with popular mandate," which should "act as the ultimate guarantor of democratic accountability and compatibility of economic policy in Europe with the political and social 'acquis européen.'"[32] In contrast to that, the Troika institutions were more reluctant to recognize the EP as an accountability holder. The European Commission in particular, and to a certain extent also the ECB, increasingly accepted the EP's accountability functions and cooperated in monitoring activities. However, the IMF successfully refused to become part of the accountability relationship. It did not respond to the inquiries by the EP committees and did not send any of its representatives to the hearings organized by the EP (da Conceição-Heldt 2016; Parra 2017; Salomon 2015, 530).

To sum up, the EP has become an important accountability holder regarding human rights violations associated with the Troika's austerity measures. By establishing human rights as a standard to be respected when implementing financial assistance programs, monitoring the implementation of the measures, and publicly sanctioning the Troika for its negative effect on fundamental rights, different committees of the EP together contributed to the emergence of a pluralist accountability framework. However, pluralist accountability varied across the different Troika institutions: it was only recognized by the European Commission and the ECB, not by the IMF.

Important Standard Setting and Monitoring by Other International Organizations

While the most comprehensive accountability framework was established by European institutions, other IOs also undertook important standard-setting and monitoring activities. The UN Human Rights Council mandated an

[32] Alexis Tsipras 2015: Letter to the President of the European Parliament, August 19, 2015 (document on file with the author).

Independent Expert on Foreign Debt and Human Rights to develop guidelines for member states and international financial institutions implementing austerity programs to "ensure that compliance with the commitments derived from foreign debt will not undermine the obligations for the realization of fundamental economic, social and cultural rights."[33] These "Guiding Principles" were adopted by the Human Rights Council in 2012 and made it clear to both the institutions designing the austerity measures and the states implementing them that they should respect core human rights standards. The Independent Expert was also mandated to monitor the human rights situation in the countries under austerity programs and to investigate the effect of EU institutions on human rights.[34]

In addition to that, the UN High Commissioner for Human Rights investigated the effect of austerity measures on economic and social rights in 2013.[35] The UN Children's Fund also provided important insights on how the rights of children have been violated in Portugal by public spending cuts (Canotilho 2015, 71, 83; Ortiz et al. 2011). These reports, however, monitored the effect of austerity measures across the world without a particular focus on examining the actions of the Troika.

In contrast, the accountability activities undertaken by the International Labor Organization very much focused on the effect of the Troika, particularly in Greece and Portugal. Its committees collected complaints related to the violation of workers' rights in response to the crisis (Kilpatrick and De Witte 2014). The organization not only issued several reports, but also engaged in monitoring by deploying a high-level mission to Greece in 2011. In meetings with the Greek government, it became clear that the International Labor Organization was considered to be the only institution through which the government could voice concerns about the effect of the Troika austerity measures on social rights (Salomon 2015, 530). In April 2013, the International Labor Organization held a meeting to discuss potentially becoming a member of the Troika, during which a representative of the EP was also present. This proposal, however, was rejected and not pursued further. Instead, the International Labor Organization contributed to the EP's efforts

[33] United Nations Human Rights Council 2011, Report of the Independent Expert, April 10, 2011, UN doc. A/HRC/20/23, para. 9.

[34] United Nations Human Rights Council, Reports of the Independent Expert, UN doc. A/HRC/25/50/Add.1, UN doc. A/HRC/31/60/Add.2, UN doc. A/HRC/34/57/Add.1.

[35] United Nations 2013: Report of the United Nations High Commissioner for Human Rights on Austerity Measures and Economic and Social Rights, available at: https://www.ohchr.org/Documents/Issues/Development/RightsCrisis/E-2013-82_en.pdf (last access October 9, 2018).

to enhance accountability through its reports and by participating in the hearing organized by ECON in 2014 (Ivanković Tamamović 2015, 159).

Pluralist Accountability by Domestic Courts

Rather unexpectedly, pluralist accountability was fostered at the domestic level through the judicial branch, in particular through decisions by the Portuguese Constitutional Court. The left minority government that had signed the MoU with the Troika in 2011 had already resigned at the stage of signature, but the two main opposition parties explicitly endorsed the MoU (Canotilho et al. 2015, 157; Coroado et al. 2017, 294). However, when Portugal adopted the austerity package a couple of months later under a center-right majority government, which had been in power since July 2011, the EU did not expect that the conditions attached to the financial assistance were reviewed by domestic institutions.

Following widespread domestic protest, the Portuguese Economic and Social Council criticized the pension cuts imposed by the austerity measures (Canotilho 2015, 70) and the Portuguese parliament rejected an austerity package in March 2011 (Figueiredo and González 2014, 308). The Troika institutions, however, did not recognize these domestic attempts at holding the implementing actors accountable. This only changed significantly with the decisions of the Portuguese Constitutional Court (Violante 2019).

The court's first decision on pay cuts in 2011 still confirmed the constitutionality of the state budget. It argued that "within certain 'limits of sacrifice'... it is acceptable that this may be a legitimate and necessary way to reduce the State's expenses" (Canotilho et al. 2015, 162). This reassured the government and the Troika that the implementation of the austerity measures would not be challenged further. It came, therefore, as an unexpected turning point when the court in 2012 rejected the budget that included additional pay cuts as unconstitutional. This decision then triggered a wave of further decisions against austerity. In 2013, the court decided that the proposed cuts were unconstitutional without granting the government any further suspension that would allow it to postpone the implementation of the court's decision (Canotilho et al. 2015, 164). In seventeen decisions that included fifty-four rulings on cases of constitutional review, the court declared that certain austerity measures violated fundamental constitutional rights (Coroado et al. 2016, 294; Cisotta and Gallo 2014). While the initial two cases reviewing the state budget in 2011 and 2012 had been originated from complaints by a group of members of parliament, more cases had been brought forward by a variety of domestic political and legal actors, including members of the Portuguese parliament, the President of the Republic, and the Portuguese Ombudsman.[36]

It is important to note, though, that the court rejected these austerity measures as being measures that the Portuguese government introduced and did not take into consideration the role of the Troika. Furthermore, the court rejected some of the measures as unconstitutional because they violated the principle of equality, not because they violated core social rights (Canotilho 2015; Canotilho et al. 2015, 158, 183; Cisotta and Gallo 2014, 10). However, these judgments "dropped the bomb" and made the court the "only counter-power to European institutions and to national political institutions" (Fasone 2014, 41). This role as an accountability holder created a public wave of sympathy, with demonstrators wearing T-shirts portraying "I love the Constitutional Court," a sign of affection uncommon in relation to state institutions (Canotilho 2015, 71). Even if the court decisions were directed toward the Portuguese government as the implementing actor, it provided a strong signal to the Troika that its austerity policies needed to be designed in line with fundamental human rights obligations, otherwise they would be overturned by domestic accountability holders.

The reactions by the Troika and the Portuguese government show that the court was taken seriously in its role as an accountability holder. In response to the court rulings on budget cuts in 2013, the Troika scheduled an extra visit to the country to discuss the implications with the government.[37] The European Commission proposed to grant Portugal an extension in reaching the bailout targets.[38] The Portuguese government revised some of its austerity measures and eventually decided not to apply for the final tranche but to withdraw from financial assistance provided by the EU in 2014.[39]

Out of the three countries under similar bailout programs, Greece, Ireland, and Portugal, the Portuguese Constitutional Court certainly had the largest effect on the evolution of pluralist accountability. The courts of Greece and Ireland were operating within a much smaller legal framework. Nevertheless, a

[36] According to the Portuguese Constitution, preventive review can only be asked for by the president, whereas successive review of a bill after its ratification can be demanded by a variety of actors, including the president of the parliament, the prime minister, the ombudsman, the attorney general, and one tenth of the members of parliament (Canotilho et al., 2015, 159).

[37] Portugal News 2013: Troika Back in Portugal, April 11, 2013, available at: http://theportugalnews.com/news/troika-schedules-emergency-visit/28174 (last access October 9, 2018).

[38] Statement by President José Manuel Durão Barroso on the situation in Portugal, April 8, 2013, available at: http://europa.eu/rapid/press-release_MEMO-13-315_en.htm (last access October 9, 2018).

[39] Press Release: Statement by the EC, ECB, and IMF on Portugal, No. 14/277, available at: https://www.imf.org/en/News/Articles/2015/09/14/01/49/pr14277 (last access October 9, 2018).

few decisions by the supreme administrative court in Greece, the Council of State, are worth mentioning as sanctioning mechanisms with regard to the austerity measures under Troika supervision. The court initially ruled on several instances that due to exceptional circumstances, austerity measures that violated social rights could be regarded as constitutional (Poulou 2014, 1175). However, in a decision on further wage cuts in 2012, the court for the first time rejected these measures on the basis of principles of proportionality and equality (Sciarra 2018, 13). Nevertheless, the effect of these decisions remained rather limited in comparison with the Portuguese Court and did not have any significant consequences for the design of the further bailout programs for Greece.

The European courts, by contrast, were very reluctant in accepting claims in relation to austerity measures. Despite the fact that the European Court of Human Rights and the European Court of Justice were approached repeatedly to exercise accountability over the Troika, both courts refrained from sanctioning. In several decisions regarding austerity measures in Greece and Portugal, the European Court of Human Rights decided that the exceptional circumstances of the crisis justified the measures and rejected those complaints as inadmissible (Nolan 2015, 12; Pervou 2016).[40] The Portuguese Constitutional Court referred a number of cases regarding the salary cuts that were introduced in the context of the austerity measures in 2011 to the European Court of Justice (Kilpatrick and De Witte, 2014, 7).[41] The European Court of Justice, however, dismissed these cases, as it did with a number of complaints by Greek unions and individuals from Greece and Portugal.[42] In its landmark *Pringle* v. *Government of Ireland* decision, the court argued that the ESM was situated outside the scope of EU law, that the Troika did not have any decision-making powers according to EU law, and, therefore, could not be held accountable by the court for the austerity measures violating rights guaranteed by the EU Charter on Human Rights (Fischer-Lescano 2014; Rittberger 2014; Salomon 2015, 533).[43] With this decision, the court thus did not contribute to an accountability framework vis-à-vis the Troika.

[40] See, e.g., European Court of Human Rights 2013: *Koufaki and Adedy* v. *Greece*, App. Nos. 57665/12 and 57657/12, May 7, 2013; European Court of Human Rights 2013: *Mateus and Januário* v. *Portugal*, App. Nos. 62235/12 and 57725/12, October 8, 2013, available at http://hudoc.echr.coe.int (last access October 9, 2018).

[41] C-127/12, *Sindicato dos Bancários do Norte*, Order of March 7, 2013; C-264/12, *Sindacato Nacional dos Profissionais de Seguro* v. *Fidelidade Mundial*, Order of June 26, 2014.

[42] European Court of Justice 2012: *ADEDY and others* v. *Council*, Case T-541/10, General Court order of November 2, 2012, available at: http://curia.europa.eu (last access October 9, 2018); *ADEDY and Others* v. *Council*, Case T-215/11, General Court order of November 27, 2012.

[43] European Court of Justice 2012: *Pringle* v. *Government of Ireland*, Rs. C-370/12, November 27, 2012.

To sum up, pluralist accountability with regard to the Troika's austerity measures was enhanced mainly by two European institutions, the EP and the Council of Europe, as well as the Portuguese Constitutional Court. Both the role of the EP and the Portuguese Court have been regarded as exceptional in how they established a system of checks and balances regarding decisions imposed by the Troika. Together, the three accountability holders established fundamental rights as a standard to be respected when implementing austerity measures, undertook significant monitoring activities that increased the transparency of the austerity programs to an unprecedented degree, and sanctioned the Troika institutions and the implementing governments for violating individuals' rights. This also shows a variation in accountability across the three Troika institutions and across the different countries that participated in the bailout program. The European Commission and the ECB, although the latter to a lesser extent, were the addressees of the EP's efforts to enhance accountability, whereas the IMF remained mainly outside of pluralist accountability. The court's decisions enhanced accountability only in the case of Portugal, whereas the other two cases with comparable bailouts, Greece and Ireland, remained largely unaffected by pluralist accountability.

Nevertheless, court decisions, or rather the shadow of potential decisions, against austerity measures complemented the activities undertaken by the Council of Europe's Commissioner for Human Rights. By framing his monitoring and shaming activities in the context of potential legal breaches, the commissioner referred to the courts as further accountability holders when interacting with members of the Troika.[44] Each of the accountability holders thus made use of the accountability functions exercised by the other institutions. This demonstrates the exceptional complementarity of the network of pluralist accountability exercised by the European institutions and domestic courts, in particular.

Competition as a Driving Factor for Pluralist Accountability

What motivated the EP, the Council of Europe, and the Constitutional Court of Portugal to engage in pluralist accountability? I demonstrate in this section

[44] "When I was talking with commission officials, I was saying: Listen, you have to look at the human rights obligations of these countries. You are imposing this [i.e. the austerity measures] on them and then afterwards they are forced to reverse policies, because national courts or constitutional courts are saying, you can't do this. Once a number of these measures actually had been overturned in national courts, they began to pay more attention to this line of argumentation. But it took a while" (author's telephone interview with the former Council of Europe Commissioner for Human Rights, Nils Muižnieks, July 2, 2018).

that all three institutions faced competition at different points in time related to resources and reputation, which triggered their activities as accountability holders.

Institutional Competition: European Parliament

The Lisbon Treaty of 2010 was the last in a row of treaties that had gradually increased the influence of the EP in the EU's decision-making process (Hix 2002). The history of the EP has been described as a "continuous struggle for power and influence" among the EU institutions (Rittberger 2014). The Lisbon Treaty eventually gave the EP "shared legislative power" in the co-decision-making procedure that created a "dramatic increase in interactions between EP and the Council" (Raunio 2017, 697). However, in the decision-making process on the EU's response to the financial crisis, the EP was "left dormant" by the main decision-making bodies (Fabbrini 2013, 1014). The European Council and the ECOFIN Council "totally sidelined" the EP in the process of the Troika establishment (Manoli and Maris 2015, 79). As a result, frustration grew among members of the EP that important policy decisions, for example the so-called "Six Pack" decisions, were prepared in informal, closed-door gatherings of the European Council, the so-called "ECOFIN breakfasts," which prevented them from participating (Raunio 2017, 697). Organizing hearings and requesting Troika representatives to answer questions thus became a further means for the EP to increase its standing vis-à-vis the European Council. In addition to this interinstitutional struggle for influence, there were three further strands of competition that characterized the EP in the years after the crisis: a growing competition between the different parliamentary committees, an increased competition between the different parliamentary groups, and a struggle between the EP and national parliaments about which parliamentary institution constituted the appropriate mechanism for oversight of the EU's economic governance in the aftermath of the crisis. Each of these competitive dynamics reinforced the EP's motivation to act as an accountability holder vis-à-vis the Troika.

Intercommittee competition

In the aftermath of the crisis, the EP committees were granted "extensive procedural rights" (Raunio 2017, 694). In the period between 2009 and 2014, there were twenty committees producing both legislative and nonlegislative reports. These reports gave visibility to the individual committees, both in the

EP plenary and before the general public, since they prepared the grounds for potential resolutions adopted by the EP plenary. In order to be able to produce a report, the committees must apply to the Conference of the Presidents. This increases the competition among the different committees. EMPL didn't want to leave ECON the discursive authority in interpreting the events after the crisis and decided to apply for another report to be undertaken with a different methodology. Committee requests for reports are "often turned down by the Conference of the Presidents, especially toward the end of the election period" (Mamadouh and Raunio 2003, 342). Therefore, the number of committee reports that monitored the Troika were rather exceptional in the period leading to the elections of May 2014. By adopting these reports during the election campaign, the EP gained visibility.

Ideological competition

The rapporteurs of the committee reports are appointed by the different political parties of the EP according to a point system by the committee itself. Only occasionally would a bipartisan rapporteurship be appointed as it happened in the ECON report, in which the rapporteurs came from the center-left and center-right parties of the EP. EU scholars expect competition among the different political parties to grow with the rising overall influence of the EP (Hix et al., 2005). Therefore, the rapporteurship is an important means for a political party to enhance its visibility. The bipartisan ECON report demonstrates how this interparty competition is balanced with regard to the ideological differences that shaped the assessment of the EU's response to the financial crisis.[45] While these differences about the role and the necessity of the Troika remained unresolved, the quest for greater accountability of the Troika and the importance of the EP as an accountability holder became common ground on which all EP members could agree on.

Interparliamentary competition

The EP has established several channels of communication through which it interacts with national parliaments. In the aftermath of the crisis, however, it became clear that this relationship was characterized by a strong disagreement about the nature of parliamentary oversight in the EU and the role of the EP in relation to national parliaments. In October 2013, an interparliamentary

[45] European Voice 2014: MEPs Temper Criticism of the Troika, article by Nicholas Hirst, March 13, 2014, available at: https://www.politico.eu/article/meps-temper-criticism-of-the-troika/ (last access October 9, 2018).

conference on Article 13 of the Fiscal Treaty, which entailed the EU's response to the financial crisis, revealed strong differences among the participating representatives of parliaments (Cooper 2016). These differences were less about whether the Troika and the austerity measures had been an appropriate response to the crisis, and more about whether the European Economic and Monetary Union should be scrutinized through a centralized accountability mechanism, for example the EP, or through a joint accountability mechanism that would allow both the EP and national parliaments to participate. Shortly after these differences became apparent, in late 2013 and January 2014, the EP organized its first hearings and mandated the various reports. It thereby promoted its vision of a centralized accountability mechanism.

Competition as a Trigger of Accountability Functions: The Council of Europe

As a result of the financial crisis, member states significantly reduced their contributions to the budget of the Council of Europe. As a consequence, cross-cutting budget reductions were discussed in the meetings of senior staff of the council after 2012.[46] The Commissioner for Human Rights, being the head of the smallest administrative entity of the organization, wanted to avoid cross-cutting reductions across all units regardless of their capacities. Instead, he assumed office with the goal of establishing the office as an efficient and visible actor, and thus become the visible profile of the Council of Europe:

> I tried to position the office politically in such a way that it would be as immune as possible from serious budget cuts... So we succeeded in not having to cut any posts, which I think was quite important... I tried to position the office as being an institution that really raised the profile of the Council of Europe for not a great expense.[47]

Acting as an accountability holder toward the Troika was an important strategy to enhance this profile. This strategy proved successful and helped the Commissioner for Human Rights to even increase the number of positions from twenty-five to twenty-seven staff members.

[46] Author's telephone interview with the former Council of Europe Commissioner for Human Rights, Nils Muižnieks, July 2, 2018.

[47] Author's telephone interview with the former Council of Europe Commissioner for Human Rights, Nils Muižnieks, July 2, 2018.

The Commissioner also recognized that the Council of Europe's public visibility was not very strong in comparison with the EU.[48] With growing popular distrust in EU institutions after the crisis, however, the Commissioner saw this as a chance to strengthen the Council of Europe's profile as the legally more powerful European institution:

> I would make the point that the EU and Council of Europe are complementary, because the Council for Europe has a case law, a legally binding case law in many human rights issue areas where the EU does not. Then monitoring mechanisms—it is quite rare for the EU institutions to do country specific work... So in that context I'd say there's still a very large role for the Council of Europe. Not only in non-member states of the EU, but within the EU.[49]

In addition, there was also some intra-institutional competition within the Council of Europe between the Commissioner for Human Rights and the Secretary-General:

> The Secretary General has a very different approach than the Commissioner ...a very political approach... The Secretary General is kind of the political head of the organization and there are only two officials who are allowed to speak to the media and that's the Commissioner and the Secretary General. Everybody else is in the chain of command of the Secretary General. The Commissioner is not.[50]

The Secretary-General promoted the European Court of Human Rights as an institutional accountability mechanism with limited success, as the section on international courts above has shown.[51] Instead, the accountability functions exercised by the Commissioner for Human Rights increased the public visibility of the commissioner vis-à-vis the Secretary-General.

[48] "I think the Council of Europe has been lousy at selling itself. [It does] great work, but it doesn't communicate well" (author's telephone interview with the former Council of Europe Commissioner for Human Rights, Nils Muižnieks, July 2, 2018).

[49] Author's telephone interview with the former Council of Europe Commissioner for Human Rights, Nils Muižnieks, July 2, 2018.

[50] Author's telephone interview with the former Council of Europe Commissioner for Human Rights, Nils Muižnieks, July 2, 2018.

[51] The European Court of Human Rights however was not very keen on deciding on this topic as it did not want to risk conflict with member states: "the European Court of Human Rights has been under attack in recent years, for stretching its mandate, for mission creep, I think it was very hesitant to adjudicate on issues particularly affecting social and economic rights because this would put it in the firing line on these issues" (author's telephone interview with the former Council of Europe Commissioner for Human Rights, Nils Muižnieks, July 2, 2018).

Finally, competition was also about shaping the political debate. Societal resonance to the work of the Council of Europe on the rights of minorities or homosexuality was rather limited.[52] In a time in which human rights concerns were pushed aside in the political debate, "focusing on social and economic rights was also a way of reclaiming a bit and rehabilitating the human rights narrative more broadly."[53] By positioning itself as an accountability holder for social and economic rights, the commissioner thereby managed to reintroduce human rights on the political agenda and to increase the visibility of the Council of Europe's work.

The Portuguese Constitutional Court in a Competitive Environment

The Portuguese Constitution of 1983 created a rather generous system of constitutional review that is incomparable to the constitutions of other countries under similar bailout programs. Most importantly, it enabled a variety of domestic legal and political institutions to ask the court for constitutional review, including the Portuguese Ombudsman, the members of parliament, and the President of the Republic (Violante 2019). When the austerity program under the auspices of the Troika was implemented, the general feeling among these actors was that the court remained the only mechanism of accountability available to them.[54] Originally, the potential of the court to dismiss legislation on economic reforms was considered to be a serious obstacle that needed to be addressed through constitutional changes (Violante 2019, 133). While the Portuguese society initially had accepted the austerity program as a necessity to overcome the crisis, the major societal outrage against austerity—through massive demonstrations—provided the competing parties with potential political gains to allow the court to enact accountability over the Troika during the election campaigns. As a consequence, parties dropped any proposals to change the constitution that would limit the court's jurisdiction on these issues during the elections. This enabled

[52] "In many contexts, the rights of national or sexual minorities are not very popular... If you talk about the rights of migrants or the rights of gays or the rights of Roma, then the majority of the population is saying, 'you know what, I don't really need those rights'" (author's telephone interview with the former Council of Europe Commissioner for Human Rights, Nils Muižnieks, July 2, 2018).

[53] Author's telephone interview with the former Council of Europe Commissioner for Human Rights, Nils Muižnieks, July 2, 2018.

[54] Author's telephone interview with Teresa Violante, former law clerk at the Portuguese Constitutional Court, June 11, 2018.

the court to prominently establish itself as a counter-majoritarian actor in the Portuguese political system, considered the "prime guardian of fundamental rights" (Violante 2019, 133, 138).

The judges on the court are political appointments by the Portuguese parliament. The cases assessing the constitutionality of a governmental policy, thus, are likely to follow partisan ideologies (Coroado et al. 2017). This means that the court is not free of political polarization, but competition in the political realm can invoke accountability exercised through court decisions. The landmark decision of 2012, for example, originated from a request for constitutional review from a group of small opposition parties supported by individual members of the Socialist Party who acted against the will of their party leadership (Violante 2019, 127). The competing party ideologies are further reflected by the fact that some of the court's decisions, such as the decisions on the Budget Act, were quite contentious and not unanimous. While up until 2007 30 percent of decisions were taken unanimously, the opinions of the judges increasingly disagreed in the seventeen decisions reviewing the government's austerity measures (Amaral-Garcia et al. 2009, 401, 305; Fasone 2014; Violante 2019, 130). In 2012, three new judges were appointed, two by the conservative coalition and one by the socialist party. While the hearings leading to the appointment showed that the members of parliament did not fully grasp the effect of the appointment process on the court's decisions on austerity, the two conservative appointments were key in the rulings on unconstitutionality in 2013 and 2014 (Amaral-Garcia et al. 2009).[55] Despite these political divisions, the court's judges adopted the second landmark decision on pension cuts in 2013 unanimously (Violante 2019, 130).

At the same time, the specific "constitutional identity" that needed to be protected played an important role in the court's decisions (Fasone 2014, 35). The importance of social rights and the principle of equality are two very distinct features of the Portuguese constitution that motivated the court to "preserve its role of ultimate constitutional guardian of the State" (Fasone 2014, 36; Violante 2019, 138). The competition between domestic constitutional courts and supranational institutions on a broader scheme thus was a driving factor for the increased exercise of accountability at the domestic level. Given that the supranational European courts dismissed most of the claims concerning the Troika measures, the decisions by the Portuguese Constitutional Court constituted a unique chance for the court to establish itself as the

[55] Author's telephone interview with Teresa Violante, former law clerk at the Portuguese Constitutional Court, June 11, 2018.

last bastion of domestic review against decisions that were considered to be imposed by supranational institutions.

Summary

The three main accountability holders faced different types of competition about resources and reputation at different points in time. Holding the Troika institutions accountable became a means for the Council of Europe, the EP, and the Portuguese Constitutional Court to increase their visibility and protect their standing in the respective institutional battles. Standard-setting, monitoring, and sanctioning activities enhanced the profiles of the accountability holders, and holding the Troika institutions accountable became a niche that sharpened their profiles.

Vulnerability: From Emergency Rhetoric to Human Rights Demands

The initial years after the outbreak of the crisis were dominated by a "mentality of a state of exception" and a "financial imperative" to ensure stability in fiscal and financial policies (Dowell-Jones 2015; Fischer-Lescano 2014, 20). This emergency discourse accompanied the adoption of the MoU between the Troika and member states in financial need. The public discourse dominated by governments like Germany and the EU institutions focused on "saving Greece" and saving the Euro (Salomon 2015, 523). Human rights at that time remained mostly absent from the policymaking discourse (Nolan 2015; O'Connell 2013; Saiz 2009, 277). In the mainstream discourse, socioeconomic rights were regarded as irrelevant and their advocates sidelined both in the austerity discourse as well as in the design of the bailout programs (Dowell-Jones 2015, 19). Even international courts upheld this narrative in their decisions, by accepting the "functional necessities" invoked by the implementing governments (Everson and Joerges 2013). In addition to this "decoupling" (Dowell-Jones 2015, 19) of a human rights discourse with macro-economic issues, economic stability (as the dominant paradigm guiding the actions in response to the crisis) had been established as a powerful norm to counter any human rights demands. In response to the decisions by the Portuguese Constitutional Court, for example, the European Commission invoked the counter-norm of economic stability. It argued that the court's decisions increased the instability of the Portuguese economy and appealed to the Portuguese government to "not leave the track of austerity" (Fasone 2014).[56]

The counter-norm of stability, however, started to lose some of its strength in 2013. The most crucial development that broke with the paradigm of economic stability was a report by the Independent Evaluation Office of the IMF in 2013. This report, which blamed the European Troika institutions for the effects of the austerity, led to the recognition that "austerity is associated with almost eating children."[57] This initiated a "blame game" within the Troika, leading to a "divorce" among the Troika institutions.[58] Moreover, the role of the Troika became increasingly contested among the College of Commissioners and the Justice Commissioner publicly called for the Troika to be abolished.[59] While this blame game allowed the IMF to remain relatively invulnerable, the European Commission and to some degree also the ECB were exposed to an increasingly high degree of vulnerability.

As a consequence, the European Commission tried to render itself immune against human rights demands. It shielded itself behind a complex delegation relationship to reject accountability demands and shifted the blame to the implementing national governments. When the EP for the first time expressed its concern about the human rights effect of the Troika's austerity measures and asked the Commission to explain the precautionary measures taken to ensure the protection of human rights, the Commission simply argued that it was the implementing member states' responsibility to comply with the human rights charter and that it monitored this in the Annual Growth Survey.[60] In response to the decisions by the Portuguese Constitutional Court, it declared itself as a neutral, technical advisor and rejected that the issues decided by the court had anything to do with the MoU.[61] The courts in Portugal and Greece facilitated this blame-shifting strategy by avoiding

[56] European Commission 2013: Statement of the European Commission on Portugal, Memo 13/307, Brussels, April 7, 2013.

[57] International Monetary Fund 2013: Greece. IMF Country Report No. 13/156, June 2013, Washington DC; Higgins, New York Times 2013: Europe's Economics Chief Tries to Peel Off "Mr. Austerity" Label, article by Andrew Higgins and James Kanter, May 17, 2013, available at: https://www.nytimes.com/2013/05/18/world/europe/europe-economist-rehn-rejects-austerity-label.html (last access October 9, 2018).

[58] New York Times 2013: Splits Appear in Policy "Troika" Addressing Europe's Financial Crisis, article by Andrew Higgins, June 7, 2013, available at: https://www.nytimes.com/2013/06/08/world/europe/policy-troika-for-europe-financial-crisis-has-splits.html (last access October 9, 2018).

[59] Viviane Reding 2012: Speech at the Citizens' Dialogue in Heidelberg, Speech 13/639, July 16, 2012.

[60] European Commission 2014: Answer given by Mr. Rehn on behalf of the Commission, Doc. E-013861/2013, February 13, 2013.

[61] Author's telephone interview with Teresa Violante, former law clerk at the Portuguese Constitutional Court, June 11, 2018.

any reference to EU law, thus fully "nationalizing" the issue (Cisotta and Gallo 2014, 6; Poulou 2014, 1173). Moreover, whenever accountability was demanded from the Commission at the national level, it blamed the governments as "bad cops."[62]

However, the public opinion ratings of the EU institutions, especially of the European Commission but also the ECB, were negatively affected by the fact that the austerity measures were directly attributed to them (Roth et al. 2016). Two special Eurobarometer surveys on the crisis conducted on behalf of the EP in 2011 and 2012 showed that trust in EU institutions in general significantly declined to a "historically low" point (Hobolt 2014).[63] Further polls showed that the citizens' trust in the ECB strongly declined (Farvaque et al. 2017; Jones 2009; Roth et al. 2014). This undermined the Commission's and the ECB's strategy to shift the blame to national governments and made them increasingly vulnerable to accountability demands. The European Commission became increasingly aware of this, which made it more inclined to accept being held accountable.[64]

This change in vulnerability of the European institutions was preceded by a change in the vulnerability of some of the implementing national governments, in particular the government of Portugal. Both the Greek and the Portuguese governments defended the economic necessity of the measures in terms of the "state of exception" narrative (Fonseca and Ferreira 2015; Salomon 2015, 544).[65] Initially, the majority of the Portuguese population had supported their government in response to the crisis; they were "willing to go through hard times in order to get through the crisis."[66] However, they became increasingly critical as the newly elected prime minister Pedro Passos Coelho fully embraced austerity, promising that the government would go even beyond Troika demands (Fonseca and Ferreira 2015, 683). The pressure by public mass protests increased tremendously over the years and exposed new divisions inside the ruling coalition in Portugal (Canotilho 2015). The two

[62] Author's telephone interview with Teresa Violante, former law clerk at the Portuguese Constitutional Court, June 11, 2018.

[63] See Eurobarometers 76.1 and 77.2. See also Guardian 2013: Crisis for Europe as Trust Hits Record Low, article by Ian Traynor, April 24, 2013, available at: https://www.theguardian.com/world/2013/apr/24/trust-eu-falls-record-low (last access October 9, 2018).

[64] Author's telephone interview with the former Council of Europe Commissioner for Human Rights, Nils Muižnieks, July 2, 2018.

[65] See also the statement of the Greek government to the International Labor Organization, defending the economic necessity of the measures, available at: https://www.ilo.org/wcmsp5/groups/public/—ed_norm/—relconf/documents/meetingdocument/wcms_193260.pdf para. 964 (last access October 9, 2018).

[66] Author's telephone interview with Teresa Violante, former law clerk at the Portuguese Constitutional Court, June 11, 2018.

main Portuguese workers' confederations collaborated for the first time in twenty-two years and organized several general strikes with hundreds of thousands of protesters (Figueiredo and González 2014, 13). These significant societal reactions to the austerity measures and the protests supporting the decisions of the Portuguese Constitutional Court in 2013 made the government realize its degree of vulnerability as well as potential political gains if they joined the societal opposition and shifted the blame to the Troika (Fonseca and Ferreira 2015).

The high degree of vulnerability of the Portuguese government was supported by the fact that the Portuguese constitution imposed significant limits on the government when invoking the counter-norm of economic necessity. The Portuguese constitution has a strong emphasis on the respect for social rights and equality, which makes Portugal stand out among other European countries for its "constitutional pre-commitment to social and economic rights" (Brito Vieira and Carreira da Silva 2013; Figueiredo and González 2014; Kilpatrick and De Witte 2014). This normative frame that emphasized the importance of social and economic rights thus made it difficult for the Portuguese government to resort to the counter-norm of economic stability over a longer period of time. While the constitutional court initially accepted temporary measures that affected social and economic rights, as long as they were considered proportional, its reasoning after 2013 showed that prolonged budgetary cuts could not be considered as a temporary measure any longer (Sciarra 2018).

Summary

The degree of vulnerability with regard to human rights demands varied across the different mandating and implementing actors and over time. In the immediate years after the crisis, the narrative of economic necessity helped the actors to invoke the counter-norm of stability in order to make themselves immune against human rights demands from accountability holders. By referring to their specific and narrow mandates, the IMF, and to a certain extent also the ECB, managed to render themselves invulnerable. The European Commission, however, grew increasingly vulnerable, not least because of a blame game initiated by an IMF report. While still trying to invoke the counter-norm and shifting the blame to national governments, it became clear that the Commission itself was divided on the role of the Troika. This internal division and the significant decline in public opinion support contributed to the Commission's growing vulnerability.

National governments also tried to invoke the norm of economic stability to counter any human rights demands, however, to a varying degree of success. While the Greek government continued to shift the blame to the Troika institutions, the Portuguese government was highly vulnerable to human rights demands at the domestic level due to a strong normative environment with socioeconomic rights enshrined in their constitution.

Conclusion

I demonstrated in this chapter how a variety of regional and national accountability holders established a network of pluralist accountability in response to the austerity measures adopted in complex economic governance. In the aftermath of the economic and financial crisis, the so-called Troika, composed of the European Commission, the ECB, and the IMF, concluded MoUs with several European countries asking for financial loans. The conditions of these loan policies entailed the restructuring of economic and social policies with significant negative effects on socioeconomic rights. While vertical accountability was rather limited at the outset of the adoption of these austerity measures, the Council of Europe, the EP, and the Portuguese Constitutional Court enacted a framework of pluralist accountability.

The Council of Europe and its Commissioner for Human Rights, in particular, established socioeconomic rights as standards to be respected in the implementation of austerity measures. Its monitoring and sanctioning activities further stimulated the EP to also engage in pluralist accountability. Several committees of the EP monitored the effect of austerity measures in 2013 and 2014. Some of these monitoring activities led to normative sanctioning of the Troika with regard to its effect on socioeconomic rights. The members of parliament remain active in this field still today. The Conference of the Presidents adopted a proposal by Guy Verhofstadt in 2016 that said ECON should monitor the implementation of macro-economic measures. Whether the EP should act as an accountability holder to this degree, however, is highly debated given that the members of parliament come from all EU countries whereas financial assistance is provided to Eurozone members only.[67]

[67] Politico 2015: Parliament Demands Greek Oversight Role, article by Maïa de la Baumein, July 17, 2015, available at: https://www.politico.eu/article/parliament-oversight-greek-deal-verhofstadt-schulz-tsipras-grexit-esm/ (last access October 9, 2018).

The analysis also reveals the important role of domestic courts as the last bastion for human rights accountability in complex governance arrangements. The Portuguese Constitutional Court contributed in particular to pluralist accountability by rejecting core budgetary policies that the government had adopted in the context of the Troika's austerity measures. Relying on a strong normative environment provided by the Portuguese constitution, the court could hold the government accountable with regard to socioeconomic rights. Governments in countries with constitutions that do not include adequate mechanisms of reviewing socioeconomic rights were less vulnerable to human rights demands.

Two conditions fostered the development of pluralist accountability: first, the accountability holders were stimulated by their respective competitive environments to enact accountability functions and, thereby, develop a distinct profile vis-à-vis other institutional divisions or outside actors working in the same field. Second, the implementing actors (i.e., governments) or the authorities mandating the austerity policies (i.e., the Troika) were increasingly vulnerable to human rights demands, however to different degrees. While the IMF and to a certain extent also the ECB managed to render themselves immune against human rights demands, the European Commission became increasingly vulnerable due to its broader mandate and the declining trust of the public in EU institutions' capacity to address the crisis. Most importantly, a blame game within the Troika initiated by a report by the IMF's Independent Evaluations Office about the effect of austerity measures increased the European Commission's vulnerability. This variation in vulnerability explains why pluralist accountability varied across the different Troika institutions. While there were some attempts to hold the IMF and increasingly also the ECB accountable, a pluralist accountability framework was most active with regard to the European Commission.

Finally, this chapter also demonstrates the complementarity of different actors enacting pluralist accountability. The standard-setting and monitoring activities of the Commissioner for Human Rights of the Council of Europe in the context of the Troika's austerity measures stimulated the EP to become active as an accountability holder. The sanctioning by domestic courts, in particular the Portuguese Constitutional Court, provided the basis for the Commissioner for Human Rights to engage in normative shaming of the Troika. This shows the distinct features of pluralist accountability in complex governance settings when several accountability holders interact and complement each other.

7

Pluralist Accountability in Global Health Governance

The Role of Public–Private Partnerships in Immunization and Vaccine Development

Introduction

"In a world full of complex health problems, the WHO cannot solve them alone."[1] This statement by Gro Brundtland, the then director-general of the WHO in 2002, marked the beginning of the restructuring of global health governance. Recognizing the limits of the WHO when addressing diseases across the world, Brundtland argued that the WHO "must reach out to the private sector" (Velásquez 2014). As a consequence, global health governance has become one of the most complex and fragmented governance areas (Andonova 2017, ch. 5; Holzscheiter 2014; Holzscheiter et al. 2016). This "private turn" in global health governance (Rushton and Williams 2011, 11) is most pointedly exemplified by the field of vaccination. The Millennium Development Goals (MDGs), adopted in 2000, formulated the goal of reducing the infant mortality rate by two thirds by 2015, among others. To achieve this, a number of global public–private health partnerships (GPPHP) were founded to halt the decline in global immunization rates since the 1990s, to lower the price of vaccines, and to address infant health issues more effectively.

In this complex governance scheme, the WHO still plays an important role either as a host of partnerships or as a founding member and as a member of the executive committees of individual GPPHP (Clarke 2014). The WHO hosts some of these GPPHP, such as *Roll Back Malaria* and *Stop Tuberculosis*; others act more independently, for example the *Global Alliance for Vaccines and Immunisation* (GAVI) (founded in 2000) and the *Global Fund* (founded in 2002). Moreover, the WHO remains the ultimate authority for approving

[1] G. H. Brundtland, "Address by Dr Gro Harlem Brundtland, Director-General, to the Fifty-Fifth World Health Assembly, Geneva, Monday, 13 May 2002," quoted in Velásquez, 2014, 4.

Accountability in Global Governance. Gisela Hirschmann, Oxford University Press (2020). © Gisela Hirschmann.
DOI: 10.1093/oso/9780198861249.001.0001

new vaccines to be used by the international community.[2] The significant progress made in the field of child health, vaccine development, and vaccination access would not have been achieved without the various actors participating in GPPHP (Bartsch 2011; WHO et al. 2009). The investments and advocacy of a small number of philanthropic foundations such as the Bill and Melinda Gates Foundation, which is a founding member and a major financial donor of the GAVI Alliance, has been crucial for designing and implementing the agenda of global health governance (Martens & Seitz, 2015). By cooperating with pharmaceutical companies and research institutes, the Gates Foundation has supported both the development and the provision of new and more cost-effective vaccines and drugs for infectious as well as neglected diseases like polio, malaria, tuberculosis, HIV/AIDS, hepatitis, and others.[3]

Understandably, placing a public good like child health into the hands of private foundations and companies has raised a number of concerns (McCoy and McGoey 2011; McGoey 2017). Health researchers and NGOs have criticized GPPHP for creating conflicts of interest as pharmaceutical companies keep patents on their developed drugs, while at the same time have representation at the board of a GPPHP like GAVI (Heimans 2002; Velásquez 2014). GPPHP have also been criticized for introducing expensive vaccination schemes in countries where the most basic healthcare was still lacking (Schuster 2015). A comparative analysis of four GPPHP in five African countries and India (Global Alliance to Eliminate Lymphatic Filariasis, Roll Back Malaria, Stop Tuberculosis, and Global Polio Eradication Initiative) argues that the focus on vaccination took away financial and staff resources from core basic health services that could not be performed during vaccination periods (Wemos Foundation 2005).

Most importantly for this study, scholars of global health have highlighted the challenge of holding GPPHP accountable given the complexity of these governance arrangements (Bruen et al. 2014, 3). However, the scholarly debate on the accountability of partnerships focuses on how GPPHP members hold each other accountable rather than on human rights aspects (Steets 2010). In line with the overall objective of this book to analyze the conditions for alternative accountability mechanisms in the context of human rights, this chapter demonstrates the difficulties of GPPHP's accountability in these

[2] Author's interview with representatives from Gavi, Geneva, February 22, 2018.

[3] See the Third Annual Letter of Bill Gates of 2011, available at: https://www.gatesfoundation.org/Who-We-Are/Resources-and-Media/Annual-Letters-List/Annual-Letter-2011 (last access December 14, 2018).

complex schemes of global governance, in which the lines of delegation are blurred when some actors act as principals and agents simultaneously. I first show how vertical accountability is limited in the case of vaccination and then explain why pluralist accountability failed to emerge in this case. My argument here is twofold: first, I demonstrate that there was no room for independent third parties to develop a profile as accountability holders. Second, I show that implementing actors were able to refuse to recognize external accountability holders due to the lack of formal delegation and managed to make themselves immune against human rights demands. They did so by invoking a powerful counter-norm: the right to immunization as a fundamental right to health.

Vaccination is an extremely contested topic (Wallace 2012). On the one side, there are strong advocacy groups in the Western world and in developing countries that reject vaccines and vaccination as being harmful. On the other, there are influential philanthropic foundations and researchers who emphasize the benefits of global vaccination campaigns in the fight against diseases. Any study on the side effects or deaths related to vaccine development or vaccination treatment is thus immediately politicized. Both sides support their arguments with numbers and empirical data, therefore, it is impossible to assess the reliability of any accusation that human rights are being harmed through vaccination or vaccine development. At the same time, this fierce battle takes place in a moral dilemma situation, in which actors have to make decisions about whether to accept the potential harm of a few people in order to save the lives of many others. Therefore, it is not the purpose of this chapter to prove that either side is right. Instead, I will demonstrate how this battle between pro- and antivaccination camps hindered the development of pluralist accountability with regard to human rights in the context of vaccination and vaccine development.

The case of vaccination very clearly demonstrates why a functioning accountability framework would be important, especially in such a contested policy field. While the legitimacy of individual actors participating in public–private health partnerships might not necessarily be affected by a lack of accountability, the legitimacy of vaccination as a policy field as a whole is at stake. Without effective monitoring, it is impossible to know whether negative health outcomes, such as deaths during a clinical trial or a vaccination process, are related to vaccines or not. This uncertainty allows actors that are against immunization to easily attribute these effects to vaccines (Puliyel 2013; Wallace 2012, 1293). Moreover, the opaque forms of responsibility attached to authority in complex governance settings like GPPHP create uncertainty among those affected by the policy outcomes. As a consequence, affected societies lose trust in policymakers and those implementing vaccination programs, becoming more receptive to discourses that discredit vaccination as a whole. Especially in countries like India, where the acceptance of vaccination has always faced difficulties due to various societal and historical reasons, a lack of accountability can further undermine trust, which can be detrimental to the successful implementation of health programs (Larson and Ghinai 2011; Larson et al. 2016). Thus, in the long run, a lack of GPPHP accountability benefits those who discredit vaccination in general by allowing them to take advantage of insecurities and the complexity of governance structures.

This study focuses on accountability with regard to two particular human rights concerns that are related to vaccine development and vaccination in India. In the process of developing a vaccine against the human papilloma virus (HPV), a number of clinical trials between 2005 and 2012 on 23,000 girls aged ten to fourteen years from rural Indian populations, some of which were implemented through GPPHP, were alleged to have violated the right to informed consent of the participants or their parents.[4] This has raised the concern that such trials are unethical (Terwindt 2014). Additionally, the vaccination program introducing the WHO-approved pentavalent vaccine, with financial support of the GAVI Alliance, reportedly caused a number of deaths in Asia, in particular in India (People's Union for Democratic Rights 2014, 13). Adverse events following immunization (AEFI) are not human rights violations in legal terms if the vaccine is administered correctly. However, in order to assess whether the vaccine had indeed been administered correctly and whether the deaths were related to the vaccine, this requires functioning accountability structures (Sreedhar et al. 2014). As I show below, the lack of a formal delegation relationship and the strong ideological cleavage in the situation of a moral dilemma hindered the development of pluralist accountability in both cases and enabled the implementing actors to refuse to recognize any accountability mechanisms.

Previous research looked at the issue of the responsibility and accountability of GPPHP through a hypothetical lens, analyzing the potentially adverse impact of these partnerships on individual rights (Clarke, 2014). By contrast, I take the aforementioned allegations as a starting point to analyze the conditions that hindered the development of pluralist accountability in the

[4] Economic Times 2014: Controversial Vaccine Studies: Why Is Bill & Melinda Gates Foundation Under Fire from Critics in India?, article by Naranayar Kumar, August 31, 2014; Michael Carome 2014: Unethical Clinical Trials Still Being Conducted in Developing Countries, available at: http://www.huffingtonpost.com/michael-carome-md/unethical-clinical-trials_b_5927660.html (last access December 14, 2018).

cases of vaccine development and vaccination in India. I first outline the complex delegation relationship that characterizes vaccination and vaccine development in India. I then proceed to outline the lack of vertical accountability in this case. Thereafter, I analyze why pluralist accountability failed to evolve in cases of HPV vaccine development and pentavalent vaccination in India. I demonstrate how the ideological cleavages about vaccination and the complexity of the delegation relationship restricted the space for independent accountability holders. Acting within a moral dilemma situation with a strong counter-norm, the implementing actors were able to refuse to recognize any potential external accountability holders, while retaining their legitimacy within their respective communities.

Vaccine Development and Vaccination: Complex Global Immunization Governance

Vaccine development and vaccination are two separate processes in global health governance, but both involve the participation of private actors. Unlike peacekeeping, in which the UN Security Council has the central authority to mandate an operation to be implemented by a variety of cooperating partners, there is no formal delegation relationship between the various actors in vaccine development and vaccination. The WHO does not have the authority to mandate clinical trials for vaccine development, and only in a minor number of cases does it authorize clinical trials. Instead, private companies and foundations finance and conduct most clinical trials. However, for vaccines to be included in global immunization programs, they need to undergo a process of prequalification by the WHO. At the same time, the WHO does not authorize GPPHP like GAVI to undertake vaccination programs in individual countries. However, as a founding member and a member of the GAVI executive board, WHO representatives have an important voice in the decisions about which vaccines to include in the GAVI portfolio and about approving countries' applications to GAVI for financial support. In the following section I illustrate this complexity in global vaccination governance with regard to, first, the clinical trials developing a HPV vaccine and, second, the pentavalent vaccination.

The HPV vaccine was developed to protect women from developing cervical cancer; GAVI endorsed the vaccine in 2008 and included it in their immunization portfolio in 2013 (Gallagher et al. 2017, 73; Kane et al. 2012). When developing a new vaccine, clinical trials are a crucial step in vaccine development because they examine a drug's efficacy and potential side effects (Milford et al. 2006, 2). While the early stages of clinical trials include healthy volunteers, the more advanced stages test the therapeutic effect of a drug and surveil its safety within larger groups of people who have been affected by or exposed to the diseases. Clinical trials thus involve the participation of human beings and increasingly they take place outside the Western world (Bard 2015; Petryna 2007; Wemos Foundation 2005). India has become one of the "world's preferred destinations for clinical trials" (WHO 2008). In the last two decades, several clinical trials to develop an HPV vaccine have taken place in India (Terwindt 2014). Two international companies, GlaxoSmithKline and Merck, developed the drugs for the tests, the nonprofit health organization Program for Appropriate Technology in Health (PATH) conducted the trials, while the Bill and Melinda Gates Foundation financed the trials.[5] Both PATH and the Gates Foundation had already carried out cervical cancer screening and HPV testing trials in India (Srinivasan et al. 2018). In 2009, the WHO issued a position paper in which it reviewed the trials with the two drugs Gardasil and Cervarix on the basis of the insights of its Strategic Advisory Group of Experts on Immunization. The WHO thereby recommended "that routine HPV vaccination should be included in national immunization programmes, provided that: prevention of cervical cancer or other HPV-related diseases, or both, constitutes a public health priority . . . and sustainable financing can be secured" (WHO 2009). The WHO also included both drugs in its list of vaccines prequalified for being implemented by UN agencies and other core international actors of the global immunization community.

The approval and inclusion of these drugs in WHO's list of prequalified vaccines is crucial for the implementation of vaccination in developing countries.[6] The prequalification assures the safety and effectiveness of the vaccines used in international immunization campaigns and provides a system to regularly monitor the effects of immunization. Once the HPV vaccine was approved by the WHO, GAVI included it in its portfolio and started supporting governments in HPV vaccination programs in 2013.[7] The GAVI Alliance is one of the key actors that has enabled HPV vaccination in low-income countries since then (Hanson et al. 2015; Kane et al. 2012). It is a public–

[5] Economic Times 2014: Controversial Vaccine Studies: Why Is Bill & Melinda Gates Foundation Under Fire from Critics in India?, article by Naranayar Kumar, August 31, 2014.

[6] WHO n.d.: A System for the Prequalification of Vaccines for UN Supply, available at: http://www.who.int/immunization_standards/vaccine_quality/pq_system/en/ (last access December 17, 2018).

[7] GAVI Vaccine Investment Strategy 2008: HPV Analysis Documentation, available at: https://www.gavi.org/about/strategy/history-of-vaccine-investment-strategy/ (last access December 17, 2018).

private partnership that was founded in 2000 by the WHO, the Bill and Melinda Gates Foundation, the UN Children's Fund (UNICEF), PATH, and the World Bank. GAVI's structure and functioning resemble those of an IO, which has allowed GAVI to obtain immunity from domestic jurisdiction (Clarke 2014, 69). In contrast to other health partnerships such as Stop Tuberculosis and Roll Back Malaria, GAVI is not formally hosted by the WHO but acts as an independent organization with its own headquarters in Switzerland (Clarke 2014, 78). As a consequence, the WHO does not have a mandate over GAVI as it does over other partnerships it is hosting. Nonetheless, it holds one of four permanent seats on the eighteen-seat GAVI board, its main decision-making organ, together with UNICEF, the World Bank, and the Gates Foundation.[8] The other board members are government representatives and private actors, such as pharmaceutical companies that develop drugs that are later included in GAVI's vaccination portfolio.[9] GAVI considers itself primarily a financing mechanism in support of governments' vaccination campaigns. It provides grants to low-income countries that apply for GAVI funding to introduce a new vaccine (Levin et al. 2014).

In the case of HPV, the WHO expert group expressed concerns that high vaccines prices could hinder countries to adopt them into their immunization programs (WHO 2009). For this reason, the financial support by GAVI is crucial for the implementation of HPV vaccines. Once the new vaccines had been included in the list of prequalified vaccines by the WHO, the inclusion of HPV vaccination in GAVI's portfolio allows countries to apply for vaccination programs that also included HPV. Among the countries that GAVI supports, India has a rather special role in terms of its size, economic development, and as a vaccine-manufacturing country.[10] While in other countries GAVI finances the introduction of a new vaccine across the whole country, India only receives partial funding for an initial period of time while the government covers the remaining costs. The government of India under Prime Minister Narendra Modi applied to GAVI for support to introduce new vaccines, including HPV. GAVI approved the funding and agreed to commit US$500 million between 2016 and 2021 as a catalytic support.[11]

[8] GAVI n.d.: Board Composition, available at: https://www.gavi.org/about/governance/gavi-board/composition/ (last access December 17, 2018).

[9] Boseley, 2011, available at: https://www.theguardian.com/society/2011/jun/06/analysis-vaccination-programmes (last access March 21, 2018).

[10] Author's interview with representatives from GAVI India (March 9, 2018, via telephone) and from GAVI Geneva (March 22, 2018, in person).

[11] Author's interview with representatives from GAVI Geneva, March 22, 2018.

It is important to note that the relationship between GAVI and the Indian government is very different than the relationship between GAVI and other funding applicants. Indian manufacturers produce more than 60 percent of all the vaccines included in GAVI programs, which gives GAVI an incentive to maintain good relations with the Indian government.[12] Moreover, the size of the country is incomparable in the GAVI portfolio. This gives India "market-shaping power" in global vaccination governance: a vaccine introduced in the Indian vaccination program shapes the global availability of the drug and, thus, the ability of GAVI to provide this vaccine also in other programs.[13] At the same time, GAVI funding to India is limited to partial or periodical funding of the government's immunization program, whereas the majority of the financial contributions and long-term financing is provided by the government itself.

The WHO included the first pentavalent vaccine, a combined vaccine against diphtheria, pertussis, tetanus, Hepatitis B, and Haemophilus influenzae type b, in its list of prequalified vaccines in 2006. This allowed GAVI to approve US$165 million in 2009 of financial support for the Indian government to introduce the vaccine into India's Universal Immunization Program (Nair et al. 2011, 32). The National Technical Advisory Group for Immunization (NTAG) recommended to restrict the implementation of pentavalent to an initial pilot study in the states of Kerala and Tamil Nadu, before it was to be introduced throughout the country.[14] Implementing vaccination is a complex governance scheme. While national health workers and doctors actually vaccinate children, three IOs play a crucial role in all vaccination processes.[15] The UNICEF supply division in Copenhagen is responsible for acquiring the vaccines from the manufacturers and providing them to those countries. Within the country where vaccination takes place, the offices of UNICEF and the UN Development Programme mobilize communities for vaccination, supply the vaccines to the individual regions, and oversee the cold chain management, ensuring that the vaccine is stored at the right temperature during transport.[16] Finally, the WHO country office trains national health workers and supports the government's capacity to carry out vaccination programs.

[12] Author's interview with representatives from GAVI India (March 9, 2018, via telephone) and from GAVI Geneva (March 22, 2018, in person).

[13] Author's interview with representatives from GAVI Geneva, March 22, 2018.

[14] Governancenow 2016: Needle of Suspicion. Vaccine Leaves Experts on Pins and Needles, article by Sreelatha Menon, April 23, 2016, available at: https://www.governancenow.com/views/columns/needle-suspicion-vaccine-leaves-experts-pins-needles (last access December 17, 2018).

[15] Author's interview with representatives from GAVI Geneva, March 22, 2018.

[16] UNICEF n.d.: Expanding Immunization Coverage, available at: https://www.unicef.org/immunization/index_coverage.html (last access December 17, 2018).

To sum up, the complex governance scheme in immunization has two processes: vaccine development and vaccination. In the process of developing the HPV vaccine, private actors such as the Gates Foundation and PATH were crucial in enabling clinical trials that tested the effects of HPV vaccines. Since the Gates Foundation is also one of the biggest financial contributors to both the WHO and GAVI, this adds a layer of complexity (Clinton and Sridhar 2017; McGoey 2017). What is particularly striking in this context is that it is therefore impossible to delineate clear responsibilities of a formal delegation relationship. Once the WHO approves the vaccines and includes them in the list of prequalified vaccines, the GAVI Alliance together with UNICEF, the UN Development Programme, and the WHO facilitate the vaccination process. Given the important role of the WHO in the approval of vaccines for use by the international immunization community, this still ascribes the WHO some responsibility for protecting human rights in vaccine development and vaccination (Clarke 2014, ch. 6). One would thus expect the WHO to act as a vertical accountability holder in the context of public–private health partnerships. However, as I show in the following section, the accountability framework in the processes of vaccine development and vaccine implementation has been rather limited since the WHO decided to engage in GPPHP.

Accountability Framework for Vaccine Development and Vaccination

Most of the literature on accountability of public–private health partnerships focuses on whether GPPHP implement their mandates effectively or how they manage their finances (Bartsch 2007; Buse and Walt 2002; Caines et al. 2004; Richter 2004; Steets and Blattner 2010). In such research, scholars rarely examine GPPHP accountability with regard to human rights. Instead, the accountability of GPPHP is primarily "judged in relation to its [i.e., the partnership's] own objectives" (Hesselmann 2011, 15). This implies that accountability of a GPPHP is mostly conceived in terms of vertical accountability, that is, how accountable the partnership is toward its members. By contrast, this chapter builds on the notion that "partnership accountability can differ from the one performed by its members" (Steets 2010). By adding a human rights perspective to the discussion on GPPHP accountability, I thus reveal the limitations of accountability in current complex global health governance.

Although human rights are regarded as a normative basis for the MDGs, the concrete actions that were developed to implement these goals were formulated without referring to a human rights framework (Alston 2005; Zaidi 2010). This has significant implications for the standards by which global actors implement specific actions such as immunization. When GPPHP started to shape global immunization governance in 2000, the accountability framework with regard to human rights aspects was thus rather limited in terms of vaccine development and vaccination.

The principles outlined in the Declaration of Helsinki, which the World Medical Association adopted in 1964 and revised in 2000, are the most relevant standards with regard to the rights of clinical trial participants in the context of vaccine development.[17] These guidelines include the conditions for using placebos, for example, and they emphasize the necessity of informed consent in clinical trials. These standards, which were directed to individual doctors and medical researchers, represent the core ethical principles to be adhered to in medical research with human subjects. The WHO incorporated them into its Guidelines for Good Clinical Practice, which made them customary international law and superior to any national or international legislation (Carlson et al. 2004; Gøtzsche 2011; WHO 1995, para. 9).[18]

The 2000 WHO guidelines for partnerships in the health sector outline more concrete standards for WHO's cooperation with private actors. However, these guidelines do not refer to a human rights framework. Instead, they outline the conditions under which the WHO can accept financial contributions from companies or cooperate with private actors for developing a new drug (WHO 2000). Moreover, these guidelines only apply to the trials that the WHO has arranged. However, PATH and the Gates Foundation, not the WHO, arranged and conducted the clinical trials testing HPV vaccines (Jain 2013). Even if these private actors later cooperated with the WHO when implementing the vaccination program, the WHO guidelines for partnerships are not directly applicable to these clinical trials.

To enhance the monitoring of vaccine development, the WHO established an international clinical trials registry in 2005 that aims at making clinical trials abroad more transparent. By hosting the registry's secretariat, the WHO had an improved basis for increased monitoring.[19] Despite the fact that registration is not legally required, the number of clinical trials registered in

[17] See Declaration of Helsinki 2001, available at: http://www.who.int/bulletin/archives/79 per cent284 per cent29373.pdf (last access December 17, 2018).

[18] See the current version of the Declaration of Helsinki, available at: https://www.wma.net/policies-post/wma-declaration-of-helsinki-ethical-principles-for-medical-research-involving-human-subjects/ (last access December 17, 2018).

[19] See the WHO International Clinical Trials Registry, available at: http://www.who.int/ictrp/about/en/ (last access December 18, 2018).

the database has significantly increased (Moorthy et al. 2015). Part of this increase is due to the support of international researchers for the registry: the International Committee of Medical Journals Editors announced they would not publish any research on the basis of clinical trials that had not been registered (Gülmezoglu et al. 2005). This policy clearly enhanced the incentives to register trials in the database. However, the monitoring of clinical trials in India was rather limited. Only since 2009 were clinical trials registered with the Indian Council of Medical Research and, as a consequence, trials with no effects or negative effects were usually not reported, thereby skewing the results of the tests (WHO 2008).

In vaccination, health activists have voiced human rights concerns most often after sudden illnesses or deaths occurring among participants of the vaccination programs (People's Union for Democratic Rights 2014). In order to develop clearer standards for how to assess whether these illnesses and deaths can be attributed to the vaccination, the WHO financed the Brighton Collaboration on AEFI, which started in 2001 (Kohl et al. 2005). In parallel, one of the WHO's core tasks in the context of global immunization campaigns is to monitor vaccination—including any adverse effects, deaths related to vaccination, or other complaints.[20] On the basis of the advice of experts from the Global Advisory Committee on Vaccine Safety, which was established in 1999, the WHO assesses vaccine safety concerns with regard to their seriousness. During the vaccination campaign, however, the core monitoring activities still are expected to be undertaken by the country itself that receives support from international actors in its vaccination programs to undertake core monitoring activities.[21] For this purpose, India established the NTAG as the main institution that recommends and monitors new vaccines. This advisory group originally met once per year but has increased the number of its meetings and expanded its membership over the years (John 2010). Alongside governmental officials and independent medical experts, representatives from UNICEF and the WHO are also members of this body.[22]

[20] Author's interview with representatives from GAVI Geneva, March 22, 2018; author's interview with a representative from WHO India, March 12, 2018; GAVI n.d.: The World Health Organization, available at: https://www.gavi.org/about/partners/who/ (last access December 17, 2018).

[21] Author's interview with a representative from WHO India, March 12, 2018; GAVI 2000: Board Meeting, Oslo, 13–14 June, available at: http://lobby.la.psu.edu/020_compulsory_licensing/Organizational_Statements/GAVI/GAVI_3rd_Board_Meeting_061300.pdf, 36–7.

[22] UNICEF in Action, available at: http://unicef.in/Whatwedo/3/Immunization (last access December 17, 2018).

Claims to Enhance Pluralist Accountability with Regard to Vaccine Development

In light of the weak existing accountability framework for GPPHP with regard to human rights, several attempts to enhance accountability were undertaken at the international level. With regard to clinical trials, the UN Special Rapporteur on the right of everyone to the enjoyment of the highest attainable standard of health, Paul Hunt, developed the Human Rights Guidelines for Pharmaceutical Companies in Relation to Access to Medicines in 2008. Taking into consideration the increased tendency for clinical trials to take place in non-Western countries, these guidelines emphasized that clinical trials "should observe the highest ethical and human rights standards" and emphasized that this was particularly relevant in states with "weak regulatory frameworks."[23] A collaborative monitoring initiative, however, failed because a majority of pharmaceutical companies was not willing to participate (Khosla and Hunt 2008, 10).

In parallel to these international efforts, further claims to enhance accountability were undertaken at the domestic level. The case of India, in particular, demonstrates the effects and the limits of these claims with regard to enhancing an accountability framework for vaccine development and vaccination. With regard to the clinical trials testing the HPV vaccine that were undertaken by PATH and financed by the Gates Foundation, several civil society actors mobilized to pressure the Indian government from 2009 onwards to stop the trials until "concerns relating to safety, efficacy and cost effectiveness of the planned interventions [were] re-evaluated."[24] In 2009 and 2010, human rights activists sent two memoranda to the Indian Minister of Health and Family Welfare, alleging the trials had violated informed consent. As a consequence, the Indian Council for Medical Research suspended PATH's HPV trials as "demonstration projects" in the two states Andhra Pradesh and Gujarat (Sarojini et al. 2010). The Indian government established an inquiry committee to investigate these allegations, highlighting that any research with human

[23] United Nations General Assembly 2008: Report of the UN Special Rapporteur on the Right to the Highest Attainable Standard of Health, UN document A/63/263, August 11, 2008.

[24] See the memorandum "Concerns around HPV Vaccine," http://feministlawarchives.pldindia.org/wp-content/uploads/Memorandum-to-health-minister-by-Health-organisations-and-activists-on-HPV-vaccines-2009-.pdf (last access December 17, 2018) and the memorandum "Opposing HPV Vaccination" sent to the Indian Minister of Health and Family Welfare, April 7, 2010, available at: https://samawomenshealth.wordpress.com/2010/04/08/memorandum-to-the-health-minister-on-world-health-day-opposing-hpv-vaccinations/ (last access December 17, 2018).

participants needed to follow the established guidelines (ECCHR 2014).[25] After a debate held in April 2010, the Indian Parliament asked the Parliamentary Standing Committee on Health and Family Welfare to investigate the claims. In its report, the committee concluded that the trials conducted by PATH with the help of Indian governmental officials were unethical, claiming that Indians were used as "guinea pigs" and asking the government to undertake steps to hold PATH accountable (Bagla 2013; Jain 2013). The Ministry of Health "issued a warning against PATH" but argued that it did not possess any legal means to enact accountability toward an international NGO and referred to the fact that the trials had ended in 2010.[26] Finally, in 2012 and 2013, several health and human rights activists submitted petitions against clinical trials to the Indian Supreme Court to file a public interest litigation.[27] The petitioners asked the Indian government to enhance accountability vis-à-vis the implementing actors. In the case of HPV trials, the petitioners asked the court to demand clear guidelines on liability and to determine the responsibility of the various implementing actors, such as PATH and the health workers from the Andhra Pradesh and Gujarat local governments (ECCHR 2014).

These public interest litigations showed two main effects. First, the court pushed the Indian government to enhance the monitoring procedures regarding clinical trials by suspending the approval procedures of the Indian authorities for 162 new drugs for two weeks in September 2013. The vocabulary used by one of the judges reveals that these measures were intended as "shaming" the implementing actors.[28] As a consequence, the Ministry of Health decided that informed consent had to be recorded audio-visually to be valid, while respecting the right to privacy (ECCHR 2014). Second, by allowing affidavits from other institutions, the Supreme Court engaged in important standard-setting activities that established a human rights framework for clinical trials. In the context of the HPV trials, the European Center for Constitutional and

[25] See the Final Report of the Committee appointed by the Government of India, No. V.25011/160/2010-HR dated April 15, 2010, to enquire into "Alleged irregularities in the conduct of studies using Human Papilloma Virus (HPV) vaccine" by PATH in India, February 15, 2011, section 7.1.3, available at: https://www.icmr.nic.in/sites/default/files/reports/HPV_PATH_final_report.pdf (last access December 17, 2018).

[26] Indian Express 2015: Can't Penalize US NGO for Violating Drug Trial Norms, article by Uthkarsh Anand, April 18, 2015, available at: http://indianexpress.com/article/india/india-others/cant-penalise-us-ngo-for-violating-drug-trial-norms/ (last access December 17, 2018).

[27] For all court orders since 2012 and ongoing hearings see: https://www.sci.gov.in (last access December 17, 2018).

[28] One of the judges reportedly said that "companies are *treating India* as a *heaven for clinical trials*, but it is *proving hell for India*," a statement that was widely reported in the media, e.g., https://www.dailymail.co.uk/news/article-2893485/Children-guinea-pigs-anti-cervical-cancer-drug.html (last access December 17, 2018, emphasis in original).

Human Rights decided to submit an affidavit in which it outlined which rights should be considered as crucial in clinical trials: the right to informed consent, the right to health, and the right to special care for children, women, and minorities (ECCHR 2014). In particular, they argued that the lack of informed consent would violate Article 7 of the International Covenant on Civil and Political Rights, which stipulates that "No one shall be subjected to torture or to cruel, inhuman or degrading treatment or punishment. In particular, no one shall be subjected without his free consent to medical or scientific experimentation." Furthermore, the lack of monitoring in trials would violate Article 12 of the International Covenant on Economic, Social and Cultural Rights. This affidavit can be regarded as an important attempt of standard setting for human rights-related aspects in clinical trials.

However, these attempts to involve domestic courts as accountability holders in clinical trials did not create a comprehensive pluralist accountability framework for vaccine development. The response of the two companies and PATH to the parliamentary report and the media reporting reveals that they did not recognize these domestic investigation and litigation processes as accountability mechanisms. Instead, they claimed that the reports contained an "inaccurate characterization" and false accusations, while the safety of vaccines had already been established earlier through clinical trials in India.[29] The reaction also demonstrates that there was a fundamental disagreement about what PATH and the Gates Foundation should be held accountable for: while the parliamentary report and the media talked about the "colluding" of PATH and the Gates Foundation with pharmaceutical companies, PATH emphasized that vaccines always needed to be procured from a manufacturer and that the companies were not involved in the design and implementation of the study.[30]

In sum, there have been several claims to enhance accountability regarding clinical trials in the context of vaccine development. In the case of HPV trials undertaken by PATH with the financial support of the Gates Foundation, civil society actors in India attempted to enhance domestic accountability structures through public interest litigations. In particular, these litigations confirmed the right to informed consent as a core standard to be respected by all

[29] PATH 2013: Statement from PATH: Cervical Cancer Demonstration Project in India, September 3, 2013, available at: https://www.path.org/media-center/statement-from-path-cervical-cancer-demonstration-project-in-india/ (last access December 17, 2018).

[30] PATH 2013: Statement from PATH: Cervical Cancer Demonstration Project in India, September 3, 2013, available at: https://www.path.org/media-center/statement-from-path-cervical-cancer-demonstration-project-in-india/ (last access December 17, 2018).

actors implementing clinical trials. However, the case study also showed that pluralist accountability was restricted by a lack of understanding about what the implementing actors should be held accountable for.

Claims to Enhance Accountability with Regard to Vaccination

The guidelines for monitoring vaccination required that doctors and hospitals record cases of AEFI correctly, which allegedly did not happen in some cases following pentavalent vaccination (People's Union for Democratic Rights 2014, 15). When concerns about potential AEFI became public, several countries, such as Bhutan and Vietnam but not India, withdrew pentavalent vaccines from their immunization programs (Puliyel 2013, 143). These actions, however, were not the result of effective accountability structures but rather constituted ad hoc governmental responses. A panel of international experts established by the WHO through its Global Advisory Committee on Vaccine Safety investigated the allegations with regard to AEFI in four Asian countries and concluded that the deaths were not related to the immunization (People's Union for Democratic Rights 2014, 14; WHO 2013). As a consequence, a number of countries reintroduced the vaccination program (Nair et al. 2011, 33). Only with regard to the drug Easy Five did the WHO enact a sanctioning mechanism: in 2011, it decided to remove the drug from the list of prequalified vaccines after a WHO team conducted an onsite audit to investigate whether panaceas were used under the drug's label during vaccination, before reintroducing it back onto the list in 2013 (People's Union for Democratic Rights 2014, 18).

Health activists in India, however, doubted the legitimacy of this WHO-based accountability mechanism and instead investigated the AEFI allegations on their own (People's Union for Democratic Rights 2014; Puliyel 2013).[31] Similar to what happened with regard to clinical trials, some of them filed public interest litigations in the Indian Supreme Court seeking to ban pentavalent vaccinations in 2011 and 2013 (Nair et al. 2011). The petitioners of 2011 even linked the pentavalent case to the case of clinical trials undertaken by PATH developing the HPV vaccine, to increase the court's motivation to

[31] Governancenow 2016: Needle of Suspicion. Vaccine Leaves Experts on Pins and Needles, article by Sreelatha Menon, April 23, 2016, available at: https://www.governancenow.com/views/columns/needle-suspicion-vaccine-leaves-experts-pins-needles (last access December 17, 2018).

follow their demands. One of the activists also joined the NTAG, which had recommended the initial introduction of pentavalent vaccination in the two states of Kerala and Tamil Nadu, as an expert.[32] The petitioner of 2013 claimed that the originally intended review of the pilot introduction of pentavalent by the NTAG was not completed and the government had not waited for the evaluation before expanding the vaccination to other states.[33]

These claims seem to have had some effects for enhancing accountability at least at the domestic level. In 2013, the government established the Immunization Technical Support Unit to reinforce and institutionalize the monitoring activities to be undertaken by the NTAG (People's Union for Democratic Rights 2014: 25). This unit then hosted the secretariat of the NTAG and facilitated the coordination of meetings of experts. Health activists continued to question the legitimacy of the NTAG, however, claiming that the body lacked independence due to funding provided by the Gates Foundation.[34] The government pushed for the development of a code of conduct providing the standards for NTAG membership and the declaration of conflicts of interest, which was proposed by the NTAG in 2015.[35] In response to criticism about "foreign funding," the government further clarified in 2017 that the NTAG was financially fully independent.[36] Contrary to allegations that the establishment of the Immunization Technical Support Unit would lead to a decrease in transparency in monitoring AEFI (People's Union for Democratic Rights 2014, 25), the reports by the NTAG are still available to the public.[37]

To sum up, there were several steps to enhance accountability with regard to AEFI in the context of pentavalent vaccination in India. While the WHO

[32] See the writ petition (civil) No. 13698 submitted to the High Court of Delhi, available at: https://currenthealthscenario.blogspot.com/2012/04/petition-against-pentavalent-sordid.html (last access December 18, 2018).

[33] Hindustan Times 2013: SC Asks Govt to Respond to PIL on Pentavalent Vaccine, September 2, available at: https://www.hindustantimes.com/delhi-news/sc-asks-govt-to-respond-to-pil-on-pentavalent-vaccine/story-iI7BHrYktdrPOe7hmIWDSI.html (last access December 18, 2018).

[34] Indian Express 2016: Conflict of Interest: NHM Panel Raises Questions on Bill Gates Foundation, article by Abantikha Gosh, March 30, 2016, available at: https://indianexpress.com/article/india/india-news-india/conflict-of-interest-nhm-panel-raises-questions-on-bill-gates-foundation/ (last access December 18, 2018).

[35] See the meeting minutes of the National Technical Advisory Group from August 25, 2015, available at: https://mohfw.gov.in/sites/default/files/29914318411467722384.pdf (last access December 18, 2018).

[36] Reuters 2017: India Cuts Some Funding Ties with Gates Foundation on Immunization, article by Aditya Kalra, February 8, 2017, available at: https://www.reuters.com/article/us-india-health-bmgf/india-cuts-some-funding-ties-with-gates-foundation-on-immunization-idUSKBN15N13K (last access December 17, 2018); Government of India 2017: Press Note, available at: http://pib.nic.in/newsite/PrintRelease.aspx?relid=158277 (last access December 18, 2018).

[37] Government of India 2005: Right to Information Act, available at: https://mohfw.gov.in/right-information-rti/rti-act-for-ministry/departments-health-and-family-welfare/immunization/aefi-reports (last access December 18, 2018).

relied on "fire alarm" monitoring and investigated allegations, domestic actors did not recognize this vertical accountability mechanism as legitimate. Similar to the case of HPV trials, they claimed to enhance accountability via domestic litigation. In the aftermath of these petitions, the Indian government reinforced domestic monitoring procedures to be able to better investigate AEFI.

Attempts to Enhance Human Rights Accountability in GPPHP at the Global Level

The claims to enhance accountability in India not only targeted domestic actors but also directly addressed the WHO as the global authority for approving vaccines for international use. A network of Indian activists, for example, published an open letter to the WHO's then director-general Margaret Chan, in which they openly criticized the WHO's actions with regard to the pentavalent vaccination in Asia.[38] In 2015, the WHO adopted a new policy on publishing results from trials, thereby asking to disclose the results from older, unreported trials (Moorthy et al. 2015). In addition, a number of international actors involved in the design and financing of clinical trials, such as PATH and the Gates Foundation, committed to publishing the results of trials, including serious adverse events, in the WHO's clinical trials database in 2017.[39]

The WHO also recognized the detrimental effects of the lack of consistent standards with regard to the use of placebos in clinical trials. Its Department of Ethics and Social Determinants thus convened an expert panel in 2014 to develop an ethical framework for the use of placebos "when an efficacious vaccine already exists" (Rid et al. 2014). The guidelines were to reassure donors financing ethical trials and to prevent trials from being unethical. This standard-setting activity was financially supported by PATH, the NGO financed by the Gates Foundation that was implementing the clinical trials on HPV in India. There is, however, no monitoring body within the WHO that checks on the implementation of this framework. The WHO's own Research Ethics Review Committee only monitors research that is financially or

[38] All India Drug Action Network 2012: Open Letter to DG, WHO, March 12, available at: https://aidanindia.wordpress.com/2012/03/12/open-letter-to-dg-who-pentavalent-vaccine-related-deaths-in-india/ (last access December 18, 2018).

[39] WHO 2017: Joint Statement on Public Disclosure of Results from Clinical Trials, available at: http://www.who.int/ictrp/results/jointstatement/en/ (last access December 4, 2018).

technically supported by the WHO, not the clinical trials that lead to the development of vaccines later approved by the WHO.[40]

To address the lack of accountability in vaccination, the WHO together with GAVI and other implementing partner organizations issued the Global Vaccine Safety Blueprint in 2011 and established the Global Vaccine Safety Initiative to implement the document's recommendations.[41] This was supposed to "enhance pharmacovigilance" and reinforce the implementing countries' capacities to monitor the safety of vaccines.[42] In 2014, the WHO revised its guidelines for introducing a new vaccine in national immunization programs, which included a minimum country capacity to monitor safety aspects (WHO 2014, 101). While the previous guidelines simply recommended that introducing a vaccine "would be an appropriate time to start establishing [an AEFI surveillance system]" (WHO 2005b, 27), the current guidelines thus set more clear standards and monitoring structures that needed to be implemented in vaccination.

With regard to GPPHP's human rights accountability, several attempts were undertaken at the global level. The Working Group on Global Health Initiatives and Partnerships adopted the Best Practice Principles for Global Health Partnership Activities at Country Level.[43] These principles, however, mainly recommended self-reporting and did not establish any human rights-related standards or monitoring procedures. The Global Fund recently has taken a more proactive approach to ensure that human rights violations would not occur in the Fund's programs.[44] No comparable steps have been undertaken by GAVI so far, despite the fact that human rights play an important role for GAVI's mandate, in particular, the rights of women and children as well as the right to equal access to medicines.[45] The only monitoring undertaken by GAVI has been in relation to the misuse of financial support. After its own investigations in 2011, GAVI withdrew its funds from four African

[40] See the WHO Research Ethics Review Committee, available at: https://www.who.int/ethics/review-committee/en/ (last access December 18, 2018).

[41] See the terms of reference of the Global Vaccine Safety Initiative, available at: https://www.who.int/vaccine_safety/initiative/GVSI_ToRs.pdf (last access December 18, 2018).

[42] See the Global Vaccine Safety Initiative, available at: http://www.who.int/vaccine_safety/initiative/en/ (last access December 18, 2018).

[43] Working Group on Global Health Initiatives and Partnerships 2005: Best Practices, available at: http://www.stoptb.org/assets/documents/about/cb/meetings/09/2.05-08 per cent20Bestper cent20Practiceper cent20Principles/2.05-8.1 per cent20Bestper cent20Practiceper cent20Principles.pdf (last access December 18, 2018).

[44] Global Fund 2014: Managing the Risk of Human Rights Violations in Global Fund-Supported Programs, meeting report, Geneva, 22–23 May.

[45] GAVI n.d.: Health Equity, available at: https://www.gavi.org/about/value/health-equity/ (last access December 4, 2018).

countries.[46] This financial accountability was institutionalized in GAVI's Transparency and Accountability Policy in 2014. Regarding the potential effect of GAVI programs on human rights, however, there has been no systematic institutional accountability mechanism established so far.

The aforementioned initial steps in standard setting and monitoring human rights in clinical trials and vaccination seem to be an effect of the attempts to enhance pluralist accountability at the domestic level. In particular within the WHO, but also among its implementing partners, the need for greater legitimacy through enhanced accountability have become a matter of concern (Rid et al. 2014). Despite this, the overall accountability framework of GPPHP in the fields of vaccine development and vaccination remains rather limited. While the clinical trials registry enhanced transparency, there is no overarching monitoring structure for clinical trials and their sponsors' reporting to the registry. In the context of vaccination, the Global Vaccine Safety Initiative, with its emphasis on "pharmacovigilance," highlights that monitoring remains the core responsibility of the member states who are implementing vaccination programs. I analyze in the following section what made accountability difficult in this case.

Conditions for Pluralist Accountability

The complex responsibilities in vaccine development and vaccination programs limit the potential for vertical accountability. The informal ways of cooperation that characterize global health governance blur the lines of attribution and make it difficult to identify vertical accountability holders. Without clear lines of responsibility, it remains unclear which actors that participate in GPPHP can be held accountable for what and by whom. As long as the responsibility of financial sponsors and of the WHO as the organization approving a vaccine for international use is not clarified, vertical accountability will continue to remain limited.

Additionally, two factors inhibit the development of pluralist accountability with regard to GPPHP in this case. First, the complex governance structures in the field of global health provide little incentive for international nongovernmental and governmental human rights organizations to act as independent accountability holders outside of GPPHP. This is partly a result of the

[46] Global Fund Observer 2011: Concerned about Misuse of Funds, GAVI Suspends Grants in Four Countries, article by David Garmaise, available at: http://aidspan.org/gfo_article/concerned-about-misuse-funds-gavi-suspends-grants-four-countries (last access December 18, 2018).

inclusiveness of the field since many of the potential accountability holders were also involved in the process of designing the MDGs and the subsequent Sustainable Development Goals (SDGs), which became the main driving institutional frameworks for the fragmentation of global health governance. Moreover, the implementation of the MDGs and SDGs often depends on human rights organizations, for example civil society organizations that mobilize communities for vaccination.[47] As a consequence, these organizations have established their profiles as cooperating partners, which precludes them from becoming accountability holders (Jain et al. 2015). One of the few international human rights organizations that got involved as a standard setter with regard to clinical trials research in vaccine development in India is the European Center for Constitutional and Human Rights, an international NGO that has established a distinct profile as an independent legal organization to enforce corporate accountability specifically in the Global South (Terwindt 2014).

Most importantly, however, the politicization that characterizes the fields of vaccine development and vaccination makes it impossible for an actor to establish itself as an independent accountability holder without being attributed to one or the other side of the ideological battle. Health rights activists and organizations that develop vaccines or implement vaccination accuse each other of being harmful to individuals, either by pushing for vaccination or by hindering it. In the discourse, "concerned clinicians and public health professionals speaking of AEFI are labelled as 'anti-vaccine lobby'" (People's Union for Democratic Rights 2014, 22).[48] Indeed, it is virtually impossible to distinguish whether actors monitoring the effect of vaccination do this because they intend to act as accountability holders to ensure the legitimacy of vaccination or because they reject vaccination as such. Many of the organizations involved in attempts to enhance accountability at the domestic level—the Human Rights Law Network, Sama Resource Group for Women and Health, the Karnataka-based Drug Action Forum, and the Delhi Science Forum, for example—are led by individuals who are critical of vaccination in general. Moreover, due to historical experiences with colonial practices, they tend to assume that international actors within a GPPHP would act out of ill will by default (Wallace 2012). Ultimately, this makes it rather difficult for potential accountability holders to establish an independent position within this politicized environment and thus remain legitimate in the eyes of the organizations

[47] Author's interview with representatives from GAVI, Geneva, March 22, 2018.

[48] Author's interview with representatives from GAVI, Geneva, March 22, 2018; author's telephone interview with a representative from WHO India, March 12, 2018.

sponsoring, implementing, or approving vaccine development. The incentive to engage in accountability, therefore, remains rather low.

The second condition that inhibited the development of pluralist accountability results from a moral dilemma that is inherent to the field of vaccine development and vaccination programs. This is the core dilemma of accepting the potential to harm a few people in order to save the lives of many others. AEFI, which might or might not be causally related to the vaccination, cannot be completely precluded from happening.[49] Representatives of GPPHP argue that these events are to a certain extent unavoidable and are regarded as a "technical issue" that the national technical advisory groups monitor with the support of the WHO.[50] Instead, both GAVI and the Gates Foundation argue that vaccination helped to prevent around 10 million deaths among children up until 2017, or an estimated amount of 2.5 million deaths per year.[51] Actors who claim to enhance accountability, however, argue that a number of fifty-four potentially vaccine-related AEFI cases in India "calls for some serious re-assessment of the decision to introduce pentavalent vaccine in the universal immunization program in India" (People's Union for Democratic Rights 2014, 3). This dilemma makes it impossible to clearly establish what the implementing actors should be held accountable for.

Nevertheless, the increased reporting about AEFI decreased the trust in international actors that developed and administered vaccines, not only in India but also globally. The WHO recognized that AEFI reporting had led to a "climate of concern" that required a more systematic monitoring and follow up of AEFI, otherwise AEFI could "undermine confidence in a vaccine and ultimately have dramatic consequences for immunization coverage and disease incidence."[52] In March 2012 the WHO launched the Global Vaccine Safety Initiative to increase "pharmacovigilance" in order to monitor vaccine safety (Maure et al. 2014). In its 2013 meeting in Delhi, the members of the Global Vaccine Safety Initiative issued a statement: "Active surveillance studies in developing countries are important with increased vaccine uptake. Vaccines are being introduced earlier or exclusively in developing countries

[49] WHO n.d.: Global Vaccine Safety, available at: https://www.who.int/vaccine_safety/initiative/detection/AEFI/en/ (last access December 18, 2018).

[50] Author's interview with representatives from GAVI, Geneva, March 22, 2018.

[51] GAVI n.d.: Mission, available at: https://www.gavi.org/about/mission/; Bill and Melinda Gates Foundation n.d.: Vaccine Delivery: Strategic Overview, available at: https://www.gatesfoundation.org/What-We-Do/Global-Development/Vaccine-Delivery (last access December 10, 2018).

[52] WHO n.d.: Global Vaccine Safety: Adverse Events Following Immunization (AEFI), available at: https://www.who.int/vaccine_safety/initiative/detection/AEFI/en/ (last access December 10, 2018).

with incomplete safety profiles."[53] This demonstrates that the WHO has become aware of the increasing vulnerability of the actors implementing vaccination. Over the years, antivaccination activists have also physically attacked vaccination teams, for example, in 2013 in Nigeria and in 2015 in Pakistan.[54] In India, although mistrust in vaccination was geographically restricted, the actors implementing vaccination programs were nevertheless aware of their growing vulnerability.[55]

In this situation of moral dilemma and increasing vulnerability, a strong counter-norm has evolved that ultimately enabled the actors involved to make themselves invulnerable to human rights demands. In 2005, the World Health Assembly adopted the Global Immunization Vision and Strategy, which issued the guideline to "reduce vaccine-preventable deaths by two thirds by 2015" (WHO 2005a). Since then, all international actors participating in GPPHP have committed themselves to prevent diseases through vaccination. Private foundations have in this context established their reputation for being "benign agents" (Moran 2011). The WHO has declared the years 2010 to 2020 as the "Decade of Vaccines" for which the Global Vaccine Action Plan formulated a clear goal in 2012: "A world in which all individuals and communities enjoy lives free from vaccine-preventable diseases."[56] This has become the guiding principle for developing and implementing vaccines. Vaccination is thus intrinsically linked to the right to life and the right to health. Using human rights as a counter-norm, actors promoting and implementing vaccination could successfully refute any claims to greater accountability.

In sum, the case study shows how two factors inhibited the development of pluralist accountability in vaccine development and vaccination programs.

[53] Report of the 2nd Meeting of the Global Vaccine Safety Initiative, 19–20 November 2013, New Delhi, India, available at: https://www.who.int/vaccine_safety/publications/GVSI_meeting2_india_Nov_2013_report.pdf.

[54] New York Times 2015: Polio Team Attacked in Pakistan, article by Salman Masood, February 14, available at: https://www.nytimes.com/2015/02/15/world/asia/attack-on-polio-vaccination-team-in-pakistan-leaves-one-dead.html; New York Times 2013: Gunmen Kill Nigerian Polio Vaccine Workers in Echo of Pakistan Attacks, article by Donald G. McNeil, Jr., February 8, available at: https://www.nytimes.com/2013/02/09/world/africa/in-nigeria-polio-vaccine-workers-are-killed-by-gunmen.html (last access December 18, 2018).

[55] Vaccine Confidence Project 2015: The State of Vaccine Confidence 2015, available at: https://www.vaccineconfidence.org/wp-content/uploads/2018/10/VCP_The-State-of-Vaccine-Confidence_2015.pdf (last access December 10, 2018). In a survey of 2016, India was ranked in the lower half of sixty-seven developing and developed countries, just above Germany (Vaccine Confidence Project 2016: The State of Vaccine Confidence 2016, available at: https://www.vaccineconfidence.org/wp-content/uploads/2018/10/VCP_The-State-of-Vaccine-Confidence_2016.pdf, 297). Only recently, the Indian government reportedly stopped the introduction of HPV vaccination (Das 2018).

[56] The Decade of Vaccines Collaboration Leadership Council includes representatives from GAVI, the WHO, UNICEF, the Gates Foundation, as well as a number of national or regional organizations (see https://www.gavi.org/about/ghd/dov/, last access December 18, 2018).

First, the characteristics of the governance structures that shape global immunization programs hinder the ability of third parties to act as accountability holders outside of GPPHP. This is partly due to the fact that the design of both the MDGs and SDGs relies on an inclusive network of implementing actors. More importantly, since vaccination is an extremely politicized topic in which actors are easily delegitimized, human rights organizations risk their reputation if they are supportive of vaccination in general. Second, there is a lack of understanding about what implementing actors should be held accountable for because of the moral dilemma that exists between accepting a potential harm to a few people in order to save the lives of many others. Despite the fact that the vulnerability of the international community had partially increased due to the growing mistrust on the ground, the Decade of Vaccine initiative has established a strong counter-norm that links vaccination to the right to life and the right to health. This strong normative environment in which vaccine development and vaccination take place has restricted the evolution of independent accountability mechanisms. It thus allowed the implementing actors to recur to a human rights framework when refusing to recognize potential claims to enhance accountability.

Conclusion

This chapter highlights the difficulties of holding actors in complex global health governance accountable. While formal delegation relationships with IOs as the mandating authorities characterize many other fields of global governance, global health governance is fragmented and consists of primarily informal governance structures. In order to implement the MDGs and later the SDGs, the WHO decided to open up global health governance to private actors, which led to the foundation of numerous GPPHP such as the GAVI. This chapter illustrates the complexity in vaccination governance by analyzing how private companies together with the Gates Foundation developed the HPV vaccine, and how international actors cooperated with private and national actors when implementing the HPV and pentavalent vaccines. GAVI also provided financial assistance to governments that decided to introduce a new vaccine.

These complex and informal governance structures have made traditional, vertical accountability impossible because there is no mandating authority that could act as an accountability holder. The fragmentation of global health governance in the process of developing and implementing the MDGs and

SDGs has led to a network of shared and unclear responsibilities in which a number of potential accountability holders rely on each other, both financially and structurally. The WHO's role is more that of a coordinator or orchestrator (Abbott et al. 2015), rather than a delegating authority. Despite this, the WHO has a very important function in the context of vaccination as it approves the vaccines for international vaccination programs. This distinguishes the WHO's authority from the role of other actors involved in global health governance. However, despite this important function, the role of the WHO as an accountability holder remains limited. The case study on vaccine development and vaccination in India shows that the organization conceives its role primarily as one of supporting national governments in strengthening domestic monitoring procedures. Other than that, the WHO's most important steps to enhance accountability for vaccine development and vaccination include conducting an ad hoc investigation into allegations of AEFI, establishing the international clinical trials registry, launching the Global Vaccine Safety Initiative, and revising the guidelines for introducing a vaccine in national immunization programs that now require a minimum structure of safety monitoring. While these are important steps toward enhancing accountability, human rights-based standard setting, systematic monitoring, and sanctioning remain limited.

GAVI in turn does not consider itself to be an accountability holder. While its competitor in the field of vaccination, the Global Fund, has acknowledged potential human rights-related effects of its programs and taken initial measures, GAVI representatives refer to the WHO and the national governments for enhancing accountability. It remains to be seen whether increased competition between GAVI and the Global Fund, for example in the field of malaria vaccination, will stimulate these partnerships to act as accountability holders toward its implementing partners in the future.[57] So far, any steps toward some standard setting, monitoring, and sanctioning comparable to vertical accountability remain limited in GPPHP.

At the same time, vaccination is an extremely politicized topic, not only in India and other developing countries but also in Western countries. While some researchers claim that the politicization of the WHO has hindered accountability in health politics (Barnes and Brown 2011; Bruen and Brugha 2014), this

[57] Global Fund 2017: Partnership Supports Launch of Malaria Vaccine Pilots in Three African Countries, April 24, available at: https://www.theglobalfund.org/en/news/2017-04-24-partnership-supports-launch-of-malaria-vaccine-pilots-in-three-african-countries/ (last access December 18, 2018). See also the recently adopted Global Action Plan for Healthy Lives and Well-Being for All, available at: https://www.who.int/sdg/global-action-plan (last access December 20, 2010).

analysis demonstrated how extreme politicization also hinders the development of accountability with regard to partnerships in global health governance, even if such entities regard themselves as apolitical or technical compared with the WHO. Ideological differences about vaccination have created a highly contested normative environment in which actors fundamentally disagree about what implementing actors should be held accountable for. An agreement, however, would be necessary for an accountability relationship. Moreover, the case of HPV and pentavalent vaccination in India shows how ideological cleavages about vaccination has made it impossible for potential independent actors to act as accountability holders without taking sides in this battle. Therefore, the incentive to engage in accountability has remained rather low.

Finally, a strong moral dilemma inherent to the field of vaccine development and vaccination—that is, the question of whether it is acceptable that some individuals experience negative effects while a significant number of people benefit from the positive effects of a vaccine—further inhibits the development of accountability. In this dilemma situation, the actors that develop and implement vaccines emphasize the overall positive effect of vaccination for millions of children worldwide. Moreover, vaccination is intrinsically linked to the right to health. This normative framework has helped to render GPPHP invulnerable to any demands for greater accountability, and as a result they refuse to recognize any external accountability holders. Since facets of the general public are mistrustful of vaccination, however, the lack of accountability invites actors that advocate against vaccination to make the affected populations increasingly insecure about the benefits of vaccination. If vaccination is a human right, a clear human rights-related accountability framework would be the next step for a successful implementation of the "Decade of Vaccine."

Ultimately, this case study shows the limitations of vertical and pluralist accountability in global health governance. The lack of a clear delegating authority has rendered the governance structures in the field of vaccination and vaccine development extremely complex. My analysis reveals how both a politicized environment and a moral dilemma situation in which actors adopt a strong counter-norm to render themselves invulnerable against human rights demands inhibit the evolution of pluralist accountability. As a consequence, the legitimacy of vaccination as a whole has come under strain. Without enhanced accountability mechanisms that take into consideration the potential human rights-related effects of vaccination, the politicization will remain strong and will potentially undermine the most vulnerable populations' trust in vaccination.

8

Conclusion

Pluralist Accountability and Legitimacy

Explaining the Variation of Pluralist Accountability

The authority of global governance institutions has over the last decades increasingly affected the rights and lives of individuals. Numerous cases have become public where members or partners of IOs, or national actors operating under the mandate of IOs, violated human rights either by not acting in accordance with their mandate or by actively doing harm to individual citizens. This has put the legitimacy of IOs under additional pressure. As a consequence, demands to hold implementing actors accountable for their deeds have been put forward, under the assumption that greater accountability would enable IOs to regain their legitimacy. The complexity of global governance today, however, raises important challenges for accountability. IOs that have been mandated to implement economic, security, or health policies by their member states ever more often delegate these tasks to private actors, national actors, or other IOs. As a consequence, the lines of responsibility have become blurred. Thus, traditional vertical accountability—that is, accountability whereby implementing actors are held accountable for their actions directly by the mandating authorities—has become rather difficult to achieve in global governance. Instead, pluralist accountability, or accountability exercised by third parties, has become an important tool for holding actors accountable in complex governance.

In this book, I developed a theoretical framework for conceptualizing and analyzing this pluralist accountability. I defined accountability as the relationship between two actors by which one actor (the accountability holder) sets the standards for the other actor's behavior and monitors and sanctions the other (the accountor). Depending on who acts as an accountability holder, I distinguished two types of accountability: in vertical accountability the mandating authority is the accountability holder; in pluralist accountability third parties such as international courts or regional organizations set the standards, monitor, and sanction the implementing actor.

Accountability in Global Governance. Gisela Hirschmann, Oxford University Press (2020). © Gisela Hirschmann.
DOI: 10.1093/oso/9780198861249.001.0001

What can explain the emergence of this pluralist accountability? I argued in this book that two specific conditions need to be fulfilled. First, there must be a specific opportunity structure in which a competitive environment influences whether third parties become active as accountability holders. I based this argument on the insights of research on norm entrepreneurship and regime fragmentation. The desire to distinguish themselves from other concurring parties in the area of human rights motivates an actor to develop certain niche capacities. Acting as an accountability holder thus enables a third party to demonstrate its distinctive contribution to the promotion of human rights in a competitive environment ("profiling").

As a second condition, I argued that the degree of vulnerability of the implementing actor or the mandating authority with regard to specific norms, such as the respect for human rights, influences the development of pluralist accountability. This argument was based on insights from research on norm compliance. The implementing actors and their mandating authorities do not operate in a social vacuum. Instead, they are embedded in communities that share certain social norms, such as the protection of human rights. If actors violate these norms, their reputation within this community is damaged. The recognition of third parties as accountability holders demonstrates that the implementing actor or the mandating authority—despite the violations—is still committed to these norms and aims to rehabilitate their social status within their respective communities ("mutual recognition").

To illustrate how these two conditions enable pluralist accountability, I examined the emergence of pluralist accountability across eight cases in three different issue areas of complex global governance: peace operations, global health, and economic governance. My desire to conduct an in-depth analysis of the evolution of pluralist accountability and to understand better the causal processes that link the two conditions to the outcome variable determined my choice for this small-N study. The case design followed the logic of variation on the dependent variable: pluralist accountability evolved in five of the selected cases whereas in the other three it did not. Thus, the cases showed that even if we expect pluralist accountability to be a rising trend in global governance, it is by no means an inevitable response to legitimacy problems in complex governance structures but rather depends on the existence of specific conditions.

The two case studies on accountability for the violation of the rights of detainees in Afghanistan revealed the differences in the evolution of pluralist accountability with regard to detainees transferred by ISAF to the detention facilities of the US-led coalition forces of OEF, and those who were handed over to the Afghan government's detaining authorities. In both cases, the treatment of detainees became cause for concern as detainees were deprived of the right to due process and were tortured on numerous occasions. My analysis revealed that while pluralist accountability failed in the case of OEF detentions, it instead evolved with regard to detentions by the Afghan authorities. In the first case, the absence of third parties motivated to advocate for the rights of suspected terrorists in Afghanistan, as well as the low degree of vulnerability on the side of the US government with regard to human rights demands in the immediate aftermath of the attacks of September 11, 2001, hindered the rise of pluralist accountability. In the case of detainees transferred by ISAF to the Afghan government, however, the human rights unit within the UN-led political operation UNAMA was motivated to act as an accountability holder in order to develop a distinct profile that would allow it to separate itself from the other sections within the operation. Moreover, the transferring ISAF states became increasingly vulnerable to human rights demands, which made them more inclined to recognize the UNAMA human rights unit as an accountability holder.

The two case studies on the accountability of peace operations in Bosnia showed the difference in the evolution of pluralist accountability with regard to human rights violations committed by members of the UN and NATO peace operations in this country. In the first case study, I analyzed pluralist accountability in response to human trafficking. A significant number of international personnel under the UN mandate, partly under contract with private security companies, who were actually mandated to promote the rule of law, regularly purchased sexual services in brothels, protected the owners from brothel raids, and sometimes even "purchased" trafficked women themselves. In this case, the relationship between the IOM and the UN OHCHR provided a competitive environment in which the Bosnian Office of the OHCHR was motivated to act as an accountability holder to develop a distinct profile with regard to how to deal with human trafficking by international actors. Additionally, the UN mission in Bosnia and its international police officers became increasingly vulnerable to human rights demands at the domestic level of the contributing states, in particular in the US. This growing vulnerability, which highlighted the discrepancy between the UN's mandate and its impact, contributed to an increasing willingness to recognize third parties as accountability holders at least to some degree.

The second case study analyzed why pluralist accountability did not evolve in response to the violation of detainees' rights by the operation SFOR under NATO leadership. The arrest and detention of persons who NATO believed were threats to security caused significant concern about the violation of fundamental human rights, such as the right to counsel and independent review. In this case, however, due to the international discourse on terrorism, advocating the rights of detainees was not attractive for transnational non-governmental or intergovernmental human rights organizations. Moreover, operation SFOR was able to render itself invulnerable against human rights demands by invoking a security-related discourse as the dominant norm that it used to guide its implementation of the mandate.

The two case studies on the operation in Kosovo dealt with the violation of the rights of detainees captured in the context of UN and NATO operations. When the UN Security Council authorized the transitional administration in Kosovo in 1999, it equipped the civilian administration UNMIK and the NATO-led military operation KFOR with a high degree of authority. As the civilian authority in Kosovo, the SRSG issued executive orders to detain arrested persons that, according to international law, would otherwise have had to be released. In addition, KFOR held several hundreds of detainees in extrajudicial detentions. Especially the denial of the right to habeas corpus, as one of the fundamental principles of international law, prompted major concerns. The analysis revealed why pluralist accountability evolved in response to the violation of the rights of detainees in the case of UNMIK and why it failed to evolve in the case of KFOR detentions. In both cases, the OSCE decided to sharpen its profile as an accountability holder within the competitive structure of the operation in Kosovo. However, the difference in UNMIK's and KFOR's vulnerability with regard to human rights demands explains why pluralist accountability evolved only in the case of UNMIK. UNMIK was more vulnerable due to its explicit mandate to promote the rule of law throughout Kosovo. Moreover, UNMIK's authoritative status contributed to its vulnerability: acting like a government entailed certain human rights responsibilities—this was the argument of third parties, which wanted UNMIK to recognize external accountability holders. In contrast to UNMIK, KFOR successfully invoked security as a counter-norm to legitimize its detention practices. By arguing that extrajudicial detentions were a necessary means for the implementation of its mandate, KFOR thus managed to render itself immune against human rights demands.

The aforementioned case studies contain six pair-wise comparisons that analyzed the emergence of pluralist accountability in the context of peace operations. In addition, to probe whether the argument holds in other issue areas of complex global governance, I analyzed two additional case studies: the austerity policies in Southern Europe adopted by the Troika in response to the

2008 economic and financial crisis, and public–private health partnerships in the context of immunization and vaccine development. These cases confirmed that the degree of competition among potential accountability holders and the degree of vulnerability of the implementing actors, or the mandating authority, influence the evolution of pluralist accountability in areas beyond the issue of peace operations.

The austerity measures that EU member state governments implemented under the auspices of the Troika—composed of the European Commission, the IMF, and the ECB, in response to the financial crisis—allegedly deprived a significant part of the population access to basic health services, medicine and social security, welfare and pension benefits, as well as education. This stood in stark contrast to the fundamental social and economic rights as provided by the International Covenant on Economic, Social and Cultural Rights. My analysis revealed how the competition between national and EU institutions as well as between different EU institutions motivated the Council of Europe, the EP, and the Portuguese Constitutional Court to enact pluralist accountability. Moreover, the counter-norm of economic stability lost its strength after 2013, thus enabling pluralist accountability at the domestic and international levels. Pluralist accountability, however, varied across the different Troika institutions. What explains this difference was the varying degree of human rights vulnerability that the Troika institutions were facing. The European Commission's broader mandate and the declining trust of the public in the EU's ability to address the crisis rendered the commission more vulnerable than the ECB and the IMF, which successfully invoked the counter-norm of stability to make themselves immune against human rights demands. Consequently, the Commission was more inclined to recognize third parties as accountability holders than the ECB and the IMF.

The final case study on complex global health governance revealed the limitations of pluralist accountability. Especially since the adoption of the MDGs, public–private health partnerships such as GAVI have become dominant actors in the field of vaccination and vaccine development. While the WHO still retains the final authority to approve newly developed vaccines, pharmaceutical companies and the Gates Foundation have become the core actors in the process of vaccine development, while international actors like GAVI play an important role in cooperating with private and national actors when promoting the implementation of vaccines. My analysis investigated pluralist accountability in response to allegations of the violation of the right to consent in clinical trials and the right to physical integrity in vaccination in India. The case study demonstrated how pluralist accountability remained limited due to the fierce ideological battles that characterize the field of vaccination, which made it impossible for potential independent actors to act as accountability holders without taking a side in this battle. Moreover, the moral dilemma between the general positive effects of vaccination and the negative side effects on the individual level made the involved parties fundamentally disagree on the substance of what the implementing actors should be held accountable for. Against this dilemma, global health partnerships rendered themselves immune to human rights demands by invoking the counter-norm of serving the "greater good" and, thus, refused to recognize any external accountability mechanism.

The analysis of the causal processes in all these different cases revealed how the mechanisms of profiling and mutual recognition contributed to the emergence of pluralist accountability. In the cases characterized by a competitive environment, third parties were motivated to engage in accountability functions to develop a distinct profile. At the same time, the analysis showed how mutual recognition is a crucial process for pluralist accountability to emerge in cases where the implementing actor or the mandating authority were vulnerable to human rights demands.

There are three further empirical insights that result from the comparative analysis. First, the different case studies demonstrated the complementarity of different actors enacting pluralist accountability. This shows the distinct features of pluralist accountability in complex governance settings: individual actors seem to be unable to enact accountability on their own; instead, several accountability holders interact and complement each other.

Second, the analysis of pluralist accountability in response to human rights violations in the context of detentions reveals important similarities across the three cases studies on Afghanistan, Bosnia, and Kosovo.[1] Invoking the norm of security has become an important strategy of detaining authorities to counter human rights demands in all detention cases. Only in cases where the norm of security lost strength could accountability holders put forward demands for the respect for detainees' rights, as in the case of ISAF detainee transfers to the Afghan government.

Third, the analysis reveals that, contrary to widespread expectations, the nature and character of human rights violations does not make any difference for the evolution of pluralist accountability. The cases did not provide any systematic evidence that pluralist accountability is more likely to evolve in

[1] Two of these cases were even interlinked in practice: some of the detainees captured in Bosnia were transferred to the US detention centers in Afghanistan or Guantánamo.

response to certain types of human rights violations, e.g., the violation of the rights of detainees. On the contrary, the detention cases show a strong variation as to whether pluralist accountability evolved. Thus, instead of explaining pluralist accountability, considering different types of human rights violations might be more helpful to explain the absence or presence of vertical accountability (Heupel and Zürn 2017).

Finally, the empirical analysis provides important insights into how important effective accountability is for the legitimacy of IOs and their implementing partners. A lack of accountability is an almost natural trade-off for the denationalization of governance functions in all empirical domains, which contributes to the legitimacy deficit of IOs. Each peace operation depends on the trust of the local population, the consent of the host state, and the willingness of other countries to finance the operation (Wiharta 2009). The stabilization of a country's economy cannot be achieved if people do not trust their governments to implement appropriate measures. In vaccination, the elimination of diseases depends on parents' trust to bring their children to medical centers to receive vaccines. If human rights are severely affected by the implementation of these global policies, this leads to a decline in the legitimacy of IOs and their implementing partners. In the existing debate, accountability is an important source for legitimacy. So far, however, we know little about how different forms of accountability affect legitimacy. I will, therefore, in the remainder of this concluding chapter provide a normative assessment of whether and how pluralist accountability addresses core legitimacy demands, both in the absence of and in comparison to vertical accountability.

Accountability and Legitimacy

Legitimacy is still a relatively new concept on the agenda of IR research (Bernstein 2011; Hurd 1999, 2007; Mulligan 2006). While the concept was previously discussed predominantly in the context of national democratic governance, IOs' exercise of state-like functions has led to a debate about how to apply the concept at the transnational or global level (Buchanan and Keohane 2006; Esty 2006; Koppell 2010; Nullmeier et al. 2010; Steffek 2015; Take 2009; Tallberg and Zürn 2019; Zürn 2012; Zürn and Stephen 2010).[2]

[2] Similar efforts to develop criteria for legitimacy in nondemocratic contexts have been made by researchers at the Collaborative Research Center (SFB) 700 on "Governance in Areas of Limited Statehood" (e.g., Ladwig and Rudolf 2011; Risse 2011; Schmelzle 2011).

Most scholars agree that an authority is legitimate if it is accountable to those affected by it (Koenig-Archibugi 2010; Zürn and Stephen 2010), to its members and stakeholders (Koenig-Archibugi 2010; Woods 1999), or to certain laws or standards (Goodhart 2011). At the same time, a lack of accountability contributes to an impression that IOs and their implementing partners stand above their own rules and standards. Consequently, the IO loses trust, which in turn can seriously hamper its effectiveness and its output legitimacy. While the analysis of sociological legitimacy, i.e. legitimacy in the eyes of affected people, remains outside the scope of this study, I undertake a normative assessment of the effect of pluralist accountability on legitimacy by comparing a state-based and a society-based conception of legitimacy.

Accountability is an important criterion for legitimacy as it establishes a system of checks and balances that serves as a procedural means of control and influences both the input and output components of legitimacy (Bernstein 2004; Scharpf 1999; Take 2009; Zürn and Tallberg 2019). While participation enhances input legitimacy and the effectiveness of policies contributes to output legitimacy, accountability also enhances "throughput legitimacy" by making governance processes more legitimate (Schmidt 2013). Another "virtue" through which accountability is expected to enhance IO legitimacy is transparency: holding an actor accountable implies that the accountability holder receives critical information about its decisions and actions taken (Koppell 2010; Schedler, 1999). According to some researchers, transparency is an important (but not sufficient) prerequisite for accountability, while others consider accountability, participation, and transparency as three independent legitimacy criteria (Bovens 2007; Zürn 2012).

While accountability is an important source for legitimacy, few researchers have undertaken the task of conceptualizing and evaluating the effect of different accountability types on legitimacy (Buchanan and Keohane 2006; Risse 2008; Rubenstein 2007). Buchanan and Keohane distinguish between narrow and broad accountability; they argue that only broad accountability contributes to greater legitimacy because it allows for a critical revision of the accountability terms by external actors. Risse, in turn, links accountability and legitimacy by combining Keohane's concept of internal and external accountability and Scharpf's distinction between input and output legitimacy (Risse 2008). According to this argument, accountability toward internal stakeholders and external affected people increases input legitimacy, while external accountability also affects output legitimacy by providing the grounds for compliance by affected actors. His analysis, however, does not expand to accountability forms that are exercised by third parties. By contrast,

Rubenstein distinguishes between standard accountability, which in her conceptualization comes close to democratic accountability by the affected people, and surrogate accountability, which is exercised by third parties if standard accountability holders are too weak (Rubenstein 2007). She establishes several criteria for evaluating the different accountability types, which include whether accountability guarantees protection from arbitrary power, increases compliance, promotes certain values and civic virtues (such as deliberation), or provides useful information to everyone (i.e., transparency). She concludes that surrogate accountability is normatively inferior to standard accountability because surrogates act without authorization ("without democratic legitimation") and can themselves not be held accountable by the standard accountability holders. There is thus the danger that surrogates will engage in unwarranted paternalism (Rubenstein 2007). While this might be a legitimate claim that could be substantiated empirically, the strong emphasis on democratic accountability is a significant obstacle to an analysis of accountability beyond the democratic nation-state.

These studies remain the exception when considering the effect of different accountability types on legitimacy. The following section evaluates the value of pluralist accountability both in the absence of and in comparison with vertical accountability, in light of a legitimacy deficit of IOs in contemporary global governance. I argue that pluralist accountability can accommodate for the absence of vertical accountability at least to some degree. I then demonstrate that—in comparison with vertical accountability—pluralist accountability introduces important participatory elements to the otherwise state-centered mechanisms of control and enhances transparency for a broader audience. However, this chapter also points to the limitations of pluralist accountability as a legitimation strategy in terms of the degree of legalization and potential pitfalls, such as multiple accountability disorder. I conclude that while pluralist accountability does not satisfy components of traditional state-based legitimacy conceptions, it instead responds better to contemporary society-based legitimacy demands that might be even more relevant for IOs in today's global governance.

A Framework for Evaluating the Effect of Pluralist Accountability on IO Legitimacy

In pluralist accountability, accountability holders are neither those who have delegated power nor those who are affected by it, but third parties that play that role. Hence, how does pluralist accountability contribute to bridging the legitimacy deficit in global governance? I argue that the normative content of pluralist accountability, that is, the principles that the implementing actors are held accountable to, makes a difference for IO legitimacy. Goodhart took some first steps in the direction of this argument when he stipulated that the norms to which an actor is held accountable are more relevant for legitimacy than to whom an actor is held accountable (Goodhart 2011). Legal scholars have pursued the quest for a more normative evaluation of accountability, in particular by those advocating the concept of "Global Administrative Law," who argue that power is to be held "*appropriately* accountable" (Rached 2014, emphasis in the original).

In the absence of vertical accountability, pluralist accountability demonstrates that human rights abuses committed in complex governance arrangements do not go unnoticed. It requires the authority that committed these violations to face its actions, so that it is not above core international rules. From a normative perspective, pluralist accountability enhances IO legitimacy as long as it enhances fundamental norms that are shared within the accountability community. In this regard, the standard-setting component of accountability becomes important: the human rights standards according to which the implementing actors are to be monitored and sanctioned are crucial to pluralist accountability to enhance the legitimacy of IOs (Goodhart 2011). Pluralist accountability, thereby, strengthens fundamental principles and upholds the norm of human rights in areas where traditional accountability holders fail.

When comparing the effect of vertical and pluralist accountability on IO legitimacy, the analysis needs to consider who the appropriate constituency is, that is, the accountability forum (Risse 2008; Rubenstein 2007). This presupposes that both accountability types aim at enhancing the same normative values, such as the protection of human rights. Depending on the theoretical perspective on IO legitimacy, there are two different models that permit a comparison of different accountability types and their effect on IO legitimacy with regard to the respective appropriate accountability forum: a state-based model and a society-based model (de Wet 2008).

According to the *state-based model*, the legitimacy of IOs relies on the consent of sovereign states (Bernstein 2004; de Wet 2008). This argument is based on the notion that states are the legal representatives of their citizens in the international realm. The legitimacy of a transnational authority such as the UN Security Council, therefore, depends on the consent of its members or, as others have argued, even on the perception of UN member states in general

(Sarooshi 1999). This entails a certain responsibility for states to constrain the authority of the IO and its implementing agents (Genschel and Zangl 2008).[3] Therefore, the state-based model, which is mostly upheld by international lawyers and classical principal-agent scholars, assumes that an IO's legitimacy increases through accountability forms where its shareholders—i.e., its member states—act as accountability holders (Sarooshi 1999). According to this model, only the members of the collective authority are the legitimate accountability constituency. States thus should act as the primary accountability holders in order to guarantee that their citizens' rights and needs are respected throughout the implementation of an IO's decision. By monitoring and approving the implementation of a decision, they demonstrate a continuing consent and thereby increase the IO's legitimacy.

A typical form of state-based monitoring is self-reporting: the UN Secretariat, for example, regularly reports to the UN Security Council about the implementation of a peacekeeping operation. Alternatively, the UN Security Council member states pay visits to individual missions as ways of police patrol monitoring. While this is not sufficient to increase the democratic legitimacy of IOs, it is assumed that this accountability to member states makes global governance more transparent to their citizens, at least indirectly (Nye 2001). If states are informed about the implementation of an IO's decision, they can pass on that information to their citizens.

The state-based model, however, comes with three caveats: first, it is based on an understanding that IOs act as executive organs for their member states. It does not take into consideration the nowadays frequent practice of prolonged delegation in global governance, through which IOs independently delegate tasks to a wide range of actors. This raises the question of why member states should be the only relevant accountability holders if the implementing actors in complex delegation chains can be other IOs, state actors, or nonstate actors. As a second caveat, the model presupposes a certain type of member state: well-functioning democratic governments with a certain degree of domestic transparency, which are held democratically accountable by their citizens (Buchanan and Keohane 2006). However, the states that are supposed to represent the interests of their citizens are often undemocratic, weak, or even nonexistent. And even if they are democratic, accountability to the most influential member states threatens rather than enhances IO legitimacy, as Woods and Narlikar (2001) demonstrate in their study about the

[3] Also see the draft articles on the responsibility of IOs, Yearbook of the International Law Commission, 2011, Vol. II, Part Two.

IMF being accountable to the US. Third, in many areas of global governance, IOs operate in circumstances when there is no functioning state and take over state functions, as the UN did in Kosovo. In particular, in the context of peacekeeping operations, there are often no functioning institutional structures in the host states that can provide democratic accountability structures. Citizens of these states, who are affected by the implementation of a decision, remain outside of the scope of the state-based model of IO legitimacy.

Given these limitations of the state-based model of IO legitimacy in contemporary global governance, researchers have increasingly come to adopt another model, a *society-based model* (de Wet 2008; Scholte 2011a). This presupposes that an IO has a much broader legitimacy constituency than its member states. The difference between the two models is exemplified to a certain extent by the terms of shareholder and stakeholder accountability, whereby the shareholders of an IO are its member states and the stakeholders the people affected by its decisions and policies. The society-based model is based on the understanding that IOs operate in the context of some kind of society, without presupposing that this society is homogenous. This contextualization of IOs has become the basis for studies on the empirical or social legitimacy of IOs, which increasingly base the conceptualization of IO legitimacy on their social acceptance in terms of public opinion and value research (Dellmuth and Tallberg 2014). The underlying assumption is that IOs should be held accountable by a broader transnational community that is, implicitly, expected to represent the perspective of affected individuals.

The society-based model thus favors accountability forms that give a say to those that are in some way involved in and affected by a decision and its implementation. These can be other stakeholders, such as the addressees of a decision or the greater transnational society. These accountability forms come closest to enhancing deliberation if they include the direct participation of affected or concerned parties in the development of a common interest about what the appropriate accountability standards should be (Buchanan and Keohane 2006). By engaging the greater community in standard-setting, monitoring, or sanctioning activities, the IO can enhance its legitimacy. The expectation is that if members of the greater public, often represented by NGOs, receive information about the implementation of an IO's decision, the potential of affected parties receiving sufficient and balanced information is greater than if only member states undertake monitoring (especially if the implementation of an IO's decision affects citizens of states that are not members of the decision-making body). In particular, if the majority of member states are undemocratic and do not have institutionalized ways of passing on information to their citizens, accountability toward the transnational public can enhance an IO's legitimacy.

Pluralist Accountability: The Transnationalization of (De)legitimation

Decision making in global governance is still an exclusive domain reserved to IO member states (Tallberg et al. 2013). Pluralist accountability helps to address this imbalance by creating a post-decision-making feedback process that involves a wider audience of societal or transnational actors. In comparison with vertical accountability, pluralist accountability falls short in satisfying state-based legitimacy demands. Instead, it responds better to the demands promulgated by a society-based legitimacy conception, as it contributes to the formation of a transnational community of actors that act as accountability holders. This community is rooted in a normatively strong environment. Its standard-setting, monitoring, and sanctioning activities are shaped by the desire to constrain the IO's authority with regard to a set of shared norms. The community of accountability holders is not necessarily made up of societal actors, but their focus remains on the transnational realm. Hence, I suggest describing this as a process of transnationalization of accountability, rather than by what has been labelled as "societalization."[4] Thus, pluralist accountability, at least to some degree, compensates for one of the biggest challenges to legitimacy at the global level: the lack of a community with shared beliefs (Koppell 2010).

A good example of a pluralist community of accountability holders establishing a strong normative environment and, thereby, constraining an IO's authority is the case of the OSCE and the Council of Europe holding the UNMIK accountable. The two organizations pushed to establish an Ombudsperson Institution, which was mandated to check the compliance of UNMIK with international and European human rights norms.[5] They enabled those affected by the UNMIK's decisions to file complaints against UNMIK with the Ombudsperson Institution. Moreover, the two regional organizations enhanced transparency to the greater European public: they required the

[4] The term "societalization" refers to the writings of Albert, who developed the concept of "Vergesellschaftung" or "Verweltgesellschaftung" (Albert 2002).

[5] UNMIK Regulation on the Establishment of the Ombudsperson Institution in Kosovo, UN doc. UNMIK/REG/2000/38, June 30, 2000.

ombudsperson to regularly report to them and also sent their own investigating teams to monitor UNMIK's compliance.

Standard setting in pluralist accountability involves external accountability holders that often possess a high degree of expert authority, which enables them to define appropriate standards of behavior that are less particularistic than if they had been formulated by the IO's member states. Particularly in the area of human rights, enhanced "institutionalized cooperation" between the UN Security Council and other human rights bodies within the UN is regarded as important for the Council's legitimacy (Fassbender 2011). A good example of external experts enhancing IO legitimacy is the cooperation between the UN Secretariat and the ICRC in Geneva regarding the development of guidelines for detention. The ICRC is known for its legal and practical expertise in the field of detention and international humanitarian law. The organization is, therefore, an epistemic authority recognized by the UN that plays an important role in the human rights community. By asking the ICRC to participate as an authoritative source on international humanitarian law, the UN tried to enhance the legitimacy of its detention guidelines, as outlined in the Secretary-General's bulletin of 1999 and the new Interim Standard Operating Procedures for detention (Hirschmann 2016).

Monitoring in pluralist accountability contributes to greater legitimacy by providing a means for transparent and independent control. External actors usually report to not only their own principals but also to the wider human rights community to which they belong. Due to their expert authority, external actors might monitor more comprehensively than internal reporting in vertical accountability and can expose human rights violations at all levels of the delegation chain. External actors, grounded in a strong normative and institutional environment outside the delegation relationship, can initiate oversight procedures on their own behalf and, thereby, independently and publicly scrutinize the implementing agents' behavior.[6] Moreover, and even more important for the legitimacy of the principal, these actors can also engage in monitoring the principal itself and its decisions and actions in response to human rights violations committed by the implementing agents. This is what the European Court for Human Rights and the Council of Europe undertook when mandating the Venice Commission and the Council's High

[6] Although formally less independent, civilian components within individual operations also engage in independent and transparent monitoring. The OSCE pillar within UNMIK, for example, reviewed the SRSG's executive detention orders and practices, e.g., OSCE 2002: Review of the Criminal Justice System (September 2001–February 2002), "Independence of the Judiciary, Detention, Mental Health Issues," OSCE Mission in Kosovo, Department of Human Rights and Rule of Law.

Commissioner for the Prevention of Torture to investigate UNMIK's compliance with human rights norms in Kosovo. While these institutions did not explicitly question the UN's role as a principal and its vertical monitoring procedures, they nevertheless proposed the establishment of a Human Rights Advisory Panel with the intention of constraining the UN's authority in the context of the transitional administration.

Sanctioning in pluralist accountability finally provides "new fora for deliberation and justification to create and sustain legitimate authority" (Bernstein 2004). Sanctioning by external third parties enhances the principal's legitimacy as it provides affected parties or other groups with the possibility of claiming their rights before an independent body. In Kosovo, for example, the UN accepted the proposal by the Council of Europe to establish a Human Rights Advisory Panel to assess complaints against the UN administration in the country. Individuals whose rights had been violated by the UN could thus participate in the sanctioning process by filing complaints. Moreover, the panel made all its decisions and recommendations public, giving affected people and the international community transparent access. The externalization of sanctioning, therefore, contributed to a greater legitimacy of UN institutions from a society-based perspective. However, sanctioning by external actors not only addresses the behavior of the implementing agent but also scrutinizes the principal's reactions if human rights violations occur. A network of experienced human rights advocates, made up of nongovernmental and intergovernmental organizations, forms a community with shared beliefs that sanctions both agents and principals when certain principles are violated in the context of a peace operation.

Despite its legitimacy-enhancing effects, however, pluralist accountability can also have delegitimizing effects for IO legitimacy. Pluralist accountability often aims to hold the implementing agents accountable externally, but can also serve to hold the authorizing principal accountable. This can result in delegitimization processes regarding state-based legitimacy demands. Standard-setting activities by external third parties can result in delegitimization processes if the accountability holders disqualify the authorizing member state body of its right or ability to set appropriate standards. The standard-setting activities of the OIK certainly had delegitimizing effects in the sense that the OIK emphasized that the standards for detentions in Kosovo had to come from European human rights institutions and not from the UN or NATO.[7] The case of the European Court of Justice's *Kadi* decision is another example, as the decision had negative effects on the legitimacy of the UN Security Council's sanctions policy by referring to its incompatibility with the European human rights framework.

From the state-based perspective on IO legitimacy, this is an important danger that comes with pluralist accountability. It allows states to hide behind pluralist accountability mechanisms and, thus, abdicate their own responsibility as members of the IO to act as vertical accountability holders. Therefore, legal scholars, in particular, warn that pluralist accountability should not replace vertical accountability: there is a remaining secondary responsibility of states "to ensure the systemic integrity of international law. Otherwise it would be a simple matter for states to avoid obligations by creating an IO to which they delegate powers and then disclaim all responsibility for the way in which those powers are exercised within the organization" (Sarooshi 1999). The underlying argument is that, no matter how much authority is vested in an IO, states must still retain obligations with regard to the exercise of this authority, either as implementing actors or as part of the mandating body. This is reflected in the debate about the responsibility of IOs, in which the delegation of powers to an IO nevertheless implies responsibilities for a state, if the state "chooses to participate in or implement domestically a wrongful act committed by an IO exercising delegated powers" or if the state "aids or assists the organization in the commission of a wrongful act."[8]

While this is certainly a valuable argument from a state-based perspective on IO legitimacy, it disregards the fact that pluralist accountability often develops in cases that lack accountability exercised by member states.[9] Pluralist accountability is thus an important means for compensating for the lack of vertical accountability, especially if the implementing agents that have violated human rights are too distant in the delegation chain for the ultimate principal to exercise vertical sanctioning. Here additional checks and balances exist when domestic or regional courts exercise sanctioning. This outcome is obvious in the case of the peace operation in Bosnia, in which the British High Court decided that a UN police officer was unfairly dismissed by her employer,

[7] Ombudsperson Institution in Kosovo 2001: Special Report No. 3. The Conformity of Deprivations of Liberty under "Executive Orders" with Recognised International Standards, June 29, 2001.

[8] International Law Commission 2011: Draft Articles on the Responsibility of International Organizations. UN doc. A/66/10, para. 87, edited by United Nations, New York.

[9] In the case of Sierra Leone, the Security Council adopted the mandate of the Special Court that provided that the jurisdiction of the court also extended to peacekeepers' actions (UN doc. S/2002/246: para. 28). At the same time, the jurisdiction was made conditional upon the peacekeeper's respective national authorities' unwillingness or inability to prosecute.

a private security company sub-contracted by the US to provide peacekeeping personnel, after she revealed a systematic involvement of international police officials in sex trafficking.[10] The court also criticized the UN for not having taken its responsibility as an accountability holder seriously. Thus, the sanctioning activities of external third parties to some degree compensated for the lack of vertical sanctioning.

To sum up, pluralist accountability thus contributes to a transnationalization of the accountability constituency of IOs, which responds to the demands of a greater transnational community and a society-based model of IO legitimacy. This community might not be universal, but nonetheless assembles several actors with shared beliefs. Consequently, the potential that these beliefs reflect the perspective of those affected by the IO's actions is greater than in vertical accountability. Pluralist accountability, therefore, introduces a notion of publicness to global governance (Bovens 2007) and contributes to the "construction of new public spaces" (Albert et al. 2009).

However, it is important to keep in mind that pluralist accountability does not necessarily imply that societal actors or affected people are also included in other steps of the policy cycle, such as the IO's decision-making procedures. These new avenues of participation through "societalized accountability" do not constitute a "step to global democracy" (Bernstein 2004). It is, therefore, important not to expect that pluralist accountability enhances democratic legitimacy. Nevertheless, standard setting, monitoring, and sanctioning by third parties, often with expert authority, might establish a closer connection to those whose rights have been violated in the course of policy implementation. Greater participation thereby reduces the potential that particular interests of individual IO members dominate the accountability mechanism. To a certain degree, it addresses the problem of the lack of a global community (Scholte 2004) and can thus serve as a new source for legitimacy beyond state consent by including the greater transnational society and by providing avenues for a more active civil society. However, whether pluralist accountability provides for better inclusion of the demands of affected people remains an open question that needs to be assessed empirically.

[10] *Bolkovac* v. *Dyncorp*, Case no. 3102729/01.

Two Caveats of Pluralist Accountability: Legalization and Multiple Accountability Disorder

While pluralist accountability is an important feature for enhancing IO legitimacy, there are two important caveats that significantly constrain the effects of pluralist accountability: the degree of legalization and the danger of multiple accountability disorder. The effectiveness of pluralist accountability as a form of authority constraint depends on how legalized the accountability mechanism is. I here refer to the components of legalization of precision, obligation, and independence (Abbott et al. 2000). Precision and obligation reduce the arbitrariness of a decision and its implementation. Moreover, clear and binding standards together with independent monitoring procedures provide the basis for effective sanctioning. Without precise standards, it is difficult to sanction noncompliance.

However, there is a certain trade-off with regard to the obligation between the two legitimacy-enhancing components of participation and transparency, on the one hand, and the compliance-enhancing legalization components, on the other hand. By its nature, pluralist accountability scores high in terms of the independence component of legalization. According to the legalization literature, the delegation of claims assessment and jurisdiction to independent third parties, such as dispute-settlement bodies, is expected to guarantee a jurisprudence that is "more autonomous of national interests" (Keohane et al. 2000). Thus, the externalization of sanctioning in pluralist accountability is especially valuable as it increases independence. Sometimes, however, pluralist accountability might be established as a pretext to pretend being independent when it is not independent enough. In the case of the UN mission in Kosovo, for example, the UN Human Rights Commission expressed "concern that the Human Rights Advisory Panel established under UNMIK Regulation 2006/12 to receive and examine complaints against UNMIK lacks the necessary independence and authority."[11] Another example is the criticism levelled against the confidential reporting of the ICRC when monitoring detentions in peace operations. In this case, the release of information is conditional on approval by the detaining authority, and the standards adopted might fall short of what was proposed by external actors. Thus, while pluralist accountability contributes to greater legitimacy, its effectiveness strongly depends on the actual

[11] United Nations Human Rights Council 2006: Concluding Observations of the Human Rights Committee (Kosovo), Geneva, UN doc. CCPR/C/UNK/CO/1, August 14, 2006.

independence of the external actors, as well as on the degree of precision and legal bindingness of the standards and the sanctioning procedures involved.

In vertical accountability, the delegating authority is generally able to adopt standards that are legally binding for the implementing actors, even if it is very costly (Hawkins et al. 2006b). As an implication, the standards adopted by the ultimate principal are in general obligatory for the complete delegation relationship. The crucial problem for pluralist accountability, however, is how to create highly obligatory standards and sanctioning procedures that exercise some constraint on the authority of the principals and the implementing actors. The more external accountability holders engage in pluralist accountability—and the greater the transparency in the implementation process—the more difficult it is to create binding standards. Moreover, in addition to the number of accountability holders, their nature in terms of their legal status and their relationship to the ultimate delegating authority matters for the degree of obligation. Few external accountability holders can—on the basis of their legal status and their relationship to the delegating authority—create binding standards that induce high compliance and thus enhance legitimacy. Most third parties cannot generate binding standards, let alone binding sanctions for other transnationally operating actors.[12] While accountability exercised by courts features a high degree of obligation, the accountability exercised by transnational societal actors and other regional organizations usually does not. Therefore, while pluralist accountability contributes to greater legitimacy, the lack of ability of external accountability holders to create a strong obligation in standard-setting and sanctioning procedures—and therefore enhance the compliance of the implementing actors—seriously hampers its effectiveness. Highly legalized pluralist accountability hence remains the exception.

The second caveat regarding the effect of accountability on IO legitimacy is the potential pitfall of "multiple accountability disorder" that may result from a combination of both accountability types or even from pluralist accountability alone (Bovens and Schillemans 2011; Koppell 2005). Despite the normative advantages of pluralist accountability for IO legitimacy, a broad accountability constituency can also imply a certain danger if accountability holders disagree, and if there is no hierarchy built into the different accountability relationships. This can significantly limit the effectiveness of accountability mechanisms. For example, too many accountability relationships can

[12] See Posner, 2005 on reputational sanctioning and on the limited role of NGOs in international law.

create contradictory standards and increase the number of veto points (Keohane 2003; Steets and Blattner 2010). In extreme cases, this can paralyze the implementing actor when there is no clarity which accountability holder it should respond to. This has to be taken into consideration when identifying accountability types with a broad accountability constituency.

This trade-off between pluralist accountability and high obligation leads me to conclude that both types of accountability are necessary to address different aspects of the legitimacy of IOs. I expect that a combination of both vertical and pluralist accountability enhances IO legitimacy the most. However, a combination of different accountability types or pluralist accountability alone might also result in multiple accountability disorder. Different accountability holders might establish different standards, monitoring and sanctioning procedures, which can create new uncertainties or might hamper effective implementation and thus undermine output legitimacy. Therefore, given that the legitimacy of IOs in global governance would require a balance between both state-based and society-based accountability constituencies, future research is needed to analyze what a healthy combination of accountability types should look like. Further studies are also necessary that analyze the sociological legitimacy of IOs in the eyes of those affected by IO policies, on the one hand, and from the perspective of the IO's stakeholders, on the other.

Concluding Remarks and Implications for Future Research

There are several implications that follow from the results of this study. One implication for the research on accountability in global governance is that we need to consider IOs within the context of their respective environments. To a great extent, previous research focuses on how either the IO's member states or the bureaucracy within the IO develop greater accountability. In contrast, the results of this study reveal the importance of the IO's institutional context. The analysis of IOs and their interactions with their environments is not only fruitful for the study of accountability, but also for further studies on the effectiveness of IOs, their legitimacy, or their authority in general. The results of this study lead me to conclude that more integrated and contextualized research on IOs is warranted.

However, I am not yet able to confirm whether the increase in pluralist accountability reflects a "systemic change" in IO legitimacy (Bernstein 2004, 16). Instead, I argue that there is a complementary system of multiple accountability forms arising. Consequently, we might see a shift from accountability through states to a system of pluralist accountability holders. The findings from this book speak to the recent work on the "opening up of IOs": the general trend toward pluralist accountability goes hand in hand with the increasing interaction of IOs with nonstate actors that have greater access in certain steps of the policy cycle (Tallberg et al. 2013). Taking over core accountability functions might be one way that outside actors interact with IOs.

My findings also provide an important contribution to the literature of advocacy coalitions. The case studies reveal that NGOs remain important actors because their activities in making human rights violations public are a prerequisite for any accountability mechanism to start. Their strategy to target individual governments proved rather successful for increasing domestic pressure. In the case of ISAF detainee transfers, for example, transnational NGOs increased the pressure at the domestic level within important ISAF member states, which raised awareness among the domestic public and set the issue of detention transfers on the agenda. Moreover, the use of legal proceedings has become an effective tool for them to activate domestic accountability holders.

Nevertheless, pluralist accountability is no automatism and does not evolve every time that vertical accountability is lacking. The evolution of pluralist accountability in all cases has been independent from the accountability regimes that existed at the outset of the delegation relationships. This should reassure those who consider nonvertical accountability to be only the second-best option and who fear that pluralist accountability might replace important vertical accountability mechanisms. Despite the danger that more complex accountability regimes might result in "multiple accountability disorder," this analysis demonstrates that different types of accountability address different important aspects of the legitimacy of IOs. In particular, the findings of this analysis show that pluralist accountability is an important procedural mechanism for regaining legitimacy in contexts where democracy, as a source of legitimacy, is nonexistent, and where states do not live up to their responsibilities as the appropriate accountability holders. I provide a more fine-grained concept of accountability that can enhance principal-agent research, the study of IOs and their environments, as well as legal scholarship on accountability and IO legitimacy. This implies that future studies of IO legitimacy need to take into consideration pluralist accountability as an alternative to traditional international legitimation concepts that rely on states. How to strike an appropriate balance between the different accountability types remains a question that needs to be analyzed in future research.

In addition to the theoretical and empirical contributions, the findings of this book also carry practical relevance and concrete policy implications. In several cases, independent human rights components became important accountability holders in peace operations. Other researchers have come to a similar conclusion and pledge for an independent standing of the human rights components vis-à-vis the SRSG and the mission leadership:

> When an SRSG is not engaged in human rights advocacy for the mission or worse yet is actively impeding human rights advocacy and reporting by others, a human rights component can be paralyzed... In these cases the direct support of the High Commissioner is essential, not only to validate the human rights concerns of the field presence, but also to exercise influence in a longer-term way on the human rights accountability of SRSGs. (Mahoney and Nash 2012, 101)

Considering that coherence, interinstitutional cooperation and synergies have dominated the discussion about peace operations during the last years, this is an important point to make. For greater accountability, the integration of human rights in the institutional structure of peace operations, as it has been pursued by the UN since 2005, might not be the best option (Hannum 2006). Pluralist accountability requires parallel operating actors that are in some competition with each other, needing to develop their distinguishable profiles. Checks and balances will not exist if the delegating IO streamlines too many commands and integrates too many tasks.

Finally, it is important to highlight that effective pluralist accountability does not mean the end of human rights violations. It just means that such violations would have consequences rather than going unnoticed. In an optimal case, the normatively desired result of accountability would be to prevent and redress further rights violations. Future studies, however, are needed to examine the effects that different accountability regimes have on effective human rights protection. While not denying that IOs do important work, the analyses of this book reveal the importance of accountability in complex global governance, be it in the field of peacekeeping, economic policy or global health governance. The authority of IOs has proven itself to be a double-edged sword: on the one hand, greater authority gives IOs higher leverage to demand member states to respect human rights. On the other hand, greater IO authority also increases the chance that human rights are being violated by IOs themselves or their implementing partners. Functioning and transparent checks and balances through pluralist accountability are crucial to ensure that global governance does not stand above the law. In times when the complexities of these governance structures have blurred responsibilities and when populist and nationalist movements threaten to undermine global cooperation, pluralist accountability will remain important for the legitimacy of IOs.

References

Abass, A., 2004. *Regional Organisations and the Development of Collective Security: Beyond Chapter VIII of the UN Charter*. Oxford: Hart Publishing.

Abbott, K. W., and Snidal, D., 1998. "Why States Act through Formal International Organizations." *Journal of Conflict Resolution* 42(1): 3–32.

Abbott, K. W., Keohane, R. O., Moravcsik, A., Slaughter, A.-M., and Snidal, D., 2000. "The Concept of Legalization." *International Organization* 54(3): 401–19.

Abbott, K. W., Genschel, P., Snidal, D., and Zangl, B. (eds), 2015. *International Organizations as Orchestrators*. Cambridge: Cambridge University Press.

Abraham, E., 2003. "The Sins of the Savior: Holding the United Nations Accountable to International Human Rights Standards for Executive Order Detentions in Its Mission in Kosovo." *American University Law Review* 52: 1291–337.

Albert, M., 2002. *Zur Politik der Weltgesellschaft. Identität und Recht im Kontext internationaler Vergesellschaftung*. Weilerswist: Velbrück Wissenschaft.

Albert, M., Bluhm, G., Helmig, J., Leutzsch, A., and Walter, J., 2009. "Introduction: The Communicative Construction of Transnational Political Spaces." In *Transnational Political Spaces. Agents, Structures, Encounters*, edited by M. Albert, G. Bluhm, J. Helmig, A. Leutzsch, and J. Walter, 7–31. Frankfurt: Campus.

Allred, K. J., 2006. "Combating Human Trafficking." *NATO Policy Review* 2.

Alston, P., 1997. "Neither Fish nor Fowl: The Quest to Define the Role of the Un High Commissioner for Human Rights." *European Journal of International Law* 8(2): 321–36.

Alston, P., 2005. "Ships Passing in the Night: The Current State of Human Rights and Development Debate Seen through the Lens of the Millennium Development Goals." *Human Rights Quarterly* 27(3): 755–829.

Alter, K. J., 2014. *The New Terrain of International Law: Courts, Politics, Rights*. Princeton, NJ: Princeton University Press.

Alvarez, J. E., 2005. *International Organizations as Law-Makers*. Oxford: Oxford University Press.

Amaral-Garcia, S., Garoupa, N., and Grembi, V., 2009. "Judicial Independence and Party Politics in the Kelsenian Constitutional Courts: The Case of Portugal." *Journal of Empirical Legal Studies* 6(2): 381–404.

Amnesty International, 2000. "Federal Republic of Yugoslavia (Kosovo): Setting the Standard—UNMIK and KFOR's Response to the Violence in Mitrovica." March 13, available at: http://www.amnesty.org/en/library/asset/EUR70/013/2000/en/22ee1ca2-df79-11dd-8abb-118b2e919ec0/eur700132000en.html (last access January 31, 2015).

Amnesty International, 2001. "Federal Republic of Yugoslavia (Kosovo): Amnesty International Calls for an End to Executive Orders of Detention." August 3, AI Index EUR 70/017/2001.

Amnesty International, 2002. "Memorandum to the US Government on the Rights of People in US Custody in Afghanistan and Guantánamo Bay." April 15, AI Index: AMR 1/053/2002.

Amnesty International, 2004a. "The Apparent Lack of Accountability of International Peace-Keeping Forces in Kosovo and Bosnia-Herzegovina." March 31, AI Index: EUR 05/002/2004.

Amnesty International, 2004b. ""So does that mean I have rights?" Protecting the Human Rights of Women and Girls Trafficked for Forced Prostitution in Kosovo." May 5, AI Index: EUR 70/010/2004.

Amnesty International, 2004c. "USA: Human Dignity Denied: Torture and Accountability in the 'War on Terror.'" October 26, AI Index: AMR 51/145/2004.

Amnesty International, 2005. "US Detentions in Afghanistan: An Aide-Mémoire for Continued Action." June 7, AI Index: AMR 51/093/2005.

Amnesty International, 2006a. "Kosovo (Serbia and Montenegro). United Nations Interim Administration Mission in Kosovo (UNMIK): Briefing to the Human Rights Committee, 87th Session." July, AI Index: EUR 70/007/2006.

Amnesty International, 2006b. "Afghanistan: NATO Must Ensure Justice for Victims of Civilian Deaths and Torture." November 27, AI Index: ASA 11/021/2006.

Amnesty International, 2007a. "Afghanistan: Mounting Civilian Death Toll—All Sides Must Do More to Protect Civilians." June 22, AI Index: ASA 11/006/2007.

Amnesty International, 2007b. "Afghanistan: Detainees Transferred to Torture: ISAF Complicity?" November 13, AI Index: ASA 11/011/2007.

Amnesty International, 2012. "Outcome of Copenhagen Process on Detainees in International Military Operations Undermines Respect for Human Rights." AI Index: IOR 50/003/2012.

Andonova, L. B., 2017. *Governance Entrepreneurs: International Organizations and the Rise of Global Public–Private Partnerships*. Cambridge: Cambridge University Press.

Andreas, P., 2009. "Symbiosis between Peace Operations and Illicit Business in Bosnia." *International Peacekeeping* 16(1): 33–46.

Aoi, C., De Coning, C., and Thakur, R. (eds), 2007. *Unintended Consequences of Peacekeeping Operations*. Tokyo: United Nations University Press.

Bäckstrand, K., 2008. "Accountability of Networked Climate Governance: The Rise of Transnational Climate Partnerships." *Global Environmental Politics* 8(3): 74–102.

Bagla, P., 2013. "Indian Parliament Comes Down Hard on Cervical Cancer Trial." *Science* 362(6420).

Baldwin, C., 2006. "Implementation through Cooperation? Human Rights Officers and the Military in Kosovo, 1999–2002." *International Peacekeeping* 13(4): 489–501.

Bard, J. S., 2015. "A Taxonomy for Analyzing Legal and Ethical Issues Arising When Conducting Human Subject Research Outside the Borders of One's Own Country." *Houston Journal of International Law* 37(1).

Barnes, A., and Brown, G. W., 2011. "The Global Fund to Fight AIDS, Tuberculosis, and Malaria: Expertise, Accountability, and the Depoliticisation of Global Health Governance." In *Partnerships and Foundations in Global Health Governance*, edited by S. Rushton and O. D. Williams, 53–75. London: Palgrave Macmillan.

Barnett, M., and Finnemore, M., 2004. *Rules for the World. International Organizations in Global Politics*, Ithaca, NY: Cornell University Press.

Bartsch, S., 2007. "Accountability of Global Public–Private Partnerships in Health." *Paper presented at the Sixth Pan-European Conference on International Relations*, September 14, University of Turin.

Bartsch, S., 2011. "A Critical Appraisal of Global Health Partnerships." In *Partnerships and Foundations in Global Health Governance*, edited by S. Rushton and O. D. Williams, 29–52. London: Palgrave Macmillan.

Bauer, M. W., and Becker, S., 2014. "The Unexpected Winner of the Crisis: The European Commission's Strengthened Role in Economic Governance." *Journal of European Integration* 36(3): 213–29.

Beck, U., 2006. *Cosmopolitan Vision*. Cambridge: Polity Press.

Benner, T., Reinicke, W. H., and Witte, J. M., 2004. "Multisectoral Networks in Global Governance: Towards a Pluralistic System of Accountability." *Government and Opposition* 39(2): 191–210.

Bennett, A., and Elman, C., 2006. "Complex Causal Relations and Case Study Methods: The Example of Path Dependence." *Political Analysis* 14(3): 250–67.

Benvenisti, E., 2008. "Reclaiming Democracy: The Strategic Uses of Foreign and International Law by National Courts." *Tel Aviv University Law Faculty Papers* No. 59, Tel Aviv.

Benvenisti, E., and Downs, G. W., 2009. "Court Cooperation, Executive Accountability and Global Governance." *Tel Aviv University Law Faculty Papers* No. 108, Tel Aviv.

Benz, A., 2007. "Accountable Multilevel Governance by the Open Method of Coordination?" *European Law Journal* 13(4): 505–22.

Bergmann, N., and Porobic, J., 2008. "The Constitutional Court of Bosnia Herzegovina Decisions on Alleged Human Rights Violations during NATO-Led Stabilization Force Operations." *NATO Gazette* 18: 2–10.

Berman, E. G., 1998. "Collaboration or Abrogation? The Security Council's Increasing Reliance on Burden-Sharing." *International Peacekeeping* 5(1): 1–21.

Berman, P. S., 2007. "A Pluralist Approach to International Law." *Yale Journal of International Law* 32: 301–29.

Bernstein, S., 2004. "The Elusive Basis of Legitimacy in Global Governance: Three Conceptions." *Working Paper GHC* 4(2).

Bernstein, S., 2011. "Legitimacy in Intergovernmental and Non-State Global Governance." *Review of International Political Economy* 18(1): 17–51.

Besson, S., 2015. "International Institutions' Human Rights Duties and Responsibilities for Human Rights: A Quiet (R)Evolution." *Social Philosophy and Policy* 32(1): 244–68.

Bexell, M., Tallberg, J., and Uhlin, A., 2010. "Democracy in Global Governance: The Promises and Pitfalls of Transnational Actors." *Global Governance* 16: 81–101.

Bolkovac, K., and Lynn, C., 2011. *The Whistleblower: Sex Trafficking, Military Contractors, and One Woman's Fight for Justice*. London: Palgrave Macmillan.

Boseley, S., 2011. "Analysis: Vaccine Programmes Come under the Microscope." *Guardian*, June 6. Available at: https://www.theguardian.com/society/2011/jun/06/analysis-vaccination-programmes.

Bothe, M., and Fischer-Lescano A., 2002. "Protego et obligo: Afghanistan and the Paradox of Sovereignty." *German Law Journal* 3. Available at: http://www.germanlawjournal.com/index.php?pageID=11&artID=187 (last access January 31, 2015).

Boutros-Ghali, B., 1992. "An Agenda for Peace: Preventive Diplomacy, Peacemaking and Peace-keeping." *International Relations* 11: 201–18.

Bovens, M., 2007. "Analysing and Assessing Accountability: A Conceptual Framework." *European Law Journal* 13(4), 447–68.

Bovens, M., and Schillemans, T., 2011. "The Challenge of Multiple Accountability: Does Redundancy Lead to Overload?" In *Accountable Governance: Problems and Promises*, edited by M. J. Dubnick and H. G. Frederickson, 3–21. New York: M. E. Sharp.

Bovens, M., Schillemans, T., and Goodin, R. E., 2014a. "Public Accountability: Proliferation and Fragmentation." In *The Oxford Handbook of Public Accountability*, edited by M. Bovens, T. Schillemans, and R. E. Goodin, 1–20. Oxford: Oxford University Press.

Bovens, M., Schillemans, T., and Goodin, R. E. (eds), 2014b. *The Oxford Handbook of Public Accountability*. Oxford: Oxford University Press.

Brand, M. G., 2001. "Institution-Building and Human Rights Protection in Kosovo in the Light of UNMIK Legislation." *Nordic Journal of International Law* 70(4): 461–88.

Brito Vieira, M., and Carreira da Silva, F., 2013. "Getting Rights Right: Explaining Social Rights Constitutionalization in Revolutionary Portugal." *International Journal of Constitutional Law* 11(4): 898–922.

Brosig, M., 2010. "The Multi-Actor Game of Peacekeeping in Africa." *International Peacekeeping* 17(3): 327–42.

Brosig, M., 2011. "The Interplay of International Institutions in Kosovo between Convergence, Confusion and Niche Capabilities." *European Security* 20(2): 185–204.

Brown, L. D., and Fox, J. A., 1998. *The Struggle for Accountability: The World Bank, NGOs, and Grassroots Movement*. Cambridge, MA: MIT Press.

Bruen, C., and Brugha, R., 2014. "A Ghost in the Machine? Politics in Global Health Policy." *International Journal of Health Policy and Management* 3(1): 1–4.

Bruen, C., Brugha, R., Kageni, A., and Wafula, F., 2014. "A Concept in Flux: Questioning Accountability in the Context of Global Health Cooperation." *Globalization and Health* 10: 73–88.

Buchan, R., Jones, H., and White, N. D., 2011. "The Externalization of Peacekeeping: Policy, Responsibility, and Accountability." *Journal of International Peacekeeping* 15(3–4): 281–315.

Buchanan, A., and Keohane, R. O., 2006. "The Legitimacy of Global Governance Institutions." *Ethics and International Affairs* 20(4): 405–37.

Buerstedde, D., 2005. "Violence in Kosovo Calls for a Fresh Look at the Mission's Priorities." *OSCE Yearbook 2004*: 135–45. Baden-Baden: Nomos.

Burke-White, W., 2004. "International Legal Pluralism." *Michigan Journal of International Law* 25(4): 963–79.

Buse, K., and Walt, G., 2002. "Globalisation and Multi-Lateral Public–Private Health Partnerships: Issues for Health Policy." In *Health Policy in a Globalising World*, edited by K. Lee, K. Buse, and S. Fustukian, 41–61. Cambridge: Cambridge University Press.

Busuioc, M., 2012. "European Agencies and Their Boards: Promises and Pitfalls of Accountability beyond Design." *Journal of European Public Policy* 19(5): 719–36.

Busuioc, M., Curtin, D., and Groenleer, M., 2011. "Agency Growth between Autonomy and Accountability: The European Police Office as a 'Living Institution.'" *Journal of European Public Policy* 18(6): 848–67.

Büthe, T., and Mattli, W., 2011. *The New Global Rulers: The Privatization of Regulation in the World Economy*. Princeton, NJ: Princeton University Press.

Buzan, B., 1993. "From International System to International Society: Structural Realism and Regime Theory Meet the English School." *International Organization* 47(3): 327–52.

Buzan, B., 2004. *From International to World Society? English School Theory and the Social Structure of Globalisation*. Cambridge: Cambridge University Press.

Caines, K., Buse, K., Carlson, C., de Loor, R., Druce, N., Grace, C., Sadanandan, R., and Sancho, J., 2004. *Assessing the Impact of Global Health Partnerships*. Available at: https://assets.publishing.service.gov.uk/media/57a08cd2ed915d3cfd001636/Assessing-the-impact-of-GHPs1.pdf.

Canotilho, M., 2015. *The Impact of the Crisis on Fundamental Rights across Member States of the EU: Country Report on Portugal*. Available at: http://www.europarl.europa.eu/RegData/etudes/STUD/2015/510020/IPOL_STU%282015%29510020_EN.pdf.

Canotilho, M., Violante, T., and Lanceiro, R., 2015. "Austerity Measures under Judicial Scrutiny: The Portuguese Constitutional Case-Law." *European Constitutional Law Review* 11: 155–83.

Caplan, R., 2006. "Who Guards the Guardians? International Accountability in Bosnia." In *Peace without Politics? Ten Years of International State-Building in Bosnia*, edited by David Chandler, 157–70. Abingdon: Routledge.

Carlson, R. V., Boyd, K. M., and Webb, D. J., 2004. "The Revision of the Declaration of Helsinki: Past, Present and Future." *British Journal of Clinical Pharmacology* 57(6): 695–713.

Cerone, J., 2001. "Minding the Gap: Outlining KFOR Accountability in Post-Conflict Kosovo." *European Journal of International Law* 12(3): 469–88.

Chappell, D., and Evans, J., 1999. "The Role, Preparation and Performance of Civilian Police in United Nations Peacekeeping Operations." *Criminal Law Forum* 10(2): 171–271.

Checkel, J., 2005. "It's the Process Stupid! Process Tracing in the Study of European and International Politics." *ARENA Working Paper No. 26.*

Chesterman, S., 2002. *Justice under International Administration: Kosovo, East Timor and Afghanistan.* Available at: http://portal.uned.es/pls/portal/docs/PAGE/UNED_MAIN/LAUNIVERSIDAD/DEPARTAMENTOS/0614/INVESTIGACION/DOC_ASPJUDICIALES/JUSTICE_UNDER_INTL.PDF.

Chesterman, S., 2008. "Globalization Rules: Accountability, Power, and the Prospects for Global Administrative Law." *Global Governance* 14: 39–42.

Chesterman, S., 2009. "UNaccountable? The United Nations, Emergency Powers, and the Rule of Law." *Vanderbilt Journal of Transnational Law* 42(5): 1509–41.

Chopra, J., 2002. "Building State Failure in East Timor." *Development and Change* 33(5): 979–1000.

Cisotta, R., 2017. "The Quest for Financial Stability and Democracy in the Banking Union: Promoting Institutional Transformation and Regulatory Evolution through Unconventional Means." In *Democracy in the EMU in the Aftermath of the Crisis*, edited by L. Daniele, P. Simone, and R. Cisotta, 283–98. Basel: Springer.

Cisotta, R., and Gallo, D., 2014. "The Portuguese Constitutional Court Case Law on Austerity Measures: A Reappraisal." *LUISS Working Paper* No. 4. Available at: https://eprints.luiss.it/1298/.

Clapham, A., 2003. "The UN High Commissioner for Human Rights: Achievements and Frustrations." *Paper presented at the Symposium on the United Nations High Commissioner for Human Rights: The First Ten Years of the Office, and the Next.* New York: Columbia University Law School, February 17–18. Available at: http://www2.law.columbia.edu/hri/symposium/ClaphamPaper.htm#_ftnref1 (last access January 31, 2015).

Clarke, L., 2014. *Public–Private Partnerships and Responsibility under International Law: A Global Health Perspective.* Abingdon: Routledge.

Clarke, L., 2012. "Responsibility of International Organizations under International Law for the Acts of Global Health Public–Private Partnerships." *Chicago Journal of International Law* 12(1): 56–84.

Clinton, C., and Sridhar, D., 2017. "Who Pays for Cooperation in Global Health? A Comparative Analysis of WHO, the World Bank, the Global Fund to Fight HIV/AIDS, Tuberculosis and Malaria, and Gavi, the Vaccine Alliance." *The Lancet* 390 (10091): 324–32.

Cole, D., 2013. "Legal Affairs: Dreyfus, Guantánamo, and the Foundation of the Rule of Law." *Touro Law Review* 29: 43–57.

Coleman, K. P., 2007. *International Organisations and Peace Enforcement: The Politics of International Legitimacy.* Cambridge: Cambridge University Press.

Cooley, A., and Ron, J., 2002. "The NGO Scramble: Organizational Insecurity and the Political Economy of Transnational Action." *International Security* 27(1): 5–39.

Cooper, I., 2016. "The Politicization of Interparliamentary Relations in the EU: Constructing and Contesting the 'Article 13 Conference' on Economic Governance." *Comparative European Politics* 14(2): 196–214.

Cordesman, A. H., 2009. "Afghan Public Opinion and the Afghan War: Shifts by Region and Province." April 10, available at: http://csis.org/files/media/csis/pubs/094013_afghanpollbyregion.pdf (last access January 31, 2015).

Coroado, S., Garoupa, N., and Magalhães, P. C., 2017. "Judicial Behavior under Austerity: An Empirical Analysis of Behavioral Changes in the Portuguese Constitutional Court, 2002–2016." *Journal of Law and Courts* 5(2): 289–311.

Correia, T., Dussault, G., and Pontes, C., 2015. "The Impact of the Financial Crisis on Human Resources for Health Policies in Three Southern-Europe Countries." *Health Policy* 119(12): 1600–5.

Council of Europe, 1999. "Council of Europe's Contribution to the United Nations Interim Administration Mission in Kosovo, Committee of Ministers." *CM/Inf* 99(48), July 23.

Council of Europe, 2002. "Kosovo: The Human Rights Situation and the Fate of Persons Displaced from Their Homes. Report by Alvaro Gil-Robles, Commissioner for Human Rights for the attention of the Parliamentary Assembly and the Committee of Ministers of the Council of Europe." *CommDH*(2002)11, Strasbourg, October 16.

Council of Europe, 2004a. "Agreement between the United Nations Interim Administration Mission in Kosovo and the Council of Europe on Technical Arrangements Related to the European Convention for the Prevention of Torture and Inhuman or Degrading Treatment or Punishment." Pristina, August 23.

Council of Europe, 2004b. "Draft Opinion on Human Rights in Kosovo: Possible Establishment of a Review Mechanism, European Commission for Democracy through Law (Venice Commission)." *Opinion* 280, CDL-DI (2004)004, Strasbourg, October 1.

Council of Europe, 2007. "17th General Report on the CPT's Activities Covering the Period 1 August 2006 to 31 July 2007, Committee for the Prevention of Torture and Inhuman or Degrading Treatment or Punishment (CPT)." Strasbourg, September 14.

Council of Europe Parliamentary Assembly, 2006a. "Alleged Secret Detentions and Unlawful Inter-State Transfers of Detainees Involving Council of Europe Member States, Report to the Committee on Legal Affairs and Human Rights." Doc. 10957, June 12.

Council of Europe Parliamentary Assembly, 2006b. "Resolution 1507 (2006) on the Alleged Secret Detentions and Unlawful Inter-State Transfers of Detainees Involving Council of Europe Member States." Adopted on June 27.

Council of Europe Parliamentary Assembly, 2007. "Secret Detentions and Illegal Transfers of Detainees Involving Council of Europe Member States: Second Report to the Committee on Legal Affairs and Human Rights, Explanatory Memorandum." Rapporteur: Dick Marty, Strasbourg, AS/Jur (2007) 36.

Curtin, D. M., 2014. "Challenging Executive Dominance in European Democracy." *Modern Law Review* 77(1): 1–32.

Curtin, D. M., and Wessel, R. A. (eds), 2005. *Good Governance and the European Union: Reflections on Concepts, Institutions and Substance.* Antwerp: Intersentia.

Curtin, D. M., Mair, P., and Papadopoulos, Y., 2010. "Positioning Accountability in European Governance: An Introduction." *West European Politics* 33(5): 929–45.

da Conceição-Heldt, E., 2016. "Verantwortungszurechnung im EU- Mehrebenensystem während der Eurokrise: Wer kontrolliert die Troika- Institutionen?" *Zeitschrift für Politikwissenschaften* 26(Supplement 1): 115–29.

da Conceição-Heldt, E., Koch M., and Liese A., 2015. "Einleitung. Internationale Organisationen als Forschungsgegenstand. Oder: 'Über Blinde und die Gestalt des Elefanten.'" In *Internationale Organisationen: Autonomie, Politisierung, interorganisationale Beziehungen und Wandel. PVS-Sonderheft 49*, edited by E. da Conceição-Heldt, M. Koch, and A. Liese. Baden-Baden: Nomos.

Dai, X., 2002. "Information Systems in Treaty Regimes." *World Politics* 54(4): 405–36.

Dann, P., 2006. "Accountability in Development Aid Law: The World Bank, UNDP and Emerging Structures of Transnational Oversight." *Archiv des Völkerrechts* 44: 381–404.

Das, M., 2018. "Cervical Cancer Vaccine Controversy in India." *The Lancet* 19(2): 84.

Daugirdas, K., 2015. "Reputation and the Responsibility of International Organizations." *European Journal of International Law* 25(4): 991–1018.

Davis, D., 2007. *Negative Liberty: Public Opinion and the Terrorist Attacks on America.* New York: Russell Sage Foundation.

Dawson, M., 2015. "The Legal and Political Accountability Structure of 'Post-Crisis' EU Economic Governance." *Journal of Common Market Studies* 53(5): 976–93.

de las Casas, M., 2016. *The IMF Executive Board and the Euro Area Crisis: Accountability, Legitimacy, and Governance.* Available at: http://www-ieo.imf.org/ieo/files/completedevaluations/EAC__BP_16-02_02__The_IMF_Executive_Board_and_the_Euro_Area_Crisis_-_Accountability__Legitimacy__and_Governance.PDF.

de Wet, E., 2008. "Holding International Institutions Accountable: The Complementary Role of Non-Judicial Oversight Mechanisms and Judicial Review." *German Law Journal* 9: 1987–2010.

de Wet, E., 2010. "Holding International Institutions Accountable: The Complementary Role of Non-Judicial Oversight Mechanisms and Judicial Review." In *The Exercise of Public Authority by International Institutions: Advancing International Institutional Law*, edited by A. v. Bogdandy, R. Wolfrum, J. v. Bernstorff, P. Dann, and M. Goldmann, 855–82. Berlin: Springer.

Deeks, A., 2008. "Administrative Detention in Armed Conflict." *Case Western Reserve Journal of International Law* 40(3): 403–13.

Dellmuth, L. M., and Tallberg, J., 2014. "The Social Legitimacy of International Organisations: Interest Representation, Institutional Performance, and Confidence Extrapolation in the United Nations." *Review of International Studies* 41(3): 451–75.

Deshman, A. C., 2011. "Horizontal Review between International Organizations: Why, How, and Who Cares about Corporate Regulatory Capture." *European Journal of International Law* 22(4): 1089–113.

Dimitriu, G., 2013. "Interrogation, Coercion and Torture: Dutch Debates and Experiences after 9/11." *Intelligence and National Security* 28(4): 547–65.

Dingwerth, K., 2007. *The New Transnationalism: Transnational Governance and Democratic Legitimacy*, Houndmills: Palgrave Macmillan.

Dowell-Jones, M., 2015. "The Economics of the Austerity Crisis: Unpicking Some Human Rights Arguments." *Human Rights Law Review* 15(2): 193–223.

ECCHR, 2014. *Q & A on Clinical Trials and the HPV Case.* Available at: https://www.ecchr.eu/fileadmin/Q_As/Q_A_on_clinical_trials_and_the_HPV_Case__6_20160727.pdf.

Eide, K., 2012. *Power Struggle over Afghanistan.* New York: Skyhorse.

Esty, D., 2006. "Good Governance at the Supranational Scale: Globalizing Administrative Law." *Yale Law School Faculty Scholarship Series.*

Everson, M., and Joerges, C., 2013. "Who Is the Guardian for Constitutionalism in Europe after the Financial Crisis?" *LEQS Paper* No. 63. Available at: https://ssrn.com/abstract=2287111.

Fabbrini, S., 2013. "Intergovernmentalism and Its Limits: Assessing the European Union's Answer to the Euro Crisis." *Comparative Political Studies* 46(9): 1003–29.

Farvaque, E., Hayat, M. A., and Mihailov, A., 2017. "Who Supports the ECB? Evidence from Eurobarometer Survey Data." *World Economy* 40(4): 654–77.

Fasone, C., 2014. *Constitutional Court Facing the EU Crisis: Italy, Portugal and Spain in a Comparative Perspective*. Available at: http://cadmus.eui.eu/handle/1814/33859.

Fassbender, B. (Ed.), 2011. *Securing Human Rights? Achievements and Challenges of the UN Security Council*. Oxford: Oxford University Press.

Federal Court of Canada, 2008. "Amnesty International Canada and British Columbia Civil Liberties Association v. Chief of the Defence Staff for the Canadian Forces, Minister of National Defence and Attorney General of Canada." Court File Number T-324-07, Ottawa, March 12. Available at: https://www.asser.nl/upload/documents/DomCLIC/Docs/NLP/Canada/A.I.Canada_and_BCCLA_v_Canadian_Defence_Dismissal_and_Grant_of_Standing_05-11-2007.pdf (last access September 18, 2019).

Ferstman, C., 2017. *International Organizations and the Fight for Accountability*. Oxford: Oxford University Press.

Figà-Talamanca, N., 1996. "The Role of NATO in the Peace Agreement for Bosnia and Herzegovina." *European Journal of International Law* 7(1): 164–75.

Figueiredo, A., and González, P., 2014. "The European Social Model in a Context of Crisis and Austerity in Portugal." In *The European Social Model in Times of Economic Crisis and Austerity Policies*, edited by D. Vaughan-Whitehead, 291–340. London: Edward Elgar.

Finnemore, M., and Sikkink, K., 1998. "International Norm Dynamics and Political Change." *International Organization* 52(4): 887–917.

Finnemore, M., and Toope, S. J., 2001. "Alternatives to 'Legalization': Richer Views of Law and Politics." *International Organization* 55(3): 743–58.

Fischer-Lescano, A., 2014. *Human Rights in Times of Austerity Policy: The EU Institutions and the Conclusion of Memoranda of Understanding*. Baden-Baden: Nomos.

Fischer-Lescano, A., and Liste, P., 2005. "Zu Trennung und Verknüpfung von Politik und Recht der Weltgesellschaft." *Zeitschrift für internationale Beziehungen* 12(2): 209–49.

Fonseca, P., and Ferreira, M. J., 2015. "Through 'Seas Never Before Sailed': Portuguese Government Discursive Legitimation Strategies in a Context of Financial Crisis." *Discourse and Society* 26(6): 682–711.

Foot, R., 2006. "Torture: The Struggle over a Peremptory Norm in a Counter-Terrorist Era." *International Relations* 20(2): 131–51.

Forsythe, D. P., 2007. "United States Policy toward Enemy Detainees in the 'War on Terrorism.'" *Human Rights Quarterly* 28(2): 465–91.

Gallagher, K. E., Howard, N., and Kabakama, S., 2017. QHuman Papillomavirus (HPV) Vaccine Coverage Achievements in Low and Middle-Income Countries 2007–2016." *Papillomavirus Research* 4: 72–8.

Ganghof, S., 2005. "Kausale Perspektiven in der vergleichenden Politikwissenschaft: X-zentrierte und Y-zentrierte Forschungsdesigns." In *Vergleichen in der Politikwissenschaft*, edited by S. Kropp and M. Minkenberg, 76–93, Wiesbaden: VS Verlag für Sozialwissenschaften.

García-Orrico, D., 2009. "Kosovo." In *Security Council Resolutions under Chapter VII. Design, Implementation and Accountabilities. The Cases of Afghanistan, Côte d'Ivoire, Kosovo and Sierra Leone*, edited by B. Antonini, 117–55. Madrid: FRIDE.

Gehring, T., and Faude, B., 2014. "A Theory of Emerging Order within Institutional Complexes: How Competition among Regulatory International Institutions Leads to Institutional Adaptation and a Division of Labor." *Review of International Organizations* 9(4): 471–98.

Genschel, P., and Zangl, B., 2008. "Metamorphosen des Staates - vom Herrschaftsmonopolisten zum Herrschaftsmanager." *Leviathan* 36(3): 430–54.

George, A. L., and Bennett, A., 2005. "Process-Tracing and Historical Explanations." In *Case Studies and Theory Development in the Social Sciences*, edited by A. L. George and A. Bennett, 205–32. Cambridge, MA: Harvard University Press.

Geyer, F., 2007. "Fruit of the Poisonous Tree: Member States' Indirect Use of Extraordinary Rendition and the EU Counter-Terrorism Strategy." In *CEPS Working Document No. 263*. Center for European Policy Studies. Available at: http://www.ceps.eu/files/book/1487.pdf (last access January 31, 2015).

Ginsborg, L., 2017. "The Impact of the Economic Crisis on Human Rights in Europe and the Accountability of International Institutions." *Global Campus Human Rights Journal* 1: 97–117.

Goertz, G., 2006. *Social Science Concepts: A User's Guide*. Princeton, NJ: Princeton University Press.

Goodhart, M., 2011. "Democratic Accountability in Global Politics: Norms, Not Agents." *Journal of Politics* 73(1): 45–60.

Gøtzsche, P. C., 2011. "Why We Need Easy Access to All Data from All Clinical Trials and How to Accomplish It." *Trials* 12: 249–63.

Government of Canada, 2005. "Arrangement for the Transfer of Detainees between the Canadian Forces and the Ministry of Defence of the Islamic Republic of Afghanistan." Kabul, December 18.

Government of Canada, 2007a. "Supplement." Kabul, May 3.

Government of Canada, 2007b. "Exchange of Letters on Access to Detainees Transferred to the Government of Afghanistan from NATO Partners to Office of the National Security Council." Afghanistan, September 6.

Government of the United Kingdom, 2006. "Memorandum of Understanding between the Government of the United Kingdom of Great Britain and Northern Ireland and the Government of the Islamic Republic of Afghanistan Concerning the Transfer by the United Kingdom Armed Forces to Afghan Authorities of Persons Detained in Afghanistan." September 30.

Grant, R. W., and Keohane, R. O., 2005. "Accountability and Abuses of Power in World Politics." *American Political Science Review* 99(1): 29–43.

Grigorescu, A., 2008. "Horizontal Accountability in Intergovernmental Organizations." *Ethics and International Affairs* 22(3): 285–308.

Grigorescu, A., 2010. "The Spread of Bureaucratic Oversight Mechanisms across Intergovernmental Organizations." *International Studies Quarterly* 54(3): 871–86.

Gronke, P., Rejali, D., Drenguis, D., Hicks, J., Miller, P., and Nakayama, B., 2010. "US Public Opinion on Torture, 2001–2009." *PS: Political Science and Politics* 43(3): 437–44.

Gülmezoglu, M., Pang, T., Horton, R., and Dickersin, K., 2005. "WHO Facilitates International Collaboration in Setting Standards for Clinical Trial Registration." *The Lancet* 365(9474): 1829–31.

Guzman, A. T., 2005. "The Design of International Agreements." *European Journal of International Law* 16(4): 579–612.

Hafner-Burton, E. M., and Tsutsui, K., 2005. "Human Rights in a Globalizing World: The Paradox of Empty Promises." *American Journal of Sociology* 110(5): 1373–411.

Hannum, H., 2006. "Human Rights in Conflict Resolution: The Role of the Office of the High Commissioner for Human Rights in UN Peacemaking and Peacebuilding." *Human Rights Quarterly* 28(1): 1–85.

Hanson, C. M., Eckert, L., Bloem, P., and Cernuschi, T., 2015. "Gavi HPV Programs: Application to Implementation." *Vaccines* 3: 408–19.

Harsch, M. F., 2012. *NATO and the UN: Partnership with Potential?* Available at: https://www.swp-berlin.org/fileadmin/contents/products/research_papers/2012_RP02_har.pdf.

Häußler, U., 2010. "Human Rights Accountability of International Organisations in the Lead of International Peace Missions." In *Accountability for Human Rights Violations by International Organisations*, edited by J. Wouters, E. Brems, S. Smis, and P. Schmitt, 215–68. Antwerp: Intersentia.

Hawkins, D. G., Lake, D. A., Nielson, D. L., and Tierney, M. J., 2006a. "Delegation under Anarchy: States, International Organizations, and Principal-Agent Theory." In *Delegation and Agency in International Organizations*, edited by D. G. Hawkins, D. A. Lake, D. L. Nielson, and M. J. Tierney, 3–38. Cambridge: Cambridge University Press.

Hawkins, D. G., Lake, D. A., Nielson, D. L., and Tierney, M. J. (Eds), 2006b. *Delegation and Agency in International Organizations*. Cambridge: Cambridge University Press.

Heimans, J., 2002. *Multisectoral Global Funds as Instruments for Financing Spending on Global Priorities*. Available at: https://www.cbd.int/financial/doc/desa-globalfunds2002.pdf.

Held, D., 2006. "Democratic Accountability and Political Effectiveness from a Cosmopolitan Perspective." In *Global Governance and the Role of Non-State Actors*, edited by G. F. Schuppert, Vol. 9–30. Baden-Baden: Nomos.

Heldt, E., 2017. "Regaining Control of Errant Agents? Agency Slack at the European Commission and the World Health Organization." *Cooperation and Conflict* 52(4): 469–84.

Henderson, C., 2014. "Authority without Accountability? The UN Security Council's Authorization Method and Institutional Mechanisms of Accountability." *Journal of Conflict and Security Law* 19(3): 489–509.

Henning, C. R., 2017. *Tangled Governance: International Regime Complexity, the Troika, and the Euro Crisis*. Oxford: Oxford University Press.

Hesselmann, E., 2011. "The Limits of Control: The Accountability of Foundations and Partnerships in Global Health." In *Partnerships and Foundations in Global Health Governance*, edited by S. Rushton and O. D. Williams, 228–52. Basingstoke: Palgrave Macmillan.

Heupel, M., 2013. "With Power Comes Responsibility: Human Rights Protection in United Nations Sanctions Policy." *European Journal of International Relations* 19(4): 773–96.

Heupel, M., 2017. "Human Rights Protection in World Bank Lending: Following the Lead of the US Congress." In *Protecting the Individual from International Authority: Human Rights in International Organizations*, edited by M. Heupel and M. Zürn, 241–72. Cambridge: Cambridge University Press.

Heupel, M., and Zürn, M. (Eds), 2017. *Protecting the Individual from International Authority: Human Rights in International Organizations*. Cambridge: Cambridge University Press.

Heupel, M., Hirschmann, G., and Zürn, M., 2018. "International Organisations and Human Rights: What Direct Authority Needs for Its Legitimation." *Review of International Studies* 44(2): 343–66.

Hirschmann, G., 2016. "Accountability Dynamics and the Emergence of an International Rule of Law for Detentions in Multilateral Peace Operations." In *The Rule of Law in an*

Era of Multilevel Governance and Global Legal Pluralism, edited by M. Heupel and T. Reinold. London: Palgrave Macmillan.

Hirschmann, G., 2017a. "NATO Peacekeeping and the Protection from Sexual Exploitation and Human Trafficking." In *Protecting the Individual from International Authority: Human Rights in International Organizations*, edited by M. Heupel and M. Zürn, 203–19. Cambridge: Cambridge University Press.

Hirschmann, G., 2017b. "NATO Peacekeeping and the Protection of the Right to Due Process in Detentions." In *Protecting the Individual from International Authority*, edited by M. Heupel and M. Zürn, 220–35. Cambridge: Cambridge University Press.

Hirschmann, G., 2017c. "United Nations Peacekeeping and the Protection of Due Process Rights in Detentions." In *Protecting the Individual from International Authority*, edited by M. Heupel and M. Zürn, 186–202. Cambridge: Cambridge University Press.

Hirschmann, G., 2017d. "When Protectors Become Perpetrators: United Nations Peacekeeping and the Protection of Physical Integrity." In *Protecting the Individual from International Authority: Human Rights in International Organizations*, edited by M. Heupel and M. Zürn, 157–85. Cambridge: Cambridge University Press.

Hirschmann, G., 2019. "Guarding the Guards: Pluralist Accountability for Human Rights Violations by International Organisations." *Review of International Studies* 45(1): 20–38.

Hix, S., 2002. "Constitutional Agenda-Setting through Discretion in Rule Interpretation: Why the European Parliament Won at Amsterdam." *British Journal of Political Science* 32(2): 259–80.

Hix, S., Noury, A., and Roland, G., 2005. "Power to the Parties: Cohesion and Competition in the European Parliament, 1979–2001." *British Journal of Political Science* 35(2): 209–34.

Hobolt, S. B., 2014. "Public Attitudes towards the Euro Crisis." In *Democratic Politics in a European Union under Stress*, edited by O. Cramme and S. B. Hobolt, 48–66. Oxford: Oxford University Press.

Hoffmann, F., and Mégret, F., 2005. "Fostering Human Rights Accountability: An Ombudsperson for the United Nations?" *Global Governance* 11(1): 43–63.

Holzscheiter, A., 2014. "Restoring Order in Global Health Governance: Do Metagovernance Norms Affect Interorganizational Convergence?" Available at: http://aei.pitt.edu/67186/1/CES_OFWP_23.pdf.

Holzscheiter, A., Bahr, T., and Pantzerhielm, L., 2016. "Emerging Governance Architectures in Global Health: Do Metagovernance Norms Explain Inter-Organisational Convergence?" *Politics and Governance* 4(3): 5–19.

Hood, C., 2002. "The Risk Game and the Blame Game." *Government and Opposition* 37(1): 15–37.

Hooghe, L., Marks, G., Lenz, T., Bezuijen, J., Ceka, B., and Derderyan, S., 2017. *Measuring International Authority: A Postfunctionalist Theory of Governance*. Oxford: Oxford University Press.

Human Rights First, 2011. "Detained and Denied in Afghanistan How to Make US Detention Comply with the Law." Washington, DC. Available at: https://www.humanrightsfirst.org/wp-content/uploads/pdf/Detained-Denied-in-Afghanistan.pdf (last access September 18, 2019).

Human Rights Watch, 2002a. "Hopes Betrayed: Trafficking of Women and Girls to Post-Conflict Bosnia and Herzegovina for Forced Prostitution." New York.

Human Rights Watch, 2002b. "Trafficking of Women and Girls to Bosnia and Herzegovina for Forced Prostitution: A Submission for the United Nations Committee on the Rights of the Child from the Human Rights Watch Children's Rights Division." Available at:

www.crin.org/docs/resources/treaties/crc.39/Bosnia_HRW_ngo_report.doc (last access January 31, 2015).

Human Rights Watch, 2007. "Better Late Than Never: Enhancing the Accountability of International Institutions in Kosovo." April 13.

Human Rights Watch, 2009. "You Will Be Punished: Attacks on Civilians in Eastern Congo." December.

Human Rights Watch, 2015. "At Your Own Risk: Reprisals against Critics of World Bank Group Projects." No. 978-1-6231-32491, June.

Hurd, I., 1999. "Legitimacy and Authority in International Politics." *International Organization* 53(2): 379–408.

Hurd, I., 2007. *After Anarchy: Power and Legitimacy of the United Nations Security Council.* Princeton, NJ: Princeton University Press.

Hurd, I., 2013. "Torture and the Politics of Legitimation in International Law." In *The Legitimacy of International Human Rights Regimes*, edited by A. Follesdal, J. K. Schaffer, and G. Ulfstein, 165–89. Cambridge: Cambridge University Press.

Ignatieff, M., 2014. "Rights Inflation and Role Conflict in the Office of the High Commissioner for Human Rights." In *The United Nations High Commissioner for Human Rights: Conscience for the World*, edited by Felice D. Gaer and Christen L. Broecker, 35–45. Leiden: Nijhoff.

International Law Association, 2004. *Final Report: Accountability of International Organizations.* Berlin Conference.

Ivanković Tamamović, A., 2015. *The Impact of the Crisis on Fundamental Rights across Member States of the EU: Comparative Analysis.* Available at: http://www.europarl.europa.eu/RegData/etudes/STUD/2015/510021/IPOL_STU(2015)510021_EN.pdf.

Jain, A., 2013. "HPV Vaccination as a National Health Priority: No Easy Answers." *British Medical Journal*, 347–8.

Jain, M., Taneja, G., Amin, R., Steinglass, R., and Favin, M., 2015. "Engaging Communities with a Simple Tool to Help Increase Immunization Coverage." *Global Health, Science and Practice* 3(1): 117–25.

Jetschke, A., and Lenz, T., 2013. "Does Regionalism Diffuse? A New Research Agenda for the Study of Regional Organizations." *Journal of European Public Policy* 10(20): 626–37.

John, T. J., 2010. "India's National Technical Advisory Group on Immunisation." *Vaccine* 28S: A88–90.

Johnson, T., 2014. *Organizational Progeny: Why Governments Are Losing Control over the Proliferating Structures of Global Governance.* Oxford: Oxford University Press.

Jones, E., 2009. "Output Legitimacy and the Global Financial Crisis: Perceptions Matter." *Journal of Common Market Studies* 47(5): 1085–105.

Jones, J. R. W. D., 1996. "The Implications of the Peace Agreement for the International Criminal Tribunal for the Former Yugoslavia." *European Journal of International Law* 7(1): 226–44.

Kane, M. A., Serrano, B., de Sanjosé, S., and Wittet, S., 2012. "Implementation of Human Papillomavirus Immunization in the Developing World." *Vaccine* 30S: F192–200.

Karantinos, D., 2014. *An Evaluation of the Social and Employment Aspects and Challenges in Greece.* Available at: http://www.europarl.europa.eu/RegData/etudes/note/join/2014/497760/IPOL-JOIN_NT%282014%29497760_EN.pdf.

Kelly, M., 2005. "The UN, Security and Human Rights: Achieving a Winning Balance." In *The UN, Human Rights and Post-Conflict Situations*, edited by N. D. White and D. Klaasen, 118–48. Manchester: Manchester University Press.

Kentikelenis, A., Karanikolos, M., Reeves, A., McKee, M., and Stuckler, D., 2014. "Greece's Health Crisis: From Austerity to Denialism." *The Lancet* 383(9918): 748–53.

Keohane, R. O., 1984. *After Hegemony: Cooperation and Discord in the World Political Economy*. Princeton, NJ: Princeton University Press.

Keohane, R. O., 2003. "Global Governance and Democratic Accountability." In *Taming Globalization: Frontiers of Governance*, edited by D. Held and M. Koenig-Archibugi, 130–59. Cambridge: Cambridge University Press.

Keohane, R. O., Moravcsik, A., and Slaughter, A.-M., 2000. "Legalized Dispute Resolution: Interstate and Transnational." *International Organization* 54(3): 457–88.

Kersbergen, K. v., and Waarden, F. v., 2004. "'Governance' as a Bridge between Disciplines: Cross-Disciplinary Inspiration Regarding Shifts in Governance and Problems of Governability, Accountability and Legitimacy." *European Journal of Political Research* 43(2): 143–71.

Khosla, R., and Hunt, P., 2008. *Human Rights Guidelines for Pharmaceutical Companies in Relation to Access to Medicines*. Available at: http://repository.essex.ac.uk/4425/1/human-rights-guidelines-pharmaceutical-companies-access-medicines.pdf.

Kickbusch, I., 2000. "The Development of International Health Policies: Accountability Intact?" *Social Science and Medicine* 51: 979–89.

Kiewiet, D. R., and McCubbins, M. D., 1991. *The Logic of Delegation: Congressional Parties and the Appropriations Process*. Chicago, IL: University of Chicago Press.

Kilpatrick, C., and De Witte, B., 2014. "A Comparative Framing of Fundamental Rights: Challenges to Social Crisis Measures in the Eurozone." *European Journal of Social Law* 1: 2–11.

Kingsbury, B., Krisch, N., and Stewart, R. B., 2005. "The Emergence of Global Administrative Law." *Law and Contemporary Problems* 68(3/4): 15–61.

Koenig-Archibugi, M., 2004. "Transnational Corporations and Public Accountability." *Government and Opposition* 39(2): 234–59.

Koenig-Archibugi, M., 2010. "Accountability in Transnational Relations: How Distinctive Is It?" *West European Politics* 33(5): 1142–64.

Koenig-Archibugi, M., and Zurn, M. 2006. "Conclusions II: The Modes and Dynamics of Global Governance." In *New Modes of Governance in the Global System*, edited by M. Koenig-Archibugi and M. Zürn, 236–54. New York: Palgrave Macmillan.

Kohl, K. S., Bonhoeffer, J., Braun, M. M., Chen, R. T., Duclos, P., Heijbel, H., Heiniger, U., Loupi, E., and Marcy, S. M., Brighton Collaboration, 2005. "The Brighton Collaboration: Creating a Global Standard for Case Definitions (and Guidelines) for Adverse Events Following Immunization." In *Advances in Patient Safety: From Research to Implementation, Volume 2: Concepts and Methodology*, edited by K. Henriksen, J. B. Battles, E. S. Marks, and D. I. Lewin, 87–102. Rockville, MD: Agency for Healthcare Research and Quality.

Koppell, J. G., 2005. "Pathologies of Accountability: ICANN and the Challenge of 'Multiple Accountabilities Disorder.'" *Public Administration Review* 65(1): 94–108.

Koppell, J. G., 2010. *World Role: Accountability, Legitimacy, and the Design of Global Governance*. Chicago, IL: University of Chicago Press.

Koremenos, B., Lipson, C., and Snidal, D., 2001. "The Rational Design of International Institutions." *International Organization* 55(4): 761–99.

Korkelika, K., 1999. "The CIS Peace-Keeping Operations in the Context of International Legal Order." Available at: http://www.nato.int/acad/fellow/97-99/korkelia.pdf.

Koskenniemi, M., 2004. "International Law and Hegemony: A Reconfiguration." *Cambridge Review of International Affairs* 17(2): 197–218.

Kramarz, T., and Park, S., 2016. "Accountability in Global Environmental Governance: A Meaningful Tool for Action?" *Global Environmental Politics* 16(2): 1–21.

Krisch, N., 2010. *Beyond Constitutionalism: The Pluralist Structure of Postnational Law.* Oxford: Oxford University Press.

Kuyper, J., Bäckstrand, K., and Schroeder, H., 2017. "Institutional Accountability of Non-state Actors in the UNFCCC: Exit, Voice, and Loyalty." *Review of Policy Research* 34: 88–109.

Kvale, S., and Brinkmann, S., 2009. *InterViews: Learning the Craft of Qualitative Research Interviewing*, Second Edition. Thousand Oaks, CA: Sage.

Ladwig, B., and Rudolf, B., 2011. "International Legal and Moral Standards of Good Governance in Fragile States." In *Governance without a State? Policies and Politics in Areas of Limited Statehood*, edited by T. Risse and U. Lehmkuhl, 199–231. New York: Columbia University Press.

Lake, D. A., 2007. "Delegating Divisible Sovereignty: Sweeping a Conceptual Minefield." *Review of International Organizations* 2: 219–37.

Lake, D. A., and McCubbins, M. D., 2006. "The Logic of Delegation to International Organizations." In *Delegation and Agency in International Organizations*, edited by D. G. Hawkins, D. A. Lake, D. L. Nielson, and M. J. Tierney, 341–68. Cambridge: Cambridge University Press.

Larson, H. J., and Ghinai, I., 2011. "Lessons from Polio Eradication." *Nature* 473: 446–7.

Larson, H. J., de Figueiredo, A., Xiahong, Z., Schulz, W. S., Verger, P., Johnston, I. G., Cook, A. R., and Jones, N. S., 2016. "The State of Vaccine Confidence 2016: Global Insights through a 67-Country Survey." *EBioMedicine* 12: 295–301.

Lenz, T., Bezuijen, J., Hooghe, L., and Marks, G., 2015. "Patterns of International Organization: Task Specific vs. General Purpose." In *Internationale Organisationen: Autonomie, Politisierung, Interorganisationale Beziehungen Und Wandel. Politische Vierteljahresschrift (PVS), Sonderheft 49*, edited by E. da Conceicao-Heldt, A. Liese, and M. Koch. Baden-Baden: Nomos.

Levin, A., Wang, S. A., Levin, C., Tsu, V., and Hutubessy, R., 2014. "Costs of Introducing and Delivering HPV Vaccines in Low and Lower Middle Income Countries: Inputs for GAVI Policy on Introduction Grant Support to Countries." *PloS one* 9(6): e101114.

Liese, A., and Beisheim, M., 2011. "Transnational Public–Private Partnerships and the Provision of Collective Goods in Developing Countries." In *Governance without a State? Policies and Politics in Areas of Limited Statehood*, edited by T. Risse. New York: Columbia University Press.

Lipson, M., 2008. "Clash of Delegations? Coordination in UN Integrated Missions." Paper prepared for presentation at the panel on Delegation to International Organizations: Dilemmas and Resolutions, Annual Meeting of the American Political Science Association, Boston, MA.

Lyck, M., 2009. *Peace Operations and International Criminal Justice: Building Peace after Mass Atrocities*. New York: Routledge.

Lyne, M. M., Nielson, D. L., and Tierney, M. J., 2006. "Who Delegates? Alternative Models of Principals in Development Aid." In *Delegation and Agency in International Organizations*, edited by D. G. Hawkins, D. A. Lake, D. L. Nielson, and M. J. Tierney, 41–76. New York: Cambridge University Press.

Macdonald, K., 2014. "The Meaning and Purposes of Transnational Accountability." *Australian Journal of Public Administration* 73(4): 426–36.

Macdonald, T., and Macdonald, K., 2006. "Non-Electoral Accountability in Global Politics: Strengthening Democratic Control within the Global Garment Industry." *European Journal of International Law* 17(1): 89–119.

Mahoney, J., 2012. "The Logic of Process Tracing Tests in the Social Sciences." *Sociological Methods and Research* 41(4): 570–97.

Mahoney, L., and Nash, R., 2012. "Influence on the Ground: Understanding and Strengthening the Protection Impact of United Nations Human Rights Field Presences." Available at: http://www.fieldviewsolutions.org/fv-publications/Influence_on_the_Ground.pdf (last access September 22, 2019).

Mamadouh, V., and Raunio, T., 2003. "The Committee System: Powers, Appointments and Report Allocation." *Journal of Common Market Studies* 41(2): 333–51.

Manoli, P., and Maris, G., 2015. "The Role of the European Parliament in Managing the International Economic Crisis." In *The European Parliament and Its International Relations*, edited by S. Stavridis and D. Irrera, 70–91. London: Routledge.

Marshall, D., and Inglis, S., 2003. "The Disempowerment of Human Rights-Based Justice in the United Nations Mission in Kosovo." *Harvard Human Rights Journal* 16: 95–146.

Martens, J., and Seitz, K., 2015. "Philanthropic Power and Development: Who Shapes the Agenda?" Available at: https://www.globalpolicy.org/images/pdfs/GPFEurope/Philanthropic_Power_online.pdf (last access September 22, 2019).

Martens, K., 2011. "Civil Society and Accountability of the United Nations." In *Building Global Democracy? Civil Society and Accountable Global Governance*, edited by J. A. Scholte, 42–57. Cambridge: Cambridge University Press.

Martin, L. L., and Simmons, B. A., 1998. "Theories and Empirical Studies of International Institutions." *International Organization* 52(4): 729–57.

Martin, L. L., and Simmons, B. A., 2002. "International Organizations and Institutions." In *Handbook of International Relations*, edited by W. Carlsnaes, T. Risse, and B. A. Simmons, 326–51. London: Sage.

Mattli, W., and Woods, N. (eds), 2009. *The Politics of Global Regulation*, Princeton, NJ: Princeton University Press.

Maure, C. G., Dodoo, A. N., Bonhoeffer, J., and Zuber, P. L., 2014. "The Global Vaccine Safety Initiative: Enhancing Vaccine Pharmacovigilance Capacity at Country Level." *Bulletin of the World Health Organization* 92(9): 695–6.

Mayntz, R., 2004. "Mechanisms in the Analysis of Social Macro-Phenomena." *Philosophy of the Social Sciences* 34(2): 237–59.

McCoy, D., and McGoey, L., 2011. "Global Health and the Gates Foundation: In Perspective." In *Partnerships and Foundations in Global Health Governance*, edited by S. Rushton and O. D. Williams, 143–63. London: Palgrave Macmillan.

McCubbins, M. D., and Schwartz, T., 1984. "Congressional Oversight Overlooked: Police Patrols versus Fire Alarms." *American Journal of Political Science* 28(1): 165–79.

McGoey, L., 2017. *No Such Thing as a Free Gift*. London: Verso.

Mégret, F., and Hoffmann, F., 2003. "The UN as a Human Rights Violator? Some Reflections on the United Nations Changing Human Rights Responsibilities." *Human Rights Quarterly* 25(2): 314–42.

Mendelson, S. E., 2005. "Barracks and Brothels: Peacekeepers and Human Trafficking in the Balkans." *Reference and Research Book News* 20(3).

Messineo, F., 2009. "The House of Lords in Al-Jedda and Public International Law: Attribution of Conduct to UN-Authorized Forces and the Power of the Security Council to Displace Human Rights." *Netherlands International Law Review* LVI: 35–62.

Milford, C., Wassenaar, D., and Slack, C., 2006. "Resources and Needs of Research Ethics Committees in Africa: Preparations for HIV Vaccine Trials." *IRB: Ethics and Human Research* 28(2): 1–9.

Momirov, A., 2012. "Local Impact of 'UN Accountability' under International Law: The Rise and Fall of UNMIK's Human Rights Advisory Panel." *International Peacekeeping* 19(1): 3–18.

Moorthy, V. S., Karam, G., Vannice, K. S., and Kieny, M.-P., 2015. "Rationale for WHO's New Position Calling for Prompt Reporting and Public Disclosure of Interventional Clinical Trial Results." *PLoS Med* 12(4): e1001819.

Moran, M., 2011. "Private Foundations and Global Health Partnerships: Philanthropists and 'Partnership Brokerage.'" In *Partnerships and Foundations in Global Health Governance*, edited by S. Rushton and O. D. Williams, 123–42. London: Palgrave Macmillan.

Müller, H., and Wolff, J., 2011. "Demokratischer Krieg am Hindukusch? Eine kritische Analyse der Bundestagsdebatten zur deutschen Afghanistanpolitik 2001–2011." In *Sonderheft der Zeitschrift für Außen- und Sicherheitspolitik 2011: Zehn Jahre Deutschland in Afghanistan*: 197–221.

Mulligan, S. P., 2006. "The Uses of Legitimacy in International Relations." *Millennium—Journal of International Studies* 34: 349–75.

Nair, H., Hazarika, I., and Patwari, A., 2011. "A Roller-Coaster Ride: Introduction of Pentavalent Vaccine in India." *Journal of Global Health* 1(1): 32–5.

Nanz, P. and Dingwerth, K., 2016. "Participation." In *Oxford Handbook of International Organizations*, edited by J. K. Cogan, I. Hurd, and I. Johnstone. Oxford: Oxford University Press.

NATO, 2006a. "Standing Operating Procedures: Detention of Non-ISAF Personnel (SOP 362)." August 13. Available at: http://info.publicintelligence.net/ISAF-DetaineeSOP.pdf (last access September 22, 2019).

Nimkar, R., 2009. "From Bosnia to Baghdad the Case for Regulating Private Military and Security Companies." *Journal of Public and International Affairs* 20(1): 1–24.

Nolan, A., 2015. "Not Fit For Purpose? Human Rights in Times of Financial and Economic Crisis." *European Human Rights Law Review* 21(4): 358–69.

Nolan, A., and Dutschke, M., 2010. "Article 2(1) ICESCR and States Parties' Obligations: Whither the Budget?" *European Human Rights Law Review* 10(3): 280–9.

Nollkaemper, A., 2018. "The Duality of Shared Responsibility." *Contemporary Politics* 24(5): 524–44.

Nullmeier, F., Biegon, D., Gronau, J., Nonhoff, M., Schmidtke, H., and Schneider, S. (eds), 2010. *Prekäre Legitimitäten. Rechtfertigung von Herrschaft in der postnationalen Konstellation*. Frankfurt: Suhrkamp.

Nye, J. S., 2001. "Globalization's Democratic Deficit: How to Make International Institutions More Accountable." *Foreign Affairs* 80(4): 2–6.

O'Brien, D., 2000. "The Search for Subsidiarity: The UN, African Regional Organizations and Humanitarian Action." *International Peacekeeping* 7(3): 57–83.

O'Connell, P., 2013. "Let Them Eat Cake: Socio-Economic Rights in an Age of Austerity." In *Human Rights and Public Finance: Budgets and the Promotion of Economic and Social Rights*, edited by A. Nolan, R. O'Connell, and C. Harvey, 59–76. Oxford: Hart Publishing.

O'Donell, G. A., 1994. "Delegative Democracy." *Journal of Democracy* 5(1): 55–69.

O'Flaherty, M., 2004. *Human Rights Monitoring and Armed Conflict: Challenges for the UN*. Geneva: United Nations for Disarmament Research.

Ohlin, J. D., 2010. "The Torture Lawyers." *Harvard International Law Journal* 51(1): 183–256.

Ombudsperson Institution in Kosovo (OIK), 2001a. "Special Report No. 3. The Conformity of Deprivations of Liberty under 'Executive Orders' with Recognised International Standards." June 29, Pristina.

Ombudsperson Institution in Kosovo (OIK), 2001b. "Special Report No. 4. Certain Aspects of UNMIK Regulation No. 2001/18 on the Establishment of a Detention Review Commission for Extra-Judicial Detentions Based on Executive Orders." August 25, Pristina.

Ombudsperson Institution in Kosovo (OIK), 2002. "Second Annual Report 2001–2002. Addressed to SRSG Michael Steiner." July 10, Pristina.

Organization for Security and Co-operation in Europe (OSCE), 1999. "Decision No. 305, PC Journal No. 237, Agenda item 2, Permanent Council, PC.DEC/305." July 1.

Organization for Security and Co-operation in Europe (OSCE), 2000. "First Review of the Criminal Justice System (February 2000–July 2000)". Department of Human Rights and Rule of Law, Pristina.

Organization for Security and Co-operation in Europe (OSCE), 2001. "Review of the Criminal Justice System, Mission in Kosovo (September 2000–February 2001)." Department of Human Rights and Rule of Law, Pristina.

Organization for Security and Co-operation in Europe (OSCE), 2002. "Review of the Criminal Justice System (September 2001–February 2002), 'Independence of the Judiciary, Detention, Mental Health Issues.'" Department of Human Rights and Rule of Law, Pristina.

Organization for Security and Co-operation in Europe (OSCE), 2003. "Review of the Criminal Justice System (March 2002–April 2003), 'Protection of Witnesses in the Criminal Justice System.'" Department of Human Rights and Rule of Law, Pristina.

Ortiz, I., Chai, J., and Cummins, M., 2011. *Austerity Measures Threaten Children and Poor Households: Recent Evidence in Public Expenditures from 128 Developing Countries.* New York: UNICEF.

Østensen, Å. G., 2013. "In the Business of Peace: The Political Influence of Private Military and Security Companies on Un Peacekeeping." *International Peacekeeping* 20(1): 33–47.

Pacquée, D., and Dewulf, S., 2006. "International Territorial Administrations and the Rule of Law: The Case of Kosovo." *Essex Human Rights Review* 4(1): 1–14.

Papadopoulos, Y., 2003. "Cooperative Forms of Governance: Problems of Democratic Accountability in Complex Environments." *European Journal of Political Research* 42(4): 473–501.

Papadopoulos, Y., 2007. "Problems of Democratic Accountability in Network and Multilevel Governance." *European Law Journal* 13(4):469–86.

Parra, S. de la, 2017. "The Economic Dialogue: An Effective Accountability Mechanism?" In *Democracy in the EMU in the Aftermath of the Crisis*, edited by L. Daniele, P. Simone, and R. Cisotta, 101–20. Cham: Springer.

Pauwelyn, J., Wessel, R., and Wouters, J. (eds), 2012. *Informal International Law-Making.* Oxford: Oxford University Press.

Pejic, J., 2011. "The European Court of Human Rights' *Al-Jedda* Judgment: The Oversight of International Humanitarian Law." *International Review of the Red Cross* 93(883): 837–51.

People's Union for Democratic Rights, 2014. "In the Name of Science and Public Health: Concerns about the Safety of Pentavalent Vaccine." Available at: http://www.esocialsciences.org/Download/repecDownload.aspx?fname=A2014610171115_20.pdf&fcategory=Articles&AId=5912&fref=repec (last access September 22, 2019).

Pervou, I., 2016. "Human Rights in Times of Crisis: The Greek Cases before the ECtHR or the Polarization of a Democratic Society." *Cambridge Journal of International and Comparative Law* 5(1): 113–38.

Peters, A., 2011. "The Security Council's Responsibility to Protect." *International Organisations Law Review* 8(1): 15–54.

Petryna, A., 2007. "Clinical Trials Offshored: On Private Sector Science and Public Health." *BioSocieties* 2: 21–40.

Pierson, P., 2000. "Increasing Returns, Path Dependence, and the Study of Politics." *American Political Science Review* 94(2): 251–67.

Pingeot, L., 2012. *Dangerous Partnership: Private Military and Security Companies and the UN*. New York: Global Policy Forum.

Pollack, M. A., 1997. "Delegation, Agency, and Agenda Setting in the European Community." *International Organization* 51(1): 99–134.

Posner, E. A., 2005. "International Law and the Disaggregated State." *Florida State University Law Review* 32: 797–843.

Poulou, A., 2014. "Austerity and European Social Rights: How Can Courts Protect Europe's Lost Generation?" *German Law Journal* 15(6): 1145–76.

Puliyel, J., 2013. "AEFI and the Pentavalent Vaccine: Looking for a Composite Picture." *Indian Journal of Medical Ethics* 10(3): 142–6.

Rached, D. H., 2014. "Doomed Aspiration of Pure Instrumentality: Global Administrative Law and Accountability." *Global Constitutionalism* 3(3): 338–72.

Ratner, S. R., 2005. "Foreign Occupation and International Territorial Administration: The Challenges of Convergence." *European Journal of International Law* 16(4): 695–719.

Raunio, T., 2017. "Control and Scrutiny: Parliaments as Agents of Administrative Law." *Research Handbook on EU Administrative Law*, edited by C. Harlow, P. Leino, and G. della Cananea, 316–43. Cheltenham: Edward Elgar.

Raustiala, K., 2004. "Police Patrols and Fire Alarms in the NAAEC." *Loyola International and Comparative Law Review* 26: 389–413.

Reinisch, A., 2001. "Securing the Accountability of International Organizations." *Global Governance* 7(2): 131–50.

Reinisch, A., 2005. "Accountability of International Organizations According to National Law." *Netherlands Yearbook of International Law* 36: 119–67.

Reinisch, A., 2010. "Aid or Assistance and Direction and Control between States and International Organizations in the Commission of Internationally Wrongful Acts." *International Organizations Law Review* 7(1): 63–77.

Richter, J., 2004. "Public–Private Partnerships and International Health Policy-Making: How Can Public Interests Be Safeguarded?" Helsinki: Ministry of Foreign Affairs of Finland.

Rid, A., Saxena, A., Baqui, A. H., Bhan, A., Bines, J., Bouesseau, M.-C., Caplan, A., Colgrove, J., Dhai, A., Gomez-Diaz, R., Green, S. K., Kang, G., Lagos, R., Loh, P., London, A. J., Mulholland, K., Neels, P., Pitisuttithum, P., Sarr, S. C., Selgelid, M., Sheehan, M., and Smith, P. G., 2014. "Placebo Use in Vaccine Trials: Recommendations of a WHO Expert Panel." *Vaccine* 32(37): 4708–12.

Risse, T., 2002. "Transnational Actors and World Politics." In *Handbook of International Relations*, edited by W. Carlsnaes, T. Risse, and B. A. Simmons, 255–74. London: Sage.

Risse, T., 2008. "Transnational Governance and Legitimacy." In *Governance and Democracy: Comparing National, European, and International Perspectives*, edited by A. Benz and Y. Papadopoulos, 179–99. London: Routledge.

Risse, T., 2011. "Governance in Areas of Limited Statehood: Introduction and Overview." In *Governance without a State? Policies and Politics in Areas of Limited Statehood*, edited by T. Risse and U. Lehmkuhl, 1–35. New York: Columbia University Press.

Risse, T., and Ropp, S. C., 2013. "Introduction and Overview." In *The Persistent Power of Human Rights: From Commitment to Compliance*, edited by T. Risse, S. C. Ropp, and K. Sikkink, 3–25. Cambridge: Cambridge University Press.

Risse, T., Ropp, S. C., and Sikkink, K. (eds), 2013. *The Persistent Power of Human Rights: From Commitment to Compliance*. Cambridge: Cambridge University Press.

Rittberger, B., 2014. "Integration without Representation? The European Parliament and the Reform of Economic Governance in the EU." *Journal of Common Market Studies* 52(6): 1174–83.

Rixen, T., and Viola, L. A., 2015. "Putting Path Dependence in Its Place: Toward a Taxonomy of Institutional Change." *Journal of Theoretical Politics* 27(2): 301–23.

Rogers, B. D., 2006. "Maintaining Legitimacy in Combined Operations: Managing the Impact of US Detainee Policy." Paper submitted to the Faculty of the Naval War College in partial satisfaction of the requirements of the Department of Joint Military Operations, Newport, RI. Available at: https://apps.dtic.mil/dtic/tr/fulltext/u2/a463690.pdf (last access September 23, 2019).

Roth, F., Gros, D., and Nowak-Lehmann, F. D., 2014. "Crisis and Citizens' Trust in the European Central Bank: Panel Data Evidence for the Euro Area, 1999–2012." *Journal of European Integration* 36(3): 303–20.

Roth, F., Jonung, L., and Nowak-Lehmann D. F., 2016. "Crisis and Public Support for the Euro, 1990–2014." *Journal of Common Market Studies* 54(4): 944–60.

Rubenstein, J., 2007. "Accountability in an Unequal World." *Journal of Politics* 69(3): 616–32.

Ruffert, M., 2011. "The European Debt Crisis and European Union Law." *Common Market Law Review* 48(6): 1777–806.

Rushton, S., and Williams, O. D. (eds), 2011. *Partnerships and Foundations in Global Health Governance*. Basingstoke: Palgrave Macmillan.

Ryngaert, C., 2012. "Arrest and Detention." In *International Prosecutors*, edited by L. Reydams, J. Wouters, and C. Ryngaert, 647–99. Oxford: Oxford University Press.

Saiz, I., 2009. "Rights in Recession? Challenges for Economic and Social Rights Enforcement in Times of Crisis." *Journal of Human Rights Practice* 1(2): 277–93.

Salomon, M. E., 2015. "Of Austerity, Human Rights and International Institutions." *European Law Journal* 21(4): 521–45.

Sapir, A., Wolff, G. B., de Sousa, C., and Terzi, A., 2014. "The Troika and Financial Assistance in the Euro Area: Successes and Failures." Available at: http://bruegel.org/wp-content/uploads/imported/publications/20140219ATT79633EN_01.pdf (last access September 22, 2019).

Sari, A., 2008. "Jurisdiction and International Responsibility in Peace Support Operations: The Behrami and Saramati Cases." *Human Rights Law Review* 8: 151–70.

Sarojini, N. B., Srinivasan, S., Madhavi, Y., Srinivasan, S., and Shenoi, A., 2010. "The HPV Vaccine: Science, Ethics and Regulation." *Economic and Political Weekly* 45(48): 27–34.

Sarooshi, D., 1999. *The United Nations and the Development of Collective Security: The Delegation by the UN Security Council of Its Chapter VII Powers*. Oxford: Oxford University Press.

Scharpf, F. W., 1997. *Games Real Actors Play: Actor-Centered Institutionalism in Policy Research*. Boulder, CO: Westview Press.

Scharpf, F. W., 1999. *Regieren in Europa. Effektiv und demokratisch?* Frankfurt: Campus.

Schedler, A., 1999. "Conceptualizing Accountability." In *The Self-Restraining State: Power and Accountability in New Democracies*, edited by A. Schedler, L. Diamond, and M. F. Plattner, 13–28. London: Lynne Rienner.

Schedler, A., Diamond, L., and Plattner, M. F. (eds), 1999. *The Self-Restraining State: Power and Accountability in New Democracies*. London: Lynne Rienner.

Schillemans, T., 2011. "Does Horizontal Accountability Work? Evaluating Potential Remedies for the Accountability Deficit of Agencies." *Administration and Society* 43(4): 387–416.

Schillemans, T., and Busuioc, M., 2014. "Predicting Public Sector Accountability: From Agency Drift to Forum Drift." *Journal of Public Administration Research and Theory* 25: 191–215.

Schimmelfennig, F., 2006. "Competition and Community: Constitutional Courts, Rhetorical Action, and the Institutionalization of Human Rights in the European Union." *Journal of European Public Policy* 13(8): 1247–64.

Schmelzle, C., 2011. "Evaluating Governance: Effectiveness and Legitimacy in Areas of Limited Statehood." *SFB-Governance Working Paper Series* Nr. 26. Berlin.

Schmidt, V. A., 2013. "Democracy and Legitimacy in the European Union Revisited: Input, Output and 'Throughput.'" *Political Studies* 61(1): 2–22.

Scholte, J. A., 2004. "Civil Society and Democratically Accountable Global Governance." *Government and Opposition* 39(2): 211–33.

Scholte, J. A., 2011a. "Global Governance, Accountability and Civil Society." In *Building Global Democracy? Civil Society and Accountable Global Governance*, edited by J. A. Scholte. Cambridge: Cambridge University Press.

Scholte, J. A., 2011b. "Towards Greater Legitimacy in Global Governance." *Review of International Political Economy* 18(1): 110–20.

Schrijver, N., 2013. "Beyond Srebrenica and Haiti: Exploring Alternative Remedies against the United Nations." *International Organizations Law Review* 10: 588–600.

Schuster, B. M., 2015. "For the Love of Drugs: Using Pharmaceutical Clinical Trials Abroad to Profit off the Poor." *Seattle Journal of Social Justice* 13(2): 1015–67.

Sciarra, S., 2018. *Solidarity and Conflict: European Social Law in Crisis*. Cambridge: Cambridge University Press.

Seawright, J., and Gerring, J., 2008. "Case Selection Techniques in Case Study Research: A Menu of Qualitative and Quantitative Options." *Political Research Quarterly* 61(2): 294–308.

Sikkink, K., 2013. "The United States and Torture: Does the Spiral Model Work?" In *The Persistent Power of Human Rights: From Commitment to Compliance*, edited by T. Risse, S. C. Ropp, and K. Sikkink, 145–63. Cambridge: Cambridge University Press.

Silverstein, G., and Hanley, J. I., 2010. "The Supreme Court and Public Opinion in Times of War and Crisis." *Hastings Law Journal* 61(1): 1453–502.

Simmons, B. A., 2002. "Capacity, Commitment, and Compliance." *Journal of Conflict Resolution* 46(6): 829–56.

Simmons, B. A., and Martin, L. L., 2002. "International Organizations and Institutions." In *Handbook of International Relations*, edited by W. Carlsnaes, T. Risse, and B. A. Simmons, 192–211. London: Sage.

Singer, P. W., 2003. "Peacekeepers." *Policy Review* 119.

Smith, C. A., and Smith, H. M., 2011. "Human Trafficking: The Unintended Effects of United Nations Intervention." *International Political Science Review* 32(2): 125–45.

Sperling, V., 2009. *Altered States: The Globalization of Accountability*. Cambridge: Cambridge University Press.

Sreedhar, S., Antony, A., and Poulose, N., 2014. "Study on the Effectiveness and Impact of Pentavalent Vaccination Program in India and Other South Asian Countries." *Human Vaccines and Immunotherapeutics* 10(7): 2062–5.

Srinivasan, S., Johari, V., and Jesani, A., 2018. "Cervical Cancer Screening in India." In *Ethics Dumping: Case Studies from North-South Research Collaborations*, edited by D. Schroeder, J. Cook, F. Hirsch, S. Fenet, and V. Muthuswamy, 33–48. New York: Springer International.

Stahn, C., 2008. *The Law and Practice of International Territorial Administration: Versailles to Iraq and Beyond*. Cambridge: Cambridge University Press.

Steets, J., 2010. *Accountability in Public Policy Partnerships*. London: Palgrave Macmillan.

Steets, J., and Blattner, L., 2010. "Partnership Accountability Need Not Be Democratic Accountability." In *Democracy and Public–Private Partnerships in Global Governance*, edited by M. Bexell and U. Mörth, 55–78. New York: Palgrave Macmillan.

Steffek, J., 2010. "Public Accountability and the Public Sphere of International Governance." *Ethics and International Affairs* 24(1): 45–68.

Steffek, J., 2013. "Explaining Cooperation between IGOs and NGOs: Push Factors, Pull Factors, and the Policy Cycle." *Review of International Studies* 39(4): 993–1013.

Steffek, J., 2015. "The Output Legitimacy of International Organizations and the Global Public Interest." *International Theory* 7(2): 263–93.

Steffek, J., and Nanz, P., 2008. "Emergent Patterns of Civil Society Participation in Global and European Governance." In *Civil Society Participation in European and Global Governance: A Cure for the Democratic Deficit?*, edited by J. Steffek, C. Kissling, and P. Nanz, 1–29. Basingstoke: Palgrave Macmillan.

Stone Sweet, A., 2009. "Constitutionalism, Legal Pluralism, and International Regimes." *Indiana Journal of Global Legal Studies* 16(2): 621–45.

Strøm, K., 2003. "Parliamentary Democracy and Delegation." In *Delegation and Accountability in Parliamentary Democracies*, edited by K. Strøm, W. C. Müller, and T. Bergman, 55–106. Oxford: Oxford University Press.

Stuckler, D., and Basu, S., 2010. *The Body Economic: Why Austerity Kills*. New York: Basic Books.

Take, I., 2009. *Legitimes Regieren jenseits des Nationalstaats. Unterschiedliche Formen von Global Governance im Vergleich*. Baden-Baden: Nomos.

Tallberg, J., 2002. "Delegation to Supranational Institutions: Why, How, and with What Consequences?" *West European Politics* 25(1): 23–46.

Tallberg, J., and Uhlin, A., 2011. "Civil Society and Global Democracy: An Assessment." In *Global Democracy: Normative and Empirical Perspectives*, edited by M. Koenig-Archibugi and R. Marchetti, 210–32. Cambridge: Cambridge University Press.

Tallberg, J., and Zürn, M., 2019. "The Legitimacy and Legitimation of International Organizations: Introduction and Framework." *Review of International Organizations*.

Tallberg, J., Sommerer, T., Squatrito, T., and Jönsson, K., 2013. *The Opening Up of International Organizations: Transnational Access in Global Governance*. Cambridge: Cambridge University Press.

Tarrow, S., 2013. "War, Rights and Contention: Lasswell v. Tilly." In *Varieties of Sovereignty and Citizenship*, edited by S. R. Ben-Porath and R. M. Smith, 35–57. Philadelphia, PA: University of Pennsylvania Press.

Terwindt, C., 2014. "Health Rights Litigation Pushes for Accountability in Clinical Trials in India." *Health and Human Rights Journal* 16(2): 84–95.

Teubner, G., 1996. "Global Bukinowa: Legal Pluralism in the World Society." In *Global Law without a State*, edited by G. Teubner, 3–28. Dartmouth: Brookfield.

The Economist, 2001. "Charlemagne Paddy Ashdown, Latest Balkan Proconsul." March 9. Available at: https://www.economist.com/europe/2002/03/07/paddy-ashdown-latest-balkan-proconsul (last access September 22, 2019).

Tierney, M. J., 2006. "Delegation of Authority in International Relations: The Promise and Limits of Agency Theory." Paper presented at the Discussion Paper Prepared for Duke Conference.

Trenkov-Wermuth, C., 2010. *United Nations Justice: Legal and Judicial Reform in Governance Operations.* New York: United Nations University Press.

Uhlin, A., 2011. "National Democratization Theory and Global Governance: Civil Society and the Liberalization of the Asian Development Bank." *Democratization* 18(3): 847–71.

United Kingdom Royal Court of Justice, 2010. "Case between Maya Evans and the Secretary of State for Defence, Case No: CO/11949/2008." June 25.

United Nations Assistance Mission in Afghanistan (UNAMA) and UN Office of the High Commissioner for Human Rights (OHCHR), 2011. "Treatment of Conflict-Related Detainees in Afghan Custody." October, Kabul.

United Nations Assistance Mission in Afghanistan (UNAMA) and UN Office of the High Commissioner for Human Rights (OHCHR), 2013. "Treatment of Conflict-Related Detainees in Afghan Custody One Year On." January, Kabul.

United Nations Department for Peacekeeping Operations (DPKO), 2004. "Best Practices Unit, Human Trafficking Resource Package." December. Available at: https://www.un.org/ruleoflaw/files/DPKO,%20Human%20Trafficking%20Resource%20Package,%202004.pdf (last access September 22, 2019).

United Nations Department for Peacekeeping Operations (DPKO), 2009. "A New Partnership Agenda: Creating a New Horizon for UN Peacekeeping." Available at: https://peacekeeping.un.org/sites/default/files/newhorizon_0.pdf (last access September 22, 2019).

United Nations Department for Peacekeeping Operations (DPKO) and Department of Field Service (DFS), 2008. *United Nations Peacekeeping Operations: Principles and Guidelines (Capstone Doctrine).* New York: United Nations.

United Nations General Assembly, 2005. "Report of the Secretary General, A Comprehensive Strategy to Eliminate Future Sexual Exploitation and Abuse in United Nations Peacekeeping Operations, 'Zeid Report.'" UN doc. A/59/710.

United Nations Human Rights Commission, 2002a. "Report of the Special Representative of the Commission on Human Rights on the Situation of Human Rights in Bosnia and Herzegovina and the Federal Republic of Yugoslavia, Jose Cutileiro." UN doc. E/CN.4/2002/41, January 8.

United Nations Human Rights Commission, 2002b. "Report of the Secretary-General on Activities of United Nations Bodies and Other International Organizations Pertaining to the Problem of Trafficking in Women and Girls." UN doc. E/CN.4/2002/80, January 25.

United Nations Human Rights Council, 2006. "Concluding Observations of the Human Rights Committee (Kosovo)." UN doc. CCPR/C/UNK/CO/1, August 14, Geneva.

United Nations Human Rights Council, 2010. "Joint Study on Global Practices in Relation to Secret Detention in the Context of Countering Terrorism." A-HRC-13–42, February 19.

United Nations Mission in Kosovo (UNMIK), 1999a. "UNMIK Regulation on the Authority of the Interim Administration." UNMIK/REG/1999/1, July 25.

United Nations Mission in Kosovo (UNMIK), 1999b. "UNMIK Regulation on the Law Applicable in Kosovo." UN doc. UNMIK/REG/1999/24, December 12.

United Nations Mission in Kosovo (UNMIK), 2000a. "UNMIK Regulation on the Establishment of the Ombudsperson Institution in Kosovo." UN doc. UNMIK/REG/2000/38, June 30.

United Nations Mission in Kosovo (UNMIK), 2000b. "UNMIK Regulation on the Status, Privileges and Immunities of KFOR and UNMIK and Their Personnel in Kosovo." UN doc. UNMIK/REG/2000/47, August 18.

United Nations Mission in Kosovo (UNMIK), 2001a. "UNMIK Regulation on the Establishment of a Detention Review Commission for Extra-Judicial Detentions Based on Executive Orders." UN doc. UNMIK/REG/2001/18, August 25.

United Nations Mission in Kosovo (UNMIK), 2001b. "UNMIK Regulation on the Rights of Persons Arrested by Law Enforcement Authorities." UN doc. UNMIK/REG/2001/28, October 11.

United Nations Mission in Kosovo (UNMIK), 2006a. "UNMIK Regulation on the Ombudsperson Institution in Kosovo." UN doc. UNMIK/REG/2006/6, February 16.

United Nations Mission in Kosovo (UNMIK), 2006b. "UNMIK Regulation on the Establishment of the Human Rights Advisory Panel." UN doc. UNMIK/REG/2006/12, March 23.

United Nations Mission in Kosovo (UNMIK), 2009. "UNMIK Administrative Directive on Implementing UNMIK/REG/2006/12." UN doc. UNMIK/DIR/2009/1, October 17.

United Nations Office of the High Commissioner for Human Rights (OHCHR), 2000. "Annual Report 2000: Implementation of Activities and Use of Funds." Available at: https://www.ohchr.org/Documents/AboutUs/annualreport2000.pdf (last access September 22, 2019).

United Nations Office of the High Commissioner for Human Rights (OHCHR), 2002. "Recommended Principles and Guidelines on Human Rights and Human Trafficking." E/2002/68/Add.1, May 20. Available at: http://www.unhcr.org/refworld/docid/3f1fc60f4.html (last access September 22, 2019).

United Nations Office of the High Commissioner for Human Rights (OHCHR), 2003. "Report of the Working Group on Contemporary Forms of Slavery 3/ 2003." E/CN.4/2004/2-E/CN.4/Sub.2/2003/43, October 20.

United Nations Secretary-General, 1996. "Report of the Secretary-General Pursuant to Security Council resolution 1035 (1995)." UN doc S/1996/820.

United Nations Secretary-General, 1999a. "Report on UNMIK." UN doc. S/1999/779, July 12.

United Nations Secretary-General, 1999b. "Secretary-General's Bulletin on the 'Observance by United Nations Forces of International Humanitarian Law.'" UN doc. ST/SGB/1999/13, August 6.

United Nations Secretary-General, 2000. "Report of the Secretary-General on the United Nations Interim Administration Mission in Kosovo." UN doc. S/2000/1196, December 15.

United Nations Secretary-General, 2004. "Report of the Secretary-General on the United Nations Interim Administration Mission in Kosovo." UN doc. S/2004/348, April 30.

United Nations Secretary-General, 2007. "Report on the Situation in Afghanistan and Its Implications for International Peace and Security." UN doc. S/2007/555, September 21.

United Nations Security Council, 1995a. "Resolution 1031." December 15.

United Nations Security Council, 1995b. "Resolution 1035." December 21.

United Nations Security Council, 1996. "Resolution 1088(1996)." December 12.

United Nations Security Council, 1999a. "Resolution 1244(1999)." June 10.

United Nations Security Council, 1999b. "Resolution 1265(1999)." September 17.

United Nations Security Council, 2001a. "Resolution 1368(2001)." September 12.

United Nations Security Council, 2001b. "Meeting on Kosovo (Federal Republic of Yugoslavia)." UN doc. S/PV.4430, November 27.

United Nations Security Council, 2002. "Resolution 1401(2002)." March 28.

United Nations Security Council, 2003a. "Letter Dated 23 April 2003 from the President of the Security Council Addressed to the Secretary-General." UN doc. S/2003/504, April 28.

United Nations Security Council, 2003b. "Report of the Security Council Mission to Afghanistan, 31 October to 7 November 2003." UN doc. S/2003/1074, November 11.

United Nations Security Council, 2007. "Resolution 1776(2007)." September 19.

United Nations Security Council, 2008. "Resolution 1806(2008)." March 20.

United States Department of Defense, 2003. "Assessment of DoD Efforts to Combat Trafficking in Persons. Phase II – Bosnia-Herzegovina and Kosovo." *Office of the Inspector General* Case Number H03L88433128, December 8.

United States Department of Defense, 2004a. "Memorandum of the Deputy Secretary of Defense Paul Wolfowitz for Secretaries of the Military Departments." January 30.

United States Department of Defense, 2004b. "Memorandum of the Secretary of Defense Donald Rumsfeld for Secretaries of the Military Departments." September 16.

United States Department of Defense, 2004c. "Final Report of the Independent Panel to Review DoD Detention Operations (Schlesinger Report)." August. Available at: http://www.prisonexp.org/pdf/SchlesingerReport.pdf (last access September 22, 2019).

Vandenberg, M. E., 2007. "Peacekeeping and Rule-Breaking: United Nations Anti-Trafficking Policy in Bosnia and Herzegovina." In *Human Trafficking, Human Security, and the Balkans*, edited by H. R. Friman and S. Reich, 81–95. Pittsburgh, PA: University of Pittsburgh Press.

Velásquez, G., 2014. "Public–Private Partnerships in Global Health: Putting Business before Health?" Available at: http://apps.who.int/medicinedocs/documents/s21394en/s21394en.pdf (last access September 22, 2019).

Verdirame, G., 2011. *The UN and Human Rights: Who Guards the Guardians?* Cambridge: Cambridge University Press.

Violante, T., 2019. "The Portuguese Constitutional Court and Its Austerity Case Law." In *Political Institutions and Democracy in Portugal*, edited by A. Costa Pinto and C. P. Teixeira, 121–43. New York: Palgrave Macmillan.

Visoka, G., 2011. "The Obstacles to Sustainable Peace and Democracy in Post-Independence Kosovo." *Journal of Conflict Transformation and Security* 1(2): 25–37.

Visoka, G., 2012. "The 'Kafkaesque Accountability' of International Governance in Kosovo." *Journal of Intervention and Statebuilding* 6(2): 189–212.

von Bogdandy, A., and Steinbrück Platise, M., 2012. "DARIO and Human Rights Protection: Leaving the Individual in the Cold." *International Organisations Law Review* 8(1): 67–76.

Wallace, S. K., 2012. "Global Health in Conflict: Understanding Opposition to Vitamin A Supplementation in India." *American Journal of Public Health* 102(7): 1286–97.

Warren, M. E., 2014. "Accountability and Democracy." In *The Oxford Handbook of Public Accountability*, edited by M. Bovens, R. E. Goodin, and T. Schillemans, 39–54. Oxford: Oxford University Press.

Waters, C. P. M., 2007. "Nationalising Kosovo's Ombudsperson." *Journal of Conflict and Security Law* 12(1): 139–48.

Weaver, C., 2008. *Hypocrisy Trap: The World Bank and the Poverty of Reform*, Princeton, NJ: Princeton University Press.

Weiss, T. G., 2016. *What's Wrong with the United Nations and How to Fix It*, Third Edition. Cambridge: Polity.

Wellens, K., 2002. *Remedies against International Organizations*. Cambridge: Cambridge University Press.

Wemos Foundation, 2005. "Risky Remedies for the Health of the Poor: Report on the Implementation of four GPPIs in Five African Countries and Three Indian States." Available at: http://www.bibalex.org/Search4Dev/files/338442/172026.pdf (last access September 22, 2019).

White House, 2002a. "Remarks by the President and the Chairman of the Afghan Interim Authority Hamid Karzai." January 28. Available at: http://transcripts.cnn.com/TRANSCRIPTS/0201/28/se.04.html (last access September 22, 2019).

White House, 2002b. "State of the Union Address by President Bush." January 29. Available at: https://georgewbush-whitehouse.archives.gov/news/releases/2002/01/20020129-11.html (last access September 22, 2019).

White House, 2002c. "Memorandum of the President of the United States on the Humane Treatment of Taliban and al Qaeda Detainees." February 7, Washington, DC.

White House, 2002d. "National Security Presidential Directive (NSPD)-22 'Combating Trafficking in Persons.'" December 16, Washington, DC.

White House, 2003. "Statement by the Press Secretary on the Geneva Convention." May 7, Washington, DC.

WHO, 1995. "Guidelines for Good Clinical Practice (GCP) for Trials on Pharmaceutical Products." Report No. 850. Available at: http://apps.who.int/medicinedocs/pdf/whozip13e/whozip13e.pdf (last access September 22, 2019).

WHO, 2000. "Guidelines on Working with the Private Sector to Achieve Health Outcomes. Report by the Secretariat." EB107/20. Available at: http://apps.who.int/iris/bitstream/10665/78660/1/ee20.pdf (last access September 22, 2019).

WHO, 2005a. "Global Immunization Vision and Strategy 2006–2015." Available at: http://apps.who.int/iris/bitstream/handle/10665/69146/WHO_IVB_05.05.pdf?sequence=1 (last access September 22, 2019).

WHO, 2005b. "Vaccine Introduction Guidelines." Available at: http://www.who.int/immunization/hpv/plan/vaccine_introduction_guidelines_who_2005.pdf (last access September 22, 2019).

WHO, 2008. "Clinical Trials in India: Ethical Concerns." *Bulletin of the World Health Organization* 86(8): 577–656.

WHO, 2009. "Human Papillomavirus Vaccines. WHO Position Paper." *Weekly Epistomiological Record* 15(84): 118–31.

WHO, 2013. "Global Advisory Committee on Vaccine Safety: Report on Pentavalent in Asian Countries." *Weekly Epistomiological Record* 29(88): 301–12.

WHO, 2014. "Principles and Considerations for Adding a Vaccine to a National Immunization Programme." Available at: http://apps.who.int/iris/bitstream/handle/10665/111548/9789241506892_eng.pdf;jsessionid=3E3AAE8A28B5CED3C21DA860D3B0132E?sequence=1 (last access September 22, 2019).

WHO, UNICEF, and Bank., W., 2009. *State of the World's Vaccines and Immunization*, Third Edition. Geneva: World Health Organization.

Wiharta, S., 2009. "The Legitimacy of Peace Operations." In *SIPRI Yearbook 2009: Armaments, Disarmament and International Security*, edited by S. I. P. R. Institute, 95–116. Oxford: Oxford University Press.

Wilde, R., 2006. "Enhancing Accountability at the International Level: The Tension between International Organizations and Member State Responsibility and the Underlying Issues at Stake." *ILSA Journal of International and Comparative Law* 12(2): 395–416.

Wille, A., 2010. "Political-Bureaucratic Accountability in the EU Commission: Modernising the Executive." *West European Politics* 33(5): 1093–116.

Winkler, T., 2010. "The Copenhagen Process on Detainees: A Necessity." *Nordic Journal of International Law* 78: 489–98.

Woods, N., 1999. "Good Governance in International Organizations." *Global Governance* 5(1): 39–61.

Woods, N., 2001. "Making the IMF and the World Bank More Accountable." *International Affairs* 77(1): 83–100.

Woods, N., and Narlikar, A., 2001. "Governance and the Limits of Accountability: the WTO, the IMF and the World Bank." *International Social Science Journal* 53(170): 569–83.

World Public Opinion, 2006a. "American and International Opinion on the Rights of Terrorism Suspects." July 17.

World Public Opinion, 2006b. "Afghan Public Opinion amidst Rising Violence." December 14.

World Public Opinion, 2008. "World Public Opinion on Torture." June 24. Available at: http://worldpublicopinion.net/wp-content/uploads/2016/06/WPO_Torture_Jun08_packet.pdf (last access September 22, 2019).

Wouters, J., and Schmitt, P., 2010. "Challenging Acts of Other United Nations' Organs, Subsidiary Organs and Officials." In *Challenging Acts of International Organizations Before National Courts*, edited by A. Reinisch, 77–110. Oxford: Oxford University Press.

Wouters, J., Brems, E., Smis, S., and Schmitt P. (eds), 2010. *Accountability for Human Rights Violations by International Organisations*. Antwerp: Intersentia.

Yamashita, H., 2012. "Peacekeeping Cooperation between the United Nations and Regional Organisations." *Review of International Studies* 38(1): 165–86.

Zagel, G. M., 2018. "International Organisations and Human Rights: The Role of the UN Covenants in Overcoming the Accountability Gap." *Nordic Journal of Human Rights* 36 (1): 74–90.

Zaidi, S., 2010. "Millennium Development Goal 6 and the Right to Health." *SUR* 12.

Zangl, B., 2006. *Die Internationalisierung der Rechtsstaatlichkeit*. Frankfurt: Campus.

Zangl, B., Helmedach, A., Mondré, A., Kocks, A., Neubauer, G., and Blome, K., 2011. "Between Law and Politics: Explaining International Dispute Settlement Behavior." *European Journal of International Relations* 18(2): 369–401.

Zaum, D., 2006. "The Authority of International Administrations in International Society." *Review of International Studies* 32(3): 455–73.

Zaum, D. (eds), 2013. *Legitimating International Organisations*. Oxford: Oxford University Press.

Zinck, K., Rogers, M., Pollock, J. C., and Salvatore, M., 2014. "Nationwide Newspaper Coverage of Detainee Rights at Guantanamo Bay: A Community Structure Approach." *Atlantic Journal of Communication* 22(3–4): 245–58.

Zürn, M., 2012. "Autorität und Legitimität in der postnationalen Konstellation." *Leviathan* 40(Sonderband 27): 41–62.

Zürn, M., 2018. *A Theory of Global Governance*. Oxford: Oxford University Press.

Zürn, M., and Stephen, M., 2010. "The View of Old and New Powers on the Legitimacy of International Institutions." *Politics* 30(S1, Special Issue "Perspectives on the Changing Global Distribution of Power"): 91–101.

Zwanenburg, M., 2005. *Accountability of Peace Support Operations*. Leiden: Martinus Nijhoff.

Index

Note: Tables and figures are indicated by an italic "*t*" and "*f*", respectively, following the page number.

For the benefit of digital users, indexed terms that span two pages (e.g., 52–53) may, on occasion, appear on only one of those pages.

The manufacturer's authorised representative in the EU for product safety is Oxford University Press España S.A. of el Parque Empresarial San Fernando de Henares, Avenida de Castilla, 2 – 28830 Madrid (www.oup.es/en or product.safety@oup.com). OUP España S.A. also acts as importer into Spain of products made by the manufacturer.

www.ingramcontent.com/pod-product-compliance
Lightning Source LLC
LaVergne TN
LVHW011753200926
848484LV00003B/690

9780198861249